T0355134

Heir through Hope

Heir through Hope

Thomas Jefferson's Lifelong Investment in William Short

PETER THOMPSON

Oxford University Press is a department of the University of Oxford. It furthers the University's objective of excellence in research, scholarship, and education by publishing worldwide. Oxford is a registered trade mark of Oxford University Press in the UK and certain other countries.

Published in the United States of America by Oxford University Press
198 Madison Avenue, New York, NY 10016, United States of America.

CIP data is on file at the Library of Congress

ISBN 978-0-19-754683-3

DOI: 10.1093/oso/9780197546833.001.0001

Printed by Sheridan Books, Inc., United States of America

Contents

Acknowledgments   vii

A Note on Translation and Nomenclature   ix

Introduction: An Unfulfilled Patriarch   1

1. Springs Set in Motion: Establishing Separate Lives in France   18

2. Living in a Woman's Country: Jefferson's and Short's Reflections
   on French Culture   44

3. "A Poor Dry Business": William Short's Diplomatic Career   72

4. The Earth Half Desolated: Reckoning with Terror   101

5. "You Are My Husband": Rosalie de La Rochefoucauld and
   William Short   130

6. Money, Slaves, and Land: Jefferson's Ties to William Short   157

7. A Serpent's Tooth: William Short's Later Life Relationship with
   Jefferson   184

Epilogue: Jefferson's Hopes, and Short's Fears   207

Notes   219

Index   275

Acknowledgments

THIS BOOK COULD not have been completed without generous research leave granted by the Division of Humanities of the University of Oxford and assistance from its Faculty of History. My thanks in particular to Professor John Watts and Professor Robert Iliffe for their support and encouragement.

During a residential fellowship at the Robert H. Smith International Center for Jefferson Studies at Monticello I enjoyed generous intellectual support from the Center's director, Professor Andrew O'Shaughnessy; from my peer group of Fellows; and from J. Jefferson Looney, Editor-in-Chief of the Papers of Thomas Jefferson Retirement Series.

I have presented early versions of this research to scholars at Michael Zuckerman's Early American Salon in Philadelphia, the Robert H. Smith Center, and the Rothermere American Institute at the University of Oxford. I wish to thank the audiences present on those occasions for their insightful and encouraging comments.

In the writing of this book, I acquired some proficiency in reading eighteenth-century French but would have been lost without the help and expertise of Dr. Olivia Durand, formerly of the University of Oxford, and Lisa V. Francavilla, Roland H. Simon, and Paula Viterbo of the Thomas Jefferson Papers Retirement Series.

I wish to offer thanks for the assistance of archivists and librarians at the following repositories: the American Philosophical Society; the David M. Rubinstein Rare Book and Manuscript Library, Duke University; the Historical Society of Pennsylvania; the James Madison Reading Room of the Library of Congress; the Louis Round Wilson Library's Special Collections at the University of North Carolina; the Albert and Shirley Small Special Collections at the University of Virginia; and the Special Collections Research Centre of the Swem Library, College of William and Mary.

For their support and input I wish to thank Zara Anishanslin, Andrew Burstein, Frank Cogliano, Nicholas Cole, Gareth Davies, Annette Gordon-Reed, Chuck Grench, Patrick Griffin, Andrea Hopkins, Tim Horgan, Nancy Isenberg, Kathy Kelly, Peter Onuf, Adam Smith, Nadine Zimmerli, and Michael Zuckerman.

I benefitted greatly from thoughtful reports provided by three anonymous readers commissioned by Oxford University Press.

I wish to thank my agent, Chris Rogers, for his encouragement and wise counsel, and my editor, Susan Ferber, for her support and wisdom.

I dedicate this book to my wife, Andrea, to her daughter Helena, and to my son, Walter.

A Note on Translation and Nomenclature

With one exception, the translation of French language material cited in this work has been supplied by me or is provided in the source cited (e.g., in later volumes of the *Papers of Thomas Jefferson*) and is clearly identifiable as such. The exception concerns quotations from letters, sometimes taking the form of an extended memoir, written by Marie-Jacinthe Botidoux to Martha Jefferson. This manuscript material, held in the University of Virginia's Alderman Library Special Collections, is extremely difficult to translate. I gratefully acknowledge the generous assistance of Lisa V. Francavilla, Roland H. Simon, and Paula Viterbo of the Papers of Thomas Jefferson: Retirement Series, as well Series' Editor J. Jefferson Looney, who gave me advance access to their translations of Botidoux's letters. (These have since been published online at the Monticello's Jefferson Quotes and Family Letters website in translations made by Roland H. Simon.) I also gratefully acknowledge the invaluable assistance of Dr. Olivia Durand, formerly of the University of Oxford, whose reading of the correspondence between William Short and Rosalie de La Rochefoucauld checked, corrected, and improved my translations. The American Philosophical Society holds very nearly all surviving manuscript letters from Rosalie de La Rochefoucauld to William Short, together with some letters to Short written by Charles Rohan-Chabot, Madame de Tessé, and the Italian aristocrat Pauline Castiglione. Soon after they were acquired Rosalie's letters were translated by A. Emsgarth. Typescripts of these unpublished translations are available in the American Philosophical Society's Reading Room, although their English now appears dated. Almost the entirety of correspondence between Rosalie de La Rochefoucauld and William Short held by the American Philosophical Society has been reprinted in its original French in *Lettres de la duchesse de La Rochefoucauld à William Short: Texte Inédit*, edited by Doina Pasca Harsanyi (Paris: Mercure de France,

2001). In one or two endnotes, I offer very brief extracts from letters in their original French to allow interested readers to check my reading of nuance.

I have anglicized French titles of nobility. In citations from letters written in English by anglophone authors, I have silently corrected inconsistently or incorrectly spelled personal names, diminutives, and surnames. The Papers of Thomas Jefferson, for example, following Jefferson's usage, identifies Madame d'Anville, Madame d'Enville, and the Duchess d'Enville as the author of material addressed to Jefferson. I have also followed in the main text and endnotes conventionally accepted contractions of personal names and titles. Marie-Joseph Paul Yves Gilbert du Moustier, Marquis de La Fayette appears as Lafayette; Louise Élisabeth Nicole de La Rochefoucauld appears as Madame d'Enville or Duchess d'Enville, and her granddaughter, Alexandrine-Charlotte-Sophie de Rohan-Chabot, Duchess de La Rochefoucauld d'Enville, as Rosalie or Duchess de La Rochefoucauld.

Heir through Hope

Introduction

AN UNFULFILLED PATRIARCH

IN THE COMPANY of his daughters and their extended families, Thomas Jefferson found "everything which is pleasurable to me in this world." Jefferson's success in enlisting his daughter Martha and her half-sister Sally Hemings to fashion a family environment that functioned exactly to his liking was unusual in an age in which the lived experience of most families, including some branches of Jefferson's, was far removed from idealized ties of affection. Visitors to Monticello commented on Jefferson's evident enjoyment of a life regulated by modern values of affectionate domesticity, but noted the presence of more traditional assumptions and aspirations. For all his hostility to aristocracy and monarchical rule, Jefferson was drawn to the image of the planter as patriarch. Managing land and slaves led him to sympathize with the worldview expressed by Virginian planter William Byrd II in 1726: "Like one of the Patriarchs, I have my flocks and my herds, my Bond-men and Bond-women . . . so that I live in a kind of independence on everyone but Providence." Describing his retirement plans as he prepared to leave Washington's administration at the close of 1793, Jefferson told Angelica Schuyler Church "I have my houses to build, my fields to farm." One daughter had made a good marriage and lived with him. "If the other [daughter] shall be as fortunate in due process of time, I shall imagine myself as the most blessed of patriarchs." Two years later he presented himself to Edward Rutledge as living "like an antediluvian patriarch among my children and grandchildren."[1]

As Jefferson well knew, sons were an essential blessing to any man aspiring to the status of a patriarch. Yet, like George Washington, Jefferson was a Founding Father with no acknowledged male heir. Jefferson's two daughters by his wife Martha Wayles Jefferson were a source of delight to him,

Heir through Hope. Peter Thompson, Oxford University Press. © Peter Thompson 2023.
DOI: 10.1093/oso/9780197546833.003.0001

and Jefferson treated "all my grandchildren as if they were my children." He developed an especially close and loving relationship with his daughter Mary's son Francis, who was born in 1801. Following Mary's premature death, John Wayles Eppes, Francis's father, encouraged Jefferson to treat Francis as a son, considering Jefferson's "claim" as "equal to my own." John regularly left Francis to stay at Monticello, where Jefferson delighted in his company. When the boy was five, Jefferson described him to John as "our dear Francis." The "company of my dear Francis has been a great comfort to me this winter" Jefferson wrote in 1810, while promising to "restore" him to John soon. As Francis approached maturity the limits of a grandfather's relationship with a grandson began to emerge. Jefferson thanked John for allowing him to make plans for the young boy's education "somewhat of the parental character." He was careful to add that he did not seek to diminish Francis's love for his father or respect for his authority. He "reserved" for John the rights of a parent. Even the closest relations with male grandchildren could not fully compensate Jefferson for the lack of a son.[2]

In an extraordinary letter to Elbridge Gerry written in 1812, Jefferson asked "How many children have you?" swiftly adding "you beat me, I expect, in that count; but I you in that of our grandchildren." Jefferson was father to three young sons by Sally Hemings when he asked his question of Gerry. Over a span of years Sally Hemings bore at least six children by Thomas Jefferson, the last of them, Thomas Eston Hemings in 1808, when Jefferson was sixty-five. Four of Sally and Thomas's children survived into adulthood. Jefferson's coy suggestion that he "expected" Gerry had more children than him (Gerry had fathered seven children) supports Madison Hemings's calculation of the place Jefferson's second family held in his affections. Hemings recalled that "although uniformly kind to all," Jefferson was "not in the habit of showing partiality or fatherly affection to us children." Jefferson did not disown, but could not fully acknowledge, William Beverley, James Madison, or Thomas Eston Hemings as sons (nor Harriet as a daughter).[3]

Like Washington, Jefferson exercised guardianship on behalf of the sons of friends and developed close relationships with his wards. But a guardian was not a parent. Like Washington, Jefferson addressed paternal instincts by creating male protégés and offering advice, encouragement, occasionally criticism to them. While such relationships could be warm, they had hard boundaries. Sooner or later Jefferson sought through advice or even overt manipulation to bring his friendships with younger men within the confines of his political conscience. Jefferson wanted to believe that, since the Earth properly belonged to the living generation, his generation should not tie the hands of future legislators. Yet he was proud of his generation's achievements and did not wish to see them squandered. Virginia's Bill for Establishing Religious Freedom, which Jefferson particularly wished to be remembered for, addressed this issue by stating that any attempt by a future legislature to dismantle the settlement he had defined in 1779 would be an intolerable infringement of natural right. He was confident that, in this case, successor generations would accept his definition of "natural right." But Jefferson lived long enough to see his legacy threatened by the "treason" he detected in the "unwise and unworthy passions" expressed by the "sons" of "the generation of 1776." Viewing rising generations with a paternal, even regal eye, Jefferson was pained by their apparent disrespect for the Founders' wisdom. These men were his heirs, and he invested his hopes in them.[4]

Jefferson's relationship with one younger Virginian in particular, William Short, brought together Jefferson's personal situation and his political frustration. Acting as a patron Jefferson launched Short's public service career. He later managed Short's financial affairs. Yet the duty of care Jefferson expressed toward Short ran deeper. His emotional ties to the young man addressed his lack of a white male heir.

———

William Short was born in Surry County, Virginia, in September 1759. His was an established family, with modest holdings in land and slaves and ties of kinship to Martha Wayles Jefferson. Short, like Jefferson, came of age at the College of William and Mary, where he studied law with George Wythe, whom he revered. Short matriculated in 1779, the same year that Jefferson became a Visitor of the college and busied himself in its reform. Since Jefferson also admired Wythe and worked with him on the reforms, it is not surprising that Short came to Jefferson's attention. By 1780, Jefferson knew the student well enough to entrust him with a precious copy of the arguments he had used in the case of *Bolling v. Bolling*. When Short completed his studies in September 1781, Wythe examined him for a license to practice law, a board Jefferson sat in on. Jefferson subsequently signed the necessary petition recommending Short for admission to the bar. By that time the two men had laid the foundations for a deeper relationship.[5]

Short was a guest at Monticello in the summer of 1781, when British raiders came close to capturing Jefferson. He may have accompanied Jefferson's daughters in the "flight from the mountain." He was certainly present at John Coles's Enniscorthy estate where Jefferson rejoined his family. On July 18,

1781, Jefferson recorded borrowing £330 from Short and two days later noted the repayment. On July 25, he borrowed £150 from Mr. Short and repaid him the next day. That Jefferson asked Short for a loan at all, the substantial sums he asked for, and the speed with which the loans were repaid, all speak to the crisis in Jefferson's affairs that summer. In that crisis, an enduring bond of trust and obligation was established. Short had demonstrated that he was ready to do anything he could to help Jefferson. Jefferson did not forget.[6]

Each man had each lost a parent at a vulnerable age: Short was twelve when his mother died, Jefferson was fourteen when his father died. Each maintained a distance from his siblings. Short was sociable, he was a member of his college's debating society, and an elected officer of the Phi Beta Kappa fraternity, but he found it difficult to maintain friendships. Jefferson was a generous host but positively craved isolation. His earliest surviving letter complains of the demands company made on him. In Paris, Jefferson often retreated from the American legation's official residence to privately rented rooms in the monastery of Mount Valérien. Later in life, Jefferson routinely escaped from Monticello to his "retreat home" at nearby Poplar Forest. He avoided conflict through reticence. As he told Abigail Adams, "I do not love difficulties . . . I am fond of quiet." In contrast, Short seemed drawn to difficulties. Complex lawsuits and convoluted wrangling punctuated his adult life. He was a close observer of distinctions of status and esteem among his contemporaries. Possessed of an inflated sense of worth, Short manifested a thin skin for perceived slights.[7]

These character traits were barely apparent when Jefferson launched Short's career. Soon after his young protégé was admitted to the bar Jefferson drafted letters on Short's behalf to James Madison, to the financier Robert Morris, and to congressmen Richard Peters and Thomas McKean. He commended Short's "genius," "erudition," and "merit." Jefferson gave Short his first legal commission, hiring him to work on the settlement of John Wayles's estate, a brief that introduced Short to the nitty-gritty of the slave trade. At this stage in their relationship Jefferson was not overly troubled by the appearance of favoritism. He lobbied for Short to be appointed to Congress by the Virginia legislature, but, even before Jefferson accepted a posting to Paris, Short hankered after an overseas appointment. Jefferson warned him that diplomatic employment without domestic political support provided at best uncertain opportunities for advancement. That Congress declined to appropriate funds to furnish Jefferson with his own personal secretary in Paris soon highlighted the point that no reliable career path existed within the diplomatic establishment. Yet Jefferson offered Short a position in his household when he accepted the post of minister to France. His decision to employ Short as a private secretary, paying his salary himself, must have appeared to Short to have been a continuation of Jefferson's previous preferential treatment. The young man was convinced he was going places under Jefferson's patronage and was impatient to make his mark on the world. Their complementary ambitions promised a harmonious partnership.[8]

———

Although Short was the recipient of one of the most sensational letters Jefferson ever wrote, the so-called "Adam and Eve" letter justifying the violence of the French Revolution's Terror, he is not a well-known figure, even to professional historians. This book does not aim to offer a full-scale biography but rather to examine Short's life in relation to Thomas Jefferson's. Within their relationship the personal and political came together, fused by Jefferson's extraordinary and enduring interest in the younger man. They shared concerns—money, politics, marriage, slavery—commonplace in male interactions at the time, yet of wider interest precisely because Jefferson expressed paternal feelings toward Short while the younger man regarded Jefferson as a father figure. Their relationship, viewed from Short's perspective, illuminates the wider difficulties faced by members of the Founding Fathers' successor generations as they struggled to establish a personal, moral, and political independence in their dealings with venerated "demi-gods." Jefferson gambled with Short's money, trust, and discretion, never fully accepting Short as an intellectual equal. Short was prepared to challenge Jefferson's values or, more often, ignore them. By doing so he wounded Jefferson. Although the two were not related, viewing Jefferson in an all too human bind—that of the father whose son just won't listen—helps explain the personal forces shaping a political morality Jefferson sharpened through his relationship with the younger man.[9]

Short's decision to take lodgings with a bourgeois family on the outskirts of Paris rather than board permanently at the official American residence soon alarmed Jefferson. The younger man's developing criticism of the French Revolution and his disinclination to marry spurred Jefferson to clarify his thinking on two distinct moral hazards: those associated with leaving republican America to live in decadent *ancien regime* France and those associated with returning to America and, in particular, to the slave society of Virginia. Jefferson was an exceptionally eloquent and perceptive analyst of both risks. Soon after he had introduced Short to the best and the brightest of French society Jefferson began advising young American men not to travel to Europe. He believed that, in France especially, they would acquire a love of aristocracy, a distrust of republican simplicity, and an appetite for extramarital sex. As Short embraced French culture while insisting that his head had not been turned, Jefferson developed his fears in ever greater detail. While in France Jefferson oversaw the publication of his masterwork *Notes on the State of Virginia*. Here Jefferson identified the moral hazard bound up in the "boisterous passions" of the master–slave relationship. "The man must be a prodigy who can retain his manners and morals undepraved by such circumstances," he wrote. He proposed to Short and to other correspondents measures to mitigate the risk posed by living in Virginia among those "whom fortune has thrust upon us," but he also attempted to justify holding slaves as an individual's Christian duty. Short was reluctant to accept this reasoning. He disliked the institution of slavery and did not wish to return to life in a slave society.[10]

Jefferson's advice to Short soon began to develop recurrent themes. Short should return to Virginia both for the good of his career and for the health of his morals. Jefferson encouraged Short to become a republican statesman in Congress if he really wished to serve his country. To achieve this goal he should marry, settle to a profession (ideally the practice of law), and serve in elected office long enough to form the political connections that were as important as experience and ability in advancing a career in public service. Were Short to take this path, Jefferson assured him, he might eventually be appointed to diplomatic positions of distinction where he might earn fame.

Had Short followed Jefferson's advice by marrying and fathering children he would have become the head of a family. As a patriarch in his own right, the conventions governing a son and father, or pupil and teacher and defining the relationship between him and Jefferson would have lost their relevance. And as Short developed his own political connections, his reliance on Jefferson's patronage would have receded. Jefferson respected his son-in-law Thomas Mann Randolph's independence and generally refrained from offering him admonition of the kind he directed at Short. Although Short valued Jefferson's advice, he balked at acting on it. By 1789, as Jefferson prepared to return to the United States, the relationship between the two men was stuck somewhere between that of equals and that of mentor and protégé. Either might have disowned their intimacy in France and walked away from a discordant relationship. Yet, at the end of his sojourn abroad, Jefferson dubbed Short his "adoptive son."

Jefferson was desperate to stay in France to witness and influence political developments there that reached revolutionary intensity following the storming of the Bastille, but, by 1789, a number of factors made a return to Virginia a matter of urgency. He faced financial ruin. His political career risked being eclipsed while the new federal government organized in his absence. He had begun his affair with Sally Hemings. According to Hemings family memory, reliable in other matters, Sally was pregnant by Jefferson in the summer of 1789 and therefore had a pressing incentive to sue for her freedom on the basis of residency in France. Meanwhile Jefferson's eldest daughter Martha (nicknamed Patsy) had expressed an interest in taking holy orders and a wish to rid Virginia of slavery. William Short presented a different problem. Jefferson had advised Short to return America at the earliest opportunity for the sake of his moral well-being and political future. But Jefferson's application for a leave of absence allowing him to return to the United States to sort out his affairs was predicated on the supposition that Short would stay in France to cover for him, and Jefferson had told Short this. In Jefferson's absence, Short would become the senior American diplomat in revolutionary France. Jefferson had not yet directly criticized the younger man's political judgment but his developing misgivings about Short's lifestyle weighed on him as he considered his options. The situation required management, and Jefferson addressed the problem in the manner of a plantation patriarch accustomed to moving members of his household around like chess pieces. In May 1789, without consulting Short, who was touring southern Europe, Jefferson offered Short's position to Connecticut-born artist John Trumbull, a mutual acquaintance of both men.[11]

Jefferson described Short's job to Trumbull, who was then based in London, in terms that Short might have found insulting. It involved, Jefferson said, little work and afforded ample time for travel. But Trumbull had visited the American legation in Paris on several occasions and he knew of Short's fondness for the city. Moreover, when Trumbull returned from his first trip to Europe in 1783, his own father, like Jefferson, had urged him to settle in America and take up the practice of law "as the profession which in a republic leads to all emolument and distinction." Trumbull was no more inclined to follow this path to a position in American society than Short. Though he did not specify what he would do were Short to be so "imprudent" as to leave his current situation, he assured Jefferson that, should Short return to the United States, "no situation in life could be so agreeable to me as one which would place me near you, and under the protection of your advice and example."

This demurral spurred Jefferson to spell out for Trumbull what would be prudent for a man in Short's position, as well as his own.

> I am going out of life, Mr. Short is coming in. He has never viewed his
> present situation but as temporary. . . . His views are justly directed to
> something permanent, independent, in his own country, and which
> may admit him to marry. His talents, his virtues, and his connections
> ensure him anything he may desire [there]. Perhaps he has already let
> pass the most favorable opportunity of putting himself in the way of
> preferment. But these opportunities will recur. His letters to me during
> his absence shewed to me that he thought it time to return to his own
> country, and some expressions in conversation make me suppose he
> means to do it on my return. I have not asked his decision, lest he
> might mistake my wishes. He put himself under my guidance at 19. or
> 20. years of age. He is to me therefore as an adoptive son, and nothing
> is more interesting to me than that he should do what is best for him-
> self. It is on this principle alone that I shall acquiesce under his leaving
> me; because I am persuaded he will obtain better positions.[12]

Within the narrative Jefferson spun around this scheme, both Trumbull
and Short gained from their patron's self-sacrifice and republican disinterest-
edness. Trumbull's artistic career would benefit from leaving London for Paris
since London was not a suitable place for a republican painter, particularly
one planning to specialize in a series commemorating American heroes and
their victories. Moreover, living in Paris and supported by income from an
undemanding job, it would be relatively easy for Trumbull to take time off to
tour the cultural sites of Europe. Meanwhile Short would benefit, as would
any young American man of his station, from a return to Virginia and re-entry
into republican society. However, although both young men had expressed a
willingness to serve him, Jefferson couldn't command them in the manner of
a patriarch instructing bondsmen or family members. For all that Jefferson
spoke of "acquiescing" in Short's supposed plan to return to the United States,
he couldn't be sure that Short would commit to leaving France.[13]

Short solved Jefferson's dilemma for him. On his return from Italy, he
told Jefferson that "with respect to my remaining at Paris during your absence a sufficient inducement would be that you should desire it . . . provided
it should be thought proper to name me *chargé des affaires*." Short would
stay, albeit in the expectation of promotion, and thereby enable Jefferson to
leave. Jefferson's concerns about the effects a continuing residence in France

might have on Short's character remained. He redoubled his efforts to coax an errant son to return home, for his good as well as for Short's. "Adoptive son" may have been a metaphor but Jefferson used it only for Short and the phrase referenced emotional vulnerability as well as parental direction. In a detailed letter of advice to Short, Jefferson revealed his need for the younger man: "nothing can be more dreary than my situation when you and my daughters shall have left me."[14]

———

Despite dubbing him a "son," Short was never fully integrated into Jefferson's domestic world. In France, he chose to reside elsewhere yet threatened to disrupt, through his interest in Patsy, emotional support structures that Jefferson was coming to regard as essential to his well-being. At the same time, despite their differences in age and Jefferson's love of privacy, while in France William Short came to know the private, personal Jefferson in a manner distinct from any other male acquaintance Jefferson made during his life. For both, the result was a singular and enduring relationship grounded neither in shared intellectual activity, nor political conviction, nor even formal familial ties.

In France, the two men shared in common friendships with society hostesses, particularly Madame de Corny and Madame de Tessé, which Jefferson might have preferred to have kept to himself. These women and others included remarks addressed to and discussing Short in their correspondence with Jefferson. They viewed Short as an intimate of Jefferson's while treating other young Americans, such as John Trumbull, as satellite members of Jefferson's circle. Although Jefferson did not encourage his friends to see his relationship with Short in this light, he could not escape the conclusions contemporaries drew from the young man's place in his life. In Paris, Short witnessed the development of an adulterous affair between Jefferson and Maria Cosway. Cosway drew Short into this relationship by including items of gossip directed at him in her letters to Jefferson, with the implication that Jefferson should relay the tidbits and thus their source. During Jefferson's tour of southern Europe Short took a particular interest in Jefferson's daughter Patsy and relayed snippets of their conversation. He socialized with Patsy's circle of teenage female friends. One of them, Marie-Jacinthe Botidoux, who admired Short, reflected fondly on laughter-filled evenings the girls had spent in Short's company. She later closed a letter to Patsy with the salutation "Give my best regards to Sally." Sally Hemings was at least occasionally part of Patsy's circle and therefore Short had opportunities to observe her outside her domestic duties and, before long, to judge from her fine clothes that she was something other than a house servant. If, as is likely, Sally was pregnant when she accompanied Jefferson on his return journey to Virginia in 1789, Short might have noticed that, too.[15]

For his part Jefferson witnessed the beginnings of a charged senti-mental friendship between Short and their mutual acquaintance Duchess Alexandrine-Charlotte-Sophie (known as Rosalie) de La Rochefoucauld. Later, reading between the lines of Short's letters, he followed its progress as it deepened in a manner that his own briefer affair with Maria Cosway had not. Jefferson was also aware of Short's desire to please older women, such as their mutual friend Madame de Tessé, and his interest in younger girls, such as Lilite Royer, the daughter of the family with whom Short lodged. Madame de Tessé commented to Jefferson on Short's evident interest in the Royers, commentary that may have made both men uncomfortable.[16]

Incomplete knowledge and informed speculation concerning one another's lives in Paris did not make the two men confidantes. Short never claimed to completely "know" Jefferson. Jefferson returned the compli-ment, never directly commenting on Short's personal affairs but instead of-fering general moral instruction presented with paternal rhetoric. Jefferson and Short were reluctant to discuss what lay half-established but unstated between them. Jefferson, intensely private, avoided the implied equality of a free discussion of personal emotions with another man in favor of more structured relationships—father–son, minister–agent—that he thought he could control. Short meanwhile struggled to find the words to express his feelings toward a father figure who was sometimes his employer and at others his creditor. Bound up with their personal desires and frustrations were the politics of intergenerational relationships.

———

While in France Jefferson came up with arguably his most protean insight: a declaration of independence on behalf of generations as yet unborn whom he would never encounter. Expanding on Kant's insight that it was a crime to impose a perpetual adolescence on the rising generation through patriar-chal micro-management, Jefferson famously considered the propositions that stewardship of the Earth rightly belonged to the living generation, and each generation was distinct, sovereign, and answerable to itself alone. Succeeding generations possessed an absolute right to rebel against the supposed wisdom of their predecessors (although Jefferson hoped they would not exercise that right lightly). While Jefferson believed that his generation had a duty to equip Short's generation for independence, his generation could not offer its children republicanism through catechism. To paraphrase the Puritan view of salvation, republicanism had to come to the rising generation through faith and understanding. Believing both that mankind possessed an ineradicable moral sensibility and also that its innate morality could be warped by the imposition of external structures such as religious instruction, Jefferson concluded that, ultimately, Short's generation and its successors had to develop an appropriately republican morality through their own efforts. Emotional bonds, the parent's desire to instruct the child, and the child's desire to receive instruction and reassurance complicated Jefferson's pristine vision but did not, in his view, make it unrealizable.[17]

In a letter to his grandson Thomas Jefferson Randolph, Jefferson explained how he had acquired a moral compass through "self-catechising habit." As a young man, he told Thomas, he was often in the society of horse racers as well as distinguished men. At the victory of a favorite horse, he told his grandson with a straight face, he would ask himself whether he wanted the reputation of a jockey or "an honest advocate of his countries rights." To help him decide, Jefferson would ask himself what his former teachers and mentors, William Small, George Wythe, or Peyton Randolph, would have done. In the moments that defined his life, Short seems not to have been in any hurry to ask himself "What would Jefferson do?" Then again Short had little need to pose the question. The republican truths Jefferson developed through judging, albeit tolerantly, the error of Short's ways were offered freely in his letters to his adoptive son and to other younger men.[18]

The most immediate setting in which Jefferson imagined an appropriately republican moral compass could develop was in a household built around a conjugal union. There power and responsibility would be shared between husband and wife, children and servants. Yet Jefferson's wife died at the relatively young age of thirty-three. Moreover, for Jefferson, "household" was a term necessarily encompassing the presence of slaves and slavery. That Jefferson had no white male heir made it easier for him to evade the question of whether the political morality of his own white children had been damaged by slavery. Nevertheless, his status as a widower and slaveowner encouraged Jefferson to imagine relationships located in a space beyond a plantation slaveowner's family hearth. Jefferson dreamed of creating a community of like-minded friends who would settle on farms around Monticello and create the antithesis of plantation society, a neighborhood in which reason could be indulged and moral conduct inculcated.

When James Monroe announced that he, too, intended to settle in Albemarle County, a delighted Jefferson replied: "Short will establish himself there, and perhaps Madison may be tempted to do so. This will be society enough, and ... [a] great sweetener of our lives." This vision of neighborliness resembled the "academical village" of the University of Virginia as much as it did a casually assembled community of friends and farmers. "Life is of no value but as it brings us gratifications," Jefferson told Madison. "Among the most valuable of these is rational society. It informs the mind, sweetens the temper ... and promotes health." Idealized community, operating in tandem with idealized families, also lay at the heart of Jefferson's advice to Short. "In this country," Jefferson later told Short at a moment when William was contemplating a return to Paris, "a family for leisure moments, and a farm or profession for those of employment are indispensable for happiness. These mixed with books, a little letter writing, and neighborly and friendly society constitute a plenum of occupation and of happiness which leaves no wish for the noisy and barren amusements and distractions of a city." Jefferson made extraordinary and sustained efforts to have Short settle in the vicinity of Monticello. Yet Short preferred to live in Philadelphia, a city that had moreover, by the 1790s, taken French manners and culture to its heart, thereby continuing, in Jefferson's eyes, to place Short's moral health at risk.[19]

Rejecting Jefferson's advice did not make Short a spokesman for his generation and cannot in itself establish a wider generational dissatisfaction with the wisdom of its fathers. Nevertheless, reflecting his generation's wisdom, Jefferson doubted the "attachment" of a man who did not have family in his country. Short's character as the bachelor prodigal who never returned to Virginia therefore reintroduces a key question. What, in the end, led each man to carry forward an investment in an imaginary yet heartfelt father–son relationship rather than, as patron and client, do one another's bidding or, as two mature adults, agree to disagree?[20]

Although the relationship between Jefferson and Short was forged during their shared residence in France, it was carried forward through the exchange of letters over the far greater number of years they spent apart. Even by the standards of the age both Jefferson and Short treated correspondence with a formality bordering on obsession: logging, copying, and preserving letters sent and received. At his death Short informed his testators: "The following is a list of the letters I have received and which have been kept by me. Many of them are old and entirely useless by now. . . . The numbers indicate the pi-geonhole in which they are placed." Retained within this "mass" were over two hundred letters written by Jefferson to Short over a thirty-year period. Jefferson addressed an incendiary defense of French revolutionary violence and, later, an agonized appraisal of the Missouri Crisis to the younger man. During Jefferson's retirement the two men discussed religious morality with some freedom although Jefferson dismissed Short's claim to be an Epicurean. A far greater number of letters exchanged between Jefferson and the likes of James Madison or John Adams survive, and these consistently discuss weightier intellectual and political themes than the bulk of the Jefferson–Short correspondence. Jefferson sometimes wrote to Short as if to an over-grown child and seldom addressed him as an intellectual equal. It is reasonable to suppose that some of Jefferson's letters must have made for painful reading, yet Short kept very nearly all of them. His deathbed claim to the contrary, there are good reasons to suppose that Short did not regard Jefferson's letters to him as part of a jumble which had survived by happenstance. Short valued them. At the very least he considered using them as a basis for an authorized biography.[21]

Jefferson also hoarded letters and for similar reasons. In 1823, declining Robert Walsh's request to be granted access to his correspondence, Jefferson argued that "the letters of a person, especially one whose business has been chiefly translated by letters, form the only full and genuine journal of life; and few can let them go out of their hands while they live. A life written after these hoards become opened to investigation must supersede any previous one." Preempting such investigation, sections of Jefferson's *Autobiography*, no-tably his account of the French Revolution, relied heavily on letters written, copied, and saved at the time. Jefferson retained over three hundred letters written by Short. Short offered Jefferson jeremiads on politics in France and in the United States. He presented views on race, slavery, and emanci-pation just as sensational, though less well known to a modern audience, as Jefferson's defense of revolutionary violence. Some of Short's letters might have made Jefferson uncomfortable. Still the common themes of Short's per-sonal correspondence with Jefferson were business or professional concerns of more obvious interest to the writer than to the recipient. Short was a needy, repetitious, and self-absorbed correspondent. Ever sensitive to perceived slights, Short seldom accepted that interruptions in correspondence might be occasioned by chance. He chided all his correspondents for not writing more frequently while often acknowledging letters received with effusive thanks for the regard they showed him. These tendencies are readily apparent in his letters to Jefferson, where they were amplified by Short's anxiety for preferment.[22]

Jefferson was unwilling, even when able, to satisfy Short's need for reassurance and encouragement. This asymmetry led Short on more than one occasion to send Jefferson a string of letters he subsequently wished he could recall and that he asked Jefferson to forget. In 1791, and again in 1809, Short asked Jefferson to burn any of his letters still in his possession. Burning correspondence suggested that the contents of the letters destroyed were of emotional value to writer and reader. It was on these grounds that Jefferson destroyed his extant correspondence with both his mother and his wife Martha. That Jefferson ignored Short and retained very nearly all the correspondence he received from him does not mean that he regarded Short's letters as valueless. As much as Short's letters recorded anxieties that Jefferson could not resolve or offered opinions he declined to address, they are also paeans to a form of emotional bond which Jefferson understood. Bound up in the business of writing and retaining their shared correspondence was an active force of self-revelation that shaped their orientation toward one another and their investment in a continuing relationship.[23]

A key objective of the epistolary friendships which Short, Jefferson, and others idealized was the act of "unbosoming." The concept possessed deep roots in civic humanist understandings of the art and purpose of letter-writing. Unbosoming created a presumptive equality between correspondents in a space beyond criticism or moral censure. Short believed that nobody but Jefferson could enter into the "true spirit" of Short's letters concerning his career as a diplomat. Jefferson prized "unbosoming," hoping that the process would surmount misunderstandings rooted in "the texture of the human mind" and the "slipperiness of human reason." Friendships based in the recognition of shared integrity stood above partisan distinctions and so cemented the republican edifice. By this definition the Short–Jefferson correspondence was neither friendly nor republican. Short never embarrassed Jefferson by endorsing Federalist positions and he never publicly criticized Jefferson's republicanism, yet he regarded much of Jefferson's politics as misguided. Testily fielding letters complaining that he had not exerted himself on Short's behalf, Jefferson claimed that he longed to unburden himself of the emotions occasioned by the politics of appointing a minister to France because, once he had, his friendship for Short would be apparent and they could move on to loftier terrain. But a climatic unburdening never occurred. Emotional reticence swung the relationship between the two men away from that of friend and equal and back toward that of father and son. Justifying the violence of the French Revolution to Short, Jefferson reflected that "while old men are sensible enough of their own advance in years, they do not sufficiently rec- ollect it in those whom they have seen young." However, this recognition of Short's independence was undermined by Jefferson's explanation that his decision to write to Short in "the stile to which I have always been accus- tomed with you" was born of "fostering anxieties." By retaining Short's letters Jefferson was acting against the wishes of a professed friend and expressing a variant of the thread of paternalism woven into their relationship.[24]

Despite their sometimes incendiary, sometimes hurtful, and often patronizing content, Short was happy to retain Jefferson's letters. There was "not one which you could object to being seen by any of those who are to come after me." That Jefferson's correspondence was often didactic and advice-laden did not lessen its value in Short's eyes. The letters saved were part of Short's larger, lifelong attempt to gain perspective on Jefferson's personality and world view. "It often occurs to me to repass in my mind your manner of viewing political subjects," Short wrote Jefferson in 1814. The acts of offering, seeking, and rejecting advice and affection often clarify family relationships, and, in this case, they shaped an equally strong imaginary bond. Through their correspondence Jefferson and Short carried forward an investment in a heartfelt yet artificial father–son relationship, despite the fact that this im- plied bond was seemingly observed in the breach. From their shared years in France onward, Jefferson found a singular emotional as well as political fulfillment through the exercise of an arm's-length, tough love, quasi-parental affection for William Short. Judging Short, he gave endlessly of his advice and encouragement to him but then, like a parent, tolerated and even indulged Short's repeated failures to follow his guidance.[25]

———

This book traces the up and downs of a relationship that swung away from the implied contract of a patron and client, toward distrust and emotional coolness, and finally back toward trust and a measure of equality. Chapter One examines the lives the two men established for themselves in France. Belying the terms of his employment Short lived largely apart from Jefferson and, for the first year of his sojourn, did little work for him. Short's absence stimulated Jefferson's paternal feeling, however, Short's behavior in France led Jefferson to question the younger man's commitment to his familial and political values. Short seemed to crave aristocratic society, whereas Jefferson tolerated it. Jefferson sought intellectual stimulation in France, Short sought social life. The key issue shaping their divergent responses to life in France was the position of women within French society. Jefferson fashioned from his observation of French mores an idealization of virtuous republican marriage. Through his engagement with French women Short developed an interest in virtuous attachments outside marriage. The development of this distinction is the subject of Chapter Two.

Short's apparent deviation from the prescriptions of republican morality fueled an unease in Jefferson which soon spilled over into distrust and eventually outright condemnation of Short's political judgment. While Short never realized his dream of succeeding Jefferson as minister to France, from 1789 to 1794, he pursued a diplomatic career that is the subject of Chapter Three. As resident minister in Holland Short handled with diligence and care the negotiation of loans from the Dutch to address America's debts to the French. Financial diplomacy brought him to the attention of Washington's cabinet and embroiled him in a larger struggle to define America's policy toward revolutionary France. Short's official despatches, increasingly critical of the French Revolution, fueled in Jefferson a suspicion that Short's judgment had been warped by his fondness for the social life of a decadent society. Magnified by distance, the gap between Jefferson's confidence in his own assessment of the aims and progress of the French Revolution versus his distrust of Short's opinion and the sources informing it produced the "Adam and Eve" letter to William Short, in which Jefferson, from the safety of the United States, informed Short that French revolutionary violence was justified. This letter, its context, and its influence of their relationship are discussed in depth in Chapter Four.[26]

Jefferson's heartless response to the murder of mutual friends was all the more painful to Short because, from 1790, Short was engaged in a relationship with Rosalie de La Rochefoucauld that lasted, with interruptions, for twelve years. Rosalie, whose family suffered grievously in the Terror and had herself been placed under house arrest, wished Short to remain in France after the termination of his diplomatic career, whereas Jefferson wanted to him to settle as a neighbor in Albemarle. Short's relationship with Rosalie is the subject of Chapter Five. In 1795 and again in 1798, Rosalie as good as asked Short to marry her. Short wavered, but in 1802, resolved his indecision by returning to the United States. Meanwhile, in 1795, Jefferson used a power of attorney granted him by Short to purchase an estate in Albemarle County, Indian Camp (now known as Morven), in the expectation that Short would return to Virginia. Although he never settled into a life as Jefferson's neighbor, Short demanded and received Jefferson's continuing assistance in the management of Indian Camp. For his part Jefferson used Short's assets to covertly fund the operation of the Monticello nailery. By the time Jefferson assumed the presidency he owed Short a substantial sum of money, which he struggled to repay. The pair's intertwined financial affairs, seen in the light of their disagreements over slavery and commerce, are discussed in Chapter Six.

Jefferson was fifty-nine when Short returned to the United States in 1802, Short was forty-three. Their relationship over the last twenty-four years of Jefferson's life is discussed in Chapter Seven. By that point both men were set in their ways. Their relationship, ruptured by Jefferson's insensitivity to the human cost of revolutionary violence that he considered necessary and, concomitantly, his extreme sensitivity to any criticism that threatened his political position within the United States, survived in part thanks to Short's willingness to suppress his disagreements with Jefferson. Still, in later life, Short's letters displayed only outward conformity to a set of ideas that Jefferson would have regarded as central to republicanism. Crucially, Short did not believe that a viable republic could be fashioned around the sovereign will of the people as expressed through their representatives in popularly elected legislative assemblies. Jefferson failed to disabuse him of this heresy. Meanwhile, in his penultimate surviving letter to Short, written in January 1826, Jefferson gently but firmly squashed Short's dream of ameliorating slavery by converting slaves into serfs. In this, as in so many other matters, Short never changed Jefferson's mind. These failures within a relationship of independently minded men who wished nonetheless to be tied to one another by trust and affection reveal in microcosm central tensions within the transmission of republican culture in the early republic.[27]

ONE

Springs Set in Motion

ESTABLISHING SEPARATE LIVES IN FRANCE

IN DECEMBER 1781, Jefferson, enraged by criticism of his performance as Governor of Virginia, resigned his seats in the Virginia legislature and Continental Congress. He told friends that he possessed no ambition other than to return to Monticello and family life. When Marquis de Chastellux visited him in the spring of 1782, he found him in his chosen setting with "a gentle and amiable wife, charming children whose education is his special care, a house to embellish, extensive estates to improve, the arts and sciences to cultivate." However, Jefferson's dream of retirement was shattered by the death of his wife, Martha, on September 6, 1782. For three months he lived in "a stupor of mind," "as dead to the world as she was whose loss occasioned it." Jefferson had previously turned down foreign appointments, but as he began to emerge from the depths of his grief, he was of a mind to accept one. Deflecting a suggestion that he replace Robert R. Livingston as Confederation Congress' Secretary for Foreign Affairs, Jefferson sought an overseas posting. His preference was for France.[1]

The emotionally scarred widower did not seek a life-changing experience. Writing of his favorite author Laurence Sterne's picaresque *A Sentimental Journey Through France and Italy*, Jefferson outlined the approach he would adopt toward his own sojourn in France. "We neither know nor care whether [Sterne] really went to France" Jefferson told his friend Robert Skipwith. "Everything," even vicarious travel, "is useful which contributes to fix us in the principles and practice of virtue." Foreign travel, indeed actual residence abroad, Jefferson theorized was useful insofar as it threw up situations and dilemmas that reinforced preexisting principles of virtue; it should not become the vehicle by which one set of values might be replaced by another.

Heir through Hope. Peter Thompson, Oxford University Press. © Peter Thompson 2023.
DOI: 10.1093/oso/9780197546833.003.0002

Jefferson had received some lessons in French—from a Scotsman. His intellectual development had taken place in settings such as royal Governor Fauquier's self-described *parties quarées* in Willamsburg, where French contributions to the arts, science, and the spread of Enlightened values were praised. He had amassed a library of French-language texts. American popular culture, expressed through widely read works such as *The American Wanderer Through Various Parts of Europe . . . By a Virginian* (a crude, plagiarized, adaptation of Sterne's *A Sentimental Journey*) might depict France as the home of a frivolous, insincere, overly sexualized, and therefore immoral culture, but Jefferson had no intention of "going native."[2]

William Short's interest in a residence abroad was rooted in his ambition rather than in any desire to develop his character. He was twenty-four years old and already bored with the practice of law when Jefferson began considering a foreign posting. As soon as he heard that Congress was considering appointing Jefferson to its Peace Commission, Short wrote to him angling for a position as secretary to an overseas legation—without specifying a country.

Short wished for, perhaps expected, advancement from Jefferson comparable to that which David Humphreys had received from George Washington. Humphreys had served as an aide-de-camp to George Washington during the Revolutionary War, and Washington had signaled his regard for Humphreys by choosing him to present Washington's official dispatch and the captured British standards to Congress when the British surrendered at Yorktown. On his arrival in Philadelphia Humphreys was feted by an ecstatic Congress. When subsequently Washington presented himself to Congress to resign his commission in person, Humphreys accompanied him. His status as Washington's protégé was sealed. When they discussed his future employment at Mount Vernon in 1783, Humphreys indicated that he wanted to take up command of a regiment in the army, or the post of secretary to a foreign commission, or perhaps "the office of Secretary of Foreign affairs." Washington duly secured Humphreys official secretarial appointments to Congress' Peace Commission and its successor, the Commission for Negotiating Foreign Treaties of Amity and Commerce. These postings, whose origin in Washington's patronage was common knowledge, established Humphreys' residence in Europe.[3]

Short's wish to emulate Humphreys by achieving a position through appointment became a source of tension between him and Jefferson. Jefferson expected Short to serve an apprenticeship in legislative politics before claiming the prize of a foreign posting. After all, he had. In April 1783, when news of the signing of a preliminary peace treaty with Great Britain led Congress to withdraw Jefferson's commission as Minister Plenipotentiary to the Peace

Commission, Jefferson had returned to Confederation Congress as leader of Virginia's delegation. Years later, in his *Autobiography*, Jefferson indicted the congressmens' "morbid rage for debate." "Day after day" was wasted "on the most unimportant questions." How, he asked, "could it be otherwise in a body to which the people send 150 lawyers, whose trade it is to question everything, yield nothing, and talk by the hour." In 1784, however, as the moment of his own departure neared, there was one more lawyer Jefferson wanted to send to Congress—William Short. "His talents are great," Jefferson told Madison, and "I see the best effects produced by sending our young statesmen here."[4]

The absolute necessity for any aspiring public servant to present himself for election to state or national legislatures would be a recurrent theme in Jefferson's advice to Short and others. Jefferson believed that service in Congress was character-forming. Short had already dismissed service in Congress as a "fall upstairs" but he understood Jefferson's reasoning. Characteristically he had offered his brother Peyton precisely the advice he himself refused to take. There was "no post in this government so respectable and so desirable for a young man as a seat in the legislature," Short told Peyton: "I must insist on your offering [yourself] at the first election." William Short disliked the business of electioneering and political log-rolling, as did Jefferson. Jefferson, mistreated by elected officials during his bereavement, had earned the right to disdain them. Short had not.[5]

Jefferson had already demonstrated a willingness to advance Short's career, and, in the spring of 1784, going against the grain of much of his previous advice, he did so once more. In April, Congress added Jefferson to its Commission for Negotiating Foreign Treaties of Amity and Commerce. He would be joining John Adams and Benjamin Franklin in Paris. The day after he received final confirmation of his appointment, Jefferson formally offered Short a position as his personal secretary. He had already warned Short that he could offer nothing but free room and board, that Short would have to lay out roughly one hundred guineas to acquire suitable clothing, and that he would need to accept any offer swiftly since Jefferson expected other applications for the post. On May 7, Jefferson told Short to be ready to depart from Philadelphia by May 25. He also asked for help ensuring that his slave James Hemings, who Jefferson intended to take with him to Paris, be sent to Philadelphia as swiftly as possible. This would be the last Short would hear from Jefferson for eleven months. Jefferson had myriad matters of his own to attend to and he was not accustomed to offering explanation to a subordinate when he set plans in motion.[6]

It is possible that Jefferson expected, even hoped, that Short would turn down his offer and advance his career by running for elective office after all. The formulation by which Short accepted Jefferson's invitation on May 14— "my determination is what it has long been, to accompany you in any capacity whatsoever"—passively hinted at the difficulties posed by it. The first involved money, the second status. Short's father had recently died. As an executor of his father's estate, Short was in the midst of settling and collecting debts. He confessed to being "at a loss" as to how he might support himself in Europe until a settlement had been achieved. Although Jefferson had told Short that Congress would not fund a private secretary for individual commissioners, Short continued to believe that they might. This suggests that Short found the proposed recompense meager, despite it coming from Jefferson's own stretched pocket.[7]

Short's concerns about how his future status might further his ambitions emerged as a no less powerful obstacle to his swift acceptance of Jefferson's offer. While in Richmond, steeling himself to act on Jefferson's instructions, Short met William Alexander. A friend of Benjamin Franklin's who made a cameo appearance in the best-selling *American Wanderer in Europe*, Alexander, Short told Jefferson, was "perfectly acquainted with all the . . . situations at Paris and with the light in which everyone will be received in every station." He recommended that Short accompany Jefferson as a private individual, not as a private secretary. French society would treat any private secretary, however well regarded by his employer, as a higher-order servant. "If you were in Paris either as a private Man, or with Mr. Jefferson only as his Friend," Alexander advised, then Jefferson's "countenance" and recommendations would introduce him to agreeable and desirable circles and "you would then be received as Mr. Short." Although exceedingly anxious to be known as "Mr. Short," he told Alexander, and tactlessly repeated to Jefferson, "my design in going was to get what improvement was to be obtained in the diplomatic line." He therefore needed an official connection to the commissioners. Echoing Jefferson, Alexander advised Short that, if he was determined to pursue a diplomatic career and at the same time overcome the prejudices of French society, then it would be imperative "to get Congress to take some notice of you by some means or other . . . anything, of any description which can be a kind of *Coup d'Eclat* . . . will do."[8]

Short's desire to make a mark was not completely incompatible with Jefferson's need for a dependable secretary, nor with Jefferson's general desire to advance Short's interests. But Short acted on Alexander's advice in ways

that strained his subsequent relationship with the man he considered his patron. It was tactless of Short to rehearse the niceties of diplomatic accreditation with Jefferson as if they bore on him alone. On the eve of his departure
Jefferson confessed to Monroe that he feared Congress might provide him
instructions so drafted that "we shall be at Paris but private citizens . . . liable to the jurisdiction of the country." Aside from the obstacle that insufficient or nonexistent diplomatic status would present to the conduct of the
legation's work, it would also render one member of the household, James
Hemings, subject to the laws of the French mainland and hence eligible to sue
for freedom. In a further manifestation of Short's desire to be his own man, in
May 1784, he risked irritating his employer by not complying with Jefferson's
request that he ensure James Hemings joined his owner's party in time for
their departure. The logistics of securing James's attendance were more complicated than Jefferson realized, and Hemings had his own ideas as to when
and how he might rendezvous with Jefferson's party. However, Short's reluctance to drop everything and deliver Hemings to Jefferson reflected in part a
dislike of the business of slavery, which was becoming visible that summer as
he settled his father's estate.[9]

In the days before his departure for France, Jefferson waited impatiently
for Short. Mutual acquaintances had offered to speed Short on his way if they
saw him. However, following Alexander's advice, and indulging a morbid fear
of sea travel that he had not confessed to Jefferson, Short instead hung around
Richmond seeking to make his mark with local politicians. He busied himself
in the practical details of the legislature's decision to commission a statue of
George Washington from a Parisian studio. He also angled to retain his seat
on Virginia's Executive Council while in France. Alexander had planted in
Short's mind the idea that perhaps one day Short might succeed Jefferson
as America's representative to France, which he "blushed" to mention to
Jefferson, but did anyway.[10]

Short put the best face he could on a residence in Richmond which, as
it dragged on, seemed to imply that he regretted that Jefferson had made
his offer in the first place. Jefferson should doubt not Short's "earnest desire to be with you." Since it would have been impossible to have traveled
with Jefferson, he might as well settle his affairs and take a later sailing. At
least the delay had allowed him to visit Jefferson's two youngest daughters,
Lucy and Mary (known as Polly), who Jefferson had entrusted to the care
of Francis and Elizabeth Eppes. "You may count on me as if present," Short
wrote Jefferson from Richmond with some swagger in late July, adding nervously that he hoped in the meantime "no body may be allowed to supplant

me . . . in your partiality or your confidence." Short had reason to be nervous. Jefferson disembarked at Le Havre on July 31, while Short delayed his departure for Europe until October, some five months after Jefferson had offered him the post. He arrived six weeks after the three American commissioners had held their first meeting.[11]

By the time Jefferson and Short began their sojourn in France, their tacit patron–client relationship had already been strained. Letters in which Short attempted to explain to Jefferson his reservations and hence his delayed departure went unanswered. Decisions made by Jefferson in the meantime altered their future working relationship. Yet mutual expectations had to remain undiscussed until Short's arrival in Paris. Thereafter, uneasy about his status, both in Jefferson's regard and in the eyes of French society, Short redoubled his efforts to present himself as something other than a subordinate member of Jefferson's household.

The five years they shared in France laid the foundation of the lifelong relationship between William Short and Thomas Jefferson. At either end of their shared sojourn abroad Jefferson used heartfelt familial metaphors— "good boy," "adoptive son"—to reference a man who responded in kind, by acknowledging Jefferson as a father as well as a friend and yet ignored advice and entreaty alike. Short chose to live at some distance from Jefferson, even as he sought a place in his family. Jefferson considered cutting his ties to Short and yet chose not to. Somehow they avoided a decisive split. Doubts and silences remained, but gradually the pair fashioned an accommodation in their personal and professional lives. In consequence, the two men created a peculiar relationship, one they could not quite describe and one that they did not, perhaps, enjoy.

———

Two days before Short finally arrived in Paris Jefferson had expressed his impatience with the young man in a letter to James Madison: "his delay is unaccountable." It is hard to imagine that Short did not go straight to Jefferson's residence on reaching Paris, but he didn't stay there. Short later reminisced that, on arrival in Paris, "chance" directed him to take up lodgings with the Royer family in St. Germain-en-Laye, on the outskirts of the city. He was probably steered to the Royers by Savary de Valcoulon, a Frenchman based in Richmond who had previously taught him some spoken French. Short said he lodged with the comfortable bourgeois family to improve his French in isolation from English-speaking friends. The twenty-five-year-old was soon doting on the women of the Royer household, presenting both the Royer's thirteen-year-old daughter Anne-Hipolyte-Louise, nicknamed Lilite, and her mother with little gifts: ice-cream for Lilite, an oyster breakfast for her mother. The whole family, said Short, treated him "like a son" and "true friend." He made frequent visits to Paris. Entries from Jefferson's memorandum books record payments made on behalf of Short and a loan from Short to Jefferson, but Short did not commit himself to living in Jefferson's household. Letters from his Virginian friends and, crucially, from Jefferson, were addressed in care of the Royer family.[12]

An air of estrangement between the two men originated in the fact that, while Short delayed his departure, Jefferson secured alternative secretarial support from Washington's protégé David Humphreys. While waiting for his ship Jefferson had encountered Humphreys, who was also about to sail for France to take his position as official secretary to the three American Commissioners to Europe. Although Humphreys was duty-bound to support all three commissioners, Jefferson asked him to take up quarters with him in Paris "if no previous connection nor engagement with either of my colleagues [Franklin and Adams] should prevent it." Humphreys was pleased to report to his brother that Jefferson had "insisted" that he should live with him at Congress' expense. He was present at the first meeting of the American Commissioners, held at Franklin's house in Passy on August 30, and at subsequent meetings. While Short performed little, if any, secretarial work for Jefferson over the winter of 1784–1785, Humphreys reeled off to his mentor George Washington a string of diplomatic activities in which he had been involved. Meanwhile, Jefferson's household was managed by a French servant, Emanuel Petit, and by the Swiss-born Charles Williamos, who was Jefferson's "constant dinner companion" during his first winter in Paris. When Short arrived in Paris he found that Jefferson had little apparent need of him as a secretary, household manager, or "particular friend." He appreciated his growing intimacy with the Royers all the more.[13]

Abigail Adams, who was favorably disposed toward Short, praised his "resolution" in learning French through an immersion in family life. During his first residence in Paris, John Adams had concluded that the swiftest means by which an American might acquire the French language were to take a mistress and frequent the theater. While Adams didn't take a mistress, he and his family enjoyed the Comédie and the Opera, as did Short. Adams sought out places where French was spoken swiftly—notably taverns and posthouses—and he listened carefully to the "chatty" conversational French spoken by female shopkeepers. An incomplete manuscript dictionary of colloquialisms compiled by Short indicates that he took a similar approach to Adams. There is no evidence that he employed a formal tutor.[14]

In time, Short would receive compliments on his written French, and Jefferson, professing an awkwardness with the written language, came to rely on Short's proficiency. Biographical sketches of Short suggest a fluency in spoken French, but perhaps Short's French friends flattered him. The Adamses' daughter Abigail believed that he was not noticeably proficient in spoken French. Jefferson, boasting that his daughter Martha (known as Patsy) spoke French as easily as English due to her immersion in a convent school, nevertheless claimed that, after nearly a year in France, he, Humphreys, and Short were no more fluent than when they had first arrived. Although later in life Jefferson grudgingly acknowledged that total immersion was the best way to learn the language, he also concluded that "while learning the language in France a young man's morals, health and fortune are more irresistibly endangered than in any country in the universe." Within six months of Short's arrival Jefferson had concluded that the young man was in danger.[15]

In the spring of 1785, Jefferson asked in a letter to Short "when are we to see you?" The question, as well as its mode of delivery, suggests a distance between the two men that intermittent face-to-face encounters over the winter had not alleviated. Describing to Short the grand spectacle of a Te Deum sung in Notre Dame to honor the birth of an heir to the French throne, Jefferson added the admonition "come home like a good boy and you will always be in the way of these wonders." At the end of April Jefferson was confirmed as Benjamin Franklin's successor as the United States' Minister to France. On May 2, he informed Short that there was to be no official secretary to the French legation; instead Colonel David Humphreys would continue to prioritize Jefferson's needs. Jefferson had come to dislike Humphreys, who was conservative, an anglophile, and fond of wearing the uniform of the Society of the Cincinnati (the recently formed hereditary association of former officers in the Continental Army). He assured Short that, if it was in his power to appoint a secretary, Short would be his choice—and on merit. For the moment, since there was no official position for him, Short kept up his residence in St. Germain.

In the spring of 1785, Jefferson, with a hint of sarcasm, invited Short to dinner with Lafayette and the Adamses on the "day on which you have flattered us with your return." But Short did not come home. Jefferson reported to their mutual friend Philip Mazzei that Short was well but "at" St. Germain. In May, Abigail Adams reported to her friend Lucy Cranch that Short had been living there exclusively for the past two months. As the first fourth of July that either man had spent abroad approached, Jefferson told Short, by letter, that he had invited "some friends" to dine with him on the day. Short was apparently not included in the invitation.[16]

By that summer the relationship between the two men was at a crossroads. Short's choices led Jefferson to a series of reflections about republican morality and the behavior that should be expected of a "good boy" let loose in France. Yet he did not give up on Short. He included Short alongside Monroe and Madison in his evolving plans to found a "rational society," centered around Monticello, on his eventual return to the United States. He might have wondered about Short's interest in the Royer family, yet he politely acknowledged Short's interest in his own. Instead of abandoning him to his fate, Jefferson set about reclaiming Short by finding him work.[17]

In July 1785, Jefferson used his influence to offer Short an opportunity to step out from David Humphrey's shadow and the Royer family's embrace. At his behest, the American Commissioners ordered Short to travel, via London, to the Hague for a meeting with Baron de Thulemeier, the King of Prussia's envoy to Holland. The pair were to address outstanding procedural issues preventing the formal ratification of a recently negotiated treaty of amity and commerce between the United States and Prussia. Short was to take with him duplicate copies of the treaty, in both French and English, prepared in Paris by Humphreys and signed by Jefferson. John Adams, in London, was to check the treaty's terms and sign in correct form before Short carried the paperwork to Holland. At the Hague he was to satisfy himself of Thulemeier's authority, collect his signature on a copy of the treaty to be returned to the United States, and give Thulemeier the copy signed by Adams and Jefferson to be returned to Berlin. It ought to have to been an uncomplicated, if cumbersome, errand, and Jefferson suggested as much when he informed Thulemeier that the American commissioners—and their secretary Humphreys—were too preoccupied to conduct it in person. However, anticipating that Thulemeier might feel snubbed by having to act through an apparent inferior, Jefferson was careful to describe Short as a "Special Secretary" and a man of talent and merit. In letters of introduction to Dutch acquaintances, Jefferson described Short as "among my most particular friends . . . though young his talents and merit are such as to have placed him in the Council of state of Virginia." Citing fear of a robbery, Jefferson gave Short just enough cash to get to London and asked John Adams to help him out from there.[18]

In London, Abigail Adams "feared" that, partly for want of younger company, Short would form an unfavorable impression of England. She was right. An abiding and unsophisticated dislike of Britain and the British was one lasting consequence of the trip. Short told Jefferson that, with the exception of St. Paul's Cathedral, the buildings of London were inferior to those of Paris. He purported to be unimpressed by what he called the "variety" of London society, as if a twenty-six-year-old Virginian could justify such an impression after ten days' residence that coincided with the capital's summer retreat. While on this mission a tendency to overestimate his understanding of his place in Jefferson's confidences also surfaced for the first time. Short passed on to Jefferson an aside critical of John Adams: "I do not know whether he is writing to you as fully as you wished." Unaware that Jefferson and Adams had agreed to communicate independently of Short he continued to overplay his hand. From the Hague Short told Jefferson that Adams "did not write because he thought it unnecessary and communicated to me, as he said, what he wished you to know." Meanwhile to Adams Short offered flowery thanks for hospitality received in London and gallant compliments to his daughter Abigail (nicknamed Nabby).[19]

When Short presented himself to Thulemeier a "simple matter of etiquette" arose. Jefferson had identified, on behalf of the American Commissioners, some areas where the terms of the treaty as rendered in French did not convey its meaning as expressed in English. But the Prussians were only prepared to accept and sign as the true record a French-language text of the treaty's instruments. While Thulemeier forwarded Jefferson's concerns to Berlin and awaited instructions, Short took advantage of the delay to make a brief tour of Holland. Letters he wrote to Jefferson during this trip reinforced his capacity for clumsy, ill-considered expression. Short artlessly informed Jefferson that he had skipped an appointment to meet Jean Luzacs, the celebrated and extremely influential editor of the *Leyden Gazette,* which Jefferson had arranged. He arrived at Breda so late that he had only a very brief meeting with Jefferson's admirer Gisbjert van Hogendorp. Truthfully, if tactlessly, Short reported that Amsterdam's merchants blamed a decline in their trade on American independence.[20]

Jefferson and Adams were resigned to news of Prussia's insistence on the primacy of a French-language text and accepted Short's characterization of the outstanding discrepancies as mere "errata" he could correct. Returning to the Hague, Short concluded his business with Thulemeier and was able to report on September 11 that the signing was complete. The United States' official copy of the treaty—the first of its kind—was carried to Congress by another Virginian, William Fitzhugh, blunting congressional recognition of Short's modest achievement. Soon after the signing, in a letter copied to John Jay, Jefferson informed Short: "Finding the assistance of a private Secretary necessary in my office I would wish you to accept of the appointment. In this case it will be necessary for you to abandon your plan of continuing [to live] at St. Germain's." Jefferson was not able to "say with certainty what is the salary allowed," and he warned Short that the appointment could be overruled at any moment by Congress. Short might have thought this offer was a reward for his work on the treaty. In fact, Jefferson had already informed John Jay and James Monroe that he simply had to have a "scribe" or official private secretary and was going to appoint Short. Short's efforts in the Hague were an added bonus. Short swiftly accepted but, defying Jefferson's wishes, continued to divide his time between the American legation and the Royers. When Short suffered an attack of jaundice in December 1785 and Abigail Adams sent a folk-remedy for his relief, Jefferson tartly noted that he was well enough to travel from Paris to St. Germain.[21]

———

Jefferson committed no direct comment on Short's relationship with Lilite Royer or her family to paper. His pointed injunction, "come home like a good boy," and his sour remark that Short had not in fact learned much French in the Royer household suggests that, in his view, something else was drawing Short to St. Germain. Jefferson was no prude. He was capable of taking a relaxed view of other men's entanglements with French women, which were, after all, "the vice of the age." Occasionally Jefferson teased those young American men of his acquaintance who, like the poetic David Humphreys, fell for the "allurements" of French women. Lilite Royer, however, was barely of an age to exercise that "female intrigue" which Jefferson believed responsible for the entanglement of American men with French women. That mutual friends such as Madame de Tessé did not condemn as immoral Short's relationship with the Royers, mother as well as daughter, might have persuaded Jefferson to hold his tongue. Nevertheless, while there is no evidence that Jefferson condemned Short's relationship with the Royers, there is no proof that he condoned it.[22]

It is not clear what the Royers thought of Short's intrusion into their life. However, William Stephens Smith, who had met the Royers at Short's invitation, had a shrewd idea of the family's view of his friend. The Royers, he told Short, deserved "everything . . . you can give them and for their sakes I wish heaven had been doubly bountiful to you." If the family had "any more" of Short they would be "over stocked," but Smith was sure that the family did not look "for more from the lamb than his fleece" and that they were reasonable enough to appreciate that "the second shearing is better than the first."

Far from acting as the family's grand patron and as Lilite's Pygmalion, Smith believed that Short was in fact being controlled by the Royers. So, while mindful of the injunction, "evil be to him who evil thinks," Smith suggested that Short move on to seek happiness elsewhere.[23]

Short maintained contact with the Royers long after Lilite had married. Playing the role of *paterfamilias* Short helped the eldest of her sons, Henri-Raphael, emigrate to the United States to take up a job with a merchant in New Orleans. He advanced him $60 a quarter during his stay there. After a younger son, Alexandre-Marie, became a notary, Short introduced him to Parisian friends. As late as 1836, he entrusted Alexandre-Marie to remit a large sum of money for him. Short regarded himself as a member of the Royer family.[24]

———

Short's emotional investment in Lilite Royer and her family does not in itself establish that Short felt estranged from Jefferson and his household during their shared time in France. However, Short's relationship with Jefferson's daughters was in its way as complicated as his relationship with Lilite Royer and her parents. In the first eighteen months of their French sojourn, Jefferson had urged Short to reside permanently as a member of his household in the American legation. Short had refused. Later it was Short who sought a closer engagement with Patsy and, eventually Polly, and Jefferson who established distance. Early in 1786, Jefferson traveled to London to consult with John Adams. This was the first time he had left Patsy alone in Paris, and he tasked Short with forwarding any letters or news from her. Stretching Jefferson's instructions, Short visited Patsy at the convent to solicit a letter. "She is well and wanting only to hear more frequently from you to render her still more happy," Short wrote to Jefferson. A thread of implied criticism as well as unwarranted familiarity ran through reports of this kind, which Jefferson acknowledged with polite but discouraging thanks. Jefferson rigorously excluded him from one of the greatest events in his family's life.[25]

In January 1785, Jefferson learned from Virginia that his daughter Polly had survived a bout of whooping cough but that her younger sister Lucy had not. The account of the death Jefferson received from the attending physician James Currie suggested a certain degree of inaction on the part of Francis and Elizabeth Eppes, despite the loss of their own two-year-old daughter in the attack. Through mischance the Eppes's account of Lucy's death and Polly's survival arrived months after Currie's report. Short would surely have been aware of Jefferson's anxiety, grief, and his resulting determination to bring Polly to

Paris. Polly was reluctant to make the journey, which was necessarily sensitive and difficult to arrange from a distance. Jefferson discussed these matters in general terms with Short, who took the liberty of suggesting an Englishwoman who might accompany Polly on her Atlantic crossing. However, as plans became firmer, Jefferson withheld the details from Short.

In December 1786, Jefferson told Abigail Adams that he intended to send Polly to London in the care of "her nurse, a black woman" on a ship scheduled to sail in May. He asked Abigail to look after Polly until he could send for her. In March 1787, Short forwarded to Jefferson extracts from a gossipy letter he had received from his kinsman Fulwar Skipwith announcing, incorrectly, that Polly would sail for London aboard the *Judith Randolph* in the care of a Captain Roberts. Short also told Patsy that she would soon be reunited with Polly. Writing from Aix-en-Provence, Jefferson acknowledged receipt of Short's letter without comment. His letters to Short during the spring and early summer made no mention of Polly's imminent return or his thoughts on how she (and Sally Hemings) might be brought from London to Paris.[26]

Polly, accompanied by Sally Hemings, sailed from Virginia aboard the *Robert*. Docking in London in June 1787, the two girls were escorted to John and Abigail Adams by the *Robert*'s captain. In expectation that Jefferson would come to collect Polly in person, Abigail asked him to bring Patsy with him to help persuade Polly to make the final leg of her journey. Jefferson sent word that he would not be coming to London. Although Captain Ramsay of the *Robert* volunteered to escort Polly and Sally to Paris, Jefferson considered the offer "unnecessary" and instead sent a man he described as a "trusty servant," namely the major domo of his official residence, Adrien Petit. Petit had limited English and was unknown to the Adamses. Abigail Adams told Jefferson that his daughter had complained that her father had sent a man she "could not understand to fetch her" across the Channel. Jefferson subsequently admitted that Polly had at first refused to leave the Adamses with Petit.[27]

Setting aside why Jefferson decided not to make the journey to London himself, why didn't he send William Short? Short was a Virginian who could speak French, he knew England, and was known and liked by Abigail and John Adams. He was a distant, although unacknowledged kinsman of Sally Hemings, and Jefferson had previously trusted Short to deliver Sally's brother James to him. It is hard to imagine that, if asked, Short would have refused to escort Polly and Sally to Paris. The incident established "Mr. Short's" distance from Jefferson's household and inner family.[28]

In January 1786, David Humphreys announced his intention to return to the United States. This decision left the French legation and its minister without an official secretary. Short had already asked James Monroe whether Congress contemplated creating a permanent secretary or *chargé des affaires* to the legation, but Jefferson had independently suggested that there was hardly enough official business in France to warrant the creation of a congressionally funded permanent secretary to the minister. The best Monroe could do for Short was to tell him, through Jefferson, that he had the support of Virginia's delegation should Congress change its mind and decide to appoint a permanent official. Meanwhile Mr. Short remained Jefferson's temporary employee, paid through Jefferson's allowable ministerial expense claims rather than directly by Congress. Short continued to divide his time between Paris and St. Germain. He was so distant from the day-to-day operation of Jefferson's official residence that it was Philip Mazzei who detected malfeasance among Jefferson's household staff and "turned them out" of employment. The relationship between Jefferson and Short had settled into a state of limbo somewhere between that of equal adults or minister and *chargé*.[29]

When he later offered John Trumbull Short's job, Jefferson dismissed it as consisting of little more than copying papers, with the occasional "squall" of more demanding work. As he left Paris on what turned out to be a four-month tour of southern France Jefferson instructed Short to follow his own inclination as to the amount of time he devoted to official business at the legation; he estimated that as little as one day's attendance a week might be sufficient. In his *Autobiography* Jefferson described, in exaggerated terms, the powerful aid and assistance of Lafayette in America's commercial diplomacy but made no mention of Short. In truth, for as long as Jefferson remained in France, most of Short's official duties, even those arising from America's increasing involvement in France's debt crisis, were those of dogsbody. Short did what he could, but complained that, without the formal title of *chargé des affaires*, officials like French Finance Minister Charles-Alexandre de Calonne treated him as a common messenger or member of Jefferson's household staff. Jefferson's reply, that French officials knew he spoke for Jefferson and that he was therefore Secretary of Legation in all but name, hardly provided reassurance. After all, as Short knew, French ministers often treated Jefferson with scant regard.[30]

In periods between squalls of work, Short compiled digests of French news for Congress and for the other American legations in Europe (though these would always be superseded by Jefferson's ministerial letters). He performed routine consular duties. He sometimes joined Jefferson in entertaining visiting

Americans, among them the New England explorer John Ledyard, who came to Paris to seek permission from the Russian minister to travel overland to Siberia. Short gave Ledyard some financial assistance, which Ledyard acknowledged as coming from a private individual. It fell to Short, as it had fallen to Humphreys before him, to bring to fruition a particularly irksome chore imposed by Congress and expanded by Jefferson: the striking of a series of medals commemorating "interesting events and conspicuous characters of the American Revolution" to be presented to the crowned heads of Europe (Britain excepted) and to the colleges of America. For want of die-makers in the United States, Jefferson recommended Parisian craftsmen and deputized Short to handle arrangements. Overseeing this business offered Short a pretext to address John Jay, Secretary of Congress' Foreign Committee, independently of Jefferson but his supervision hardly augured an act of *éclat* of the sort that William Alexander had urged an aspiring diplomat to present to America's lawmakers. The chore instead put Short on a collision course with Congress—and Jefferson—when a servant Short had entrusted to pay the makers of the medals' presentation cases ran off with the cash. Short fretted he would be billed for the loss.[31]

Jefferson's own achievements in the arena of formal diplomacy during his tenure as minister to France were limited and short-lived. After months of wrangling, Jefferson induced French trade ministers to adopt protocols allowing for freer trade in tobacco. He promoted the claims of American exporters of whale oil to French markets. Gains in these areas were largely negated by growing turmoil within the French government. Likewise, Jefferson painstakingly negotiated a consular convention with France which the French abrogated soon after they had signed it. He lacked the authority to meaningfully address the major issue in Franco-American relations, the United States' failure to repay loans made to it by the French government during the Revolutionary War. Jefferson's main achievements during his years in France lay in the field of cultural diplomacy, managing and molding French views of the United States. In this arena, Jefferson had little need of, and seldom sought, William Short's assistance.[32]

───

Soon after his arrival in Paris Jefferson acted swiftly to correct a report in the *Journal de Paris* that John Dickinson was the author of the Declaration of Independence. Short's opinion on the matter would have carried little weight. Jefferson went to great lengths to ensure that Jean Nicolas Démeunier's entries on Virginia and the United States in the *Encyclopédie Méthodique* were as accurate as possible. Démeunier did not seek Short's opinion. Jefferson reminded the campaigner Honoré Gabriel Riqueti, Count Mirabeau, that Virginia's Act for Establishing Religious Freedom predated French discussions of religious liberty. His voice had the authority of an author. Jefferson soon discovered the limits of the French appetite for learning about the United States from Americans. Prominent friends of America, notably Hector St. Jean de Crèvecoeur, Brissot de Warville, Louis-Alexandre de La Rochefoucauld, and Condorcet, produced for a French audience ostensibly objective accounts of America's life, manners, political system, or potential for change with the ultimate intention of critiquing contemporary French values. Jefferson was reluctant to let misleading statements concerning American life made by French authors whose intentions he admired pass unchallenged, but correcting misapprehensions risked rupturing friendships. As a Virginian in Paris, known to be a friend of Jefferson's and thought to have his ear, Short was drawn into these contests.[33]

Crèvecoeur's highly stylized presentation of the natural simplicity of American life, presented in the French-language editions of his *Letters of An American Farmer* in 1784 and 1787, encouraged false expectations among potential emigrants to the United States. Jefferson was reluctant to disavow the spirit of Crèvecouer's work or deal with one consequence of its popularity: a string of complaints made against America land companies by disappointed French investors. Short did what he could to restrain American promoters, among them Joel Barlow, and counsel their clients. Jefferson and Short were drawn into a spat between French friends of France prompted by Brissot de Warville. In his polemic *De la France et des États-Unis* (1786), Brissot joined Crèvecoeur in criticizing the Marquis de Chastellux's *Travels in America*. Brissot, who had not yet visited America, found the Marquis's account "aristocratic" in viewpoint and cited its sympathetic discussion of slavery, which reflected Jefferson's influence, as a case in point. Both Jefferson and Short liked Chastellux. Equally, Jefferson believed Brissot was a "great enthusiast for liberty." He corrected Brissot on several minor points—among them the prevalence of drunkenness in America (more pronounced then in France but less common than in England) and the correct collective noun for Americans— Jefferson preferred "federo-Americans" to Brissot's "free Americans." But Brissot's claim that any inferiority in the condition of America's blacks was a product of slavery and not race taxed Jefferson's reserves of tact.[34]

Brissot de Warville played a leading role in founding the abolitionist Société des Amis des Noirs. Condorcet, whose friendship both Jefferson and

Short valued, was also among the group's charter members. Although invited by French friends, Jefferson did not join the Amis des Noirs. He addressed issues of race indirectly by sending Brissot a copy of *Notes on the State of Virginia*. Short, in contrast, joined the society and furnished Brissot with letters of introduction ahead of his journey to the United States. When a list of members of the Amis des Noir was published in a polemic commissioned by the planters of St. Domingue and their supporters, Short was drawn into French debates over slavery and the slave trade.[35]

Although Short's reports of Parisian responses to the great slave uprising on St. Domingue would scarcely mention ideas of freedom, either as a trigger for the revolt or a worthy aspiration, Short was in a position to observe how disagreements over slavery and race intruded into Jefferson's relationships with prominent French intellectuals. He was sometimes present at meetings between Jefferson and Condorcet, with whom he continued his acquaintance after Jefferson's return to America. Condorcet's *The Influence of the American Revolution in Europe*, published in 1786, had increased Jefferson's already sizeable admiration for its author. While statements such as "the declaration by which she declared her independence is a simple and sublime statement of . . . sacred and long forgotten rights" must have pleased Jefferson, Condorcet's qualification "it is true that negro slavery still exist in some of the United States . . . all enlightened men feel both the shame and the danger of this error" invited Jefferson's engagement. In 1788, Jefferson offered to produce an English-language translation of Condorcet's condemnation of the institution of slavery. The project soon foundered because Jefferson could not agree with Condorcet's assessment that any lack of moral awareness and cultural achievement among enslaved black people originated in the condition of slavery and not in any racial characteristics. Short witnessed this disagreement but if Condorcet asked for his views on the matter, Short did not record it.[36]

As a Virginian Short shared Jefferson's concern that the first English-language edition of *Notes on the State of Virginia* accurately reflect its author's intentions. He criticized a translation of *Notes* being undertaken by a Frenchman, hoped that an English-language edition would not be embellished by a British editor, and procured an accurate, high-quality, engraved map of Virginia for the edition eventually published in London by John Stockdale. Sharing Jefferson's desire to present an accurate view of the United States to European audiences, Short also assisted Philip Mazzei in the completion of his *Researches on the United States*—planned as a riposte to the work of Abbé Raynal, French travel accounts, and the arguments made by John Adams in his *Defense of the Constitutions of Government of the United States of America*. Short undertook to learn Italian in order to translate Mazzei's notes into English. To hasten publication and, in turn, ease the author's financial situation, Jefferson gave Mazzei permission to incorporate into *Researches* more or less verbatim sections of *Notes on the State of Virginia*, while Condorcet allowed Mazzei to incorporate his *Lettres d'un Bourgeois de New-Haven*. Predictably, Mazzei remembered Jefferson and Condorcet's help more vividly than Short's, while Jefferson made scant acknowledgment of Short's assistance in the production of the first English edition of *Notes on the State of Virginia*.[37]

Although a by-stander rather than an active participant, Short enjoyed his engagement with the literary world of Paris. He used the knowledge he acquired to pose as a world-weary sophisticate to long-suffering American friends. Madame de Tessé had insisted he read Gabriel Sénac de Meilhan's *Considerations sur l'Esprit & les Moeurs*, he told his friend William Nelson. "I shall be obliged to praise it to her," Short concluded with an almost audible sigh. Elsewhere Short professed to be unimpressed by the intellectual pretentions he encountered in French society. He assured William Nelson that many academicians, Condorcet excepted, "lose much of their *éclat* on being closely examined." Lacking Jefferson's conviction, expressed in *Notes on the State of Virginia*, that an error corrected was a truth established, Short ducked substantive engagement with fashionable intellectual debates, preferring instead to view himself as a realist for whom the social world of Parisian *salons* was of more interest than the ideas encountered within them.

To a greater extent than Short realized, Jefferson accepted his desire to be "Mr. Short"—the secretary who lodged at St. Germain and was only marginally interested running the legation or advancing his cultural diplomacy. This did not mean, however, that Jefferson accepted Short's estimation of his own character and it helps explain why Jefferson did not open up to Short about one of the most important moments in his emotional life.[38]

———

Jefferson was introduced to twenty-seven-year-old Maria Cosway in August 1786 by John Trumbull when she accompanied her husband, artist Richard Cosway, to Paris. Contemporaries praised Maria's complexion, her carriage, and her piercing blue eyes. She was English, but having been raised in Italy, spoke with a beguiling accent. Her husband, seventeen years her senior, had arranged a marriage she could not refuse by agreeing to provide for Maria's

mother while at the same time settling a sum on his bride. She was an accomplished artist and musician. Richard encouraged Maria to develop her
artistic talent so long as it did not threaten his own business, the production on commission of miniature portraits. Maria dutifully bolstered her
husband's ego and furthered his business interests by keeping a renowned
house whose Sunday evening music nights showcased her talents. The couple
were well-known in fashionable London. Richard had the reputation of being
"an absurd little coxcomb" who was a sycophantic member of the Prince of
Wales' set. Biographer James Boswell thought that Maria used her power over
men to treat her admirers like dogs, while other, more charitable observers
thought she was slightly spoiled and overly ambitious. Jefferson found Maria
"modest" and came away from their first encounters enthralled by her beauty
and talent. In the two months she spent in Paris in 1786, Jefferson completely
fell for Maria. Although ultimately his passion for her did not survive and
seems never to have been physically consummated, this was the one moment
during Jefferson's residence in France when he contemplated renouncing the
moral restraint of an American widower to embrace European, bohemian
self-expression.[39]

Jefferson's preoccupation with Maria Cosway could no more have escaped
Short's notice than his own attendance on Lilite Royer could have escaped
Jefferson's. Sensing that Jefferson's interest in Maria was emotionally deeper
than his flirtatious relationships with society hostesses such as Madame de
Corny, Short tried to keep his distance from the pair. However, Maria kept
weaving him into her correspondence with Jefferson. "I hope Mr. Short will
not be out as his usual [sic] when I have the pleasure to come to you," she
wrote to Jefferson on the eve of one of their meetings. From London, Maria
wrote Jefferson with news of a woman who had taken Short's fancy. "How is
Mr. Short? Pray remember me to him in the kindest manner, the beauty he
lost his heart by is keeling every body with her beweeching eyes." Jefferson
wanted Maria for himself alone. "You make everyone love you," he told her
reproachfully, "you are sought and surrounded therefore by all." Although
Jefferson disliked being lumped together with Short in letters from Maria,
he was prepared to drag other men, notably John Trumbull, whom he used
as a courier, into third-party involvement in his affair. "Tell Mrs. Cosway she
is inconstant," Jefferson wrote Trumbull in London on the eve of his departure for the south of France, "she was to have been in Paris long ago, but she
has deceived us." Here, as in other letters to Trumbull, Jefferson attempted a
light-hearted, gallant tone to discuss his interest in Maria. Since Short was
more frequently in Jefferson's company than Trumbull, and since Maria had

taken a shine to Short, Jefferson might possibly have shared conversational banter about Maria's "constancy" with him. In his letters to Short, however, Jefferson did not rehearse the conflict between head and heart that was taking shape within him. Equally, Short never committed his feelings for Lilite Royer to paper. Yet the suspicions and preliminary conclusions each man drew from his observation of the other man's affairs were no less powerful for being unverified.[40]

Short's workload increased when Jefferson met Maria Cosway and began taking time away from the legation. On a stolen day off with Maria in September 1786, Jefferson injured his right wrist while attempting to impress her by vaulting a fence. Soon after this Jefferson painstakingly wrote, with his left hand, a dialogue between head and heart for her. While his right wrist healed, Jefferson relied on Short to produce his official correspondence. The squall of work produced by Jefferson's infatuation and injury had silver linings for Short. He deputized for Jefferson at a spectacular ceremony staged to commemorate the presentation of a bust of Lafayette to the city of Paris. Advised to take the waters in Aix-en-Provence to cure his wrist, Jefferson left Short in charge of the United States' official business while he made an extended tour of southern France and Italy in the spring of 1787. Short met regularly with Lafayette and occasionally with French Minister for Foreign Affairs Armand-Marc Montmorin. Further flattering Short's sense of self-importance, Jefferson encouraged Short to write directly to Congress' Secretary for Foreign Affairs, John Jay, during his absence, if and when doing so would show Short to his advantage. Short took up the invitation, discussing with Jay the repayment of America's debt to France. For good measure he opened an independent correspondence with James Madison in which he offered some catty reflections on John Adams's *Defence of the Constitutions of Government* and his thoughts on the likelihood of Virginia ratifying the Federal Constitution.[41]

Short's imperfect knowledge of Jefferson's affair with Maria Cosway and his suspicions of a growing attraction between Jefferson and Sally Hemings had the effect of encouraging Short to see himself as Jefferson's "particular friend" and confidante. As part of Jefferson's earlier efforts to induce Short to "come home" to his official residence, and as a sign of affection, he had introduced Short to the households of several grander female acquaintances, notably those presided over by Madame d'Enville, Madame de Tessé, and Madame de Corny. These women took a liking to Short, which his connection to Jefferson only increased, and became friends the two men shared in common. Short indulged a natural desire to gossip about society women in letters written to Jefferson during his absences from Paris. While Jefferson stayed in Aix-en-Provence, for example, Short sent him an account of the social life surrounding the Easter promenades at Longchamps that referenced his relations with both Madame de Tessé and Madame de Corny. Later, when Jefferson traveled to Holland on official business, Short wrote to him that Madame de Corny was "cross" that he had not replied to a letter in which she had asked to take Patsy and Polly on a day out. He added in affected flourish, conveyed in French, that Madame de Corny was "furious" with John Adams and America's Dutch bankers for keeping Jefferson from her. Jefferson didn't request such reportage from Short, and his reserved replies suggest that he found the air of familiarity offered in such unsolicited banter intrusive. As Short would discover, Jefferson remained an intensely private man. The explanatory device Jefferson eventually used to describe his relationship with Short—the metaphor of adoptive son—did not suggest an equality of status or even, perhaps, any particular liking. Moreover, Jefferson had no desire to see Short as a son-in-law.[42]

When traveling, Jefferson could delegate some matters relating to his daughter Patsy, such as paying the Abbess of the Panthémont convent school, to his major domo Petit. However, from his first trip to London in the spring of 1786, Jefferson relied on Short to facilitate correspondence between him and Patsy in his absence. It proved difficult, and to some extent undesirable, to keep exchanges of information between Short and Jefferson on the subject of Patsy's well-being strictly matter of fact. Despite the fact that father and daughter wrote to one another independently of Short, both relied on him to a degree as a source of context. In May 1787, during Jefferson's tour of southern France, Short rather casually mentioned that "Miss Jefferson has been indisposed but has recovered. I send you a letter from her which will probably mention it." This prompted an anguished request for further information. "My daughter's [letter] mention[s] her illness and that she was recovering," Jefferson wrote. "Your last, saying nothing of her, proceeds I hope from her being well: but it would be a relief to me know that this is the case as soon as possible."[43]

Short spun from the business of attending to Patsy's needs a language of shared familiarity. "On my way to dinner yesterday," Short wrote Jefferson in March 1787, "I called on Miss Patsy to receive her commands for you . . . I can join my testimony to hers that she is perfectly well." In April, Short made inquiries about Patsy to round out a letter to Jefferson. "She is well and wanting only to hear more frequently from you to render her still more." As Jefferson prepared to cross into Italy, Short reported, "I went to the Panthémont yesterday and informed Miss Jefferson of your intended silence for three weeks at least; and I comforted her at the same time that you were well." His letters during Jefferson's trip to Holland, and then the Rhineland, in the winter of 1788, presented himself as a confidante of Patsy and Polly and as a friend of "the little family" to its father. Jefferson should free himself, Short wrote, from "any uneasiness" on account of an illness afflicting Polly that "could not be less than alarming to a parent." Short's letters to Jefferson began to suggest a developing sense of supervision—analogous to the behavior he displayed in his relationship with the Royers.[44]

Patsy's schoolfriend Caroline Tufton knew the "amiable" Mr. Short was a frequent visitor to the Panthémont and, as the Jefferson family prepared to depart for America, concluded that he must have been quite a "resource" for her. Caroline's sister Elizabeth, writing soon after Patsy's departure, avoided writing Short's name for fear of giving Patsy "offence." Marie-Jacinthe Botidoux ("Bot"), a particular friend, referenced directly Short's amatory interest in Patsy. In her first communication following Jefferson's departure from France, which was received in April 1790 and the took the form of an effusive letter-cum-journal, Bot referred casually to an earlier infatuation on Short's part that her friend Patsy had turned aside. Short, Marie-Jacinthe told Patsy breathlessly, had visited her in January 1790, to tell her that he had received a letter from Jefferson informing his friends in France of the family's safe arrival in Virginia. Bot wondered why then she had not received a letter from her friend "Jeff" via the same ship. Learning of her "despair" at not hearing from Patsy, Short told Bot that he would collect and forward her extended letter to Patsy. When he made good on his promise: "Our conversation was only of you. He told me he thought you were <u>insensitive</u>, that you have surely forgotten me already, and speaking of your departure he said that it had been up to you alone whether to stay in France." Bot agreed "that he might be right in thinking you are not very sensitive, that you are <u>very young and silly</u> and that I blamed you for not writing to me as soon as you arrived." As for Short's suggestion that it had been up to Patsy to decide whether to stay in France, "I pretended not to understand what he meant and answered that you would have preferred even the convent to leaving, but that your father would surely not have let you stay here." Finally, cutting through her own "chatter," Bot told her friend: "I would think, however, that he is angry for your having refused him, but that he is no longer in love." Bot had earlier chided Patsy, "I think that it would have been very good for you to do him justice, and that he would have made you very happy."[45]

Bot did not date the events in question. Any infatuation probably developed during Jefferson's tour of southern France and Italy in 1787. It might have come to a head during Jefferson's brief tour of the Rhineland in the spring of 1788, but it was certainly over when Short departed on his own Grand Tour in the second half of 1788. Bot may have exaggerated or misunderstood the nature and depth of Short's feelings for Patsy, and the offer Short made and Patsy refused may not have been a marriage proposal. Yet if Short truly believed Patsy had been free to choose to stay in Paris while her father returned to Virginia, then, as Bot understood, Patsy would have either had to stay in the convent or live under Short's protection. The latter option would have required marriage or, at the very least, a formal engagement, as Patsy realized but Short, apparently, did not.

In 1787 Patsy, then aged fifteen, had joined Short in taking a decidedly sophisticated view of a *cause celebre* that was the talk of France: the suicide of the cuckholded husband of the beautiful Madame de Simiâne. If every husband in Paris who believed his wife did not love him committed suicide, then, Patsy suggested to her father, "there would be nothing but widows left." Two years later she had internalized her father's views on marriage and completely accepted the fulfillment of his needs as her duty. There was little likelihood that she would have entertained a proposal that kept her in France and apart from her father. Still, memories lingered. Years later, during his final visit to Paris, Short made a point of tracking down Marie-Jacinthe. Once again the pair discussed the romantic interest Bot believed she had witnessed in "laughter filled dinners" they had shared with Patsy. Bot made a point of reminding her friend of those times.[46]

No correspondence between William Short and Martha Jefferson survives. Neither of them nor her father alluded to the possibility of Patsy choosing to remain in Paris if Jefferson returned to the United States. Yet it seems likely that Jefferson knew that an offer of some sort had been made. Somewhat against the grain of previous advice, in the summer of 1788, Jefferson actively encouraged Short take a tour of southern Europe. He supplied Short with travel advice and generous letters of introduction. During his tour, in a reversal of previous roles, Short found himself in the position of soliciting news of Jefferson's daughters from their father. Jefferson volunteered information about Patsy in almost aggressively neutral tones. In January 1789, he wrote that, as a consequence of extreme cold in Paris, "my eldest daughter had a fever for about a fortnight, the younger has had one of the nervous class [for] two months." Short's responses to such news followed for the most part Jefferson's lead. Writing from Rome he confessed to feeling "an anxiety to which I am not accustomed in learning [of] the severe indisposition of your family." He offered Jefferson "unfeigned thanks" for sharing the news, seeing it as a proof of Jefferson's continuing friendship. Elsewhere a thread of resentment ran through Short's references to Jefferson's daughters. In an otherwise chatty travelogue offering an appreciation of the wines he had sampled on his journey, Short added as a concluding thought: "be so good Sir as [to] present my most respectful compliments to the amiable and agreeable part of your family at Panthémont and yet I can hardly flatter myself that they will be received by the two little prudes."[47]

Following the family's return to America, Jefferson implied through the use of decidedly frosty language some developing knowledge of earlier incidents in Short's relationship with Patsy. Acknowledging in April 1790 the arrival of the package in which Short had forwarded Bot's extended letter to Patsy, Jefferson noted the receipt of "a packet from Miss Boutidor [sic] for my daughter." He used the same formulation, "my daughter," when informing Short, almost as an afterthought (the third item in a string of "small news"), that Patsy had married Thomas Mann Randolph. Short attempted a similar air of detachment. In his first letter to Jefferson since the family left Paris, Short enclosed a letter for "Miss Jefferson" given to him by her admirer the British minister plenipotentiary Lord Robert Fitzgerald. But Short was hurt both by the news of Patsy's marriage and the fact that she apparently didn't tell him directly. Short wrote to Jefferson as if he would share his feeling of abandonment. "The friends of your daughter here," Short wrote from Paris, "complain much of her having entirely forgotten them." Jefferson wouldn't have minded in the slightest if Patsy had put Paris behind her.[48]

———

Even if Jefferson did not want Short as a son-in-law, he did not regard him as a "blockhead" of the sort he feared his eldest daughter might marry. Short was among a handful of younger men whom Jefferson positively encouraged to settle near him in Albemarle County. Leaving France, Jefferson extended the invitation once again since "affection and the long habit of your society have rendered it necessary to me." His need of Patsy was greater. Jefferson would never have consented to any marriage proposal that involved his daughter living away from Virginia. Although Short's prior attendance on Lilite Royer, his developing attachment to Rosalie de La Rochefoucauld, and Patsy's seeming dislike of Short's proposal would all have influenced Jefferson's thoughts on a potential match, his oft-repeated invitation to Short to settle near him, marry, and raise a family genuinely reflected heartfelt hopes.[49]

For his part Short reluctantly admitted to friends that life in France offered pleasures he would miss on returning to America, but he was careful to tell Jefferson that he intended to come home. As Short toured southern Europe his letters suggested that he would return to the United States sooner rather than later. He was "persuaded" that he was "made for the kind of life to which we are accustomed in America" and that "those pleasures which are within the grasp of everybody in Europe are transient and not at all adapted to captivate me." As if to demonstrate to Jefferson that he was thinking seriously about a return, Short wrote from northern Italy that he was studying the *metayer* system of land tenure since it seemed "well adapted" "for the genius of negroes"—presumably those of Virginia. Nevertheless, Short continued to doubt that he could find a proper station in the United States through the practice of law or the pursuit of elective office. He cited the case of James Madison, whose peers in Virginia had recently declined to elect him to the United States Senate, in support of the latter argument. Short's suggestion that his claims to respect and position were comparable to Madison's was entirely in keeping with his sense of self-worth. Jefferson did not rise to this particular expression of hubris because, just as Short was indicating a reluctant willingness to leave Europe, he was hatching plans that would end Short's indecision by requiring him to stay in France.[50]

In the winter of 1788–1789, Jefferson formally applied to John Jay for a temporary leave of absence. "Mr. Short, who had had thoughts of returning to America," Jefferson told Jay, "will postpone that return till I come back. His talents and character allow me to say with confidence that nothing will suffer in his hands." Jefferson asked Jay to consider naming Short the United States' official *chargé des affaires* in his absence so he could attend diplomatic functions. He estimated the extra cost in salary to be 170 guineas and asked Madison to use his good offices to secure "immediate" approval of his request. Having offered Short's job to John Trumbull in order to nudge him toward a return, Jefferson now secured a promotion for Short to induce him to stay.[51]

By 1789, the relationship between the two men had seemingly defaulted to its origins in the conventions of patronage. Jefferson had placed Short. Short feared being turned out of his new post in favor of a political appointee of lesser qualifications. That, he said, would be "mortifying." Not so subtly appealing for protection, he told Jefferson "I am so little known to those who will compose" the new federal legislature that congressmen would not "turn their attention towards me unless invited to it by some person who knows me better"—that is, Jefferson. Short's ambition, as well as his feelings for Patsy, sharpened his desire for a place within Jefferson's family. "You cannot doubt," he told Jefferson, "that it is your suffrage which I value above that of all others. . . . [I] beg one thing more and that is that you will be so good as to preserve me always a place in your remembrance and in your friendship, and that you will never doubt of the unalterable attachment of your friend and servant." Short used "suffrage" here in the sense of support and approval, and that, in turn, led him to cast his desire for continuing preferential treatment in terms of a state of quasi-filial dependency. Jefferson's concern for Short's well-being remained, yet Short continued to act independently.[52]

The years Jefferson and Short shared in France added an emotional complexity to their relationship that was lacking in David Humphrey's transactions with George Washington or Jefferson's with John Trumbull. Any feelings of guilt that Jefferson might have had from seeming to manipulate Short were only partially assuaged by the consideration that Short would derive consolation from his French friends and a recognized diplomatic post. What drove the relationship between the two men forward from the point of Jefferson's supposedly temporary departure from France was a consciousness of unfinished business, a shared need for "unbosoming." Shared experiences, friends, and conversations might have drawn the two men together, but an awareness of divergent responses to these stimuli instead pushed them apart. Jefferson and Short were prone to feeling they had failed one other. Short had delayed his departure, had then chosen to live apart from Jefferson's household, and was showing signs of defying Jefferson's advice by remaining in France as a bachelor. Jefferson had failed Short by inviting him to France in the first place rather than insist that he stand for elective office. Thereafter he had kept Short at arm's length, despite his concerns for the young man's moral well-being, before ultimately steering him into prolonging his residence abroad. Meanwhile, whether the intensely private Jefferson liked it or not, through shared interactions with Maria Cosway, Sally Hemings, and society hostesses Short had acquired a degree of presumptive knowledge regarding Jefferson's inner character that discomforted his erstwhile father. Jefferson, having invited Short to come "like a good boy" and live in closer proximity to him, was troubled by doubts concerning Short's character. In letters to Jefferson protesting that he had not renounced his native country and that he really did intend to return home, Short displayed an awareness of quasi-paternal scrutiny. In response, Short began to work through his feelings toward his native country and ambivalence toward marriage. His irresolution was overshadowed as well as framed by a more important influence on their continuing relationship: the bedrock certainties Jefferson developed from his social life in France, which took in Short's behavior and his own, and were triggered by his observation of French women.

TWO

Living in a Woman's Country

JEFFERSON'S AND SHORT'S REFLECTIONS ON FRENCH CULTURE

WHILE MINISTER TO France Jefferson spent a fortune he did not possess on handsome French clothes for himself and his entourage, fine wine for his table, and a fashionable carriage for public appearances. Biographers have suggested that during his time in Paris Jefferson was able "to be the sort of man he wanted to be." That Jefferson was at ease abroad, more nimble in Parisian society than, for example, John Adams—often presumed to be stiff and slightly awkward—is a stubbornly entrenched feature of both men's popular images. William Short is generally portrayed as being even more acculturated to French society than Jefferson. After all Short lived with a French family, ate into his patrimony to fund a Parisian lifestyle, and eventually conducted an extended affair with a French aristocrat. Surely, it seems, Short seized the opportunity to be the sort of man he wished to be.[1]

In France, both men, though Jefferson especially, responded to the stimuli of the society they experienced by briefly considering a new, cosmopolitan identity for themselves. Each became interested in identifying transcendent universal values through an interrogation of differences within and between individuals and nations. Both men, but especially Jefferson, entertained the idea that affective ties grounded in values shared by citizens of the world might conjure into being elements of a progressive, supranational new world order. Where learned societies led, democrats would follow. In the summer of 1785, Jefferson drafted a remarkable treaty that would have dissolved national distinctions by proposing that visiting citizens of one country would enjoy all the rights of their host country for the duration of their residence. At least initially Jefferson saw the acquaintances he made in French society as potential

Heir through Hope. Peter Thompson, Oxford University Press. © Peter Thompson 2023.
DOI: 10.1093/oso/9780197546833.003.0003

fellow travelers, collaborators in a grand historical project. Yet Jefferson and, to a lesser extent, Short also believed that the American Revolution had presented the world they inhabited with its first articulation of practical and progressive republicanism. The dawning realization that French society did not and would not accept the United States of America as a cultural and po‐litical template for a distinctively French Revolution led Americans to reflect on a tension between values that were ideally universal and practices that were distinct unto nations. During their time in France, Jefferson, and especially Short, came to accept that each nation would have to develop according to its own manners and customs.[2]

What is striking in the letters Jefferson and, to a lesser extent, Short wrote during their residency in France is the absence of any narrative of gradual adjustment signaled by the resolution of initial difficulties of languages and manners. Jefferson's letters in particular convey a growing detachment from France and disappointment with Paris. He came to believe that French cul‐tural influences were insidious and potentially harmful. Jefferson's peers, no‐tably Benjamin Franklin and John Adams, as well as William Short, shared Jefferson's pride in America's republican culture while, at least initially, largely discounting Jefferson's fears that foreign influences might corrupt it. According to his daughter Nabby, John Adams easily adapted to French fashion while in Paris (and, in Jefferson's eyes, even more so to British mores while in London). Yet, in John Trumbull's account, as soon as Adams had attended his last diplomatic function and was free to return to the United States, he symbolically divested himself of foreign ways by having all the powder brushed out of his hair. Adams never feared that residence in London or Paris had turned him into a monarchist. Jefferson warily acquiesced in the demands of French manners insofar as these were compatible with his view of republican morality while condemning those aspects of the French way of life that were not. He not only defended America's manners, but also asserted their superiority over French, let alone British, mores. The clarity which the experience of living in France brought to his republicanism would have a de‐cisive impact on Jefferson's relationship with William Short.[3]

Jefferson spun from his observation of the behavior of French women in particular a series of conclusions regarding the perceived instability of mar‐riage in France and the superiority of American marital norms. The renun‐ciation of these norms by younger men like William Short would damage America's republican project. His observations, developing as certainties, encouraged Jefferson to frame his relationship with Short as that of a father instructing a son. He believed that Short should put the attractions of France aside and return home to marry and settle down. From his perspective Short needed to be reclaimed, and the energy which Jefferson devoted to this task demonstrates the value he placed on the morality he sought to inculcate in the younger man. Short, who understood but only partially accepted Jefferson's reasoning, found himself in the role of an errant junior called upon to justify his behavior. He was more willing than Jefferson to experiment with French ways but this did not, in his eyes, diminish his commitment to the United States. He struggled to reconcile internal conflicts, rejecting Jefferson's republican certainties while failing to develop fully formed alternatives of his own.

Short, who resisted what he would describe as the "yoke" of marriage, was not a theorist of bachelorhood or a cosmopolitan existence. Unlike Thomas Paine, a true citizen of the world who ended a life spent at the heart of the transatlantic Age of Revolutions as a citizen of nowhere, Short never renounced his native country. Yet, largely because of his experience of living in France, Short returned to the United States alone and as a stranger to his family and former friends. To understand the lasting impact that life in France had on both men and their continuing relationship requires an examination of how they conducted themselves in a French society whose tone, set by aristocrats and assertive women, was unfamiliar and unsettling.

———

Jefferson had sailed to Europe with letters of introduction to the great and good of French society. "I hope you'll be pleased with our social scene, which is the shining side of our nation," Hector St. Jean de Crèvecoeur, who supplied a number of introductions, told Jefferson on the eve of his departure. Crèvecoeur was particularly eager that Jefferson meet Duke Louis-Alexandre de La Rochefoucauld and his formidable mother, Duchess Élisabeth d'Enville. The La Rochefoucaulds, Crèvecoeur assured Jefferson, offered "a c[enter] of re[union] where men of genius and abilities often meet." Jefferson duly accepted an invitation from the Duke, and Short accompanied him. The sociability they subsequently experienced among this family and its circle quickly became woven into the narrative of their lives in France and shaped the manner in which each formed his attitudes toward wider French culture.[4]

Few of the social settings which Jefferson and Short encountered shone more brightly than that they encountered at the country seat of the La Rochefoucauld family, the chateau La Roche-Guyon in Normandy. The chateau was built on the site of an early medieval castle situated atop a cliff overlooking the Seine and guarding the approaches to Paris. Over the centuries the intertwined La Rochefoucauld and Liancourt families added stone-faced reception buildings tied horizontally to the cliff face. Around the mid eighteenth-century, Élisabeth, Duchess d'Enville, added a new residential wing in the Palladian style, a terraced garden, and an impressive oversized stable block. The English agronomist Arthur Young, who visited in 1788, described La Roche-Guyon as "the most singular place I have seen," while the French artist Hubert Robert presented it as a *capriccio*, a whimsical mixture of the sinister and the charming. It was unlike any building Short and Jefferson had known in the United States. They were familiar with more designedly fantastic surroundings in France, notably François de Monville's garden of follies and the Désert de Retz in nearby Marly, but the chateau La Roche-Guyon was first and foremost a family home whose quirky splendor played an important part in projecting the La Rochefoucauld clan's expansive self-image.[5]

Even French observers found the La Rochefoucaulds striking. The celebrated hostess Madame du Deffand concluded that the family presented themselves as "a tribe of Israel," exiles from another age and curators of past patrimonies. Their most illustrious forbear, François VI, second Duke de La Rochefoucauld, had written the aphoristic collection *Maximes* (1665), still widely read and admired in fashionable society. Although guests of the La Rochefoucaulds commented on their hosts "modesty," the family owned substantial estates in Charentes, Poitou, and the Auvergne in addition to their lands in Normandy. When Louis XVI convened the États-Général, six members of the extended family were represented. They were the grandest of grand families, personifying to both Jefferson and Short the culture of France's aristocracy.

Philip Mazzei, who joined Crèvecoeur in urging Jefferson to meet the La Rochefoucaulds, advised him that Madame d'Enville, the matriarch of the family, was one of the "greatest" and "most singular geniuses of the age." She had a contrarian streak. Over the years she had encouraged clever people, notably Turgot and Condorcet, from a variety of social backgrounds. She took up Jefferson, John and Abigail Adams, and, especially, Short, presenting them with an immediate and troubling example of forms of female conduct and expression unknown in the United States.[6]

Abigail Adams described a visit to the La Rochefoucaulds in horrified tones to her friend Elizabeth Cranch.

> We found the [Duchess d'Enville] sitting in an Easy chair, around her
> sat a circle of Academicians and by her side a young Lady [Rosalie].

Your uncle [John Adams] presented us, and the old Lady rose and gave us a Salute . . . that she had no paint, I could put up with it, but when she approached your cousin [John Quincy Adams] I could think of nothing but death taking hold of Hebe. . . . The duchess is near 80, very tall and lean. She was dressed in a silk chemise with very large sleeves coming half way down her arm, a large cape, no stays a black velvet Girdle round her waist . . . the lace [round her neck] was not sufficient to cover the upper part of her neck which old time had harrow'd. She had no cap on . . . her venerable white hair in full view. The dress of old women and young girls in this Country is *detestable* to speak in the French stile. The latter at the age of seven being clothed exactly like a woman of twenty and the former have such a fantastical appearance that I cannot endure it. The old lady has all the vivacity of a Young one. She is the most learned woman in France. Her house is the resort of all Men of literature with whom she converses upon the most abstruse subjects.

Being the most learned woman in France did not, in Abigail Adams's view, compensate for dressing and acting in a manner inappropriate to a woman's age. "It is manners more than conversation which distinguish a fine woman in my eye," Abigail Adams told Royall Tyler. She hoped she could find some French women whose behavior was more consistent with her ideas of decency. Otherwise she would become a "mere recluse."[7]

Becoming a recluse was not an option for Jefferson, part of whose job it was to see and been seen in society and to maintain connections with opinion-formers like Madame d'Enville's son Louis-Alexandre, Duke de La Rochefoucauld. Louis-Alexandre had a wide range of interests but was not noted for his depth of understanding. He translated America's state constitutions into French, but John Adams believed that his reading in the science of government was superficial. Although he was an early member of the Société des Amis des Noirs, the English abolitionist Thomas Clarkson believed that Louis-Alexandre was an ineffectual campaigner. Agricultural improvement interested the duke, but Arthur Young found him disinclined to translate theories into practical reform. As befitted a patron of Condorcet, master of the mint, Louis-Alexandre involved himself in financial policy but he wrote on it with more ambition than insight. He collected both fossils and geologists. He dabbled in philanthropy, helping his more determined cousin the Duke de La Rochefoucauld-Liancourt found what became the École des Arts et Métiers, a progressive educational institution. Gouverneur Morris thought Louis-Alexandre a well-meaning windbag, and Short, though later prone to praise the duke's influence in order to bolster his own, tended to agree. Jefferson persevered with him in hopes of influencing a French transition to constitutional monarchy.[8]

Louis-Alexandre's second wife, Alexandrine-Charlotte-Sophie de Rohan-Chabot known as ("Rosalie"), Duchess de La Rochefoucauld d'Enville, was eighteen years her husband's junior. Arthur Young praised what he took to be Rosalie's "simplicity of character" and disinterest in the "foppery of rank." She was a devotee of Rousseau; happier in the gardens of the family's Parisian townhouse than in its state-rooms, happiest of all in a secluded chalet located in the flood plains near La Roche-Guyon. Jefferson, in a rhetorical flourish offered to Rosalie's husband, suggested that "were her system of ethics and government the system of every one, we should have no occasion for government at all." Yet there was more steel in Rosalie's character than such compliments recognized. A granddaughter of the celebrated Madame d'Enville could hardly have been unaware of the advice offered to young French noblewomen by Madame de Puisieux: "If to speak well is the mark of a good education, to write well is the mark of a woman of wit." Rosalie's carefully composed letters, which eschewed the phonetic spelling associated, pejoratively, with women of her class reveal that she had received a formal education rarely offered to daughters of the aristocracy. Rosalie possessed a reading knowledge of German and English. She was bookish, having been raised conscious of her family's self-appointed role as arbiters of taste and civility. When Short remarked to Rosalie that he was applying himself to a serious study of Voltaire, Rosalie promptly drew up an ambitious reading list to help him appreciate "our good French poets."[9]

Although the La Rochefoucaulds considered themselves reformers, their house was markedly less "advanced" than that presided over by Madame de Tessé, also frequently visited by both Jefferson and Short. Madame de Tessé endeared herself to Jefferson by greeting the abolition of aristocratic titles and feudal privileges with "joy" since their "silly arrogance" affronted universal liberty. Gouverneur Morris grumpily dismissed Madame de Tessé as a republican of the "first feather" and avoided her circle of friends. In contrast, Rosalie joined her grandmother, brother, and husband in ostracizing their former friend Condorcet after his conversion to republicanism. Rosalie's sympathies lay with the royal family when a revolutionary crowd invaded the palace of the Tuileries—and not just because her brother stood his ground at the King's side. Her letters to Short treated most assemblymen (her husband Louis-Alexandre excepted) and all popular leaders as dangerous demagogues.

No reactionary, Rosalie was nonetheless bred to the aristocracy and under-stood her obligations to her family and, indirectly, to her rank. Jefferson was quicker than Short to realize the implications of these loyalties.[10]

In 1789, taking his leave of Madame d'Enville, Jefferson paid her and the La Rochefoucauld family handsome compliments while expressing his conviction that, despite a few "thorns" along the way, the revolution under way would pro-ceed peacefully and successfully, demonstrating that "God did not make man in his wrath." Madame d'Enville's reply matched Jefferson, "No, God did not make man in his anger, this passion belongs to us and we . . . lend it to him." The La Rochefoucauld family's sufferings during the Terror, a point of common reference for the two men, would shape their divergent views of the French Revolution. More immediately, the La Rochefoucauld's lifestyle, their modes of speech and behavior, and their attitude toward privilege drew responses from Jefferson and Short that, in turn, wove themselves into the fabric of their relationship.[11]

At least initially the unfamiliar worlds created by French hostesses who spoke their minds interested Jefferson. Following his first encounter with the La Rochefoucaulds in the summer of 1785, Jefferson ventured to Sannois, ten miles from Paris, to "commence an acquaintance" with another of Crèvecoeur's friends, "the old Countess d'Hocquetot." The Countess, who been Jean-Jacques Rousseau's muse and a friend of Benjamin Franklin's, presided over one of the most famous salons in France. Jefferson hoped the visit would open a new "door of admission for me to the circle of literati with which she is environed." It did. Yet, after a year in France and exposure to the best of French society, Jefferson posed a rhetorical question to Charles Bellini, the man he had appointed to a professorship of French and Modern Languages at the College of William and Mary. "You are perhaps curious to know how this new scene has struck a savage of the mountains of America?" "Not advantageously," Jefferson quickly assured him. He had had chance to examine "the condition of the great, to appreciate the true value of the circumstances in their situation which dazzle the bulk of the spectators." He wasn't star-struck, finding "the general fate of humanity here most deplor-able." He admired French achievements in architecture, art, and music, yet, after eighteen months in Paris he told Eliza House Trist that he wished he were among his "lazy countrymen" in Virginia. "We all pant for America, as will every American who comes to Europe," Jefferson told Francis Eppes at the end of 1785. He was, he claimed, "past the age for changing habits."[12]

Neither Jefferson nor Short wished to give correspondents back home the impression that they had forsaken their native country or adopted a foreign one. Jefferson in particular was acutely aware that Congress, let alone the American electorate, regarded a diplomatic establishment as a luxury and would not welcome gushing accounts of French culture. He possessed the rhetorical skills to turn American political prejudices on their head. Inviting James Monroe to visit him in Paris, Jefferson justified the trip on the grounds that it "will make you adore your own country, its climate, its equality, liberty, laws, people and manners. My God! How little do my country men know what precious blessings they are in possession of." Similar political considerations led him to assure conservative John Rutledge that his son should undertake a grand tour of the European capitals in order to appreciate the simplicity of American government, as "only the Indians have less law than we." "The best schools for republicanism," Jefferson claimed, were "London, Versailles, Madrid, Vienna, Berlin."[13]

Abigail Adams was among those few Americans who understood Jefferson's unease. In February 1785, she told Mary Smith Cranch that eight months in Europe had taught her the wisdom of the observation "daily example is the most subtle of poisons." She found her taste reconciling itself to habits and customs that at first disgusted her, and, like Jefferson, she concluded "everything I have yet seen, serves to endear my own country more and more to me." Life in France led Abigail to wonder how she would "tarry out" the years of husband John's ministry. As a more recent arrival, Jefferson undertook a light-hearted defense of Paris and its amiable society for her—"I do love this *people* with all my heart"—but expressing the thought led Jefferson to the fearful realization that to love the people was to embrace their system. "I think that with a better religion and a better form of government," Jefferson told Abigail and himself, the condition of the French people and France itself "would be most enviable." Jefferson feared not so much a corruption of morals as a dilution of political principle. It was almost his duty to go only so far down the road to accommodation.[14]

John Adams recognized this concern and more than matched Jefferson in expressing it. "What absurdities, inconsistencies, distractions and horrors would [French] manners introduce into our republican governments in America," Adams concluded of France, "no kind of republican government can exist with such national manners as these. Cavete Americani." However, in the 1780s, John Adams didn't think it likely the French manners would pollute American republicanism. He chose to take his son with him on his first mission to France, and John Quincy and Nabby accompanied their parents on his second sojourn in Europe. John and Abigail drew the line at allowing Nabby to perfect her French in a "convent," "not having entertained so favourable an opinion of those abodes as some who have placed their children there." Jefferson's decision to place his daughter Patsy in the Panthémont convent, as well as his invitation to William Short to accompany him to France, represented notable concessions to French culture. Despite this, in Jefferson and Short's correspondence, expressions of discontent with France or, more accurately, with the France they knew quickly became a dominant motif. Jefferson's exchanges with correspondents such as John and Abigail Adams and John Banister, Jr., who knew the world he was inhabiting, took disenchantment and frustration to a level that exceeded any perceived need to pose as an unimpressed bystander. From the late summer of 1785, barely a year after his arrival, Jefferson began actively discouraging Americans, especially young Americans, from traveling to France.[15]

In April 1785, Walker Maury wrote to Jefferson to report that he had taken on Jefferson's nephew Peter Carr as a private pupil. Maury requested his permission to have Carr instructed in French while perhaps dropping the study of Anglo-Saxon. Jefferson told Maury that he had considered sending for Carr to be educated in Paris but had developed the opinion that, "of all the errors which can be possibly be committed in the education of youth, that of sending them to Europe is the most fatal. I see clearly that no American should come to Europe under 30 years of age." "The hollow, unmeaning, manners of Europe," he said, were "not to be preferred to the simplicity and sincerity of our own country." When Carr repeated an interest in visiting France, Jefferson again counseled firmly against it. Perhaps he had William Short in mind when he told Carr that the young man abroad learned "new habits which cannot be gratified when they return home."[16]

Two months after Jefferson's first letter to Carr, it was the Virginian John Banister Jr.'s turn to be offered a lecture on the dangers of France. Banister had been in France for a year and was in Avignon nursing his health when he wrote asking where in Europe his brother might most advantageously pursue a college education. Jefferson treated Banister to a comprehensive statement of his hostility to prolonged foreign travel. The Virginian abroad "acquires a fondness for European luxury and dissipation and a contempt for the simplicity of his own country." He would become fascinated with aristocrats, partial to monarchs, and view "with abhorrence the lovely equality which the poor enjoys with the rich in his own country." Foreign travel jeopardized the pursuit of a career in American public life. The men Americans most trusted, respected, and promoted, Jefferson assured him, were "those who have been educated among them, and whose manners, morals and habits are perfectly homogeneous with those of the country." Even one of the principal perceived advantages of a sojourn in France, the opportunity to learn French, was more illusory than real and, in any case, led to a man speaking and writing in his native tongue as if a foreigner, for "no instance exists of a person writing two languages perfectly." "It appears to me," Jefferson told Banister, "that an American coming to Europe for education loses in his knowledge, in his morals, in his health, in his habits, and in his happiness." He had become convinced that "the consequences of foreign education are alarming to me as an American."[17]

William Short was destined to hear repeated sermons on the perils of residence in France throughout his years abroad, and not only from Jefferson. In May 1785, his friend William Nelson admonished "Those who are sent abroad for their education leave their native country so early that they are insensible of the distinctions of government—perfect equality and liberty can scarcely be understood by a child—but the pomp and ostentation of a monarchy and improvement in the arts of luxury cannot pass unnoticed by him." Friends back in Virginia regularly warned him of the damage extended foreign residence inflicted on career prospects in the United States. Accordingly, as the years of his European residence rolled by, Short periodically announced plans to return to the United States and repented of the "folly and vanity" of a life in Europe spent "rambling without house or home." He followed Jefferson's lead when advising his brother Peyton to prevent his children from crossing the Atlantic to advance themselves, for "the happiest state on earth is that of an American citizen living at home, being industrious, providing for his family, unconnected with all other parts of the world." "Do not think" of coming to Paris, Short implored his brother in the summer of 1800, telling him his situation in frontier Kentucky was infinitely preferable.[18]

Short regularly protested that his head had not been turned by the experience of living abroad and encountering aristocracy. "No attraction in France," Short told William Stephens Smith, "can ever weaken those already formed in youth. . . . I mean the attachments to a free country." Smith, having visited Short in Paris, was not inclined to believe him. Short insisted: "I feel I have had enough of Paris . . . the scenes which pass in such a place . . . have charms at first and novelty gives a thousand enchantments, but a constant repetition of the same brings on indifference." Short claimed to be bored by travel writing and offered little detailed description of France even to friends who asked for it. Jefferson had greater opportunity to judge Short's reactions, and, as his sense of the moral hazard faced by young Americans living in France increased, so, too, did the intensity of his desire that men in Short's shoes firmly embrace American values.[19]

Gouverneur Morris pithily encapsulated the problem that Jefferson in particular found with France. It was, he said, "a woman's country." Morris had in mind high society settings where he, Jefferson, and Short encountered proudly independent and well-informed women. Jefferson's unease with French gender norms was also fueled by his observation of settings less exalted than Parisian drawing rooms. During his tour of southern France in 1787, Jefferson reflected on the great derangement of a natural, proper order of things caused by what he took to be evidence of men performing women's work and women encroaching on male roles. In France, so Jefferson reasoned, it was men who dressed hair, made clothes, and ran kitchens, while women drove carts, reaped fields, and smote anvils. Since white women were not, in his view, suited to heavy manual labor and could find in it no fulfillment of an innate need to attract men, French women, especially of the laboring classes, were drawn to positions as prostitutes and concubines. These were "easier" ways of making a living than carting or smithying. Yet prostitutes needed clients, and kept women needed keepers. Jefferson could have laid the responsibility for the "vice of the age" at the feet of men, but he chose to locate it in the actions of French women. A subsequent tour of Germany confirmed his prejudices. He noted that, although German women could often be observed employed in "dirt and drudgery," some "tag of ribbon, some ring or bit of bracelet, earbob or necklace will shew" that the "desire of pleasing" men was not suspended by their employment. In France, however, the desire of pleasing men had been removed from its roots in normal life and placed in an independent sector of immoral employment.[20]

What disturbed Jefferson, and some French moralists, about the extent and standing of sexualized relations between men and women was not so much the evidence it gave of widespread immorality but its role in destabilizing a supposedly normative world of stable marriages. In the first of a string of letters describing negative reactions to life in France written around the first anniversary of his arrival, Jefferson told Charles Bellini: "Conjugal love having no existence among them, domestic happiness, of which this is the basis, is utterly unknown. In lieu of this are substituted pursuits which nourish and invigorate all our bad passions, and which offer only moments of extasy [sic] amidst days and months of restlessness and torment." Jefferson offered young John Banister, Jr., the same opinions. In France, a man learned to consider fidelity to the marriage bed as an ungentlemanly practice. The "intrigues" of European women, their "voluptuary dress and arts," led a young American man to pity and despise the "chaste affections and simplicity" of the women of his own country. Jefferson's thinking was uncomfortably close to the widely circulated, misogynistic analysis offered by Rousseau's popularizer, Louis-Sèbastian Mercier. Since French ladies had lost what Mercier, echoing Rousseau, described as "the most endearing qualities of their sex," to whit "bashfulness, simplicity of manners, and delicacy of sentiment," "love, properly speaking, is now, at least in Paris, no more than a kind of tempered libertinism." Jefferson acknowledged in a letter to Madison that Mercier presented the "dark side" of private manners in Paris but nevertheless urged Madison to read Mercier's *Tableau de Paris*, telling him that it would acquaint him with the city as if he had lived there for years.[21]

Abigail Adams described the 52,000 registered prostitutes of Paris as "unmarried women," making essentially the same point as Jefferson. But she, and other American observers of the mores of French marriages, viewed women with greater sympathy. The woman who came closest to meeting Abigail Adams's exacting standards was Marie-Adrienne de Noailles, wife of the Marquis de Lafayette, and the terms on which she did so are as noteworthy as the exclamation points with which Adams highlighted them: "Madam de la Fayette . . . is a good and amiable Lady, exceedingly fond of her Children and attentive to their education, passionately attached to her Husband!!! A French Lady and fond of her Husband!!!" Adams explained to Mercy Otis Warren that Marie-Adrienne "disapproved very much the Manner in which the conjugal connection was formed in this Country," and since she had been married before, she was capable of love. Adams assured her friend that Madame de La Fayette had nevertheless made it the study of her life to perform her duty in the domestic sphere, and, in consequence, her life was more fulfilling than those of her countrywomen who sought pleasure in "dissipation and amusement." Even if relatively few of the women Abigail encountered were as dutiful, she had to admit that "a real well bred French Lady" "has the most ease in her manners that you can possibly conceive of." Such ease was studied by French women "as an art."[22]

None of Jefferson's surviving letters links general statements such as "in France domestic happiness is unknown" to a discussion of likely causes of this unhappiness or a denunciation of its unjust consequences for women, children, and, indeed, men in France. Yet Jefferson must have been aware of the causes and prevalence of arranged marriages in higher French society; the vivid example of the La Rochefoucauld family should have offered a goad to his imagination. In order to preserve the La Rochefoucauld estate and its name, Madame d'Enville had been forced at the age of fifteen into an arranged marriage which produced a male heir, Louis-Alexandre. Widowed at thirty, she felt a duty to her son and his heirs not to dilute their inheritance by remarrying. Louis-Alexandre became the sixth Duke de La Rochefoucauld. Dynastic considerations also dictated that Madame d'Enville's daughter should marry a cousin with two titles, Louis-Antoine-Auguste, Duke de Rohan-Chabot and Prince de Léon. That marriage produced a daughter, Rosalie. On the death of Louis-Alexandre's first wife, the preservation of the family estate led him, with Madame d'Enville's encouragement, to marry his niece, Rosalie. The Duchess d'Enville was therefore Rosalie's grandmother as well as her mother-in-law. Louis-Alexandre and Rosalie felt no pressure to conceal this consanguinity. They shared La Roche-Guyon and a Parisian townhouse amicably enough, though they did not have children and lived largely independent lives.[23]

Abigail Adams understood that arrangements of this kind undermined marriage and produced women who looked elsewhere to compensate for the shortcomings of domestic life. Jefferson, in contrast, foregrounded as an explanation what Abigail Adams took to be a consequence: French women were, whether by choice or by the opportunity afforded them by men, too forward, too independent. Here again Jefferson's views echoed those of writers such as Mercier, who believed that "our women, who have by degrees crept into all public places, and mix with the other sex, have taken the haughtiness, the looks and the very gait of the latter." Jefferson witnessed one consequence of the La Rochefoucaulds' family life and history, the beginning of Short's developing affair with Rosalie. This seemed to substantiate the fear of moral seduction Jefferson offered John Banister, Jr. It was one more scintilla of evidence shaping the conclusions Jefferson drew from his observation of French women and their marriages: an idealized view in which stable conjugal unions, and the morality which nurtured and protected them, would form the bedrock of a republican society—in America.[24]

If it was true, as Jefferson told Eliza House Trist in 1785, that in France, "the domestic bonds here are absolutely done away" then the question arose "where can their compensation be found?" Jefferson had a ready answer. Happiness would be found within a wholesome republican marriage in the United States, preferably in a setting such as Albemarle County. The "tranquil permanent felicity" of "domestic society" in America was a blessing that allowed its inhabitants "to follow steadily those pursuits which health and reason approve." When Jefferson wrote this, in Paris, he had been widowed for three years; he had yet to meet Maria Cosway, and Sally Hemings was still in Virginia. One might conclude that Jefferson idealized domestic bonds precisely because he was not currently—nor would he ever again be—a party to marriage. Within American culture bachelors were objects of lingering suspicion, and he wished to deflect this by foregrounding his status as a widower. Yet the extent to which Jefferson regarded male existence outside domestic bonds as unnatural is striking. "Tell me who has married and who has hanged themselves because they could not marry?" he asked Eliza House Trist in a morbidly revealing joke. Within marriage, Jefferson believed, a man should father a "quiver full" of children. Soon after James Madison married at fifty, Jefferson noted that he had not yet fathered a child. The emphasis Jefferson placed on marriage and fatherhood is further apparent in some uncharacteristically intrusive comments he offered William Stephens Smith, secretary to the American legation in London, who married Nabby Adams.[25]

Jefferson was disposed to like William Stephens Smith; indeed, he went out of his way to praise the "extreme worth" of Smith's character to Abigail Adams and asked her to consider the "the advantageous impressions which his head, his heart, and his manners" had made on him. After Nabby married Smith in June 1786, Jefferson composed a mock address, which he asked Smith to pass on to his wife as she prepared for motherhood. "All Hail Madame. May your nights and days be many and full of joy! May their fruits be such as to make you feel the sweet union of parent and lover, but not so many as you may feel their weight. May they be as handsome and good as their mother, wise and honest as their father, but more milky!" A few months later he risked another clumsy reference to pregnancy. Asking Smith to pass on his compliments to "Mrs. Adams" and to "Mrs. Smith," he hoped "the former is very well, and that the latter is, or has been, very sick, otherwise I would observe to you that it is high time." Jefferson's wife had been pregnant or lactating throughout their marriage. Fathering children, preferably within a relationship that could be acknowledged, was a matter of such pressing concern for Jefferson, apparently celibate while in Paris, that it surfaced clumsily in what he doubtless intended to be lighthearted banter with the Smiths. Had Short married an American and fathered children, a mental reservation regarding his character would have been removed from Jefferson's mind and with it the need to insistently offer advice and admonition.[26]

Jefferson turned a blind eye to marital infidelity in others while ultimately declining to engage in it himself. The allure of refined women such as Maria Cosway or Madame de Corny was, in conventional interpretations of his life, insufficient to overcome the widower Jefferson's attachment to his former wife. There was one aspect of the "ease" and charm expressed by French women that Jefferson, the theorist of American republican values, was not prepared to ignore. "The Tender breasts of ladies were not formed for political convulsion; and the French ladies miscalculate much their own happiness when they wander from the true field of their influence into that of politics," Jefferson told Angelica Schuyler Church smugly in 1788. Accordingly, while in Paris, Jefferson avoided political wives and assertive hostesses like Madame de Staël. He took pleasure in the company of ladies who, like Madame de Tessé, did not challenge his political beliefs. Yet, with Madame de Tessé and still more so with Madame d'Enville Jefferson preferred to avoid politics altogether and discuss instead topics such as gardening and architecture. Meanwhile Jefferson was determined that American women should not follow their French counterparts into political expression. The "true field" of their influence was the marital home.[27]

The restrictions of the "hearth and home" future Jefferson sketched for young American women, including his own daughter, while in Paris are striking. He urged Patsy to master "the needle" and domestic economy. "In the country life of America," he told her, "there are many moments when a woman can have recourse to nothing but her needle." Jefferson did prescribe to Patsy and other girls an ambitious program of reading that offered them access to the intellectual sophistication of thought to be characteristic of well-bred French women, but the systems of education Jefferson prescribed for young American women were largely designed to help them acquire the social skills that were a necessary preparation for marriage. In the community of rational farmers Jefferson hoped to conjure into being around Monticello, Jefferson envisaged higher thought, especially on politics, would be expressed by men. His attitudes softened in later life, but the experience of living in France led him to the conviction that there could be no such useless adornment to a Virginian country house as "a girl of mere city education."[28]

Jefferson's thinking in this vein during his years abroad sits darkly alongside his shining realization formed at the same time that the earth ought to belong in usufruct to the living generation, although it was prompted by the same concerns. If each generation was sovereign unto itself, what was to prevent men and women of Short's generation from discarding the achievements of Jefferson's generation? Stable marriages and the enjoyment of family life might not guarantee the transmission of republican values across generational lines, but life in France had convinced Jefferson that chaste wives and dutiful husbands were necessary for the maintenance of the morality that undergirded a truly republican political system. Having convinced himself of this, he dispensed his advice freely to younger Americans resident in Paris, women as well as men.

A particular object of Jefferson's concern, as well as the Adamses', was Anne Willing Bingham. Twenty when she came to France, Anne was a rich, beautiful, married mother of two children. "Mrs. Bingham is a fine figure and a beautiful person, her manners are easy and affable but she ... gives too much into the follies of this Country," Abigail Adams told her friend Elizabeth Cranch. Jefferson worried that, with her husband's encouragement, Anne was spending an ample fortune in an attempt to establish herself as a fashionable political hostess in Paris. He set out to remind her of her duty, initially by contrasting the frivolity of life in Paris to the virtues of life in America. Jefferson asked her to "recollect the women of this capital, some on foot, some on horses, and some in carriages hunting pleasure in the streets, in routs and assemblies, and forgetting that they have left it behind them in their nurseries." In contrast: "in America ... the society of your husband, the fond cares for the children, the arrangements of the house, the improvements of the grounds fill every moment with a healthy and useful activity." "America's good ladies," Jefferson informed Anne as the United States debated the ratification of the federal Constitution, "have been too wise to wrinkle their foreheads with politics. They are contented to soothe and calm the minds of their husbands returning ruffled from political debate. They have the good sense to value domestic happiness above all other, and the art to cultivate it beyond all others." Jefferson had no desire for America's ladies to emulate the likes of Anne Willing Bingham or French women by setting up political salons.[29]

Anne pushed back against Jefferson's idealization of the submissive non-political wife and his treatment of womankind as a passive citizenry in terms that transcended American partisanship. "I agree with you that many of the fashionable pursuits of the Parisian Ladies are rather frivolous," she told Jefferson on her return to Philadelphia. Nevertheless, she insisted that the picture of French women that Jefferson had presented to her and to other American correspondents was "rather overcharged." Far from offering an example to be avoided by American women, French women were more accomplished, better educated, and more cultivated than those of any other country in the world. If the "Women of France" interfered in politics and gave "a decided turn to the fate of empires" that was because they had "obtained that rank and consideration in society, which [their] sex are entitled to, and which they in vain contend for in other countries." American women, Bingham maintained, were "bound in gratitude to admire and revere" French women "for asserting our privileges," in just the same way "as the friends of the liberties of mankind reverence the successful struggles of the American patriots." Pointedly, Bingham told Jefferson that his daughter Patsy, who Jefferson was at that time encouraging to take up needlework in preparation for married life in rural Virginia, was the envy of all young ladies in America for having lived in Paris.[30]

Some American men of Short's generation sympathized with Anne and tended to admire rather than fear the unfamiliar manners of the French women they encountered. John Rutledge, Jr., who met Anne Willing Bingham in Paris, reflected,

> Women in France are as well acquainted with Politics as the Men so that when that is the Subject they are as much at home as if they were talking of a Cap or Feather and do not sit mum, as the English women do on these occasions. The charmingness of the French Society arises, I am persuaded, from both sexes mixing as they do. The men have no idea of happiness without women. I believe French men have more Wit than Englishmen because they pass so much of their time in the society of amiable Women—nothing pleases them more than wit and the whole nation have a desire to please.

Short was equally disposed to favor French refinement and its importation to the United States by patriotic American women. Learning that his friend Edward Sterrett was courting a beautiful heiress in Baltimore, Short offered to purchase for her a collection of French books. "They are publishing here at present very elegant editions in petit[e] format. . . . And as the female sex are in no country better educated or better read than in this, I think there is no language in which a lady could form so perfect a library as in the French." If this "frenchified" Sterrett's future wife, then so be it. Short had no dislike of rich, beautiful, and well-educated women.[31]

But he did have a dislike of marriage. The flip side of the "hearth and home" agenda Jefferson presented to young American women was the duty of young American men to marry. That duty was well understood by male Virginians of Short's generation, if not by Short himself. Thomas Rhett Smith offered Short's friend John Rutledge, Jr. a sermon on the obligation to marry far more gloomy than Jefferson's admonitions. "In America," Smith told Rutledge, "matrimony is a thing to which we must all submit and we might as well give ourselves with a good grace while we are worth being received. Therefore pray do not put off this important business, till time shall have rendered you stiff in your limbs only and when you will be fitter for a father than a husband to the object you elect." While Short was in no hurry to assume the role of republican husband in Virginia, he would prove to be in no hurry to marry a Frenchwoman either.[32]

Jefferson was conscious of the possibility that a young man in Short's position might go off the sexual rails in Europe. A scant three months after his arrival in France Jefferson wrote to reassure Charles Thomson that a young Philadelphian acquaintance of theirs had displayed no corruption of morals—so far. Jefferson identified for Thomson the "great danger" faced by young Americans in Paris: "that of forming a connection, as is the fashion here, which he might be unwilling to shake off when it shall be proper for him to return to return to his own country and which might detain him disadvantageously here." Jefferson conceded that it was difficult to avoid such connections "where beauty is begging in every street." With John Banister, Jr. he shared his view that the young man in Europe is "led by the strongest of all the human passions into a spirit for female intrigue destructive of his own and others happiness, or a passion for whores destructive of his own health, and in both cases learns to consider fidelity to the marriage bed as an ungentlemanly practice and inconsistent with happiness." Even before he set sail for France Jefferson believed that French women would test an American's character. In the winter of 1783, when he accepted Congress's first invitation to serve in France, it was mooted by Congress that Colonel David Salisbury Franks accompany him as his secretary. Jefferson made inquiries of into Franks' character, sharing his findings with James Madison: "I have marked him particularly in the company of women where he loses all power over himself and becomes almost frenzied. His temperature would not be proof against their allurements were such to be employed as engines against him." When Franks eventually returned to Europe in a minor diplomatic capacity, William Short's college friend, Preeson Bowdoin, joked that Franks must speak very good French since he had spent so much time pursuing ladies.[33]

If Jefferson ever made an assessment of Short's behavior around women he never committed it to paper. He apparently showed no inclination to understand vicariously, let alone praise or criticize, Short's attachments to various French women or even to his own daughter. Despite their having female friends in common, Jefferson's correspondence with Short very rarely discussed specific women as women. An exception—when Jefferson twice referred to Philip Mazzei's ex-wife as a "bitch"—suggests the rule. Individual French women were generally the subject of prosy compliments—they were "angels." In contrast, French women as a category were discussed primarily with reference to their capacity to help or, more likely, hinder the creation of a virtuous political system—"amazons." Insofar as Jefferson's letters to Short discussed women at all they conveyed the absolute necessity for a man in

Short's position to marry—in the United States. But Jefferson declined to engage in matchmaking.[34]

Some of Short's friends, notably William Nelson, thought that Short might be a womanizer cut from the same cloth as Colonel Franks. Nelson, referencing the recently published *The American Wanderer*, pictured Short falling haplessly for "every hostess's daughter." While Short's relationship with Lilite Royer gave his friends pause, Short insisted that he was not the moonstruck victim of a young girl's charm. He suggested to his friends—but not, apparently, to Jefferson—that he knew what he was doing. In the spring of 1785, Short intimated to Preeson Bowdoin, then sojourning in the French town of Orléans, the depth of his feeling for Lilite. Bowdoin pledged to keep as a profound secret everything that Short said relating to the "Belle of St. Germain." He also offered some extremely worldly wise advice. "Love like other things requires practice as well as theory and you I make no doubt will pluck the finest flower of her little garden—a maidenhead is a valuable thing in France, made so by the scarcity of the article," he wrote. "I sincerely wish you may have both the *pucelage* [virginity] and the doing," Bowdoin continued, "but above all things think not of Hymen—no, no, a mistress but no wife in France." Nobody married for love in France, Bowdoin assured Short; the man who did so was sure to be cuckolded.[35]

Short's relationship with Lilite Royer seems not to have followed a narrative of purposeful seduction. He cloaked the relationship in terms of sentiment and feeling. Two years after he first met Lilite, Short told his friend William Nelson that his visits to St. Germain were directed at "one most dear to him." Nelson dismissed Short's interest in the "fair Pomona of the village" as an immature infatuation. Short plied Lilite, Madame Royer, and occasionally the entire family with little gifts: chocolates, trips to the theater, and the like. His account books also record payments to the Royer's servants. Although seemingly unable to explain his attraction to Lilite, Short maintained his interest even after she, then aged fourteen or fifteen, married Henri Denis, a solidly respectable young man who appraised and auctioned probate estates, in late 1786 or early 1787. Short continued to visit the Royers after the birth of Lilite's first child. In a partial acknowledgment of Lilite's new status as a wife, Short arranged for his mail to be forwarded to "Chez Denis, Rue de Lorraine, St. Germain-en-Laye." On the eve of his departure for the south of France in the spring of 1787, Jefferson left word with Madame de Tessé that Short would forward to her any letters Jefferson sent in care of the American legation, if, that is, he was there and not staying with the Royers.[36]

One lens through which Short's friends, indeed Short himself, might have viewed French culture and the place of women within it was supplied by the Earl of Chesterfield in his letters to his son. Widely read in America as well as in Britain, Chesterfield saw it as entirely decent and proper for a young Englishman traveling in Europe to take on the services of a *decrotteuse*—an older, experienced woman of fashion who might knock the rough edges off a young gentleman's manners. Paris was the best setting in Europe for the acquisition of this polish, and French women were particularly adept at applying it. When his twenty-one-year-old son Philip Stanhope arrived in Paris during his Grand Tour, Chesterfield commended to Stanhope's attention the *salonniere* Madame Dupin and also the seventeen-year-old Mademoiselle du Blot, the niece of a friend he had made. Madame Dupin was well read, possessed manners and delicacy, but was past the first bloom of youth. Stanhope could learn from her. Chesterfield advised that smutty banter was appropriate to a relationship with a young girl like Mademoiselle du Blot and was not overly concerned that such banter might lead to sex. "For a mere gallantry," Chesterfield suggested to his son, "I should prefer *la petite Blot*" but the enjoyment of one did not preclude the enjoyment of the other. There was a sexual undercurrent in much of Chesterfield's advice, but Chesterfield wished his son to be a man of pleasure, not a rake. He should avoid prostitutes and never entertain the idea of keeping a woman. He should appreciate beauty, grace, and manners and not become a slave to demeaning passion. Above all Chesterfield's advice was functional. The purpose of consorting with French women was to learn how to move in society and to acquire graces that would further a political career in England.[37]

Short's behavior with Lilite Royer, by contrast, seemed to Jefferson and to Short's friends without point or purpose. Jefferson saw no political advantage in consorting with Lilite or any other French woman, and, in this, he spoke for Virginian contemporaries. In August 1785, James Currie told Short with a hint of menace, "I expect to see you return a Chesterfield, Frenchified in your manners as much as a sensible Republican gentleman would wish to acquire." In his only reference to Short's relationship with the Royers and, indirectly, Lilite—the admonition "come home like a good boy" offered in April 1785— Jefferson suggested that he thought Short was moonstruck. Short believed himself to be a man of sensitivity capable of being led by female purity and innocence into those "douces reveries of which the elegant and sensitive Rousseau speaks so often and with so many charms." In the spirit of Rousseau, he regretted that "it would seem as if after a short stay at Paris one has need of finding the women dressed with taste in order to find them handsome."

Yet, even while he was plying young Lilite Royer with gifts—and especially after this particular reverie was interrupted by her marriage—Short liked the company of elegantly dressed women, some of them less obviously innocent.[38]

In the winter of 1788–1789, Short's feelings were directed toward a woman in Paris referred to by his friend the Milanese countess Pauline Castiglione as "Countess d'Al." She was Princess Louise Stolberg-Gedern, self-styled Countess of Albany, the widow of Charles Edward Stuart, the Young Pretender to the thrones of England and Scotland. The Countess was seven years older than Short. Raised in a Belgium nunnery and still technically a canoness, Louise had been married off by proxy to the Young Pretender, many years her senior, with the promise that she would be Queen of England at Charles's restoration. When she was found to be infertile, Charles abused her, the Pope protected her, and a Piedmontese poet, Count Vittorio Alfieiri, pursued her. After Charles Stuart's death in 1788, Louise and Vittorio, who did not believe in marriage, lived together openly in Paris and presided over a raffish *salon* favored by Gouverneur Morris, among other English speakers. As Short prepared for his southern tour Pauline Castiglione "rejoiced" in Short's "aptitude" to be electrified by a "charming body" and wished he might find on his travels an "explosion suitable to your feelings." When he returned to Paris, Countess Castiglione wrote hoping that his contemplation of the "ethereal beauties" of Naples and Rome would help Short recognize the Countess's "earthly excellence." With a bit more experience Short's "good qualitys [sic] and parts" would surely render his "court" "agreeable" to an appropriate woman. Yet, understanding Short's tendency to idealize women, Castiglione believed he was destined to remain unfulfilled as "poor in love Mr. Short." Short's attempts to convince himself and others that he was a realist where European women were concerned could be undermined by pomposity. Speaking of the beautiful Madame de Tott, the companion of Madame de Tessé, a woman he and William Stephens Smith dubbed "the fair Grecian," Short concluded priggishly: "I love her and several others of that soft and tender and spiritual and gay and lively sex very much, or as they say in French *infiniment,* but I love my country more." Jefferson gave no sign of recognizing this priority in Short's behavior.[39]

It is clear from surviving correspondence that Short left female friends in Virginia behind when he set off for France. William Nelson pointedly forwarded the compliments of a Miss Barret as proof that "the ladies on this side of the water are not unmindful of your former attention." John Mayo mentioned a Miss Marshall. It is impossible to ascertain what form of sexual experience or appetite Short possessed prior to his arrival in France, but he seems not to have subscribed to the view expressed by Gouverneur Morris, and derived from a selective reading of authors such as Sterne and Chesterfield, that no French woman would be offended by an attempted seduction, that "gallantry" generally succeeded, and no harm was done if it did not. A number of Short's male American friends approached French women with a sense of crude entitlement to sexual activity that was only barely disguised by the conventions of "gallant" adventurism. Abraham Bishop fully embraced sexual opportunism in France, boasting to Short that even the Spanish Inquisition would not prevent a French country girl from "indulging herself." Short, clearly interested, asked for more description. "Give me some details in your affairs of gallantry in this way and speak plainly that I may see not only what you did but the manner of its being done. Do the little village girls lend a willing ear and a ready one too to a travelling stranger?" Bishop had told Short he was currently lodged in a convent, which further encouraged Short to ask for smutty details since he supposed that, in the convent, all was holy "and that women are precluded altogether from participating in the pleasures of men." Bishop replied that, to the contrary, he was having a good time playing billiards with the female residents and implied that it was only a matter of time before sexual encounters commenced. Country girls, even convent girls, did indeed "lend a willing ear to a travelling stranger" he assured Short. "Yes, women have tender hearts and when they see a man look (as I did) as tho' 'in want of all things'—they freely give him their *little all*." Bishop invited Short to spend four weeks with him in the country, promising that he would be infinitely happy. Short declined. Preeson Bowdoin, who toured France in 1785–1786, recommended a number of women to Short and even promised to set him up with the "willing" wife of an "ugly" watchmaker recently settled in Paris. Short did not act on these suggestions.[40]

Preeson Bowdoin identified a tour of Europe as a rite of passage, accompanied by a degree of sexual license, through which a young American might acquire the cosmopolitan character of a "man of the world." He boasted of his sexual experiences to Short. Given the prevalence of such attitudes among young American men, it is striking that Jefferson sufficiently overcame his concern for Short's moral well-being as to positively encourage him to travel in France and Italy: "You should not think of returning to America without taking the tour which I have taken, extending it only further South." He stressed a tour's higher purpose, providing Short with a copy of his *Hints for Travellers* and a reading list. Jefferson also undertook to choose Short's traveling companion. He first thought that Short should be accompanied by the son of Colonel Thomas Mann Randolph, but Short thought him hopelessly improvident and hence incapable of traveling economically. Short was less able evade Jefferson's second suggestion, that he travel as far as Italy with John Paradise and his wife Lucy Ludwell Paradise. The chaotic Paradise marriage, the demands of their personalities, and a severe fever initially limited Short's opportunities for "adventures in the love line." However, in February 1789, thirty-year-old Short rendezvoused in Turin with Thomas Lee Shippen and John Rutledge, Jr. From this point Short's Grand Tour began to conform to stereotypes established in *A Sentimental Journey* or *The American Wanderer*.[41]

Short's subsequent correspondence with Rutledge recounted amorous encounters on their journey through Italy. Both Rutledge and Short acquired or experienced a recurrence of a sexually transmitted disease. Short referenced the matter in a letter written after Rutledge's return to the United States.

> I suffer most sincerely for the ill treatment you have received from your mistress. I commend it to you my dear friend not to neglect [longer?] a disorder which may injure radically your fine constitution. Take care of your health for your own sake as well as that of your family and above all for the sake of her with whom you are to pass many days and nights and of those who are to be produced by them ... [Saltpetre?] you know is reckoned an antidote to that most dangerous of all poisons. I hope you will never experience what I have done, but I think you will now consider my fears as less unreasonable than when we were at Naples.

Although his suggestion that his attack was worse than Rutledge's was characteristic, the details of where and under what circumstances Short might have contracted a venereal disease are unknown. The reasons for Short's concern—the consequences for Rutledge's marriage prospects and potential as a father—are suggestive since they might equally have applied to Short himself. Rutledge was not married when Short wrote, but fifteen months later wed the daughter of the Episcopal bishop of South Carolina. Did Short exaggerate Rutledge's condition and, by implication, his own with the intent of finding reasons not to marry? His subsequent correspondence with Jefferson made no reference to venereal disease or any other concrete explanation for a reluctance to marry and father children. Meanwhile, far from acquiring a reputation as a rake, Short was seen as an innocent by friends where women were concerned.[42]

———

While Short was in Europe his friends and family in America began to marry and settle down. Short's uncertain reactions to these events were in inverse proportion to Jefferson's certainty that such marriages were natural and laudable. Short tried to picture himself in his friends' shoes, but could not bring himself to accept the attraction of a Virginian marriage. After his friend John Mayo wed, the news nudged Short to reflect on the distinction between American manners and French culture. He was pleased to hear of Mayo's marriage and was sure that his friend's new wife would be an adornment to local society.

> I congratulate you, most sincerely on this . . . change from celibacy, that solitary, monastic, wearisome state of existence to all the tender affections and alluring endearments of matrimony. It is the state I am sure for which man was formed, is certainly that alone where he can find happiness, if he remains on that side of the Atlantic. Domestic pleasures alone are those which are worth possessing there—and if they are not more exquisite, more brilliant, more bewitching and more rapturous than those which are run after by all the world in this place—yet I am sure they are more innocent, and more lasting and consequently better deserve the pursuit and enjoyment of a rational mind.

Short's assumption that hitherto Mayo must have been wearisomely celibate was reinforced by friends who presumed that, by virtue of his residence in France, he possessed, as William Nelson put it, "the advantage of having before enjoyed pleasures unknown to many of us" as a result of "opportunities . . . which have never been presented to us." No libertine, Short continued to prudishly pit celibacy and matrimony against one another. In 1808, Short offered his friend Merit Moore Robinson a "credit and debit account" of the two states. Robinson was surprised when Short identified the pleasure of being able to sleep diagonally in a bed as one of the advantages of remaining unmarried. Robinson knew that Short had by that time conducted a co-habiting affair and might have been forgiven for assuming that had involved sharing a bed. Apparently, for Short, residence in France had offered no sexually permissive middle ground between lonely celibacy and the "harness" of matrimony.[43]

Nevertheless, as he heard of his friends' marriages, Short began to muse in his letters on "the superiority of domestic life" to that he was living in Paris. As he did so, Short, like Jefferson, tended to idealize companionate marriage and, implicitly, a return to Virginia. "By a kind of contradiction I cannot well account for," he claimed, "the inconstancy in love of the Parisians has rendered me an admirer of the opposite qualities." He told William Nelson that he "felt he was made for domestic life" and regretted an earlier missed opportunity to marry a girl he had courted in Williamsburg. Lodging in a house in southern Italy during his Grand Tour Short found "Madame" to be "quite the good Virginian wife," just as active in the management of the household and estate as the best manager he knew in America. "In the dining room are girls setting constantly at work, like the negro girls in the houses of the middling class in Virginia." Reacting to news that Nelson had married for a second time Short insisted "I am quite a convert and I am one of the most zealous votaries to Hymen." Yet Nelson noted that Short seemed "to be only half a convert" to the idea of marrying a Virginian.[44]

In none of his letters to recently married friends or family members did Short express a wish that he had been able to attend the wedding or even any particularly strong desire to meet the spouse. Instead Short referred repeatedly to marriage as a restraint—his letters to male friends back home spoke of "hymen's silken knot," the "yoke of matrimony," or of "votaries at the shrine of cupid" being "sacrificed" at the "shrine of hymen"—even while insisting that he would himself marry one day. William Nelson chided Short on this usage. Short assured him that he looked forward to enjoying the "unalloyed pleasures" of "domestick life," yet he lamented that Nelson's marriage to Abby Byrd made it unlikely that Nelson could visit him in Europe. Having characteristically suggested to John Rutledge, Jr. that "hymen's silken knot" must have been preventing him from writing to Short more frequently or in greater detail, Short nevertheless insisted that he was indeed interested in the processes by which two souls became one. He assured William Stephen Smith that he was "advanced to that time of life when a tender companion or friend is necessary to our happiness—a friend whose bosom expanded by the impression of love is formed to participate in all our pains and pleasures—whom nature has formed for our better half." Yet Short's letters gave friends like William Nelson evidence that he believed such a union of souls could be achieved outside marriage.[45]

In November 1787, Short offered Nelson a chatty account of developments in the life of their mutual friend, the Marquis de Chastellux. While taking the waters in Spa (Belgium) the Marquis became enamored of Marie Brigitte de Plunkett and proposed marriage to her, despite the fact that she was twenty years younger and had little fortune. In an act of capricious intervention favoring marriage for love, the Duchess d'Orléans, herself the wronged party in one the most notoriously unjust arranged marriages in France, made Plunkett a *Dame de Compagnie*; a position that, in addition to establishing status, came with an annual pension. Chastellux married Plunkett and returned to Paris with his new bride, who Short described as being "pretty enough without being too handsome for the peace of mind of an old husband." These developments outraged the Marquis's long-standing mistress, who railed against the Chastellux's "inconstancy." Short thought she had a point, reflecting for Nelson's benefit that, in Paris, "the offer of what is called *liaison de Coeur* or *bonne amitié* . . . has its rules and morality as well established as marriage among us—an infidelity is reckoned as base and . . . unpardonable in that case, as amongst us between husbands and wives." In drawing an equivalence between marriage and a *liaison de Coeur*, Short not only ruffled the feelings of his recently married friend but also strongly hinted which of the two states he preferred.[46]

Short liked Plunkett but did not ask himself why the Marquis de Chastellux wished to marry her rather than take her as a mistress. The notion that men and women in France and, by implication, in the United States as well, might actually value marriage was an idea that Short seems to have found novel. Studies suggest that during the French Revolution wealthy French women, along with their male partners, began to embrace companionate marriage and domesticity as part of a reaction to the perceived corruption inherent in *ancien regime* morality. This change in manners went unnoticed in the society gossip Short offered in his letters to American friends. In 1786, Condorcet married Sophie de Grouchy, a decision that angered Madame d'Enville, who believed that Condorcet owed his career to the La Rochefoucauld family. Judging that he had married beneath his station, Madame d'Enville and her daughter-in-law Rosalie de La Rochefoucauld made the newlyweds unwelcome at La Roche-Guyon. Although Short had ample opportunity to observe the Condorcets working as a husband and wife team, although he observed Condorcet's conversion to republicanism, and although he must have been aware of the couple's advocacy of citizenship rights for women, Short essentially shared Madame d'Enville's perspective. How strange that the unkempt Condorcet should marry the much younger, beautiful Sophie de Grouchy, daughter of a minor aristocrat. Condorcet had submitted to the "yoke of hymen."[47]

Short's disinclination to enter into a homespun marriage of the type Jefferson idealized was also fueled by snobbery. Short was proud of his relationships with society ladies, seemingly the grander the better. Their influence on Short's view of marriage could only be guessed at by most of Short's correspondents back in Virginia, but Short gave Jefferson insights into the influence that exposure to aristocracy had wrought on his system of values. In January 1790, Short passed on to Jefferson what he took to be a humorous remark made to him by Madame de Tessé from her exile in Switzerland with Madame de Tott and the Viscount d'Agoult. In this transplanted community, Madame de Tessé had told Short, her chief occupations were sewing coarse cloth and attending to the most common domestic operations. "Her health is much the better for it, and she thinks herself worthy of being an American wife." In passing on Madame de Tessé's *bon mot*, Short ran the risk of offending Jefferson—and probably did. It was one thing for a sophisticate such as Madame de Tessé to find the role of American wife amusing, quite another for William Short to even hint at disparaging the virtuous simplicity of American marriage. Short's behavior in France seemed to confirm the wisdom of Jefferson's warning that prolonged residence in France warped a young American's morals.[48]

During Short's lifetime companionate marriage and stable conjugal union emerged as the bedrock of a new post-revolutionary morality in the Atlantic world. As the friend with whom Short most often discussed bachelorhood, Merit Moore Robinson put it, marriage offered the "protection of mutual love against the slanders on an invidious world." It was not a harness but "a mantle which virtue and delicacy have made for love, out of materials furnished by heaven." Matrimony only became a harness when worn by avarice, ambition, or lust. Short paid lip service to such emerging sensibilities while repeatedly invoking metaphors of restraint in his discussion of American marriage. Life in France offered opportunities for meaningful relationships outside formalized marriages—*liaisons de coeurs*—which attracted Short.[49]

Short's disinclination to locate his emotional and sexual needs within a stable conjugal union, within a marriage idealized by Jefferson as a little republic, brought out the paternalist in Jefferson. However, their shared residence in France, for all their divergent responses to it, was also a common bond imparting some equality to their relationship. "We return like foreigners, and, like them, require a considerable residence here to become Americanized," Jefferson wrote to him in 1801. Both Jefferson and Short faced on their respective returns to the United States allegations that they had "gone native" while in France. That Jefferson had internalized the values of a godless French republicanism while in France was a charge frequently made by his political opponents. In fact, residence in France marked Short's character to a greater extent than Jefferson's. Nowhere is this more evident than in Short's reluctance to adopt the lifestyle Jefferson championed for American republicans. Although he developed no fully formed alternative, residence in France and observation of French society encouraged Short to reject a specifically American republican morality centered around marriage. This prompted a question in Jefferson's mind as Short began an independent diplomatic career in a France hurtling toward revolution: Was such a man trustworthy?[50]

THREE

"A Poor Dry Business"

WILLIAM SHORT'S DIPLOMATIC CAREER

WHILE MINISTER TO Great Britain John Adams described to Thomas Jefferson the challenges of selecting diplomats: "there can be no employment more disagreeable than that of weighing merit, by the grain and scruple. . . . It is worse than the business of a portrait painter as men are generally [more] satisfied with their own talents and virtues, than even with their faces." Even before Jefferson had formally accepted the post of Secretary of State claimants to the post of minister to France drew him into the business of judging claims to preferment. William Temple Franklin, the illegitimate son of Benjamin Franklin's illegitimate son William Temple, milked his connections to lobby for a position that his grandfather had let it be known he should occupy. Temple Franklin pressed his claims with considerable swagger. "As I think it not improbable that I shall soon go to Europe," he had made known to President Washington "my wish to be employed in the diplomatic line." Although Washington was "desirous of complying with my views," he had waited, so Temple Franklin believed, for Jefferson to take up the post of Secretary of State before "making any foreign arrangements." The young man put Jefferson on the spot. "Should you think me worthy of your patronage I know you will afford it me . . . I need not therefore solicit it." Jefferson had his doubts about Franklin's grandson. He had not, he told James Monroe, been able to "unravel" Temple Franklin's "unpenetrated" character. He batted away the request, replying that the nomination lay with the President and "your merit is too well known to him to need any testimony from me." In the event, Temple Franklin's plans changed, and an awkward refusal was averted.[1]

William Short's claims were not so easy to deflect. His professional life was dominated by one great ambition: to succeed Jefferson as the United States'

Heir through Hope. Peter Thompson, Oxford University Press. © Peter Thompson 2023.
DOI: 10.1093/oso/9780197546833.003.0004

minister plenipotentiary to France. He believed himself almost uniquely well-qualified for the job by virtue of his language skills, his contacts, and the time he had already spent in Paris under Jefferson's auspices. He was certain he was better qualified than any political appointee Congress might send instead. Short was prone to portray himself, disingenuously, as an outsider, experienced but unjustly condemned to be employed in low grades. Short therefore personified the problem John Adams identified and yet he subtly changed its terms.[2]

Short considered himself a journeyman who had completed his apprenticeship and was ready for an independent station. "The diplomatic career is that which I always desired to follow," he told his sister. He saw his desire to construct a career as setting him apart from adventurers like William Temple Franklin. Jefferson had already advised Short that no certain foreign service career path existed. Now, in addressing Short's claims, Jefferson found himself having also to explain why language skills or existing personal relationships with key French politicians, let alone friendship with the Secretary of State of the United States of America, did not represent demonstrable, incontrovertible qualifications for promotion to the rank of minister to France.[3]

Congress, and ultimately Jefferson himself, negatively glossed Short's knowledge of France, its language, and his contacts within its *ancien regime* government. These factors aroused the suspicion that he might lack political objectivity. Following his return to the United States Jefferson gave Short fair warning of the prevailing mood in America's new government. He thought it "likely" that the United States would "discontinue" its "foreign servants after a certain time of absence from their own country, because they lose in time that sufficient degree of intimacy with its circumstances which alone can enable them to know and pursue its interests. Seven years have been talked of." Jefferson realized that failure to be appointed his successor would break Short's heart, yet, anxious to avoid revealing his own assessment of Short's merit, he lectured Short in terms that must have seemed absurd. "One circumstance . . . in your letters must be corrected," he wrote nearly a year into his tenure as Secretary of State, "that is your idea of my influence in foreign affairs."[4]

Jefferson's freedom to maneuver was in fact constrained. One of his first tasks as Secretary was to deal with the repercussions of Congress' decision to request that France recall its minister to the United States, the Count de Moustier. Jefferson was reluctant to appoint a minister to France unless and until France replaced Moustier. The French government, affronted by Congress' action, was in no hurry to name a new minister. This matter was linked to another. Jefferson was determined to "kick" a haughty British government into "good manners" by delaying the appointment of a minister to the Court of St. James's until the British recognized American sovereignty by appointing an ambassador to the United States. In this instance, Jefferson's national pride aligned with isolationist tendencies both in Congress and the country at large, but, with major appointments delayed, the utility of the State Department itself came under further scrutiny.[5]

Many congressmen questioned the need for substantive engagement with foreign powers. Senator William Maclay of Pennsylvania maintained "I know not a single thing that we might have for a minister to do at a single court in Europe." As he dealt with claims to foreign appointments Jefferson also challenged congressional parsimony. In 1790, he prevailed upon Congress to pass the Foreign Intercourse Act, raising the pay awarded ministers plenipotentiary and *chargé des affaires*, and, crucially, expanding their allowable expenses. In recognition of congressional opinion, he paid for these reforms by restricting the rank of minister plenipotentiary to the United States' representatives in London and Paris alone. Spain, Portugal, and Holland were to be dealt with by *chargés*. Opposition to the creation of permanent and numerous diplomatic corps persisted. It surfaced again in the winter of 1791–1792, when the Senate debated nominations for the posts of minister to Britain, France, and Holland.[6]

Short took little or no account of congressional opinion. In moments of frustration, he comforted himself that Jefferson was "in a place which would necessarily [have] influence" on foreign appointments. Mutual friends in France, in particular the La Rochefoucauld family, as well as members of the diplomatic corps, encouraged Short to believe that "I should be employed here because I was known to you." Jefferson responded that if his adoptive son thought his father could fix for him a permanent appointment in Paris, then "you have forgotten your countrymen altogether, as well as the nature of our government."[7]

Jefferson's own feelings about democratic oversight were ambivalent. "Gloomy forebodings" of criticism and censure from "a public just in intention" though sometimes "misinformed and misled," had almost convinced him to decline Washington's invitation to serve as Secretary of State. It was Jefferson's "heart's desire" to "glide unnoticed through the silent execution of duty," and he did not choose to be "laid on the gridiron of debate in Congress" for "paltry" matters. He was reluctant to risk his own political capital to further William Short's desire for a diplomatic career.[8]

Yet, between 1789 and 1794, Short served as the US *chargé des affaires* in France, its financial agent in the money markets of Europe, and Resident Minister to Holland before being moved to Spain as a special envoy. He thereby fulfilled an ambition Jefferson believed unattainable. Albeit briefly, he enjoyed a public service career founded on diplomatic activity abroad. Conducting himself reasonably ably, he attracted the favorable attention of George Washington and Alexander Hamilton. Short seldom ventured into strategic policymaking. He offered Hamilton a reasoned but noncommittal assessment of the likely financial effects of an American declaration of neutrality in any future general European war. He shared with Jefferson well-developed thoughts on the need for American access to the Mississippi. He assured Spanish minister Gardoqui that the United States would never countenance entangling alliances. These statements did not challenge their recipients' preconceptions and showed little originality. Understandably, given the importance he placed on a diplomatic career, Short's lengthiest and most considered reflections on the purpose and objectives of diplomacy considered the optimal organization of the American diplomatic service: its ranks, pay grades, and standing vis à vis European diplomatic corps. Short's detractors found him unprepossessing and self-important, but few doubted his energy and attention to detail.[9]

At the heart of Short's professional self-identity was his belief that, in the midst of a global ideological ferment, he could distinguish between honest men and true patriots, who were capable of offering "wise counsel," and designing men and demagogues, who were not. He disparaged men of ideas (Jefferson and Hamilton excepted). A man like Condorcet, so Short believed, was too "theoretical" to occupy a post such as Master of the French mint. He was puzzled by the praise heaped upon both Edmund Burke's *Reflections on the Revolution in France* and Thomas Paine's *Rights of Man*. Short was no lover of monarchy yet equally believed that sovereignty could not be vested in the people at large without some form of supervision whose precise nature he could not fully articulate. He lived in Paris when, in Jefferson's view, "everybody" was trying their hands at drafting declarations of fundamental rights and constitutions to protect them. Jefferson joined this ferment, Short did not. He disdained ideological conviction, believing himself to be a pragmatist who was to all intents and purposes apolitical. This misconception was a point of origin for Jefferson's distrust.[10]

Unwilling, perhaps unable given his distance from the partisan fray, to discern in the conduct of America's politics a competition between principles, Short struggled to understand the new republic and Jefferson's position within it. Seeing little connection between events in France and America's future, he saw no reason why his relationship with Jefferson was interpreted, by Jefferson as well as by other cabinet members and congressmen, within the context of America's domestic politics. His insecurities led him to search for approval from Alexander Hamilton and engage in an ugly feud with Gouverneur Morris, thereby exacerbating Jefferson's concerns regarding his judgment and trust-worthiness. He believed he acted at all times in accordance with instructions received as well as simple common sense, but in truth he acted on his own un-examined but conservative political instincts. Much of Short's diplomacy was, as far as Jefferson was concerned, clumsily expressed and often unhelpful. His diplomatic reports tended to confirm Jefferson's suspicion that he was overly fond of a decadent French culture epitomized in liberal aristocrats' way of life. Not entirely trusting Short to act independently, and wishing to direct policy toward France himself, Jefferson set out to steer Short.

———

In the aftermath of Jefferson's departure from France, Short was a diplomat without accreditation. Acting on his own authority Jefferson had told French officials as well as key foreign correspondents, notably America's bankers in Holland, that, during his absence, Short would act as America's *chargé des affaires*. Official confirmation of Short's appointment was slow in coming, but Short's status was recognized by members of the new federal government, including Treasury Secretary Alexander Hamilton, in October 1789. From Jefferson Short heard distressingly little.[11]

Jefferson began his journey home in late September 1789, and, upon making landfall at Norfolk, on November 21, he sent Short a brief account of the voyage. In a letter dated December 14 but not received until May 1790, Jefferson told Short that he had been offered the post of Secretary of State. "My answer," he told Short, "is . . . that if the President thinks the public ser-vice will be better promoted by my taking" the position then "I shall do it" but "the office" of minister to France "is more agreeable to me." Jefferson later claimed that a "repugnance" to serving as Secretary of State made him favor a return to Paris until Washington made it clear that he expected Jefferson to accept the cabinet position. He took his time mulling over Washington's offer, keeping even political allies like James Madison in the dark. He did not write to Short again until March 1790.[12]

Reacting to rumors, in November 1789, Short wrote to Jefferson that he expected that he had accepted the Secretaryship and began discreetly angling for a permanent position as *chargé des affaires* in France, or, better still, Minister. Despite this, Short maintained outwardly for as long as possible that Jefferson was determined to return to Paris. He discounted reports that Jefferson had accepted Washington's request because the title, *Secretary* of State (not minister), suggested the status of an underling. As late as May 1790, Short addressed his official letters to John Jay, head of foreign affairs under the Confederation Congress, even though Jay had told him that Jefferson was now in charge. Watching in the company of the La Rochefoucauld circle the "rise and progress" of "the great spectacle of a revolution" that daily presented "new and great lessons in politics and morals," Short waited with great impatience for news from the United States. The "silence of Mr. Jefferson," Short told John Brown Cutting, "is one of the most puzzling and unaccountable events possible." Short wanted to hear Jefferson's news from Jefferson himself. Second-hand reports confirmed his secondary status in Jefferson's affections.[13]

All correspondence from the United States took longer than usual to reach France during the winter of 1789–1790. When they eventually arrived, Jefferson's letters to Short were not in the sequence they had been written. The first letter Short received from Jefferson in more than three months asked him to "send me if you please the continuation of Rousseau's confession . . . my address is simply 'Thos. Jefferson Secretary of State,'" while the following day an earlier letter arrived in which Jefferson announced his decision to accept the Secretaryship. In referencing the news Jefferson was laconic and self-absorbed to the point of insult. He casually informed Short of "small news" that he knew Short to be interested in: choosing first the death of Virginia's US Senator William Grayson and second "the marriage of my daughter with young T. Randolph of Tuckahoe." Finally the hammer fell: "I am therefore on my way to enter on the new office. Not a word has been said about my successor. . . . At present I must talk to you about the winding up of my affairs which I fear will necessarily give you a great deal of trouble." The remainder of this letter issued a series of commands relating to the winding down of Jefferson's Parisian establishment and the removal of his effects. The effort involved in returning Jefferson's possessions to America, securing licenses for export and exemption from double customs duties, and fielding Jefferson's incessant queries would prove immense but Short found the emotional effects of Jefferson's departure hardest to handle.[14]

The situation of 1784–1785 reversed itself, as this time Jefferson offered inadequate explanation for his decision-making. Short had hoped that "success in the career which I had adopted" would compensate for being separated from the man "who I have long looked to as father." As the news sank in, he

wrote accusingly to Jefferson "until I hear further from you and know something of my future lot, I shall be in a state of anxiety, uncertainty and uneasiness the continuance of which is worse than death itself." Switching from
self-pity to aggression Short risked accusing Jefferson of something akin to
a breach of promise. "I take it for granted that," Short wrote, "my name has
never been put in the view of him who names."[15]

From mid-summer 1790 to the winter of 1792, Short reverted to a discussion of his prospects of becoming minister to France so frequently that
Jefferson began scoring out references to the matter from Short's letters. He
later suggested that he did so because he intended to share Short's letters with
third parties, including the President, with whom "to overdo a thing is to undo
it." Yet interlining and deletions in letters Short received conveyed Jefferson's
ambivalence. In one expressing the sentiment "I have thought it better to let
your claim ripen in silence," Jefferson let Short see that he had considered, and
deleted, the alternative formulations: "to let it lie" or "not to introduce the
subject." "Your letters," Short deduced, "shew me that you have never spoken
of me to the President relative to [the position of minister to France]." He was
sure that Washington had therefore assumed that his Secretary of State had
some unstated reservation about Short's claim to ministerial appointment.[16]

Although he occasionally reassured Short that he was "steering the best
I can for you," Jefferson's uncompromising responses to Short's complaints
were conditioned by his hardening republicanism. In moments of clarity,
Short recognized that if Jefferson "conceived that the public would attribute
my appointment to partiality in you" then he would be averse to taking such
a "degree of responsibility" on himself. Even if "I were his brother," Short reasoned correctly, Jefferson would be "unwilling" to use undue influence on his
behalf. Still, while his head told Short that Jefferson would not and could
not simply appoint him minister to France, his heart, particularly influenced
by his friendship with the La Rochefoucauld circle, was tormented by the
fact "in this country no such reserve is known." Everyone in Paris, so Short
maintained, assumed that protégé would succeed patron—if the patron
wished it. Did Jefferson wish Short to succeed him? The question was deferred as Short was thrust into an area of activity he had not sought—financial
diplomacy.[17]

During the Revolutionary War, in addition to gifts of money and materiel,
France loaned the United States 24 million livres (roughly $4.4 million) and

underwrote a loan of 10 million livres (roughly $1.8 million) made by the United States in Dutch money markets. From 1786, annual interest payments due to France, including interest on arrears, exceeded $800,000. Yet, between 1786 and 1790, Confederation Congress made no payment toward any of its foreign debt obligations. France had also supplied direct military assistance to the United States, and, in a gesture of gratitude, the US had guaranteed pay and pensions to French army officers, among them the Marquis de Lafayette, who had fought with the Continental Army. The repeated failure of the new nation to meet even the interest on its obligations to the officers, although this represented a fraction of America's outstanding foreign debt, acted as a lightning rod. As Jefferson noted to Madison, "all our other debts in Europe do not injure our reputation as much" as the debt owed the French officers. Addressing a financial crisis in France partially triggered by the scale of its support for the United States during the Revolutionary War, French politicians subjected the credit worthiness of the United States to censorious language in the Assemblée des Notables. It fell to Jefferson and Short alike to defuse "dissatisfaction" with America fomented by British agents in Paris as well as the unpaid officers themselves. Yet while contradicting rumors that the United States intended to repudiate its foreign debt, Jefferson and Short were forced to acknowledge that Confederation Congress had ceased to function while the Constitutional Convention met. Jefferson hoped that while John Adams remained in Europe he would use his contacts in Amsterdam to negotiate a line of credit sufficient at least to pay the interest on the sum owed the French officers. Adams in turn urged Jefferson to apply to the US banking house Van Staphorst and Willink for a loan without waiting for Congressional approval.[18]

A subsidiary manifestation of the larger debt crisis involved the payment of America's diplomatic officers. In May 1786, Confederation Congress' Commissioners of the Treasury wrote to Jefferson that, lacking any means of defraying even domestic expenses, they proposed to meet the salaries and costs of America's diplomats by drawing on prize money raised by Captain John Paul Jones. A year later the Parisian banking house of Ferdinand Grand, which handled the United States' accounts in France, refused to advance any further credit to the Paris legation until Congress addressed outstanding repayments on existing debt owed the bank. Jefferson was away on his tour of southern Europe when the announcement came. On his return, he told Adams haughtily that Grand was a "sure" banker but "excessively cautious" and had overreacted by suspending "small demands for current occasions." Among those small demands were his own salary and Short's.[19]

Signaling his virtue, Short ordered Grand to place his own personal deposits and salary stream at the disposal of the legation's account, commenting rue-fully "so away went my scheme of becoming rich." Although Jefferson quickly wrote to the Commissioners of the Treasury on behalf of the US consuls in the Hague and Madrid, who were also paid from the account with Grand, he did so in terms that sought to distance himself from what he admitted in private correspondence was becoming a "terrible pickle." Jefferson hoped that Charles William Frederick Dumas in the Hague and William Carmichael in Madrid would adopt Short's attitude. Dumas, owed back pay and witnessing a civil war, could not afford to, and Carmichael accepted very grudgingly. Chiding Congress, Jefferson wrote that it was "disagreeable" for him to be drawn into the business of procuring salaries. Ultimately John Adams resolved Jefferson's problem by exercising discretionary powers to borrow enough from the United States' Dutch bankers to satisfy Ferdinand Grand's claims and also address the interest on the arrears in pay due the French officers. But the officers' claims remained unsettled as late as 1791, when Short begged Jefferson to apply money set aside for ransoming Algerine captives to pay off the debt owed the officers.[20]

Plans for the United States to negotiate a major loan on the Dutch markets and use the proceeds to repay its various debts to France had existed in schematic form for several years before Short became involved in them. Jefferson had investigated various options, but he wanted no part of the de-tailed negotiation of a new loan. He assured Madison that "I do not under-stand bargaining nor possess the dexterity requisite" to negotiate a major loan. "It is a business that would be most disagreeable to me . . . and for which I am the most unfit person living." He suggested that Dumas might "suffice," though it is hard to believe that Jefferson seriously contemplated entrusting such sensitive business to a non-American. In January 1788, Jefferson was able to persuade John Adams to use his expiring power as US minister to Holland to secure an emergency loan in Amsterdam. Adams grumbled, but, concluding that an additional loan was "absolutely necessary," he made the journey from London and secured one. Eagerly anticipating his return to Massachusetts, and writing on the assumption that Jefferson would now take over the business of negotiating loans, at the conclusion of his trip Adams left Jefferson with a terrible warning: "My dear friend . . . I pity you, in your situation, dunned and teased as you will be" by Dutch bankers. As Jefferson's own determination to return home increased, and as creditors pursued his private debts, he was even less inclined than Adams to treat with dunning and teasing bankers. Besides, Jefferson insisted that responsibility for dealing with the Dutch money markets did not rest with any minister to France. He maintained even into old age that he "had no powers, no instructions and no means" of negotiating any future loan. As he canvassed the remaining options, it became clear that he considered Short to possess the ambition and skill required in a future financial agent whose responsibility the "disagreeable business" would become.[21]

However, it was the United States' Dutch bankers, not Jefferson or Congress, who finally pushed Short to the forefront of financial diplomacy. The inability of the United States to make even scheduled interest payments on its foreign debts (arrears on interest alone had reached $1.6 million by the end of 1788) posed several threats to the house of Van Staphorst, Willinks, and Hubbard. In the midst of its own financial crisis, and desperate to recoup even a portion of the value of its loans to the United States, French finance minister Jacques Necker proposed either using America's debt as collateral for a loan to be raised in European money markets or to sell the debt at discount to speculators. Either course of action would further damage assessments of the United States' creditworthiness made in international markets. Van Staphorst and Willinks had purchased American securities in the expectation that America's credit would rise with the formation of a new federal government. They calculated that there was sufficient market confidence in the future stability of the United States to allow for the negotiation of a major loan on its behalf that would give the new American government breathing space in which to reorganize its debt repayments. Van Staphorst and Willinks, the United States' official Commissioners of Loans, wanted the business.[22]

Jacob Van Staphorst proposed a three-part plan. First, he urged Short, the ranking American diplomat in Jefferson's absence, to use his "utmost exertions" to prevent the government of France from selling or transferring its claims against the United States. Second, to help defeat speculation, Van Staphorst invoked what he described as his bank's discretionary powers to take out a loan of three million florins on behalf of the United States and in advance of Congressional approval. The bank remitted this money to the United States and informed the French financial community that they had done so. Van Staphorst gambled that Congress would retrospectively authorize the loan and use the proceeds to resume dependable payments to France, thereby easing pressure on the French to sell their American debt. He justified this unsolicited action in a letter to Short, reminding him that "the transfer unto the money lenders of this Country [Holland], of the debts due by the United States to France, has as you know long been a favourite measure of His Excellency Thomas Jefferson."[23]

The final element of Van Staphorst's plan was the cleverest and most relevant to Short. Writing to Alexander Hamilton, Van Staphorst testified to
Short's zeal in the service of his country. When, in the aftermath of Jefferson's
return to the United States, Short had told him that his bank was best placed
to decide upon "everything relating to the credit of the United States in
Holland," Van Staphorst had acted on the powers implied in that statement to
take out a loan on America's behalf. However, anticipating a necessity for further substantial loans to refinance America's foreign debt repayment schedule,
Van Staphorst suggested to Hamilton that either his bank be granted permission to negotiate on behalf the United States—a proposition he knew could
not be accepted—or the United States appoint an authorized agent in Europe
to handle the business. The unstated assumption behind the latter proposal
was that a man like William Short, whom Van Staphorst knew and liked,
would fit the bill.[24]

Short did not particularly wish to be appointed as an agent empowered to
negotiate loans on behalf of the United States. He regarded such business as a
"poor dry affair," a form of "drudgery" that would not bolster his claims to the
post of Minister to France. But he did want to be seen by Washington's cabinet, Congress, the French National Assembly, Parisian society, and Virginians
back home as a man of importance. So, while Short recognized that America's
Dutch bankers had "manifestly" taken out the loan in order to force Congress
into using their services, he nevertheless urged the United States to accept the
money raised. The Secretaries of State and Treasury agreed, with Jefferson, in
this instance, supporting a loose construction of the discretionary power of
bankers and Hamilton congratulating Van Staphorst and Willink for their
"zeal" in serving the interests of the United States. Congress, wrangling over
domestic funding bills, did not formally approve the Van Staphorst loan until
August 1790. Nevertheless, as Short waited for news from New York, he found
himself in the limelight. Over the summer of 1790, French finance ministers
pestered Short either to use his own authority as *chargé des affaires* to release
the proceeds of the loan ahead of congressional sanction or to give his blessing
to a scheme hatched by finance minister Jacques Necker for the French to float
a loan of their own in Holland secured by the United States' obligation to
France. For his part, Short loyally set out to leverage expected congressional
approval of Van Staphorst's loan to advance Jefferson's commercial diplomacy
and he battled speculators, further signaling, as he saw it, his integrity and
suitability for employment as a financial agent or higher position.[25]

In the last months of 1789, Short began reporting back to Jay, Jefferson,
and Hamilton on the activities of an amorphous grouping of financiers,

sometimes referring to itself as a Society of Friends to America, and involving American money-men Daniel Parker and James Swan, Genevan-born banker Etienne Clavière, French writer and politician Brissot de Warville, and New Yorker Gouverneur Morris, who was in Europe to supervise the interests of his cousin the financier Robert Morris. In the grandest version of their speculation, those associated would borrow from Dutch money market funds sufficient to purchase from France the entirety of the debt owed it by the United States. As security for their initial loan the speculating syndicate would offer as collateral American state and confederation debt acquired on the cheap but backed by the full faith and credit provision of the recently ratified US Constitution. American credit rose in Dutch markets as a result of the ratification of the Constitution, allowing the speculators to borrow Dutch florins relatively cheaply. America's debt to France was denominated in French livres, whose value against the florin was falling. Parker and Morris contemplated buying America's debt from the French using a mixture of livres and French bonds, the bonds acquired at discounted prices but presumably liable to rise in value as a result of the improvement in French finances that the purchase would bring.[26]

The speculation promised France immediate benefits: some cash, a reduction in outgoing debt-service repayments, and, if desired, the resale of French bonds. The United States would secure its international credit rating but at the cost of pledging its full faith and credit to the redemption at their original value of the obligations purchased from France by men like Parker and his associates. This was a price worth paying, the American associates argued, because by committing to acquire American debt obligations the group established an interest in seeing the United States establish financial security. If, at every point of the transaction, the speculators made substantial profits, then so be it. Gouverneur Morris was willing to take "an interest" in such schemes ("provided always there is nothing in them prejudicial to the United States or inconsistent with personal Honour and Integrity") since the pursuit of profit was simply the way of the world. As Morris told Washington, this was an instance where private greed might serve a public good.[27]

Despite their potential to alleviate France's financial crisis, maneuvers better calculated to excite Jefferson's prejudices against bankers, stock-jobbery, and corruption are hard to imagine. Determined that the US government should never be subject to the "chicaneries and vexations of private avarice," Jefferson ordered Short to inform speculators, "whether native or foreign," "that our government condemns their projects and reserves to itself the right of paying nowhere but in to the treasury of France, according to their contract." But Short viewed the speculators more in the guise of rivals for influence within a murky world of intrigue created by France's financial crisis than as villains pursuing immoral objectives. His knowledge of the wheeling and dealing associated with the speculation bolstered Short's sense that he could serve America's national interest by distinguishing honest, credit-worthy men from under-resourced or fraudulent schemers. When French foreign minister Montmorin pushed the advantages of a scheme to buy America's debt to France organized by French bankers Schweitzer, Jeanneret & Co. and the American speculator James Swan, Short reported to Hamilton in the tones of an insider that the syndicate lacked both capital and credit. Lacking Jefferson's strategic interest in ensuring that a strong, stable, and democratic France would in future serve as a counterweight to British power, Short was willing to exploit France's financial crisis even at the cost of exacerbating its political crisis. He made known to Jefferson that "a loss to France was a gain for us" and backed schemes that would have allowed the US government to profit by repaying its debts to the royal treasury in depreciated French bonds (*assignats*) rather than harder currency. Jefferson, by contrast, remained determined that the United States should not seek to exploit the depreciation of French currency and bonds.[28]

Short had told Jefferson that he was not ashamed of an "ardent desire" to acquire an "affluent fortune," and his personal dealings with Connecticut-born Daniel Parker suggested that he saw in the chicaneries of speculation an opportunity to realize his ambition. Parker was universally acknowledged to be resourceful, cunning, and determined. Even his associate Gouverneur Morris described Parker as a "devilish slippery fellow," an assessment Short shared. Yet, belying his belief that he was a good judge of character, Short gave Parker a portion of his personal savings to buy discounted American securities. When Parker went bankrupt, Short, fearing for his money, told Jefferson about this foray into speculation. But by the time Short confessed, Jefferson was no longer in charge of US policy toward the French debt.[29]

———

Congress approved the three million florin loan taken out on its behalf by Jacob Van Staphorst in August 1790. Subsequently President Washington authorized Treasury Secretary Hamilton to use Van Staphorst to borrow up to $14 million to be applied in the first instance to the annual payment of interest and principal on the United States' foreign debt or, in the event of a favorable opportunity, to repay the entire sum outstanding. Washington's instructions to Hamilton provided for the appointment of a financial agent to oversee the negotiations of loans, someone who would have to travel to Amsterdam promptly and stay there for months. When Washington asked Jefferson whether "Mr. Short" might be spared from France, Jefferson agreed that he could, "without injury to the public service." He offered Washington no explicit endorsement of Short's abilities. Vesting responsibility for the organization and administration of foreign debt repayment in the Treasury, rather than the State Department, represented a victory for Hamilton over Jefferson. Jefferson set out to limit Hamilton's influence by persuading Washington to set some restrictions on the agent's powers; not opening a loan exceeding $1 million or opening any subsequent loan until existing loans had been fully subscribed and approved by the President. Jefferson's reasoning, influenced by his critique of Hamilton's domestic financial program, reflected more his suspicion of bankers in general than of Short in particular. An impressionable "new man" arriving in Amsterdam with the authority to borrow a ten-figure sum would immediately be "beset" by "dexterous" lobbyists who would "ensnare" him. The restrictions on the agent's power Jefferson proposed were necessary to protect the agent against himself.[30]

With these safeguards in place Jefferson wrote in passive official tones to inform Short of Washington's decision. In reply, Short pledged to "use all the zeal of which I am master," but he regarded his new responsibility for conducting the nitty-gritty of commercial diplomacy within constraints set by the federal government as tantamount to a demotion. He only accepted the position, he later claimed, to enhance his chances of being appointed minister to France. Jefferson described himself as "anxious" that the mission to Holland should place Short advantageously in the public view, but told Short soon after his arrival in Amsterdam "I do not exactly see to what your . . . mission . . . may lead." Once again Jefferson urged Short to conclude his business swiftly and return to Virginia. An appointment to a US senate seat following the death of William Grayson was about to be made, and this offered an opportunity for Short "which will not recur for years, and never under such certainty."[31]

Hamilton's letters of guidance and instruction to Short, although collegial in tone, gave notice of the minefield he was entering. Distancing himself from Jefferson, he reminded Short that "however cordial our disposition to come to the pecuniary aid of France in her present . . . condition" "prudence" dictated that payments to France, especially through the expedient of "new *foreign* loans," should be attended with some advantage to the United States. Hamilton was keen to have Short secure the best possible terms for any future loan and tasked him with supplying enough information to allow the Treasury Secretary to judge from New York whether Short had done so. Arriving in Amsterdam in late 1790, Short soon agreed with Van Staphorst, Willinks, and Hubbard on the terms of a further loan of three million florins (or $1 million). He was unable to secure an interest rate lower than 5% but, after "delicate" negotiation, was able to limit commission charges to 4% and to defer for ten years the date on which payments would become due. He accepted, and advised Hamilton to accept, the advice of the bankers to delay floating the loan until February 1, 1791. He also made every effort to supply Hamilton with information on the state of European money markets and America's standing within them.[32]

The loan was offered to the Amsterdam market on February 15, 1791, and completely underwritten within two hours. Short reported an immediate clamor from the markets for him to authorize a new and larger loan. He told Hamilton that "if I had ... been in longer relation with you and better acquainted with your views I should probably have taken on myself this additional degree of responsibility." However, Short continued, in this instance he had followed his instructions to the letter, thereby guaranteeing his personal tranquility albeit at the expense of the public interest. Confident that the constraints on the financial agent's freedom of maneuver imposed by Jefferson were unnecessary, he pointedly appealed to Hamilton for greater "latitude" to be granted "to those who have your confidence on this side of the Atlantic."[33]

Short eventually had the satisfaction of hearing from Hamilton that "the manner in which you have proceeded . . . is entirely satisfactory to me and I doubt not will be equally so to the President." Hamilton was also persuaded that the restrictions imposed on the powers of America's financial agent by Jefferson were overly cautious, and he brought the President around to his position. In exchanges conducted in July 1791, Washington (without consulting or informing Jefferson) authorized the Secretary of the Treasury to remove the limitations imposed in Short's initial letter of appointment. He instructed Short to set about securing new, larger loans, at the same time hinting that these might be used to meet domestic needs as well as the repayment of the debt owed France. He paid Short the considerable compliment of trusting him to secure the lowest possible interest rates and charges. Short's reply to these new instructions was duly modest: "I have not sufficient reliance on my skill and judgement to be exempt from apprehensions that the interests of the United States may suffer in my hands."[34]

Both Jefferson and Hamilton sought to leverage the money raised in Amsterdam—though with different goals in mind. Jefferson had already informed Short that he was considering delaying repayment of the debt to France in order to extract concessions on American access to trade with the French West Indies. Hamilton eventually confirmed that only half of the three-million florin loan Short had negotiated would be remitted to France. The remainder would be applied to the United States' domestic debt. He also instructed Short to inform Van Staphorst that one-third of the sum allotted to France should be held back. Suspecting that the United States was delaying repayments in order to take advantage of France's financial crisis and anticipating French objections that he would have to field, Short risked offering Hamilton a mild criticism—"I find you use more delay in employing the money borrowed than I had supposed you would"—as well as grumbling to Jefferson. Short's qualms were superseded by discussions within Washington's cabinet, in which the question of whether and to what extent the United States should take advantage of the prevailing currency and bond markets was debated extensively over the summer of 1791. Hamilton maintained that "it must be proper to unite liberality toward France with an equitable regard to the interest of the United States." By contrast, Jefferson continued to oppose the exploitation of exchange rates and repayment schedules to repay France less than the true value of the debt owed her. Jefferson lost out.[35]

Largely unaware of the struggle within Cabinet, Short artlessly described to Jefferson the "infinite pleasure" he felt on receiving Hamilton's approval of his conduct. Pointedly he said that he felt "in need of approbation," since the negotiation of the loan had "so many sorts of delicacy" attending it that silence on Hamilton's part would have been "painful." Meanwhile he continued to complain about Jefferson's "mortifying" silences, especially on the subject of future diplomatic appointments.[36]

On his return to Paris from Holland in the spring of 1791, Short reported that the political situation in France "renders it impossible for me or any body else to be . . . useful for the present." Life as the United States' senior diplomat in France offered some sops to Short's self-esteem. He hosted the United States' official July Fourth dinner. He offered practical advice to Hamilton on the size and design of coinage to be struck by the newly established mint. He attended debates of the National Assembly where, he claimed, his views were sought after by delegates. Yet his confidence was fragile. On September 6, 1791, Short attended a reception at Madame de Staël's. As the dispersing guests waited for their carriages, Lady Sutherland, wife of the British minister to France, invited Gouverneur Morris, who was standing next to Short, to be a more frequent visitor to the British ambassadorial residence. She deliberately ignored Short. Following this snub, Morris recorded in his diary, Short's "countenance" was "decomposed and his voice broken." Morris thought it likely that "he will go home with ill-will wrankling in his heart against me because he is not taken notice of" since, as *chargé des affaires*, Short "expects from all and more especially the *corps diplomatique* a marked preference and respect." Sure enough, Short was out of sorts when Morris encountered him the following day.[37]

———

Gouverneur Morris first came to Paris in 1789, on a mission to protect his cousin Robert Morris's monopoly on the supply of American tobacco to France. Despite being obligated to pursue Jefferson's preferred policy of breaking the monopoly, Short ought to have got on well with Gouverneur Morris, who was also in his thirties, tolerant of the mores of French society, and an anglophobe. Morris had spoken out against slavery—a "curse of heaven"—at the Constitutional Convention. Short had recently joined the Société des Amis des Noir. Each man expressed frustration with pretentious political conversation encountered in fashionable salons. Neither believed that the idealism of the French revolutionaries they encountered was likely to be successfully accommodated within a stable republican government. Morris distrusted mobs, especially when they began to think and reason. Short agreed and, for good measure, dismissed most of France's assemblymen as demagogues. Despite these commonalities, Short's pursuit of promotion to the post of minister to France led him into competition with Morris and hastened the end of his diplomatic career.[38]

Short harbored an undeserved ill-will toward Morris almost from the moment of their first meeting. He presented his own diplomacy as being informed by diligent preparation, seeing Morris by contrast as "one of those privileged geniuses who possess by intuition all the knowledge he has occasion for." Morris was slightly older and considerably more worldly than Short. He enjoyed a rich, sexually charged relationship with a mistress, Adèle de Flahaut, whom he shared with Talleyrand, while Short's relationship with Rosalie de La Rochefoucauld was characterized at this time by sentimental letters and mutual indecision. Concluding as early as November 1790 that the French Revolution had "failed," Morris interested himself in schemes to restore or impose constitutional monarchy. Short, more fearful and fatalistic, reasoned that his status as a diplomat precluded any meaningful involvement in domestic French politics. Short's authority to negotiate loans originated with President Washington, but, from January 1790, when he was ordered to London, Morris could also claim the status of a presidential emissary. The two men became rivals for the attention and support of Washington and his cabinet.[39]

Morris's conduct as emissary to the court of St. James's attracted the displeasure of Washington, earned the approval of Jefferson, and set him on a collision course with Hamilton. Washington had charged Morris with resolving outstanding disputes with Britain while at the same time making known to the British the "disagreeable impression" produced by their failure to appoint a minister to the United States. Morris reported, accurately enough, that the British government was hostile to the United States and not inclined to make any concessions to American demands. Jefferson collaborated with Washington on an official letter substantially accepting Morris's reading of the current situation. Forming the impression that Morris was an ally in his battle against Hamilton's pro-British "Anglomany" as well as a friend of France, Jefferson sent an unusually warm personal follow-up.[40]

Hamilton, in contrast, believed that the British were more interested in a commercial treaty with the United States than Morris's reports allowed and that possibilities for future cooperation had been jeopardized by Morris's personal manner. Using as evidence highly charged accounts of Morris's conduct of negotiations, Hamilton defamed him as "a man of great genius, liable however to be occasionally influenced by his fancy, which at times outruns his discretion." Washington eventually concurred with this assessment and concluded that Morris was not suited to be appointed minister to London. Meanwhile Jefferson was for the moment convinced that Morris might make a tolerable minister to France. Short set out to ensure that Morris was not appointed to a position he had come to regard as his own.[41]

Short seems to have genuinely believed that Morris's political views made him an inadmissible candidate for the post of Minister-Plenipotentiary to France. In October 1791, adopting a "more in sorrow than in anger" tone, Short forwarded to Jefferson a French attack on Morris's counter-revolutionary views, adding that Morris's "aristocratical principles," "his contempt for the French Revolution and . . . [his] dogmatizing manner and assumed superiority has exposed him generally to ill will and often to ridicule." Parisian society, Short reported, said of Morris "the most disagreeable things, many of which I know he does not deserve, but it produces the same effect." Short could cite the authority of influential French friends, such as Lafayette, for the veracity of these reports, but, by the time Jefferson and through him Washington received Short's letters, Morris had been confirmed as minister to France.[42]

The decision to nominate Gouverneur Morris for the position of minister plenipotentiary to France, Thomas Pinckney to the equivalent position in Great Britain, and William Short as resident minister to Holland was made by the President. Jefferson did not overtly challenge Washington's choice or the US Senate's right of approval. In private, he held strong views on who should serve in such politically sensitive posts, and he was prepared to act on them. In the fall of 1791, he acted ruthlessly to dissuade Washington from nominating William Stephens Smith for the post of minister to Great Britain, believing Smith too Federalist, too pro-British, and insufficiently sympathetic to the needs and aspirations of the French. Smith and his wife Nabby Adams never forgave Jefferson for this betrayal of former friendship and made their anger known within their circle of remaining friends, including Short. Jefferson also sought to temper Washington's favorable impression of Morris. In his correspondence with Short, Jefferson treated the choice of minister to France dispassionately while acting against his interest in the corridors of power.[43]

In January 1792, as Senate hearings on Washington's ministerial nominations opened, Jefferson wrote Short to inform him that there was opposition to Morris's appointment (with the implication that Short might yet be switched into the French post), that Short should distrust rumor, and that he would write with reliable information by the first available means. He did not state his own preference in the matter. James Monroe led Senate opposition to Morris, on the grounds that his manners were not conciliatory and that, as a "monarchy man," he was not fit to be employed in any capacity by the United States of America and particularly not as its minister to France. Monroe preferred Short for the posting, and, as the crucial vote approached, he asked Jefferson to help him accomplish a procedural maneuver that would block Morris's nomination and likely secure Short's. Jefferson simply passed Monroe's request to James Madison, with the comment that Madison should intervene if he wished. He himself did nothing.[44]

After several days of debate in the Senate, Morris's nomination to serve in Paris was approved by a vote of 16–11 and Short's to serve at the Hague by 15–11. Almost immediately, the Senate approved without a roll call Washington's request that Short should be temporarily reassigned from his duties in Holland to join America's *chargé des affaires* in Madrid, William Carmichael, in a commission authorized to negotiate with Spain on matters relating to the southern boundaries of the United States and the opening of the Mississippi to American vessels. On January 28, 1792, Jefferson wrote a private letter to Short glossing these recent decisions.

    Jefferson admitted that Morris was an unpopular choice but claimed he
had been approved out of deference to the President. He left unstated the fact
that Short had never been considered and did not address Short's concern
that a failure to promote him to the rank of minister would signal a lack of
confidence in his abilities. Jefferson explained away the eleven votes opposing
Short's nomination to the Hague in terms of hostility to the creation of the
post itself. He expected "the Hague mission" to be "discontinued" soon and
had therefore told Washington that he would advise Short to return home.
Thereupon Washington, so Jefferson reported, informed him that William
Carmichael planned to retire and that he intended to appoint Short as minister to Spain in his place. Hence it had been Washington's idea, Jefferson
intimated, that Short should join Carmichael in negotiations with the Spanish
as preparation for his eventual promotion to resident minister in Madrid. All
in all, Jefferson concluded cheerily, "what has occurred here will convince you
I have been right" in not "raising your expectations" of appointment to the
post of minister to France. In the same letter, Jefferson announced his own
intention to leave government in March 1793, telling Short that he was the
first of his correspondents to learn this "sacred" secret. Since Jefferson knew
Short was in communication with Hamilton and yet trusted Short to keep his
secret, he displayed great faith in Short's discretion. Yet the disclosure hinted
at a discharge of duty. Jefferson had done what he could to further Short's
career and could do no more. Jefferson had moved on, and so should Short.[45]
    This was a moment of truth in the relationship between Thomas Jefferson
and William Short. Short was not prepared to accept that Jefferson had been
right all along and rehearsed his grievances at length. He suspected that his
supposed patron had steered him into dead-end jobs in Holland while sugar-
coating these acts of manipulation with the promise of future preferment in
Spain that was itself a by-product of another man's retirement plans. His new
posting would require cooperation with David Humphreys, *chargé des affaires*
in Lisbon, who, to Short's chagrin, continued to benefit from Washington's
patronage. Meanwhile Short was left to reflect on a fundamental question.
If Jefferson was prepared to exert influence to destroy the claims of a former
favorite, William Stephens Smith, why was he not prepared to act behind
the scenes to advance Short's? Jefferson's disinclination to act on his behalf
seemed to indicate a lack of confidence, especially given his willingness to
tolerate the appointment of his rival Morris as minister to France, a man who
in Short's view was not only skeptical about the likely outcome of the French
Revolution but also had little sympathy for its aims.[46]

As Short had warned, Morris's appointment was not well-received in Paris. Thomas Paine immediately criticized the choice in a letter to Jefferson. Lafayette wrote to Washington in March 1792, once more denigrating Morris's "aristocratic, indeed counter-revolutionary principles" and contrasting these with the sentiments expressed by "Mr. Short" who had acquired "esteem" in France. As late as December 1792, Madame d'Enville asked Jefferson whether "Morise" and "Mr. Schort" might yet swap posts. Travel by the canals of Amsterdam would be gentler on Morris's wooden leg than walking the paved streets of Paris she suggested.[47]

"Disordered" in both "body and mind," Short lashed out at Jefferson. "The manner in which I am affected," he raged, trumped even the "amazement" that Morris's appointment had caused "friends of the revolution of all classes in France." Parisian society supposed a "want of confidence" in Short and attributed to him "a kind of dishonour." Adding insult to injury Short had heard the news long before Jefferson's letters arrived. Gouverneur Morris himself informed Short that he had been appointed minister. Morris commiserated with Short. In contrast, Jefferson's "silence and reserve" conveyed to Short "a kind of indifference." Since Short valued Jefferson's friendship "above any place the government can give," he had hoped for far greater consideration from a man "I have so long [been] accustomed to look on as a father." He rehearsed his grievances far and wide, and to Alexander Hamilton, among others.[48]

When Jefferson eventually replied to Short's accusation of indifference his response was utterly uncompromising. "You complain of silence and reserve on my part," Jefferson wrote. Had Short done as Jefferson asked and come home like a good boy, "there should have been no silence and reserve," indeed there would have been a full "unbosoming." As it was Jefferson had dropped "pregnant" hints that Short had failed to pick up. Over time Jefferson betrayed something of a guilty conscience. He referred Short to their shared letters as proof that he had done all he could to get Short appointed minister to France. But Jefferson had not exerted himself on Short's behalf, and Short knew he hadn't. The question of trust was reversed. Could Short rely on Jefferson?[49]

———

Rather than accept defeat, Short continued his feud with Morris. Writing once again in tones of painful duty, Short reported to Jefferson that the French National Assembly's committee of foreign affairs was reluctant to accept Morris's credentials. Morris himself heard a rumor to the same effect, and

Pierre Lebrun, Minister for Foreign Affairs, eventually instructed the French minister to the United States to state revolutionary France's displeasure with Morris. Short informed Jefferson in July 1792 that an assemblyman had asked him whether, in the event that Morris's credentials were not accepted, he would act as an interim minister until a suitable replacement could be found. Short hastened to assure Jefferson that "I without any hesitation told him I would not—that my orders were to go to the Hague, and that I should obey them." However Short delayed his departure from Paris, even though he found the revolution unfolding before his eyes too "terrible" to behold. He was genuinely uncertain whether he should go straight to Spain or first to Holland, but, above all, he wanted to involve Morris, who was himself slow to journey from London to take up his new post, in a series of decisions that Short was sure he would mismanage, thus reopening the question of Morris's suitability.[50]

Short was concerned that money paid to France from loans taken out by the United States in Holland would not be properly credited or employed. He was also expecting a request from the French government for the United States to furnish money to relieve the planters of St. Domingue, offsetting sums advanced against debt unpaid. Both Jefferson and Short wished to ensure that any money remitted to the French government for this purpose would be spent purchasing provisions in the United States. Their preference was to credit the French minister in the United States with dollars rather than remit florins from the United States' Dutch accounts to the French treasury. By act of Congress any future loans made for the purpose of repaying foreign debt or any advance of money to France for the purpose of enabling it to provide aid to St. Domingue had to be offset against the United States' outstanding debt to France on terms advantageous to the United States. Interpreting this decision Jefferson instructed Morris that "we wish to avoid any loss by the mode of payment [to France], but do not choose to make a gain that would throw the loss on them." Whether continuing debt payments to France, calculating arrears and interest, or advancing to the French minister in the United States a sum in dollars to be set against the American debt, account had to be taken of the depreciation in the value of French *assignats* and livres against the Dutch florin and American dollar. The precise terms of exchange rate adjustments were to be negotiated with the French government. Citing an earlier exchange of letters, Short argued that responsibility for all matters relating to payments to France had devolved to Morris on his appointment as minister. Short set off for Holland in the spring of 1792, happily leaving a series of problems in Morris's hands and calculating that his rival would either confirm his reputation as a counter-revolutionary or betray his principles by conciliating the French government.[51]

In August, Short was unpleasantly surprised to learn from Hamilton that the Treasury Secretary continued to believe "every matter" which may concern "the reimbursement to France remains with you." Abandoning his earlier claims of a particular competence in this field Short, fearing future blame, sought to duck further responsibility. He complained to Hamilton that he was reluctant to make any future decisions on debt repayment since this was "a pecuniary operation of so much importance that it involves a kind of responsibility the most painful and disagreeable of all others... when confined to an individual." His discomfort increased when Morris, against the odds, successfully agreed with the French a valuation of debt repayments that took account of asset depreciation. The exchange rate Morris negotiated did not, in Short's opinion, represent value for money and he disapproved of Morris's decision to acquiesce to French demands that future payments be made in florins through the United States' accounts in Amsterdam. On receipt of an order from Morris, in September 1792, Short instructed Van Staphorst to direct debt repayments to the French through their own Dutch bankers. But he insisted on post-dating the first payment under the new system and demanded a receipt stating that any money transferred was "on account of the debt due to France" and was to be held "at the disposition of his most Christian Majesty." This was the most consequential decision of Short's diplomatic career.[52]

Short's decision to reference the King was deliberate. It knowingly conveyed non-recognition of the current French government which, so Short told Jefferson, had been "in the agony of death" from "the moment of its creation." Short subsequently defended his language in more measured tones, but he had unmistakably signaled a view of France's revolution at odds with Jefferson's. He was also aware of the difficulties his choice of words posed his rival. Morris objected, to both Short and Jefferson, that the caveat was gratuitously offensive to a legitimate ministry formed after the arrest and imprisonment of Louis XVI. Pierre Lebrun lodged a formal complaint against Short's actions with Morris, who declined to exploit it, telling Hamilton that, even if blame of Short were due, he would "not be instrumental in calling it forth." Morris dismissed Short as a man of little ability but made known to Hamilton his greater displeasure with Jefferson. Hamilton took his cue from Morris, filing away Lebrun's complaint for future use. Jefferson, by contrast, made sure that Washington was provided with extracts of letters from Lebrun equally critical of Short and Morris. Meanwhile Short and Morris bombarded Jefferson and Hamilton with letters justifying their actions. As France descended into the violence of the Terror, Jefferson ordered Morris to suspend debt repayments but stand ready to recognize any future French government formed "by the will of the nation substantially declared." On the basis of newspaper reports, Jefferson believed that such a government would shortly be formed. By contrast Hamilton, instructing Short to suspend debt repayment, added that "of course," given the nature of France's crisis, the "validity" of "future reimbursements" would be "questionable."[53]

Hamilton had, from the creation of the federal government, taken an expansive view of his right to influence foreign policy. He also believed that Jefferson harbored an ambition to shape America's domestic financial policy, or at least limit Hamilton's influence over it. The foreign loans negotiated by Short opened a new terrain of competition between his two masters. Hamilton had not immediately applied all monies raised in Holland to the repayment of the US foreign debt. Citing the economic wisdom of using money borrowed abroad at 5% to retire domestic bonds paying 6% and therefore invoking the national interest, Hamilton diverted some money raised for foreign debt repayment to the retirement of the newly consolidated American national debt. With Jefferson's tacit encouragement, Democratic-Republicans questioned the legality of Hamilton's actions and suggested that he had diverted funds with the true purpose of supporting the Bank of the United States. In response, Hamilton, writing as "Catullus," accused Jefferson of hypocrisy in the Federalist *Gazette of the United States*, alleging that Jefferson had earlier interested himself in schemes to pay off the American debt to France that would have benefited Dutch investors at the expense of the French government. Democratic-Republican congressmen, led in the House of Representatives by William Branch Giles, passed a series of resolutions demanding that Hamilton explain the use that had been made of foreign loans. The matter was debated in Congress and the press in January and February 1793, in a partisan atmosphere charged by the latest reports of revolutionary violence from France.[54]

Hamilton's defense of his conduct, which is generally judged to have demonstrated his brilliant best, inevitably drew Short's diplomacy into the limelight. Short's letters, both those to him conveying instructions and those in which Short explained his actions to Hamilton, Jefferson, and Morris, were central to hearings in which nuance and interpretation fueled rhetoric. Having always sought recognition and support, Short suddenly received conflicting responses to the self-portrait of a reliable, meritorious, and long-suffering public servant he had attempted to present in his correspondence.[55]

Hamilton attempted to act transparently with Short and showed regard for his feelings. During the hearings he commended Short's understanding of the Dutch money market, paying him the compliment of working his analysis into his speeches before Congress. He referred to Short's "hesitations" as entirely understandable. Since the hearings were, Hamilton wrote, "intended to prejudice me," Short should be free from anxiety. On two occasions Hamilton sent Short extracts from the congressional record so that he might judge events for himself. When Hamilton's letters caught up with him in Madrid, Short immediately asked him to "expose fully the whole of my conduct as contained in tedious and prolix correspondence with you, if any part of it should be considered questionable by anybody." While keen to establish Morris's responsibility for any questionable dealings, he showed no apparent fear of being scapegoated by Hamilton for his own actions.[56]

In contrast, during congressional hearings on the Giles resolutions, Jefferson offered Short qualified, patronizing support. He declined to follow Hamilton in offering Short the reassurance that his conduct was fully congruent with instructions received. When James Monroe wrote to Jefferson asking whether Short had in fact exceeded his authority, Jefferson replied that he was a "stranger" to the instructions given to "Mr. Short" by Hamilton and had asked Short to apprise him of them. Irritated by Hamilton's use of Short's letters, in March 1793, Jefferson told Short to be "cautious" in his correspondence with Hamilton. Hamilton was bent on sacrificing Short, Jefferson warned, offering as evidence the fact that the Treasury Secretary had laid before Congress a letter in which Morris represented Short's hostility to the French Revolution as more extreme than his own. In consequence, wrote Jefferson, without evidence but externalizing his own feelings, Short had acquired the reputation of an aristocracy-loving friend of Hamilton's. "I have done what I could to lessen the injury this did to you," Jefferson said, as if overlooking the missteps of a naughty child.[57]

Blinded by his feud with Morris and keen to signal that, however critical his own view of the French Revolution might be, his rival's hostility to it was worse, Short eventually thanked Jefferson at length for warning him against Hamilton. Sidelined in Spain, Short came to the almost paranoid conclusion that Morris was Washington's favorite and had therefore unfairly received advancement and protection from Hamilton. Hamilton and Washington, so Short chose to believe, had engineered the lengthy delay in naming a minister to France in order to gain time to maneuver Morris into place. Accepting

Jefferson's prompts, and ignoring his previous disinclination to advance his claims, Short concluded that Hamilton, not Jefferson, bore ultimate responsibility for his current "mistimed, misarranged and unfortunate" mission. Short had already likened influence-mongering within Washington's cabinet to that of the "court of the Medicis." One reason why the relationship between Jefferson and Short survived Jefferson's manipulation of Short's career is that Short wanted to believe, despite boasting of his detached, professional, independence, that Jefferson was a fatherly friend and patron at that court.[58]

———

Most public service careers contain frustration and end in disappointment. A coda to William Short's career proves the point. In 1792, Jefferson brought about Short's transfer to Spain. Jefferson presented Short's reassignment as offering a personal service as well as an opportunity. The US representative in Spain, William Carmichael, had been in the post and in increasing ill health since 1783. Citing, with justification, the insecurity of mail sent from Spain, Carmichael wrote far too infrequently for Jefferson's liking. Jefferson had already made known to Short his displeasure with Carmichael's inability to advance the United States' claims in matters relating to the southern borderlands and Mississippi trade. He asked Short to "study and communicate to me confidentially the true character of Carmichael." William Stephens Smith had warned Short that the stifling formality of the Spanish court obstructed even simple diplomatic exchanges, while its peripatetic schedule led to uncomfortable living conditions. Still Short pitied Carmichael for "lingering on" in Spain. Demonstrating his superiority to Carmichael held out the prospect of discomforting Gouverneur Morris, a friend of Carmichael's, and reengaging Jefferson's trust in his own abilities. In the event, the four years Short spent in Spain offered a disastrous illustration of the insecurity of a diplomatic career in the face of chance and contingency.[59]

Short arrived in Madrid on the very day, April 2, 1793, that Spain declared war on revolutionary France. Allied with Great Britain against France, Spain could count on British assistance when resisting any diplomatic or military pressure exerted by the United States in support of its territorial claims in the American southeast. The Spanish government had little incentive to negotiate in good faith with Short. In addition, the credentials Short presented to the Spanish court described him as a minister, not a minister plenipotentiary, which placed him in the third rank of the diplomatic corps. Short and Carmichael dealt primarily with Don Diego de Gardoqui, a former Spanish minister to the United States, and not with Godoy, the current Spanish for-eign minister. They could only meet with Gardoqui on Saturdays and even then higher-ranked diplomats took precedence. Short appealed to Jefferson's memories of his frustration with the court etiquette of Versailles in an unsuc-cessful bid to have the United States upgrade his official status. Meanwhile Short lodged in "dirty" Spanish taverns and with Carmichael and his Spanish wife, whose lifestyle he found dissolute. As Carmichael's health deteriorated, Short's workload increased.[60]

Against this unpromising backdrop Short applied himself to the task of dissolving the Anglo-Spanish alliance by encouraging Spain to make peace with France. Short's approach was imaginative and framed by his desire to pull off a great coup. Reporting that the Spanish King desired an alliance with the United States, he calculated that influential Spanish politicians shared his assessment that neither the war with France nor the alliance with Britain served Spain's best interests. He proposed inserting himself as an honest broker in talks between Spain and France aimed at ending the war between the two countries and thereby the main justification for Spain's alliance with Britain. He would travel to Paris incognito, under the guise of returning to his permanent post in Holland, carrying proposals from the Spanish for a peace treaty with France. The precondition he suggested, that Spain resolve its border dispute with the United States and grant navigation rights to the Mississippi, would, he believed, compensate Spain for the loss of an alliance with Britain with the greater strategic prize of American good will in re-maining matters relating to Spain's empire. If successful, Short would be the man of the moment.[61]

As Short's planning came together, Carmichael's application to resign his post on the grounds of ill health and return to the United States was approved. Short was appointed resident Minister to Spain, ending his op-portunity to travel to France incognito. Short was unaware that Spanish foreign minister Godoy, through Spain's agents in Philadelphia, had briefed Washington and Secretary of State Edmund Randolph that Short was an un-prepossessing character of insufficient rank to negotiate with royal ministers. In response, Washington appointed Thomas Pinckney as a presidential envoy to Spain with sole responsibility for negotiating a settlement of outstanding territorial and trade issues between the two countries. Short and Carmichael's authority to negotiate was terminated. Short was therefore denied by a pro-motion the chance to covertly insinuate himself into Franco-Spanish peace talks and debarred by an effective demotion from continuing his direct nego-tiation with Spanish ministers.[62]

Unlike Short, Pinckney inherited a situation propitious for constructive diplomacy with Spain. In 1794, US Chief Justice John Jay had negotiated a treaty with Britain which, by auguring closer relations between former enemies and weakening British commitment to support Spanish claims, pushed Spain to offer concessions to the United States. Pinckney arrived in Madrid in June 1795 and would have visibly supplanted Short had Short not already tendered his resignation from foreign service. The Treaty of San Lorenzo resolving territorial disputes between Spain and the United States, which is commonly identified by Pinckney's name and not Short's, was signed in October 1795.

Short bore Pinckney no ill will. The pair left Spain as soon as the treaty was signed, sharing a carriage and travel expenses as far as Paris. But Short felt slighted and humiliated. On the eve of his departure he wrote to Jefferson cataloguing his disappointments. The actions of Washington and Randolph in appointing a presidential envoy over his head would "embitter and perplex me [for] the rest of my life." Retirement would not heal the wounds inflicted on him during his career "but will save me from receiving others." Jefferson received this lament in February 1796, but did not respond to it or to three further letters from Short until March 1797. At that point, Jefferson was preparing to assume the vice-presidency and, claiming that he had been in "daily" expectation of Short's return from Europe, had therefore "suspended" correspondence. The message to Short was, once more, come home.[63]

Although Short took a generous view of his abilities and qualifications for a diplomatic career, his claims had substance and should be set in context. He may have lacked an ability to tolerate perceived slights and, in consequence, made enemies, but James Madison memorably remarked of Gouverneur Morris that he produced an unfavorable impression "before known and where known." Short could be vain, but Washington's favorite, Colonel David Humphreys enjoyed wearing the uniform of the Cincinatti and writing overwrought poetry. If Short wrote too much for Jefferson's liking, William Carmichael did not write enough. Jefferson ducked out of the nitty-gritty of financial negotiation; Short did not. James Monroe, Gouverneur Morris's successor as minister to France, spoke no French, nor did Robert "Chancellor" Livingston, minister to France during the formulation and failure of Napoleon's western design and the subsequent sale of Louisiana. Short lived in Europe for seventeen years. George Washington and James Madison never left the United States, while Alexander Hamilton never visited France. In sum, William Short was as qualified as any other diplomat available to have been entrusted with the affairs of the United States in Europe—Jefferson, Adams, and Franklin excepted. But that trio were titans who would have graced any country's diplomatic establishment. Short's understandable demand was that the United States should, like other countries, value and respect the utility of second-rank men such as himself.[64]

Short did not owe his career to Jefferson, but it was Jefferson, not Morris, Pinckney, Hamilton, or Washington, who effectively broke it by not supporting Short's claims to advancement and by maneuvering Short away from France. Personal and political misgivings informed Jefferson's suspicion that Short lacked loyalty to his definition of republicanism. Short had embraced French culture and, so Jefferson believed, enjoyed his friendships with grand families such as the La Rochefoucaulds to an unhealthy degree. He professed loyalty to Jefferson but had presented evidence of a desire to act independently, disastrously so, in Jefferson's eyes, by withholding debt repayments from France's first republican government. Short believed himself to be apolitical, a man above or apart from America's partisan fray. By contrast, Jefferson was utterly committed to what he viewed as a struggle to define America's democracy and interpreted events in Europe, and especially France, through a rigid political prism. Determined to establish personal control of US policy toward revolutionary France, Jefferson needed an ally abroad. Both Short's personal ambition and his diplomacy offered Jefferson a series of problems. For the most part Jefferson avoided direct criticism of Short or overt action against him. However, in one searing letter justifying revolutionary change by violence if necessary, Jefferson laid bare his underlying anger and frustration with his adoptive son's complacent politics and indicated the growing gulf between them.

FOUR

The Earth Half Desolated

RECKONING WITH TERROR

WILLIAM SHORT KNEW and was trusted by one of the first victims of the French Revolution's Terror, the Count Armand Marc de Montmorin, French Minister of Foreign Affairs. While in France Jefferson had worked closely with Montmorin, whom he admired. Both Short and Jefferson had enjoyed the hospitality of the Duke de La Rochefoucauld, who was brutally murdered days after the assassination of Montmorin. Jefferson knew that Short was especially close to the La Rochefoucauld family. Jefferson insisted to Short that he had been deeply wounded by the slaughter of these and other innocent mutual acquaintances. Yet Jefferson offered Short a defense of the aims of the French Revolution and a series of justifications for revolutionary violence in general—and France's Terror in particular—so combative and robust as to appear at best callous and at worst cruel. The scale of the violence had made a mockery of Jefferson's predictions that transition from the corruption of monarchical government to a healthy and stable republic could be achieved in France at minimal cost. Now it hardened Jefferson's conviction that, with the liberty of the whole Earth dependent on the outcome of France's revolutionary struggle, ends justified means. William Short was almost destined to become the recipient of Jefferson's most celebrated statement of principle on this point because of their shared experience of a world the French Revolution destroyed. Knowing what Short knew, Jefferson felt compelled to let Short know what he should think—at any cost to their relationship.[1]

This chapter foregrounds Jefferson's emotional investment in the French Revolution, its excesses, its potential, and its relevance for the United States. Jefferson resolved, from afar, the moral ambiguity of violence in the service of revolution by asserting principle. Having convinced himself that his

Heir through Hope. Peter Thompson, Oxford University Press. © Peter Thompson 2023.
DOI: 10.1093/oso/9780197546833.003.0005

interpretation was just as well as correct, and in the context of what he saw as his unique role in a battle for the very soul of the American republican experiment, Jefferson came close to confining the true meaning and signifi-cance of the French Revolution to its effect on his own politics and political position within the United States. This left him with little tolerance for or interest in rival interpretations of the violence of the French Revolution or even sympathy for its victims. Short's reflections on events he knew a little closer to hand than Jefferson tended to a similar degree of self-absorption. What would the Revolution do for his career prospects, his relationship with the La Rochefoucaulds, and his wider enjoyment of the civility of French culture? Neither man really understood nor showed much sustained in-terest in understanding the France that took shape after the Terror. Yet the fact remained that Jefferson and Short had lived together in the comfortable, aristocratic world of liberal reform whose proponents and institutions the Terror destroyed. Expressions of disquiet concerning revolutionary violence and its victims when voiced by Short touched on shared experiences and re-membrance and therefore held the potential to goad Jefferson's conscience. Reportage from the likes of Gouverneur Morris only served to strengthen Jefferson's convictions.

Jefferson's claim to have been wounded by the scale of the Terror and the identities of its victims had substance. He would have been inhuman had he not felt a need to unburden himself of his feelings to at least one confidant. William Short was a likely choice, not least because, in Jefferson's eyes, he was an errant republican. Setting Short straight on the French Revolution would not only clarify Jefferson's thoughts but also constitute an act of kindness to-ward his adoptive son. But this catharsis could only be achieved by treating Short's feelings for the victims of the Terror as misplaced, if not improper. Jefferson had difficulty conceptualizing a space in which Short, or anybody else, might affirm his own opinion on events in France, and, arguably, he never made the concession. His certainty consigned doubts, Short's especially, to a position of subordination as manifestations of error.

Jefferson's determination to privilege political calculation over empathy strained relations throughout the circle of friends and colleagues he had crafted during his residence in France. He seems never to have considered how they might have received his self-absorbed reflections on French revolu-tionary violence. To contemporaries, as to many modern observers, Jefferson's emotional detachment seemed unbalanced, extreme, or a mistake in need of correction. Several correspondents suggested that the timing of Jefferson's de-parture from France was fortuitous for him and excused his lack of sympathy for their suffering. He left just a scant two weeks before bread riots in Paris in October 1789 gave rise to the march of the *poissardes* (market women and fish wives) on Versailles. Replying to Jefferson's personal letter of farewell, Rousseau's muse Sophie de Houdetot referred to that "horrid outrage" when she told Jefferson, accusingly, that he had left his friends in a storm of troubles. She drew out a lesson for Jefferson's benefit. The American Revolution, unlike the French, had nothing to destroy or injure. Americans had therefore avoided all inconveniences attendant on revolution. Jefferson was not accustomed to admonishments of this kind from a woman, but there is little evidence to suggest that his faith in the ultimate outcome of the Revolution would have been shaken had he personally witnessed the march to Versailles, or the massacres of September 1792, or the execution of the royal family. Jefferson left France convinced that its revolution heralded, as he put it, the beginning of the history of European liberty. Writing a hurried note to his friend Madame de Corny as he changed ships in England on his voyage back to Virginia, Jefferson claimed to have read English newspaper reports of violence that had occurred in Paris since his departure as he "would those of a romance." Accounts of mobs and murders, he told Thomas Paine from the dockside, were like the rags in which religion robes the true God.[2]

———

By the time he departed France, Jefferson was accustomed to separating and justifying political ends from their personal and institutional costs. In September 1786, Charles Dumas, who loyally served as the agent of the United States in Amsterdam, reported to Jefferson on the violent civil war that had broken out in Holland and ultimately left Dumas and his family fearing for their lives. Jefferson's condolences were limited and confined to a political point. If the powers of the Dutch Stadtholder could be reduced and the happiness of the people increased, he told Dumas, then the outcome would be worth the shedding of even more blood. Europe's struggles, he lectured Dumas, occasioned great sacrifice but were of immense value to posterity.[3]

Entirely convinced of the necessity and transcendent value of America's violent struggle against despotism, Jefferson sometimes viewed European events as variations on an American theme. He took a lofty approach to the convening of the Estates General in France. "This event," he told Edward Carrington, would "hardly excite any attention" in a democratic America, yet "is deemed here" the "most important event of the last century." More than comfortable with the role of iconoclastic opponent of corruption, despotism, and the old order in the United States, Jefferson adopted a permissive attitude to white-on-white political violence in locales outside Virginia (and counter-revolutionary white-on-black violence within it). Reports received in France of the short-lived rebellion against the government of Massachusetts, led by Daniel Shays, prompted Jefferson to write to Madison on the subject of "turbulence" among a free people. He averred that it was an "evil productive of good." The thought led him to pronounce, "I hold it that a little rebellion now and then is a good thing, and as necessary in the political world as storms in the physical." In the course of an otherwise light-hearted letter to Abigail Adams, he dismissed her concerns over Shays's rebellion with the same metaphor—"I like a little rebellion now and then. It is like a storm in the atmosphere." William Stephens Smith received a more pointed reflection on Shays. "What signify a few lives lost in a century or two? The tree of liberty must be refreshed from time to time with the blood of patriots and tyrants. It is its natural manure." When Jefferson applied this idealized view of revolutionary violence to events in France, the effect was darker and more disturbing.[4]

On July 25, 1789, Jefferson wrote to Maria Cosway to discourage her from traveling to Paris to see him. He had begun his affair with Sally Hemings and was in daily expectation of receiving permission to return to the United States. By way of finding an excuse sufficient to deter her, he told Cosway that the state of affairs in France made travel inadvisable, attempting a light-hearted tone since he was writing about politics to a woman. "We have been here in the midst of tumult and violence. The cutting off of heads is become so much á la mode, that one is apt to feel of a morning whether their own is on their shoulders." Jefferson was writing three days after a particularly striking example of the new fashion. On July 22, Joseph-François Foulon, who had briefly served as a French government minister, had been accused of fomenting a famine in Paris. He fled the city, was recaptured, and summarily executed by a mob. His son-in-law Bertier de Sauvigny, accused of abetting Foulon, also attempted to flee and was recaptured. After he, too, was executed, his decapitated head, its mouth stuffed with grass, straw, and ordure, was paraded through the streets of Paris on a pike, with the mutilated body dragged along behind. Gouverneur Morris witnessed the gruesome procession and the crowd's savage joy. Exclaiming "Gracious God, what a People!" he contemplated an immediate return to the United States. Jefferson's response to the "massacring" was closer in spirit to that of Assemblyman Antoine Barnave who, when asked whether the killing of Foulon and Bertier was necessary, replied "What, then, is their blood so pure?" Even writing to

Cosway, Jefferson was careful to note that Bertier and Foulon's flight and recapture had excited an understandable, and therefore justifiable, spirit of vengeance. However, he declined to describe his emotional reaction to the violence. Instead he boasted to Cosway "my fortune has been singular, to see in the course of fourteen years two such revolutions as were never before seen."[5]

In his official account of the incident for John Jay, Jefferson stressed the efforts made to protect Foulon and Bertier from mob violence. Writing to James Madison a few days later, he drew from their deaths a moral for American politics. Jefferson told Madison that he wished John Adams had been in Paris to witness the "late scenes." Vice President Adams had been floating the idea of attaching an honorific, monarchical title to the office of the presidency. Surely, Jefferson told Madison, if Adams had witnessed the killing of Foulon he would not have supported investing the American Presidency with the old world flummery of title. Such straining for political effect in a letter to a correspondent as intelligent as Madison trivialized any expression of distaste for violence Jefferson was prepared to make. He was seemingly incapable of entertaining the possibility that an observer of the killing of Foulon and Bertier might be disgusted and yet remain a democrat. In the figure of Lafayette, Jefferson knew just such a man. The crowd that executed Bertier attempted to present his mutilated corpse to Lafayette as a tribute. Lafayette turned the offer aside with distaste.[6]

Both Short and Jefferson viewed bloodshed from an emotional and physical distance. Neither man was resident in France during the most violent phases of the Revolution, the massacres of August and September 1792 and the Great Terror of 1793. But what does this absence explain? The main outlines of Jefferson's attitude to revolutionary violence were in place by 1789, and he never amended his views. What made Jefferson's detachment chilling was the pragmatic conclusion he drew from his observation of horrific butchery in France: terror works. Jefferson told Thomas Paine that the exemplary killing of Foulon and Bertier would persuade obnoxious characters to lie low. He reported neutrally to John Jay that, since the "deaths" of Foulon and Bertier, the tranquility of Paris had not been disturbed. Morality was beside the point.

Jefferson's response to the killing of the Marquis de Launay, Governor of the Bastille, on July 14, 1789, cemented his grim, abstracted reaction to violence. De Launay was executed outside the Bastille by a pastry chef named Desnot after Jefferson's friend Louis de Corny had pleaded with the crowd to spare de Launay's life. De Launay preferred to die, and Desnot was keen to kill. Refusing the offer of a sword, Desnot used his pocket knife to hack, cut, and saw until he had severed de Launay's head from his body. In official dispatches as well as personal correspondence, Jefferson described the beneficial effects of what he forensically termed "decapitations" such as that inflicted on de Launay. His commentary drew on his reaction to events such as Shays's rebellion. There had never been so great a "fermentation" as that in Paris in the summer of 1789 nor one that had produced such little injury, Jefferson told Count Jean Diodati. Assuring the Count that he had observed the mobs of Paris with his own eyes and was convinced of their legitimacy, he concluded that the innocent had nothing to fear. Certainly he felt able to sleep quite safe in his bed as he awaited his departure for America. The first chapter of the history of European liberty was being written.[7]

Dumas Malone, the great biographer of Jefferson, praised his subject's dispatches from Europe and suggested that, had Jefferson the time and inclination, he might easily have become a distinguished historian. In fact, Jefferson's rush to draw a moral from events often led him to a simplistic understanding of historic forces and violent change that foregrounded the actions of corrupt aristocracies, kings, and, especially, queens. In the summer of 1787, the Dutch republic entered into civil war. Jefferson attributed its primary cause not to tensions between commercial classes and landowners, or to a struggle between patriots and backers of foreign power, but instead to the detention of the Princess of Orange on her way to excite commotions at the Hague. This, Jefferson believed, kindled the pride of her brother, the King of Prussia, who, at his sister's request, ordered 20,000 men to march instantly to take revenge. The "pride and egotism planted in the heart of every king" was likely, Jefferson told John Jay, to spread "fire, sword and desolation over half of Europe." Young republics should learn from such incidents. They should, he sermonized to David Humphreys, "besiege the throne of heaven with eternal prayers to extirpate from creation this class of human lions, tygers and mammouts called kings."[8]

Most likely Jefferson did not really believe that the whole of Europe would be laid waste simply because the Princess of Orange had been molested. What mattered was the moral. Jefferson felt that correspondents like David Humphreys, a member of the Society of the Cincinnati, needed to be reminded of the retrograde and destructive power of monarchy. Jefferson repeated the same cartoonish claims to John Rutledge of South Carolina, a Federalist, and to John Adams, who was at least as well, if not better, informed about events in Holland than Jefferson. In his reply to Jefferson, Adams developed from events in Holland a different but equally outlandish denunciation of monarchy. Where Jefferson sought to extirpate monarchy root and branch, Adams twitted the pretensions of monarchical power politics. If the Dauphin of France demanded the hand of one of Jefferson's daughters, Adams suggested, in a conceit that might have touched a nerve in Jefferson, then all of America would rejoice and even New England would declare a day of Thanksgiving. Equally any son of George Washington would have been invited to come a courting in Europe. Adams thought the claims of monarchy more ridiculous than menacing.[9]

Jefferson's official descriptions of events in France in the climactic year of 1789 were replete with references to the influence of reactionary aristocrats and clerics, the moral flaws of chief minister Necker, and, above all, to the character of a king who sought to be a friend to his people but spent his days hunting and drinking and was under the control of a queen driven by "rage, pride and fear," who knew no "moral restraint." He had previously advised American tourists to enter the "hovels" of the laboring poor to see for themselves how they were fed and clothed, but the lives and concerns of the mass of Parisians were of little interest to Jefferson except insofar as they gave proof that city life was "pestilential" and to be avoided by those who had a choice. He referenced shortages of grain and bread in his official dispatches but dismissively decoupled the economic grievances of the poor from the revolution taking shape before his eyes. In April 1789, over one hundred Parisians were killed in clashes sparked by rumors of a reduction in daily wage rates. Jefferson noted the rumor but described the protestors in his official letter to John Jay as "an unprovoked and unpitied" mob of "the most abandoned banditti." The rioters, he told William Carmichael, did not know what they wanted except to cause mischief.[10]

William Short's description of events that unfolded after Jefferson's departure referenced a slightly broader range of contributory factors than Jefferson's official dispatches to John Jay but were peppered with disparaging references to mobs and the demagogues whom he believed animated them. Short, echoing Madame d'Houdetot, eventually concluded that "it is the misfortune of this country to have too many of those who will always desire disorder and changes because having nothing to lose they have nothing to fear." The targets of Short's moralizing were populist assemblymen. Through his association with the Royer family, Short had some personal knowledge and understanding of the French bourgeoisie, whereas Jefferson had virtually none. Short took slightly more notice than Jefferson of the literary productions captivating France's new reading public, but ascribed them little influence.

Gouverneur Morris frequently sampled opinion in the cafes and coteries of the Palais-Royale. He seldom ran across Jefferson or Short there. Short's denunciation of demagoguery took little account of its societal origins.[11]

One of the ways in which both men, along with many other foreign observers, compensated for—and in the process compounded—their lack of reliable knowledge was by conjuring national character as a standard of judgment and interpretation. In consequence, through a process of refraction, Jefferson in particular made American politics the ultimate subject of his analysis of events in France. For example, the French, Jefferson believed, were exceedingly talkative. As the pressure for political reform began to assume revolutionary velocity, he informed David Humphreys that men, women, and children spoke of nothing but politics. Since there were always more speakers than listeners in French political discussions Jefferson wondered, in March 1789, how the meeting of the Estates-General would avoid operatic tumult and confusion. He piously hoped that cool and collected leaders would guide the convocation. This piety led seamlessly, in Jefferson's mind, to a comforting comparison arising from his reflection on the recent experience of constitution-making at home. In the United States, the constitution had been changed by assembling the wise men of the nation rather than armies or mobs. The resulting document was "the wisest ever yet presented to men." The comparative disadvantage under which French constitution-makers labored was further illustrated by the influence of French women on politics. "Without the evidence of his own eyes," Jefferson told Washington, an American "would not believe" the "omnipotence" of female influence on politics. This threatened orderly decision-making—in France. "Fortunately for the happiness of the sex itself," he reassured Washington, women in America did not endeavor to extend their influence "beyond the domestic line."[12]

For better or worse the view Jefferson and Short formed of the progress of the French Revolution—its successes, its failures, and its potential—was largely shaped through encounters in Parisian drawing rooms and at country estates with scheming royal ministers and financiers, with reformist aristocrats, with intellectuals turned politicians, and, above all, through their friendships with the La Rochefoucauld family and the Marquis de Lafayette. Lafayette and Louis-Alexandre de La Rochefoucauld proposed both Jefferson and Short for membership of the Société de Quatre Vingt Neuf, a grouping of aristocratic liberals seeking orderly constitutional change. Jefferson and Short accepted their invitations and, with membership, confirmation of their status as participant observers within social circles that reinforced their reading of the aims and desired outcome of the revolution. Lafayette kept a copy of the

American Declaration of Independence engraved in gold on display in the entry hall of his Paris townhouse. Next to it was an empty frame, ready to receive the French equivalent. Louis-Alexandre de La Rochefoucauld had published a French-language translation of America's state constitutions. Such prompts encouraged Jefferson to believe while he remained in France that public opinion, molded through free debate and influenced by enlightened Frenchmen of his acquaintance, would bring forth a durable and rational constitutionalism capable of protecting rights, particularly those of property, even as it abolished feudal privileges and restrictions. Jefferson conceded that, even in the United States, it took time to persuade men to act for their own good. He and, eventually, Short recognized the limitations of Lafayette's "canine appetite for popularity and fame." Nevertheless, while Jefferson remained in France he, and Short, believed, in the face of mounting evidence to the contrary as well as carping commentary in the monarchical British press, that a well-tempered constitution could be brought into operation in France with little bloodshed. The United States, especially its representatives abroad, could help bring about such an outcome.[13]

Jefferson proposed to Lafayette a Charter of Rights for France of his own devising but then worked with him to amend the Bill of Rights that Lafayette presented to the National Assembly on July 11, 1789. The fact that the French National Assembly adopted a bill of rights (the Declaration of the Rights of Man and Citizen) more radical than that which either Jefferson or Lafayette thought appropriate might have led both men to question their ability to shape events. Undeterred, however, Jefferson worked with the leaders of factional groupings in the Assembly to broker a deal between what he called "moderate royalists" (*monarchiens* to their opponents) and those he dubbed "avowed republicans" (radicals to their enemies). A defining distinction between the two groupings concerned the power to veto acts of the legislature. Royalists held out for the ultimate right of the Crown to exercise a constitutionally delineated power to veto legislation passed by an assembly. Republicans, though willing to allow an executive role to the Crown, insisted on the primacy of the legislature. The issues involved, if taken out of context, bore a resemblance to those which had been canvassed in America's constitutional convention and ratification debates. Accordingly, in July 1789, the Archbishop of Bordeaux invited Jefferson to meet a committee of the Assembly charged with drafting a constitution. Jefferson declined, citing diplomatic neutrality. Nevertheless, as he prepared to leave France, Jefferson continued to volunteer his advice in private, and leading protagonists in the wrangling remained willing to listen to him.[14]

In response to a histrionic request from Lafayette—"I beg you for liberty's sake"—on August 26, 1789, Jefferson hosted a discreet dinner party in an attempt to broker a deal among national assemblymen that would prevent the forces of "aristocracy" from stifling the revolution. Jefferson's recollection of the evening occupies a place of pride in his *Autobiography* (written in 1821). The guests, as Jefferson described them, were patriots in search of a coalition, prepared to speak candidly and capable of agreeing to disagree. Lafayette initiated their six-hour discussion while Jefferson sat as a silent, admiring witness to chaste eloquence, coolness of argument, and logical reasoning. The result was an agreement that the legislature should be composed of a single body, chosen by the people, but that the monarch be provided with the power to refer legislation back to the assembly for further consideration through a suspensive veto. This "concordat decided the fate of the constitution" Jefferson recalled. Except that it didn't. Jefferson was forced to admit to Jay that the agreement had been picked apart in subsequent proceedings of the assembly though not, he hastened to add, through the actions of the leaders who had met at his table. The meeting furnished Jefferson with an image of the true nature of the French Revolution that he carried back to the United States and subsequently burnished. In it, there was no place for mobs or murder. Jefferson left France convinced that an orderly transformation of government in France would form but the first chapter in the history of liberty in Europe. He agreed to be stoned as a false prophet if all did not end well in France.[15]

Jefferson threw a dinner party for Lafayette and Louis-Alexander de La Rochefoucauld nine days before his departure from Paris. Later, when Jefferson announced that he was not returning to France, he favored Lafayette, La Rochefoucauld, and that gentleman's mother, Madame d'Enville, with fulsome letters thanking them for their friendship and praising their patriotism. His letter to Louis-Alexandre de La Rochefoucauld included handsome compliments addressed to La Rochefoucauld's wife, Rosalie. Short would have been aware that such pleasantries had been offered, and, equally, Jefferson was aware of Short's good standing within the La Rochefoucauld circle. Replying to Jefferson's letter of farewell, Madame d'Enville praised Short as a young man who combined the gaiety of youth with a gravitas beyond his years. She told Jefferson that the family often talked of him in Short's company, particularly because he was Jefferson's protégé, a young man formed under his eyes.[16]

Short's continuing intimacy with the La Rochefoucaulds presented a source of opinion and perspective unavailable to Jefferson after 1789. Short used this intelligence to supplement the newspaper accounts, legislative decrees, and journals he forwarded and discussed in his letters to Jefferson. His use of the higher gossip amounted to more than harmless padding. For example, in December 1790, Short received in quick succession a letter from Rosalie describing the break-up of the Société de Quatre Vingt Neuf, and one from her brother, Armand-Charles de Rohan-Chabot, describing the formation in Paris of a club supporting the monarchy, composed of heterogenous elements but generally aristocratic in leaning. Its first act had been to distribute bread to the poor at a cut price and for that reason the Jacobin club had exerted pressure on the city's municipality to suppress the monarchists. Writing to Short, Charles Rohan-Chabot denounced the authorities' actions as both arbitrary and reprehensible, those of the monarchists as principled and patriotic. In January 1791, Short wrote to Jefferson, from Amsterdam, that a new club of monarchists had been formed in Paris. Its members were men "of heterogeneous principles." The club would have sunk into oblivion had the municipality of Paris not taken it upon itself, at the behest of the Jacobin club, to forbid their meetings. Short had his own quarrel with the Jacobins of Paris, who believed him to be an accomplice of La Rochefoucauld's faction, but he kept this from Jefferson. In reporting to Jefferson unattributed trivia derived from his connections with the La Rochefoucauld circle, Short was, whether wittingly or not, embracing their politics.[17]

On the night of June 10, 1791, the royal family attempted to flee France. Recognized and captured near the eastern border at the town of Varennes, they were forcibly returned to Paris. Short reported events accurately enough to Jefferson, dutifully forwarding newspapers and pamphlets to the Secretary of State. However he was unwilling to accept that the revolution had taken a decisive turn toward republicanism. Short reported with surprise that members of the National Assembly suddenly had no doubt as to their right to declare Louis XVI king or depose him as they saw fit. He blamed incendiaries and demagogues for the apparent enthusiasm for a republican form of government expressed by the people of Paris, although he also sent Jefferson examples of republican journals, reporting in astonishment that these were avidly read. While admitting that the people out of doors influenced the deliberations of the assembly, Short hoped that their influence would be limited. His contacts continued to suggest that a functioning constitutional monarchy might yet be achieved. Meanwhile Short posed as a baffled onlooker. It was impossible, he told the Secretary of State in the pivotal month of July 1791, to judge when the crisis would end or what kind of government would be established and by whom.[18]

Despite protestations of ignorance, it became harder and harder for Short to disguise his dislike of republicans and his opposition to their republicanism in his correspondence with Jefferson. In May 1791, Short reported, accurately enough, that Condorcet had joined the Jacobins. No assemblyman of Jefferson's acquaintance approved of the defection, Short added. Here Short generalized from the reaction of La Rochefoucauld circle to Condorcet's conversion. That family viewed his embrace of republicanism as an expression of ingratitude to them as well as a betrayal of friendship and political principle. After Condorcet had declaimed at length in favor of a republic in her drawing room, Madame d'Enville ordered a bust of Condorcet she had had commissioned to be banished from the state rooms of La Roche-Guyon. Rosalie's brother Charles said he would spit on Condorcet if he ever saw him again. Short told Jefferson that it was likely that Condorcet would be appointed the Dauphin's governor in preference to the Duke de La Rochefoucauld and that Condorcet would be tasked with providing the young man with a republican upbringing. He wrote as if Jefferson would share the La Rochefoucaulds' disapproval.[19]

The demand that the Dauphin be educated in republicanism had been supported by Thomas Paine, who was a particular object of Short's disdain. Reporting to Jefferson that the first volume of *The Rights of Man* had been well received in Paris, Short expressed surprise that Paine had not been arrested for treason in England. With sublime self-assurance he told Jefferson that the *Rights of Man* was entirely in Paine's style, "that is to say incorrect—with strong expressions and bold ideas." Jefferson rarely commented on Short's observations but this drew a swift and direct response. He warned Short that *The Rights of Man* had been greeted with general applause in the United States and that attacks made on it by Publicola (John Quincy Adams) had been repelled by a host of "republican volunteers." Without mentioning his own role in creating a furor over the *Rights of Man*, Jefferson sent Short a collection of anti-Publicola, pro-republican polemics. This was a taste of the criticism and conflict between the two men to come.[20]

Although vexed by the National Assembly's failings and alarmed by the rise of republicanism, Short continued to hope that counsels of moderation would somehow prevail and France might yet to return to a fondly remembered golden age. In July 1791, Short concluded a letter to Jefferson replete with references to crises in the affairs of France with a characteristic change of subject. A loaf of maple sugar refined in Philadelphia had been received in Paris, and he had promised a piece of it to Madame d'Enville, who in turn had asked Short to ask Jefferson to send her a further sample. Meanwhile Louis-Alexandre de la Rochefoucauld had begged Short to ask Jefferson to send him a few grafts of Virginian peach trees. In the very next breath, as if as an afterthought, Short welcomed the recent departure from Paris of Thomas Paine since, as an "apostle of republicanism," he had alarmed all moderate Frenchmen. Short may have believed Jefferson still shared his perspective. In fact, their interests were diverging. On this occasion Jefferson asked to be remembered to all the La Rochefoucauld family and drew out a moral on the potential for American maple sugar to supplant West Indian cane sugar in French markets. He ignored Short's criticism of Paine.[21]

Ironically, Short's reporting helped convince Jefferson that the French people had matured to the point where they could dispense with constitutional monarchy and embrace republicanism. This was a conclusion that events in the United States made attractive, even vital. The American people, so Jefferson believed, backed him in an existential struggle against American enemies he dubbed monarchists. The cause of America's republicans was legitimated by the struggle of the French people against monarchy and that of the French nation against foreign kingdoms. Jefferson, like Short, was constructing an idealized French Revolution of his own, and there was little space in Jefferson's French Revolution for obstructionists such as Duke Louis-Alexandre de La Rochefoucauld and his circle. From 1791, French documents arriving at the State Department were translated by the politically reliable Philip Freneau. In June 1792, Jefferson told James Madison, "I begin to consider" the Jacobins "as representing the true revolutionary spirit of the whole nation."[22]

Although Short pledged to stop troubling Jefferson with jeremiads on his future, over the summer of 1792, he tried to prepare the Secretary of State for what he considered to be inevitable: news of the arrest, execution, or exile of all friends of a constitutional monarchy. In late August, Short identified "Robertspierre [sic] and others of that atrocious and cruel cast" as the "prime agents of summary justice, cloaked in the guise of liberty, *egalité*, and patriotism, whose excesses would soon make humanity shudder." Such reportage was, if anything, more restrained than that which Short offered other correspondents. The storming of the Tuileries, Short assured Alexander Hamilton, delivered an "unfortunate monarch" to the fury of a "race of miscreants" and presaged "absolute anarchy." Yet Short's letters were no more alarmist than those Jefferson received from Gouverneur Morris, who, in July 1792, wondered whether the King himself, never mind the project of a moderate constitutionalism, would survive the coming storm. In August 1792, before these prophesies reached the United States, the storm hit.[23]

Rosalie de La Rochefoucauld's beloved younger brother Armand-Charles was the first of Short's aristocratic acquaintances to fall victim to emerging standards of justice. At the outset of the Revolution, Charles had espoused support for a constitutional monarchy, but he was first and foremost a loyal member of Louis XVI's bodyguard. Charles had stood at the King's side during the storming of the Tuileries. He furnished Rosalie and, through her, Short with a vivid account of what he saw as an outrage perpetrated on a courageous king. Charles despised the National Legislative Assembly, and, as the chances of establishing a constitutional monarchy evaporated after the King's flight to Varennes, Charles' passionate royalism appeared counter-revolutionary. On the night of August 10, Charles was arrested in Paris, questioned by members of the National Assembly, and imprisoned in the L'Abbaye St. Germain. The family used its remaining influence in attempts to secure Charles' release, but, on the night of September 2, he was dragged from his cell and executed.[24]

Rosalie's husband, Louis-Alexandre de la Rochefoucauld, was a natural lightning rod for emerging revolutionary justice. In 1789, he had sponsored Article 11 of the Declaration of the Rights of Man and Citizen, which held that the free communication of ideas and opinions is one of the most precious rights of man but that every citizen should be answerable for abuses of the right to speak, write, and print with freedom. This woolly proposition typified La Rochefoucauld's cast of mind. Gouverneur Morris recalled a telling incident at the dinner Jefferson gave for La Rochefoucauld and Lafayette prior to his departure for the United States. Lafayette raised the terrible threat to public order posed by a shortage of bread in Paris and called for immediate action. La Rochefoucauld responded by telling the company distractedly that someone or other had written an excellent book on the commerce of grain. Following the dissolution of the National Assembly, La Rochefoucauld assumed the presidency of the directory of the département of Paris. He was already an object of suspicion among Parisian radicals, but that suspicion turned to enmity when La Rochefoucauld signed a petition criticizing the Mayor of Paris Jerôme Pétion for first inciting the invasion of the Tuileries and subsequently taking no steps to quell the protests or punish its ringleaders. Facing calls for his arrest and impeachment, La Rochefoucauld resigned from government in July 1792. If his detractors thought him an enemy of republicanism, his allies thought him insufficiently resolute. "Entre nous, I think he has made poor exit," Short's friend Marie-Brigitte Plunkett Chastellux confided from Paris.[25]

La Rochefoucauld, accompanied by geologist Déodat Gratet de Dolomieu, slipped out of Paris in early August to lie low in the country. On August 16, Citizen Jean-Baptiste Bouffard, a one-time near neighbor of the La Rochefoucaulds, was authorized to arrest Louise-Alexandre on sight and return him to Paris to face charges of maladministration. The duke rendezvoused with his family and their traveling companions in the normally quiet town of Forges-les-Eaux, some thirty miles south of the port of Dieppe. Rosalie, her companion Madame d'Astorg, and her grandmother Madame d'Enville had been living in Forges since August 20. They had begun to form what Rosalie described as an intimate community with other wealthy, talented, and disillusioned refugees from Paris, including Charles-Michel Trudaine de La Sabliere (who, that year, had published a French-language edition of *The Federalist*) and his brother Charles-Louis Trudaine de Montigny (who, with his brother, had commissioned Jean-Louis David's celebrated painting *The Death of Socrates*). As conspicuous urbanites, they must have been a natural source for gossip within local Jacobin networks. Sensing their danger, the La Rochefoucauld party decided to leave in late August to return home to their chateau La Roche-Guyon.

Citizen Bouffard captured the traveling party in the small town of Gournay-en-Bray. There the group, but in particular Louise-Alexandre and his feisty mother, Madame d'Enville, were insulted by the locals. Bouffard took his detainees southward to a larger town, Gisors. During this journey Rosalie learned that her brother Charles had been killed. She managed to write a brief note to Short conveying the news. At Gisors the party was confronted by a body of patriotic militiamen from the Brittany regions of Sarthe and Orne who, answering the call to arms of a "nation in danger," were marching to Verdun to combat the Prussian invasion of France. Judging the party's captors overly deferential to an internal enemy, the volunteers urged immediate and summary justice. A stand-off between Bouffard, backed by the municipal authorities of Gisors, and the militiamen—"brigands" in the eyes of Madame d'Enville—was resolved when the Louis-Alexandre pledged to return to Paris to face his accusers.

However, when the party left Gisors on September 4, 1792, the militiamen followed. They forced the duke to walk on foot ahead of the carriage transporting Rosalie and Madame d'Enville. A stone thrown from a crowd "howling like 'cannibals'" knocked Louis-Alexandre to the ground. The guard protecting him melted away. He was clubbed to death and his body hacked with sabers. Louis-Alexandre's remains were carried past the carriage in full view of its occupants and hastily buried in an unmarked grave. Bouffard escorted the remainder of the party onward to La Roche-Guyon, where they were placed under house arrest.[26]

The Duke de la Rochefoucauld's cousin, Alexandre François Rochefoucauld-Liancourt thoughtfully wrote to "Monsieur Short" in Holland to confirm news of Louis-Alexandre's death and to assure him that Rosalie was unharmed. Immediately on her arrival at La Roche-Guyon, Rosalie wrote reassuring Short of her physical well-being. Soon after, Short received a letter from Madame d'Enville describing the horrible events and also a lengthy account of them from Madame d'Astorg. Short was appalled by the killings. He asked his friend John Rutledge, who had known Charles Chabot, to imagine the feelings of Madame d'Enville and Rosalie de La Rochefoucauld, who had lost a son and grandson and a husband and brother, respectively. For Short, the massacres were proof that France had descended into anarchy. He predicted—to Rutledge, but not yet to Jefferson—that the royal family would soon be sacrificed by cannibals. He prophesied that Paris would probably be set ablaze at the approach of the allied armies since "those who now govern have no kind of property to lose." Short told Rutledge—but not Jefferson—that he no longer cared about the affairs of France, only about the fate of individuals like Rosalie.[27]

The day after he wrote to Rutledge, Short composed a lengthy and self-consciously statesmanlike appreciation of recent developments in France for the Secretary of State. After discussing the disposition of the various classes within France following the suspension of the monarchy and the Prussian invasion, Short came to the September massacres. He trusted Gouverneur Morris to have supplied Jefferson with details from Paris. From his post at the Hague he reported that agonized friends of France had been obliged to turn their eyes from scenes too horrid and distressing to behold. The streets of Paris were "literally red with blood." In a clear reference to the La Rochefoucaulds, Short spoke of the massacre of men confined without trial and the murder of innocent men in the bosom of their families. Later, after announcing himself unable to dwell on the murders, Short invited Jefferson to reflect on the integrity and virtue of the victims and to contrast their desire to serve the public good with that of the "monsters" currently directing a "blind multitude." Jefferson would eventually conclude that the bloodshed had been necessary and proportionate. He did not, however, respond to this initial reference to the killing of Duke Louis-Alexandre de La Rochefoucauld.[28]

Gouverneur Morris was in Paris during the September massacres. Aware that Jefferson had been on good terms with both the Duke de La Rochefoucauld and Madame d'Enville, his letters to Jefferson drew attention to Louis-Alexandre's murder. At the same time, he informed Jefferson that the former Minister of Foreign Affairs, Comte Montmorin, who had shared a prisoner's cell in L'Abbaye with Rosalie's brother, Charles de Rohan Chabot, and whom Jefferson knew very well, was among those "slain." Jefferson did not directly respond to Morris. Given his previous relationships with them, it would not have been surprising if Jefferson had sent condolences to Montmorin's family or to Madame d'Enville's. He did not.[29]

In December 1792, when Short left the Hague to take up his new post in Spain as presidential emissary, he risked danger to travel through revolutionary France in order to visit Rosalie and her grandmother. Mindful that Jefferson might disapprove of the detour, Short insisted that the family situation was so distressed, and their friendship for him so strong, that nothing but his sense of duty could persuade him to tear himself away. During his visit Madame d'Enville gave Short a sealed letter to Jefferson which he dutifully forwarded. In it, Madame d'Enville invited Jefferson to reflect on the murder of her son. Jefferson, she said, was surely aware that the Duke de La Rochefoucauld had been an excellent citizen for whom no sacrifice for the good of France was too great. His reward, she noted saltily, was an assassination committed "under our eyes." She and Rosalie were desolate. Jefferson did not reply to her and skipped over Short's covering letter in his future correspondence.[30]

As the world they had shared together in France was torn apart Jefferson detached himself from Short. Between April 1792 and March 1793, Jefferson wrote just three personal letters to Short and only a few official communications. In none of these did Jefferson empathize with Short's concern for the safety and well-being of his friends or address the human impact of the Revolution. Jefferson was not incapable of understanding the human cost of revolutionary upheaval. Reading a newspaper report in May 1793 that three young girls recently arrived from Paris had been "butchered" by rebellious slaves in Guadeloupe and informed by Polly that the "respectable" victims might possibly have been former classmates of Patsy's, Jefferson immediately wrote to Patsy that he hoped the reports were not true. The sufferings of the La Rochefoucaulds elicited no comparable letter of sympathy to Short, but then Louis-Alexandre de La Rochefoucauld had been butchered by white Jacobins, not black. In just one letter to Short from this period did Jefferson offer a generalized view of the progress of the French Revolution, its

achievements, and its human cost. In many ways it is the most unpleasant that
Jefferson ever wrote.[31]

———

On January 3, 1793, Jefferson wrote to Short what has been presented by
distinguished Jefferson scholar Merrill Peterson as "a paean" to the French
Revolution. The theme of the letter was encapsulated in its famous question—
asked of Short but perhaps also of Jefferson's own conscience—"Was ever
such a great prize won at the cost of so little blood?" Jefferson led up to an
answer with a resumé of correspondence sent and received. This was one-
sided. Short had written far more letters to Jefferson than Jefferson had to
him over the summer of 1792. Jefferson claimed that Short's letters had for
some time given him "pain" on account of the "extreme warmth" with which
they had "censured the proceedings of the Jacobins of France." Short had indeed reported that France was torn by factions, groaning under anarchy, and
menaced by "private vengeances armed with the sword of justice and clothed
in the robes of law." Short had crossed a Rubicon of sorts by referring to the
"failure" of the unfolding revolution. Any pain such letters caused Jefferson
might have been offset by an acceptance that Short was concerned for the
welfare of his friends and was, under the circumstances, displaying either remarkable restraint or understandable exaggeration. To anyone less politically
principled than Jefferson, the degree of self-censorship he expected of Short
would have seemed unreasonable, even unattainable.[32]

   In letter 114 in their agreed system of numbering (written on October
12), Short strayed sufficiently far from a recital of reports received as to warrant Jefferson's charge that he was an "extreme" enemy of the Jacobins. Short
speculated, correctly, that as the invading armies of Austria and Prussia were
beaten back, sooner or later a member of the convention would urge that the
King be put on trial. The consequences, in his view, would be dire. The suspension of monarchy had already unbalanced the Constitution to the point
of its destruction. The next step was anarchy. Accordingly, Short wrote, the
successes of the French armies abroad represented an unquestionable "evil"
for humanity. The revolution the French sought to export was so visionary
and impracticable that it could only end in despotism for "freed" peoples,
but not before the furies whom the French worshipped under the names of
Liberté and Egalité had called forth unconscionable sacrifices of blood. This
was the straw that broke the camel's back. Short's apostacy drew forth an utterly uncompromising, emotionally austere response.[33]

Where Short saw "furies" Jefferson discerned the beginning of the history of European liberty. The Jacobins, Jefferson told Short in his letter of January 3, had correctly seen the necessity of, as he put it clinically, "expunging the authority" of a hereditary executive (the King, the Royal family, and apparatus of monarchical authority) once and for all. Opposition to the Jacobin position was unwarranted and unjustifiable, as Jefferson explained in soaring rhetoric.

> In the struggle which was necessary, many guilty persons fell without the forms of trial, and with them some innocent. These I deplore as much as any body, and shall deplore some of them to the day of my death. But I deplore them as I should have done had they fallen in battle. It was necessary to use the arm of the people, a machine not quite so blind as balls and bombs, but blind to a certain degree. A few of their cordial friends met at their hands the fate of enemies. But time and truth will rescue and embalm their memories, while their posterity will be enjoying that very liberty for which they would never have hesitated to offer up their lives. The liberty of the whole earth was depending on the issue of the contest, and was ever such a prize won with so little innocent blood? My own affections have been deeply wounded by some of the martyrs to this cause, but rather than it should have failed, I would have seen half the earth desolated. Were there but an Adam and an Eve left in every country, and left free, it would be better than as it now is.

This discussion of revolutionary violence was cast in the past tense, as if the "necessary struggle" was already over. It is often assumed that when Jefferson wrote this letter to Short he had yet to hear of September's extrajudicial slaughter. In fact, in addition to Short's general warnings, Gouverneur Morris supplied Jefferson with specific details of the murder of Louis-Alexandre de La Rochefoucauld and Charles de Montmorin in a letter which Jefferson received on January 10. Jefferson's letter to Short of January 3 contains a postscript dated the January 15. Jefferson had several days in which to consider whether, in light of news received, he should send Short a letter treating the destruction of mutual friends in such an apparently heartless fashion. He sent it anyway.[34]

Jefferson's letters to Short demonstrate the degree to which events in France had indeed engaged his "affections." To contemporaries such as John Adams, France's descent into Terror was a nearly inexplicable event warranting extreme detachment. Adams's sole comment on the murder of his friend Louis-Alexandre de La Rochefoucauld was made in early 1793, in the context of his disapproval of festivals organized in Boston to celebrate the successes of the French armies abroad. "If," he told Abigail Adams, "I had not washed my own hands of all this blood" by warning Louis XVI to change policies to stay in power, "I should feel some of it upon my soul." His advice had been ignored and what followed, while unfortunate, had nothing to do with him, or America. Jefferson, in contrast, approached events with an overriding interest in finding meanings that might define American politics. Had Jefferson confined his remarks on the French Terror to its impact on American politics his letter might have been easier for Short to receive. Unlike Adams or Jefferson, Short was far removed from, and not particularly interested in, America's partisan struggles. He was, however, heavily invested in the politics and culture of French high society, a setting that Jefferson had renounced. It was this distinction that led the father into conflict with the son, as Jefferson divested himself of what he took to be hard truths. "I have written to you in the stile to which I have been always accustomed with you, and which perhaps it is time I should lay aside," he wrote. He had no doubt of Short's republicanism but Short's reports had been too squeamish. He had been "embittered" against the Revolution by "too great a sensibility at the partial evil by which its object has been accomplished there." In particular, Short had been led by the sufferings of his friends into a temper of mind that gave rise to a painful warmth of expression. The hard truth was that Short had gone native. Jefferson undertook to reclaim him by developing faithfully in him the sentiments of his country.[35]

Jefferson claimed Short's views would be extremely "disrelished" if made known to the American public because "ninety-nine in a hundred of our citizens" agreed with Jefferson's assessment of the French Revolution. He offered as proof the feasts, fêtes, and other manifestations of "universal rejoicing" in America at the successes of the French revolutionary armies. The "death" of the King of France had attracted less condemnation from "monocrats" than might have been imagined. Thus, Jefferson neatly reversed any implication that he did not know what was really going on in France with the charge that Short did not know what was going on in America. The victory of the French army at Valmy had indeed inspired pro-French festivals in various locales within the United States. In February 1793, even Alexander Hamilton spoke of a "popular tide" in the United States favoring the direction of the French

Revolution. But Jefferson knew that many Americans, and not all of them Federalists, already viewed events in Europe from Short's perspective, which was why Short's assertion that French victories abroad were evils for humanity could not pass uncontested.[36]

The claim that President Washington agreed with Jefferson and not with Short was of a piece with Jefferson's larger purpose in writing.

> Your [letter] . . . induced [the President] to break silence and to notice the extreme acrimony of your expressions. He added that he had been informed the sentiments you expressed in your conversations were equally offensive to our allies, and that you should consider yourself as the representative of your country and that what you say might be imputed to your constituents. He desired me therefore to write to you on this subject. He added that he considered France as the sheet anchor of this country and its friendship as a first object.

By straying into a geopolitical condemnation of the Jacobin's revolution Short's dispatches threatened to push Washington's cabinet toward adopting a hostile policy toward an emerging French regime that Jefferson regarded as legitimate and admirably republican. This Jefferson would not tolerate. He viewed republicanism's epic struggle against the reactionary forces of monarchy both abroad and, crucially, at home as a zero-sum game. He was unapologetically prepared to stretch the truth to win the argument.[37]

The President and Secretary of State had met on December 27, 1792, to discuss France. At that meeting Jefferson referenced Short's letters describing the success of the French armies abroad as a disaster for humanity. On Jefferson's account, to his great delight Washington ignored Short's jeremiads and apparently urged a "stricter connection" with revolutionary France. Jefferson would later claim that Washington urged him at this moment to write a letter rebuking Short. However, there is no evidence in Jefferson's notes of the meeting or elsewhere to suggest that Washington wished Jefferson to censure Short's views and behavior. As early as 1789, Washington had predicted that the French Revolution would end in bloodshed and a "higher toned despotism than the one which existed before." Washington took lurid reports from France with a greater equanimity than Jefferson allowed. Meanwhile the criticism of Short that Jefferson attributed to Washington bears a very close resemblance to the criticism of Gouverneur Morris's conduct that Jefferson helped Washington draft at the time of Morris's appointment as minister to France. Just as Washington's criticism of Morris was offered under the guise of

friendship, so Jefferson's criticism of Short's views on the French Revolution
was presented as a friendly warning offered in the interests of the younger
man. But even as he claimed "fostering anxieties" had prompted him to write
to Short, Jefferson brought discussion around to himself.[38]

The underlying concern of his "Adam and Eve" letter to Short on the
French Revolution was Jefferson's position within the political situation of
the United States. In its conclusion, Jefferson, having expressed perfunctory
regret for the murder of mutual friends, asked Short to sympathize with his
situation.

> There are in the United States some characters ... some of them ... high
> in office, others possessing great wealth, and all of them hostile to
> France and fondly looking to England as the staff of their hope. These
> I named to you on a former occasion. . . . Excepting them, this country
> is entirely republican, friends to the constitution, anxious to preserve
> it and to have it administered according to its own republican princi-
> ples. . . . The successes of republicanism in France have given the coup
> de grace to their prospects, and I hope to their projects. . . . I have
> presented things without reserve, satisfied you will ascribe what I have
> said to its true motive, use it for your own best interest, and in that
> fulfil completely what I had in view.

While the content of Short's letters on the revolution mattered little to
Jefferson, their potential misuse by political opponents did, and for that
reason Short should treat the Terror and its human costs with the same detachment that Jefferson showed. Since Jefferson was prepared to rehearse his
sense of priority with Frenchmen and women who had actually suffered in the
great struggle, it is hardly surprising that he was prepared to tell Short to steel
himself. But where did this leave Short?[39]

In February 1793, President and Secretary of State met again to discuss French affairs. William Stephens Smith had told the President that
Gouverneur Morris no longer enjoyed the confidence of the French ministry. Later Jefferson presented Washington with letters from the French
minister to the United States detailing Parisian displeasure with Morris's
hostility toward the current regime. Jefferson also shared with Washington
with an extract from a private letter in which Short justified his behavior
toward the French government while criticizing Morris's. On Jefferson's account Washington decided there and then that Morris should be replaced as
minister to France. Various options—including that of Jefferson returning to

Paris—were discussed and dismissed. But the possibility of replacing Morris with Short was apparently never mentioned—by Washington, by William Stephens Smith, or, crucially, by Jefferson. Short was too closely attached to pre-revolutionary France. Yesterday's man, he was better off out of the way in Spain.[40]

———

Neither Short nor Jefferson amended or disavowed their views. Each quietly agreed to disagree. As he prepared to leave Holland for Spain, Short, abandoning claims to neutrality, told Jefferson that recent French victories had had the effect of prolonging a form of government that Short believed had been in the agony of its death from the moment of its creation. Civil war in France was inevitable as soon as the danger from foreign armies subsided. Under the circumstances he was glad he suspended payment of America's debt to France. Jefferson received Short's letter two days after a meeting with Washington in which he had quietly extinguished the last remaining possibility that Short might be appointed minister to France. He did not respond to the substance of Short's argument. Writing from Spain in the spring of 1793, Short restated the conclusion that had so riled Jefferson: far from elevating the continent of Europe to a new age of liberty, the French Revolution would instead plunge it into bloody chaos. Regrettably, Short told Jefferson from his new posting, it was a characteristic of the French Revolution to negatively influence France's neighbors. The execution of Louis XVI, which Short described as a horrible catastrophe, had galvanized a hatred in Spain for all things French. The Spanish government had ordered the expulsion of all Frenchmen. Short on the whole agreed with this policy. However, he warned, it would likely prompt a war between France and Spain and, therefore, make the resolution of the United States' outstanding business with the two nations harder. Jefferson forwarded Short's letter to Washington without comment and did not reply to it himself.[41]

Short received Jefferson's "Adam and Eve" letter on March 25, 1793, at a moment when he was beset by financial worries, frustrated by his secondment to Spain, and tormented by jealousy of Gouverneur Morris. He showed enough independence of character to suggest that he would be more inclined to accept Jefferson's strictures on his view of the Jacobins if Jefferson "had been in the way of seeing and examining them" with his own eyes. He assured Jefferson that "no body on earth can wish better to France than I do." Unlike Jefferson, however, Short was not concerned by the particular form of government the inhabitants of France may "give themselves," provided it secured their "happiness and prosperity." Perhaps the judgments that Jefferson objected to would prove mistaken—he would await the outcome of time and experience—but Short defended his duty to express his true sentiments on the situation of affairs in France. He continued to do so, although he used the remainder of his missive to rehearse the claim that Morris's opinions were even more extreme than his.[42]

In March 1797, Short passed on to Jefferson Madame d'Enville's desire to be remembered to him. Short assured Jefferson of her respect and attachment to him and, in addition, forwarded Rosalie de La Rochefocauld's kind regards. By chance Jefferson received this letter on the same day as another in which Marie-Brigitte Plunkett Chastellux told him that she was constantly in the company of Short, Rosalie, and Madame d'Enville, where his name was often mentioned with affection and esteem. These prompts drew a response from Jefferson, but one in which he resolutely distanced himself from the human cost of the destruction of the *ancien regime*. In reply to Short, Jefferson offered an encomium on Madame d'Enville cast very firmly in the past tense: "I considered her friendship, while in France, as one of the most precious of my acquisitions, have ever cherished the remembrance of it with tenderness, and taken a lively part in all her interests and feelings." He did not write to Madame d'Enville directly. When she died later that year, Jefferson did not reply to the letter in which Short conveyed the news.[43]

Jefferson expressed to third parties his belief that the murder of Louis-Alexandre de La Rochefoucauld had "anti-revolutionized" Short, leaving him "soured and embittered." Such acknowledgment of the suffering revolutionaries had inflicted on the Duke's family as Jefferson was prepared to make to Short were indirect and evasive. In 1798, at a moment when Short seemed on the point of a return to the United States and thus, possibly, a permanent separation from Rosalie, Jefferson asked Short to present his respectful salutations to her. For once, he acknowledged that Rosalie had been deprived of a family which, he claimed, had been most dear to him. A year earlier, Jefferson had assured Short that he was as moved by the sufferings of Madame d'Enville and her granddaughter as if they were members of his own family. Why then had he not written Rosalie even a brief note of condolence? Jefferson asked Short to believe that the difficulty of communicating his ideas "justly" in a foreign language had prevented him, but assured him that he remained entirely sensible of her merit and held her in esteem.[44]

Such spasms of conscience that Jefferson's views on revolutionary violence prompted in him were seldom expressed in correspondence and never addressed to William Short. In a brief letter written in October 1794 to John Jay's former secretary Henry Remsen, with whom he typically discussed nail-making and agricultural improvement, Jefferson offered an uncommon appraisal. He assured Remsen that he had no political ambitions other than to see the French Revolution succeed. "I cannot help hoping that the execution of Robespierre and his bloodthirsty satellites is a proof of their [the French people's] return to that moderation which their best friends had feared had not been always observed." Even this rare condemnation of Robespierre suggested that the Terror had been something of an aberration and that the further lethal force used against him and his "satellites" had been necessary. Jefferson's faith in the proposition that France's bloodshed had been justified survived the Terror and its aftermath largely intact. An exchange with Jean-Nicolas Démeunier in 1795 suggests a position that endured. Démeunier, a former President of the National Assembly, had fled France and taken exile in the United States. From the perspective of a victim, he invited Jefferson to condemn the institutionalized terror of Robespierre's regime. Jefferson's reply, sometimes cited as a clear repudiation of blood-letting in light of evidence received, was stubbornly equivocal.

"Being myself a warm zealot for the attainment and enjoyment by all mankind of as much liberty as each may exercise without injury to the equal liberty of his fellow citizens," Jefferson wrote pompously to Démeunier, "I have lamented that in France the endeavours to obtain this should have been attended with the effusion of so much blood." He had known all the leading figures of the revolution in 1789 and was convinced that their views were "upright." The principles of the leaders who followed, Démeunier presumably included, were less well known to him, although he assured Démeunier that he believed his conduct to have been entirely innocent, friendly to freedom, and undeserving of sanction. In fact, in 1786, Jefferson had, at Démeunier's invitation, involved himself in extensive correction of factual and conceptual flaws in the latter's article on the United States for the *Encyclopédie Méthodique*. The corrections indicated that Jefferson found the author's republicanism wanting. He was therefore unwilling to conclude that Démeunier, and others, had been unfairly victimized by the "arm of the people." Writing to the exile, he hoped that the Brissotins and their successors, "excepting *perhaps* the party which has lately been suppressed" (the grouping of radical Jacobins controlled by Robespierre) supported "the establishment of a free government in their country." In an accompanying disquisition on proper employment in the

United States and his own in particular—"my new trade of nail-making is to me in this country what an additional title of nobility or the ensigns of a new order are in Europe"—Jefferson came close to suggesting that tender French liberals like Démeunier were in need of a republican reeducation. In his experience, well-to-do French exiles of a philosophical turn who suddenly found themselves obliged to work for their fortunes had done best by taking up a small farm. He had recommended this pursuit to Démeunier, but, since Démeunier had chosen to settle in New York and further had announced he would not be visiting Monticello, Jefferson had little more to say.[45]

In October 1806, Jefferson returned to the consequences of the French Revolution for American politics and for William Short's career. In response to Short's request for help gaining a diplomatic appointment in Europe, President Jefferson offered the "naked state of things": Short's views on the French Revolution disqualified him from service. During Jefferson's tenure as Secretary of State the French Revolution had, so he claimed, been in the plenitude of its favor in the United States. Employing a smug past tense warranted by the suppression of Federalism that his reelection to the Presidency signaled, Jefferson reminded Short that during Washington's administration wishes for and against the success of the French Revolution had distinguished and sharply divided Republicans from Federalists, Democrats from Aristocrats. During this period of partisan division, so Jefferson claimed in 1806, disgust with the conduct of the French Revolution had manifested itself in "every letter" sent by Short from Europe. Short's critique was inappropriate and also premature because "we," wrote Jefferson, had yet to see anything in the conduct of the Revolution but what proceeded from the necessity of the situation—the Terror included.

In 1806, as in 1793, Jefferson asserted that Washington had asked Jefferson to express the President's disapproval of the tone of Short's dispatches. This time Jefferson ventured the detail that, as a favor to his adoptive son, Jefferson secured permission from Washington to do this via a personal and hence private letter. "You may remember receiving such a letter from me," Jefferson reminded Short. However, matters would have ended there had not Short also shared his thoughts on the French Revolution with Hamilton. Hamilton was largely in agreement with Short, yet, said Jefferson, he could not pass up the opportunity of ruining Short since he knew him to be an object of Jefferson's particular friendship. In 1806, Jefferson claimed that, using the pretext of a request for information on the Dutch loan, Hamilton had in 1793 made all of Short's dispatches from Europe available to the Senate. Short's letters to Hamilton were read, their "counterrevolutionary spirit" was communicated to the people of the United States, and, in consequence, Short was branded an enemy of progressive democracy. Had Short heeded Jefferson's advice and returned to the United States to cultivate congressmen, he might in time have "rectified" their opinion of him. Instead, the Senate would certainly withhold approval were Short to be nominated for a diplomatic post. This was regrettable, as much for Jefferson as for Short. On many occasions President Jefferson and his Secretary of State had been at a loss to find suitable persons to do their bidding abroad, he told Short vindictively. It was unfortunate that Short's reputation deprived them of his assistance.[46]

In 1806, Jefferson offered Short a grubby evasion of the moral issues his "Adam and Eve" letter had exposed in 1793. "I repeat what in substance I have before observed," he told Short. "In a government like ours, the power is not really and solely where it is ostensibly; and that whenever it runs counter to the public sentiment, it will be made to feel its [the public's] superior control. It is better for all parties that that conflict be not risked." This tortured construction presumed that the American public had no great problem with the morality of the French Revolution and its violence, so, therefore, no public servant should provoke a conflict with the people by presenting them with uncomfortable questions. Jefferson had often dilated, and to Short among others, on his dislike of the day-to-day realities of political life, the necessity for compromise and secrecy, the frequency with which personality and partisanship trumped principle in political debate. Yet congressmen, Jefferson now told Short, should be considered as the nation in microcosm. By not cultivating politicians in order to correct the impression that he was an un-American counter-revolutionary Short was in effect insulting the people. In this formulation, Jefferson denied his friend the space to express a principled criticism of revolutionary terror.[47]

By suggesting that it was Hamilton's reaction to and use of Short's commentary on France that was responsible for fatally damaging Short's reputation, Jefferson implied that he himself had been able to keep his disagreement with Short private. But Jefferson had not been able, in 1793, to treat Short's opinions with equanimity, and he wasn't able to do so in 1806. Short ought not to have thought as he did. Failing that, he ought not to have expressed himself as he did. An appreciation of beneficial ends should not be undermined by a discussion of unpleasant means.

His passing acknowledgment in the *Autobiography* that "atrocities" had been committed in France did not represent any substantial modification of Jefferson's views on revolutionary violence. Indeed, the *Autobiography* recycled near verbatim views and interpretations Jefferson had expressed previously in official letters and were now bolstered by claims of personal witness. For example, in 1789, Jefferson told Jay in an official dispatch that, as a result of the consolidation of the National Assembly and its demand that royal troops be withdrawn from Paris, the King "was now completely in the hands of men, the principal among whom had been noted thro' their lives for the Turkish despotism of their characters." The *Autobiography* described the King's situation in 1789 in exactly the same words. Jefferson's official letters made no claim to have personally witnessed the fall of the Bastille; his Autobiography implied that he had. In old age, Jefferson's simplistic depiction of historical process and his detestation of the French royal family, particularly Marie Antoinette, remained as pronounced as ever: her inordinate gambling and dissipations had called into action the reforming hand of the nation. Her disdain for the people had led her and the King to the guillotine. Marie Antoinette had plunged the world into crimes and calamities that would forever stain the pages of history. "I have ever believed that had there been no queen, there would have been no revolution," he averred. Passages such as this make one wonder how it was that Jefferson could be simultaneously so principled and so crude. It was William Short's misfortune to experience both facets of Jefferson's political character in his reaction to the French Revolution.[48]

The destruction of his friends and the consequences of this for him stayed with Short long after the event but he did not publicly break with Jefferson. He kept his disagreement with Jefferson's reading of the French Revolution private and in this performed a service worthy of a son's duty to a father. Had Short released Jefferson's "Adam and Eve" letter during any of the episodes of extreme partisanship in the United States inspired by the French Revolution—during the Gênet affair, the XYZ affair, or the Quasi-War with France—the damage to Jefferson's political career might have been terminal. Jefferson knew as much. "A single sentence got hold of by the Porcupines will suffice to abuse and persecute me in their papers for months," he told John Taylor at the height of the "reign of witches" in 1798. Yet if Jefferson recognized Short's discretion in not feeding the press, he did little to show his appreciation.[49]

Short asked Jefferson to imagine his feelings on being denied the post of minister to France, or being stuck in the backwater of the Hague, or suffocating under the protocol of the Spanish court. Yet he never directly asked Jefferson to imagine his reaction to the destruction of the world they had shared in France. Short had always accepted that even a relatively benign outcome to the French Revolution would likely involve bloodshed. His main concern, like Jefferson's, was that the blood that was shed did not flow from the wrong people. Even this concern could lead Short to harden his heart. When Lafayette was arrested by Austrian troops and cited his American citizenship to avoid imprisonment, Short, to the disgust of Lafayette's friends, declined to exert himself on the Marquis's behalf, arguing that to do so would make matters worse. In this specific instance, Short discussed his feelings as well as his actions with Jefferson. But Short never courted a discussion of another specific consequence of the slaughter of central importance to him, namely that Rosalie de La Rochefoucauld was free to remarry. As news of the killing of de La Rochefoucauld sank in, Short was preoccupied with his own finances and entering two years of frustrating diplomatic drudgery in Spain. Meanwhile Rosalie and Madame d'Enville languished in confinement, Madame de Corny suffered in Rouen, and Madame de Tessé had decamped to Switzerland. The world they had shared was shattered and there was nothing that Short, let alone Jefferson, could do about it.[50]

FIVE

"You Are My Husband"

ROSALIE DE LA ROCHEFOUCAULD AND WILLIAM SHORT

IN NOVEMBER 1793, Rosalie de La Rochefoucauld and her grandmother Madame d'Enville were arrested and imprisoned in the convent of the Filles-Anglaises in Paris. Following her release in late August 1794, Rosalie wrote William a vulnerable and loving letter. She was accustomed to preserving her self-esteem by claiming that the act of writing was therapeutic, that she poured out feelings of love for her own benefit not William's, and that, in any case, her letters to William might not find their way to him. Prefaced with these defenses against rejection, Rosalie declared her devotion to William. "After having lost almost all my relatives, the greater number through assassination," she wrote,

> after having lived through ten and a half months of imprisonment, after having seen my unfortunate companions in misery taken away and after having awaited the same fate a hundred times myself, my courage has been sustained only by the feeling which unites me to you, by the certainty of your devotion and by the hope that heaven would perhaps bring together two hearts made to love each other. The thought, the memory of you lent me strength, your image and the hope of seeing you consoled me, you alone have sustained me. . . . Without you, without the reassuring thought of your love for me, I should not have clung to life, which offered nothing but suffering.

While in prison she had treasured two books Short had given her, wore his ring, and cherished a lock of his hair. Though "mere trifles," they were

Heir through Hope. Peter Thompson, Oxford University Press. © Peter Thompson 2023.
DOI: 10.1093/oso/9780197546833.003.0006

"priceless" in her eyes since they brought her "closer to you my beloved, filling my heart with tender and delightful thoughts and keeping you constantly in my mind." Employing for the first time in their correspondence informal second-person forms of address, she insisted that she was not sad since she knew he loved her. On hearing, in November 1794, a rumor relayed by a friend to the effect that Short had sought leave to return to France from his posting in Spain, her heart was filled with serenity at the prospect of their reunion. These outpourings contained an invitation to action on Short's part.[1]

In July 1795, William, for the first time in their correspondence addressing Rosalie by name, announced that, with his tour of duty in Spain ending, he was about to become a "free man." His first act would be to return to France to be near his "chère Rosalie." She would hardly recognize him. The Spanish climate had aged him twenty years, turning his hair gray. He didn't doubt that they would have much to say to one another. His letters made no allusion to one potential topic of conversation, the possibility that the widowed Rosalie might marry or openly consort with William. Nor did he give any warning that Jefferson had purchased an estate for him in Virginia that summer. Rosalie likely heard news of the purchase from the facilitator of their correspondence during her detention, James Monroe, minister to France and Short's potential neighbor in Albemarle. She was discomforted. When Short reached Paris in December, he immediately sent letters to La Roche-Guyon. Rosalie replied that her grandmother would organize a party in William's honor and asked William to liaise with Madame d'Enville as if she herself would not be involved in celebrating his return. She asked William to visit her father in Paris, but she couldn't tell William where she would be spending the winter since her own plans were uncertain. In fact, early in the New Year, Rosalie and her grandmother departed for a tour of family estates in the Charente and did not return to La Roche-Guyon until June. This was one of a number of false starts in what was once billed as "the most romantic love affair in which an American has ever been engaged."[2]

———

Since the discovery in 1926 of a substantial tranche of correspondence between Rosalie de La Rochefoucauld and William Short, French as well as American writers have tended to approach the couple's relationship via the conventions of a romance novel. Since Rosalie inhabited a childless arranged marriage with a much older man who was absorbed in his political interests, commentators have taken it for granted that she needed

FIGURE 5.1 Alexandrine Charlotte Sophie (Rosalie) de Rohan-Chabot, Duchess de La Rochefoucauld d'Enville, later Countess de Castellane. Attributed to Vigeé Le Brun, undated. Pastel. National Museum, Warsaw.

at least a confidante and probably a lover of her own age. William was a well-connected young man, at ease in the company of French women. He spoke good French; she had a preliminary knowledge of English. He had prospects; she had position. Viewed through the lens of genre fiction it was nearly inevitable that an initial friendship should turn into a passionate romance. The common view is that such an affair would have carried little risk of censure.[3]

Yet Rosalie, who was twenty-seven when the affair began, had no reputation for promiscuity or history of adultery. Even if she had been looking for a soul-mate of her own age and interests Short was an unlikely suitor. His desire to be a father-figure in one set of relationships—with girls like Lilite Royer or Patsy Jefferson—and a son in another set of relationships—with Jefferson, Madame de Tessé, and possibly Madame Royer—was at least as strong, if not stronger, than his inclination to form a partnership with a woman of his own age. Short's commitment to the Royer family, which drew to close in 1787, was known to American men and French hostesses. Rosalie and her mother the Duchess d'Enville were probably among those aware that Short spent much of his spare time at St. Germain since his absences from the social scene he shared with Jefferson sometimes required explanation. It is unlikely that either woman was particularly curious about the cause of Mr. Jefferson's secretary's absences. Short had yet to make a mark, and his affair with Rosalie was not a case of love at first sight.[4]

In the aftermath of Lilite Royer's marriage and the birth of her first child, Short did not immediately turn his attention to Rosalie. He made a serious pass at Patsy Jefferson, and, around the same time, he was attracted to Princess Louise Stolberg-Gedern, self-styled Countess of Albany, but neither enthusiasm survived his Grand Tour of southern France and Italy. After his return Gouverneur Morris, in October 1789, "without jealousy," and indeed rather approvingly, noted that he had observed Short eyeing up his mistress, Madame de Flahaut. There is no evidence that, prior to his affair with Rosalie, Short had experience of a meaningful relationship with a woman of his own age. Although in the five years following her husband's murder Rosalie bared her soul to William to the point where he can have been in no doubt of her desire that he marry her, or at least cohabit with her in France, William avoided making a commitment to meet Rosalie's stated needs while clinging to the expectation that she would meet his—most dramatically by returning with him to America.[5]

Following Rosalie's release from prison in 1794 and Short's return from Spain in 1795, William found himself in a tug of love. Rosalie signaled increasingly clearly her desire that he remain, in France, with her. From a distance, Jefferson took steps to encourage Short to return to Virginia. William and Rosalie were loathe to separate but found it difficult to agree on a future path. Their affair was shaped by the intersection of three distinct revolutionary forces in the Atlantic world. The renunciations of patriarchal states set in train by the Declaration of Independence and the French Revolution was accompanied, in France, by growing condemnation of arranged marriages and an affirmation of a natural right both to a choice of marriage partners and to a divorce. Companionate conjugal unions would conjure into being a new French state grounded in a new, secular morality. Rosalie was attracted by these ideas. American men of William Short's generation experienced a different force. The late eighteenth century saw the repeal of American legislation penalizing bachelors, and cultural suspicion of unmarried men began to dissipate. William, reluctant to marry or father children, embraced bachelorhood, if only by default. With the same intention as French marriage reformers, Jefferson, among other American commentators, emphasized the political importance of conjugal unions to the maintenance of republican morality. He frequently admonished Short to settle down by marrying. Meanwhile a third force, French revolutionary violence and postrevolutionary dislocation bore directly on William and Rosalie as they attempted to construct a relationship that would meet their needs. The murder of Rosalie's husband made marriage or open cohabitation between William and Rosalie a possibility, yet the distress suffered by Madame d'Enville led Rosalie to prioritize a duty of care toward her grandmother while Jefferson's distrust of Short's attitude toward the French Revolution led him to sideline William to a post in Spain. From the beginning of their relationship both William and Rosalie experienced the sensation of being caught between all manner of competing imperatives. Some of these were of their shared making. Other dilemmas were imposed upon them by Short's regard for Thomas Jefferson and Jefferson's regard for him.[6]

The origins of the affair lay in an incident that occurred April 1790, while Short was a guest at the La Rochefoucauld's chateau La Roche-Guyon. One morning when the hosts and their guests were out walking on the banks of the Seine, Short and one of the company—Rosalie perhaps—got into a "little canoe" with a thirteen-year-old boy. Short described what happened next in a letter to his friend John Rutledge, Jr. The boy became scared of the river, which the witnesses on the bank found amusing. The adults paddled their canoe to the bank, got out, and then, in jest, one of the company pushed the craft and its scared passenger back into the stream. Short quickly took pity on the boy.

> I endeavoured to hand him a long pole so as to draw the canoe ashore—having made one or two useless efforts, and the current being

so rapid . . . I ran to a point where I saw it must pass and leaning on a
tree I stretched out the pole, when all at once the tree giving way I was
over head and ears in twelve or fifteen feet of water and carried off from
the shore in the stream.

Continuing, without any reference to the fate of the little boy, Short drove
this account to what was for him its most important point: how the adventure affected his standing with the La Rochefoucauld family. "After a short
time . . . I gained the shore by swimming. [T]he day was cold the wind high
and we were a league from the Chateau—the weight of my clothes impeded
much my march—still I arrived there a little fatigued." Short changed clothes.
Then he drank "old Madeira and other wines in quantities that astonished
everybody." He told Rutledge that he had expected to be intoxicated and everybody present was sure he would be. Yet "still I played chess after dinner with
great success, slept well and have since heard or felt nothing more of it." Short
suggested to Rutledge that he should try the same remedy if a similar accident
befell him.[7]

Consciously or not, Short had managed to establish a persona beyond
that of a well-connected, polite, young man with good French and grace on
the dance floor. He was hardy yet sensitive. He praised the countryside and
helped out with the hay harvest, but he was at ease in Paris where he was
spoken of as the next American minister to France. He was desirous of staying
France but contemplated a return to America. He was a canoeist afraid of the
sea, a man with one foot in the boat and one foot on the bank. By that same
token he was well-suited to life at La Roche Guyon among the extended La
Rochefoucauld circle of aristocratic progressives on the eve of a revolution.
He had piqued their interest.

Initially the family member most taken with Short was Rosalie's grandmother. Duchess Élisabeth d'Enville had a history of encouraging younger
men from modest backgrounds, while Short's talent for charming older
hostesses had already been demonstrated in the case of Madame de Tessé.
Within a few weeks of his adventure on the Seine, Short was on sufficiently
good terms with Madame d'Enville to ask Jefferson to supply her with a variety of seeds from which she might propagate American plants in her garden.
Before long the duchess herself was moved to write Jefferson an encomium
on Short's character. He was a man who combined the gaiety of youth with
the sound judgment of a much greater age. Short's appointment as Jefferson's
successor to the post of minister to France would provide her and her family
with consolation for the loss they felt from Jefferson's departure. A young

man trained by Jefferson could only be "infinitely interesting." Short would
have been aware that, as the matriarch of the La Rochefoucauld family, the
Duchess d'Enville was also its gatekeeper. She could certainly have prevailed
on Rosalie or her husband to ostracize Short had she wished. She never
changed her favorable opinion of Short.[8]

In his relationship with the Royer family, Short had wooed the mother,
plying her with gifts, while simultaneously courting the daughter. Buttering
up Madame d'Enville was an unlikely route to making a conquest of her
granddaughter. But William did not seek to seduce Rosalie. His previous affair with Lilite Royer had apparently never been sexually consummated. It
had satisfied instead Short's immense cravings for belonging, for being part of
a family. A similar dynamic began to emerge in his relationship with the La
Rochefoucaulds. In October 1790, after a long hiatus in his correspondence
with Jefferson, Short heard he was to be seconded to Holland. Rosalie wished
to see him before he left. On the eve of his departure Short skipped an invitation to hear Condorcet deliver a eulogy on the recently deceased Benjamin
Franklin in order to dine with the La Rochefoucaulds at their Parisian townhouse. He had entered their circle and before long Madame d'Enville was
chiding Short for ending a letter to her in formal tones more suited to a
Roman than an American. She would not employ the same formality, she
said; the feelings that Short had inspired in her would last as long as she lived.
Far from finding such correspondence objectionable, Rosalie commended
it and vouched for the depth of her grandmother's affection for Short. "She
loves you this good mother," Rosalie told William.[9]

———

Short was busy but miserable in Amsterdam. Rosalie responded sym-
pathetically to Short's evidently self-pitying assessment of his situation.
Commiserating with him on the dreadful climate of a Dutch winter, she
urged him to conclude his business promptly and return to people who
offered him "true friendship," that is, the La Rochefoucauld circle. Her letters were not yet written in the register of romantic passion. She addressed
William using the formal "vous" form (and continued to do so even after
her letters grew more expressive). William followed her usage of personal
pronouns. However, complimenting William on his written French, Rosalie
singled out his facility with unfamiliar expressions. This encouraged him
to write more ambitious letters that positioned himself within a world of
sentiment.[10]

Hearing that the French assembly had commissioned and erected a statue of Rousseau, William offered Rosalie an encomium on Rousseau's principles. Agreeing that the purity of Rousseau's vision was honored mainly in the breach, the correspondents began to conjure definitions of "true" friendship. They each strove to signal their capacity for feeling. In February 1791, Rosalie attended a performance of the ballet-pantomime *Psyché*. The sympathies of the piece lay with the lovers Pysche and Cupid who conducted their affair in defiance of Venus, the goddess of love. Rosalie found the piece "enchanting" but could not decide whether she preferred it to Pierre Gardel's *Télémaque dans l'Ile Calypso*, a play based on François Fénelon's didactic novel *The Adventures of Telemachus*. This provided another point of connection between the pair. Short knew the store that Rousseau set by Fénélon's denunciation of luxury and selfish excess. (In Rousseau's *Émile*, which Short was reading in 1791, Emile is presented with a copy of the *Adventures* by his lover Sophie as a reminder of the values of a virtuous life.) The novel was much admired by Jefferson, who reread it, in Spanish as well as in French, while in Paris. Accordingly, William replied to Rosalie that, while he longed to see *Psyché*, he could not imagine that anything, apart from "Rousseau's tales," could be as penetrating and touching as the story of Telemachus. When Short returned to Paris at the end of March 1791, the couple continued such aspirational conversations and William began courting Rosalie in earnest.[11]

Almost immediately he revealed how little he understood Rosalie's background and situation. Having apparently learned nothing from his previous proposal to Patsy Jefferson, William now pledged to Rosalie that he would remain in France, come what may, in order to draw her into an adulterous relationship in which he would be her protector. "What shall I answer to all the amiable and flattering things you said?" Rosalie asked in reply.

> A thousand reasons come to me to prevent my heart from responding to yours and you must not blame me for trying to stifle feelings that would be dangerous for both us. Consult your reason, which was intended to have some influence over us; how much would you risk in making yourself unhappy, if your attachment is truly deep, in giving yourself up to it so whole-heartedly[?] Think what must be your future and how little the natural order of things would permit you to form an attachment in this country without wholly risking your happiness. I am myself too vitally concerned over your happiness to ignore the means of assuring it . . . think of me a little and see what we would be exposing each other to if I were to permit myself to be swept

away by my feelings. . . . You know my way of thinking, you know how far removed from constraint and deception my life has been, thus you must believe that I should never find peace were I to turn aside from the duties that are marked out for me. . . . I know that I am not using a language corresponding to yours, but I believe that it is necessary to use it.

William had misunderstood French manners. Rosalie was a married woman with duties to her family and position. Any sentimental pity Short might have felt for her situation—a childless arranged marriage lived out in a gilded cage—was as misplaced as it was patronizing. What she had to offer him was "interest," not devotion.[12]

Short took this badly. He had already convinced himself that Rosalie loved people in proportion to their love for her. Since he had expressed his feelings of love for Rosalie, it seemed unfair and slightly insulting that she didn't love him enough or sufficiently in return. Hurt, he wrote to Jefferson to explore the possibility of returning to America to seek promotion to the US Senate or, failing that, employment as an undersecretary of State. Yet Madame d'Enville was quick to write to William assuring him of her continuing friendship, and, before long, Rosalie wrote to ask William to make her imminent return to Paris bearable by visiting her at the earliest opportunity. On June 25, 1791, the couple dined together at the National Assembly, on her husband's turf but in his absence. She confessed to a sense of "shame" that the demands of her situation required her to hide the true extent of her feelings for William and "the choice her heart had made." At the same time, she begged William to understand that she had to respect the conventions governing the behavior of women in her situation. A man in a relationship such as theirs had much less need to behave with caution than a woman. She pleaded with William to accept such "unpleasant restraints" as limiting the number of letters the pair could exchange.[13]

Yet despite her appeals to propriety Rosalie also continued to present herself as a woman of feeling. She was angered by manifestations of emotional reticence in William's letters to her. Why, she asked William, would he want to take from her the sweet satisfaction she would experience were he to share his feelings? Her soul, she said, needed to receive his emotions as a testament to the confidence that must necessarily exist between two people tenderly attached to one another. She found it difficult to resist acting on the "explosion of sentiment" that reproachful letters from William produced in her by responding to him in kind. "What! You suffer and [yet] you would want to keep quiet about it when writing to me?" At the same time she worried that indulging her feelings caused William suffering. She asked him to burn a particularly reproachful letter she had sent him since it amounted to a "fabric of folly," but he kept it and others in a similar vein because, in rebutting his charges of indifference, Rosalie laid herself bare to him. As in his correspondence with Jefferson, Short craved "unbosoming" in the letters he exchanged with Rosalie. In one particularly fraught exchange, initiated as Short departed for Holland and blaming Rosalie for not making herself available for a final meeting, she made an extraordinary admission.

> If you only knew all that I endure when I see you unhappy. . . . I am feeling a deep sadness, the strangest things present themselves to my sad imagination under the darkest colors; melancholy is taking hold me. . . . I add even more to your sorrow by painting mine! Yet I am only doing what you have asked me to when you wished that I would never hide from you all that I should feel. . . . If I am hurting you, you have just to warn me, and you will find me in the same eagerness to hide my pains from you that I am demonstrating today in communicating them to you.

In the near absence of surviving letters from William to Rosalie, it is difficult to judge whether he was able to match her passion in his replies.[14]

For Rosalie, the self-assertion achieved through letter-writing was liberating. She told William soon after his second departure for Holland that, although she was saddened by the need to substitute for face-to-face conversation the act of "scribbling black characters" on a piece of paper, writing itself was "an invention that makes one thank heaven for the intelligence granted to those who first imagined the means to transmit their ideas and feelings across infinite distances." During William's absences she retreated from Paris to La Roche-Guyon where she enjoyed taking long walks, sometimes by moonlight and often alone. In her solitude, she began to read Brissot de Warville's recently published *Travels in the United States of America*, professing herself curious to know more of Short's native country. Was there a specifically American system of manners? Did the "mild education of Rousseau" prevail there? In a further sign of interest, she announced plans to improve her spoken English—preferably learning from Short himself but, failing that, from a tutor in Paris. While at La Roche-Guyon she liked to retreat to a chalet on a nearby island where she could write to William in solitude. There, surrounded by flowers and greenery, she began to share with William a "reverie" reminiscent of Jefferson's vision of a community of rationally minded friends gathered around Monticello.[15]

Rosalie wrote of her desire to nurture a "little society" of her own choosing in the Normandy countryside. She envisioned life in a small, clean cottage, days spent cultivating a garden, years spent in the company of a few true friends, among whom she numbered Short. She situated Short in this society by what amounted to a direct request—"in this day dream I would settle down by my side some traveller who is readying himself to leave us"—as well as indirectly through references to the regard in which her friends held William. While Rosalie's letters employed a high-flown language of longing, they stressed William's position within the relationships of a society she had chosen for him, and they foreground her family's view of William as much as her own affections. "You are quite right to look at us as friends and even relatives," she told William in the summer of 1792, because the entire family had the same feelings for him. She encouraged William to write to her husband as well as her beloved brother Charles. By the time Short left Paris to take up his new post as Minister Resident in Holland in May 1792, beginning what became a near six-year separation, he had carved his name and Rosalie's into the bark of a tree in the gardens of the La Rochefoucaulds' Parisian townhouse. He had given her a necklace engraved with their names. The couple had exchanged locks of hair. But William had avoided answering the question of whether the prospect of a future life in Rosalie's little society pleased him. Instead, reflecting his uncertainty, Short chose this moment to reach out to his birth family.[16]

By this time the dysfunctionality of Short's actual relationship with his American family was very near complete. From Holland William complained to his "dear brother" Peyton that he depended entirely on "Mr. Jefferson" for family news. It was through Jefferson that Short learned of Peyton's first marriage and his determination to relocate, with his sisters, to Kentucky. William grumbled—to Peyton—that Jefferson could not remember the name of the gentleman from Kentucky whom his sister Jenny had married, but he did not ask his brother to name Jenny's husband or supply their address. William knew from Jefferson that during a visit to Monticello his sister Eliza had, for reasons unknown, turned down her host's offer to forward a letter to him. He resented this, yet he didn't ask Jefferson for an explanation or Peyton for help in making contact with her. Although William supplied a list of addresses at which a letter from Peyton might reach him, he advised his brother to continue to communicate through Jefferson. He did not ask Jefferson how he could communicate directly with Peyton. William offered Peyton no personal news of himself—certainly no intimation of his relationship with Rosalie. Yet after years of misdirection and noncommunication William asked his brother to believe that neither time, distance, nor indirect communication could weaken those "sentiments of fraternal affection" which had their roots in William's heart and could never be eradicated. As he prepared to make a risky overland journey through revolutionary France in the winter of 1792, he told Peyton that it was his desire to settle near him and never quit him. He wished to return to the bosom of his biological family. He repented of having ever crossed the Atlantic. "The happiest state on earth is that of an American citizen living at home, being industrious, providing for his family, unconnected with all other parts of the world."[17]

Short hid this idealization of American family life from Rosalie while he concealed his developing relationship with Rosalie from Jefferson, as well as from his brother. On his return to Paris from his first mission to Holland he told Jefferson that he did not go out very often. He was instead engaged in pulling together a library, an activity calculated to gain Jefferson's approval although also perhaps, obliquely, implying an intention to settle in France. Short had opened his "new scene" for John Rutledge in 1790, but William engaged in no subsequent elaboration with Rutledge or any other of his friends, some of whom, like William Stephens Smith or Philip Mazzei, had met Rosalie and the principal members of her extended family. Short eventually had to intimate to Gouverneur Morris how matters stood between himself and Rosalie in order to explain the urgency of his desire for news of her, but he did so grudgingly. William's relationship with Rosalie, like her relationship with him, formed his own personal, private world. The integrity of the spaces the couple had created would be tested to the point of destruction by revolutionary Terror.[18]

———

In Rosalie's first letter to William after the murders of her husband and brother, she told him that her life would be too short to cry sufficiently for the tragedies that had befallen her. She asked William to believe that all her misfortunes did not preclude the "possibility" of her loving him but the murder of her brother hung over her like a funeral shroud and marked a dividing line between her past life and a future in which any happiness would be compromised by melancholy. Moreover, since her grandmother had now been deprived of all the consolations of old age by the murders, "my life" must now "be with her." The trauma, as well as Rosalie's imprisonment, had halted

their burgeoning relationship. Short readily accepted this. He continued to
conceal the extent of his former intimacy with Rosalie and her family, leaving
it to Gouverneur Morris to inform Jefferson of the murders. To Jefferson
he claimed, disingenuously, that "with you I have been . . . long accustomed
to open every fold of my heart" but the preoccupations of letters written
to Jefferson over the winter and spring of 1792–1793 were his diplomatic
prospects or the threat to his fortune posed by the collapse of the trading
house of Donald and Burton. Jefferson offered Short a detached, political appraisal of the murder of "unarmed and helpless individuals in the bosom of
their families." Short's references to the sufferings of the La Rochefoucaulds
did not offer the counterweight of an emotional reaction written from the
perspective of a lover. His letters to Jefferson were liable to be opened and read
by both French and British police agencies—an incentive to discretion—but
discretion failed to stop Short from concluding a despairing survey of the
state of Europe with the prediction that the execution of the King, Queen,
and Dauphin was not only possible but likely.[19]

Rosalie's financial troubles were worsened by the decision of her
surviving brother, Alexandre, to seek exile in England. In time, he would be
proscribed by the revolutionary authorities and his estate sequestered. These
developments offered William a limited opportunity to play a role he had
enjoyed in his dealings with the Royer family, that of manager. During his
brief visit to La Roche Guyon en route to Spain he offered to help the La
Rochefoucaulds transfer as much of their remaining estate as possible into
foreign funds. He furnished them with a letter of introduction to the Van
Staphorsts, assuring the family that their money would be safer in Amsterdam
than in their own hands. He enlisted the help of Gouverneur Morris to secure La Rochefoucauld lands on the island of St. Domingue. The basis on
which this assistance was offered and accepted was William's position within
a family by which—as he explained to the Van Staphorsts—he was treated
during his stay in France as a son rather than as a stranger. He did not present
himself as Rosalie's lover. He chose to present himself as a dutiful son and
close friend rather than a potential husband.[20]

Despite her troubles, Rosalie had not abandoned her desire to situate
William within her little society. At some point after the murder of her husband in 1792, and before what William described as his "final departure"
for the United States (presumably in 1802), Rosalie lent him three hundred
thousand francs—on condition that he would not pay interest to her, that
he would not disclose the loan's existence, and that he would not repay her
during her lifetime but would instead settle with her heirs. Short reneged on

this last promise. In 1836, when he was seventy-seven and Rosalie was seventy-three and in straitened circumstances, he discharged the principal, which was then estimated to be worth $60,000.[21]

Surviving correspondence between the couple does not discuss Rosalie's motivation in extending the loan or William's in accepting it. Short kept obsessive accounts of his assets and the income he received from them, yet his records show no trace of the loan until the moment of repayment. The question of when the loan was offered bears on why it was offered. William had a prior history of airing his woes with Rosalie, and it is likely that they discussed the possibility of each other's financial ruin during William's brief visit to La Roche-Guyon in December 1792. Perhaps Rosalie acted to preserve family assets or shield William from bankruptcy. Either contingency would explain William's willingness to accept the money. Since it is clear that it was Rosalie who supplied the principal, and while she and her brothers had shared a substantial inheritance in 1791, it would surely have been hard for her to lay her hands on such a sum so soon after the murder of her husband and at a time when she had pressing needs of her own. More likely Rosalie offered the loan in calmer times after her release from detention. The death of Madame d'Enville in 1797 might have provided Rosalie, the duchess's heir, with both the necessary funds and an explanation, her grandmother's affection for William, sufficient for him to accept the offer. Short told Jefferson in 1798 that he expected to come into funds. The loan was made in the context of Rosalie's desire to keep William in France. It provided William with a discrete source of income from interest that would obviate his need to find another diplomatic post or return to America, thereby making a continuing residence in France feasible. It facilitated the possibility of cohabitation or marriage, not least by supplying William with a covert source of income that, paradoxically, protected Rosalie's reputation by defusing any appearance that he was sponging off her. Although Rosalie was uncomfortable with the financial dynamics of arranged marriages, her desire to keep William in France, as a member of her little society if not necessarily as her husband, is the most likely explanation for her decision to advance the loan. By accepting it, William deepened a dilemma which was of his own choosing but sharpened by Jefferson's actions as well as Rosalie's.[22]

Day-dreaming from his isolation in Spain in 1793, Short had shared with Jefferson, although not with Rosalie, a fantasy in which he imagined purchasing an estate in Virginia on which he could gradually convert slaves into *metayers* (a form of sharecropper) and, ultimately, free farmers. In 1795, as Short's diplomatic career drew to a close, Jefferson announced that he had purchased for Short, using his adoptive son's money, the Indian Camp estate in Albemarle County. Short was in a position, even without a loan from Rosalie, to live where he chose—either in France or Virginia—and with whom he chose. Rosalie had declared her love for him and her desire that he join her little society, Jefferson had purchased an estate for him to return to as a neighbor. Yet Short continued to resist choosing either option.[23]

———

Short's first decision on his return from Spain in 1795 was to act on a previously announced intention by residing apart from Rosalie in Paris. This was a form of rejection. Rosalie never asked William how he passed his days there; she imagined he frequented bookshops. Aside from indicating a trust in William not to embarrass her by consorting with another woman, her silence indicated a disinclination on her part to press further her previous declarations of devotion. William had his interests and she had hers. Aware that William wished to return to America, if only temporarily, she was saddened and irritated by his gloomy reflections on future separations. She was not inclined to allay his anxieties by accompanying him on a voyage to the United States. They should live in the present and not fret about the future.[24]

For Rosalie, living in the present meant cultivating connections with her family and friends, largely outside Paris, at her own country estate and increasingly the country residence of Boniface Louis André, Count de Castellane, the husband of Rosalie's cousin Adélaïde Louise de Rohan-Chabot, near Acosta. She defined the contours of her little society in the letters through which they maintained their relationship. In these, Rosalie's affirmations of Madame d'Enville's regard for William were coupled with references to the young children of her acquaintances. Rosalie, in her mid-thirties, reflected that nothing could be more rewarding than caring for a "darling child or kind old person." Such care developed amiability and kindness in the carer which would be reciprocated in old age, a thought, she told William, that reconciled her to the prospect of her own dotage. She offered William a more general proposition. Society was nothing more than a series of mutual exchanges in which people sought affection, kindness, and love. Thanking William for paying a visit to her father in Paris, she reminded him of the importance she gave to the "little social attentions" that kept friendly ties alive. William had no experience of such kin-keeping within his own family, and he struggled to maintain all his friendships, including that with Jefferson. As a younger man he had plied the Royer family with small gifts, advice, and attention, making him, in his mind, the dominant partner in the relationship. Despite the sentiments of dependence on William that she had expressed on her release from prison, Rosalie's firm requests that he tend to relationships within her extended family and pay courtesy calls on other members of her little society discomforted William.[25]

Jefferson made fewer demands on Short's allegiance, but the ambiguity of those that he did make was emotionally wrenching. In the spring of 1797, Jefferson gently alluded to the probable cause of Short's reluctance to make good on his promises to at least visit the United States, while at the same time softening memories of the "Adam and Eve" letter. "As I presume you are in habits of relations with Mesdames Danville and de la Rochefoucault [sic]," he wrote, "I pray you to tender them the homage of my respects, to assure them of my heartfelt sympathies in all their sufferings and that I shall ever recollect them with the same affections as if I were of their family." It was important to Short that Jefferson know, like, and approve of Rosalie. Forwarding expressions of affectionate recollection from Madame d'Enville and her granddaughter to Jefferson, Short nervously commented that he hardly supposed that Jefferson remembered her. However, "she assures me often there is no person whose friendship she would be more happy to cultivate." In reply, Vice President Jefferson told Short emphatically that his business affairs, particularly the estate at Indian Camp, required his urgent personal attention. Expecting Short's return, Jefferson said he could offer "some *gite* for a single friend" at Monticello, even though he was having the roof replaced. Having almost directly advised Short not to bring Rosalie with him on any trip to Virginia, Jefferson backtracked by adding compliments to her, albeit cast once more in the past tense. Nobody, he told Short, had been more impressed by her merit, to which he paid sincere tributes of respect. This begged the question of whether Jefferson might render such tribute in the future. Although he could console himself that Jefferson did not absolutely disapprove of his relationship with Rosalie, Short, who craved Jefferson's approval, found his friend and father's apparent evasions noticeable. Yet they were grounded in his inability to describe his feelings for Rosalie.[26]

Following a brief illness, Madame d'Enville died on May 31, 1797. Her death removed the last obvious obstacle to William and Rosalie openly admitting to their relationship. It occasioned a further breach of reserve from Rosalie, "My friend," she told William, "you have fully taken possession of my heart, and I do not want to regain its control. . . . Let us savour the pleasure of loving one another." There was, she assured him, nothing sweeter. Although Short canceled a planned trip to the United States to offer Rosalie support, Paris remained his principal place of residence. Earlier in the year he had asked his bankers to lend him $10,000 to purchase a French country estate and a townhouse in Paris. William didn't pursue the matter, possibly because it was around this time that Rosalie advanced her loan to him. Despite Rosalie's latest expressions of love, William continued to distance himself from her.[27]

William and Rosalie did not share children, a factor adding to the distance the pair experienced. Rosalie brought no children from her first marriage to their relationship, and there is no evidence that she was ever pregnant during her affair with William. She certainly took an interest in children, especially as she grew older. In 1813, she told William that her niece Adèle had wasted no time in starting a family and that she would be attending Adèle's confinement. Were there hints of jealousy or reproach in such remarks? Short, later in life, enjoyed offering advice to his nephews, but he had apparently little interest in starting a family of his own. Perhaps an attempted cure of the venereal disease he claimed to have contracted in Italy in 1788 left him impotent. Perhaps in his discussions of prostitution, disease, and the "marital yoke," Short offered a smokescreen to obscure a wider lack of interest in fatherhood or perhaps even in heterosexual sex itself. This feature of the relationship between William and Rosalie was relevant not only to the couple's understanding of each other's needs and desires but also to the view taken of it by outsiders, notably Jefferson. In Jefferson's world, a man married and fathered children, preferably a "quiver full" and preferably in Virginia. To Jefferson, if not to the couple themselves, the relationship appeared unresolved and incomplete.[28]

Short was in his forties. To stay in France without continuing some kind of relationship with Rosalie amounted to an act of emotional as well as professional self-exile. Equally, he recognized, but struggled to accept, that asking Rosalie to relocate to the United States would be asking her to begin her life anew. An obvious middle way presented itself: remain in France with Rosalie, maybe after a brief return to the United States to sort out his affairs, and in an open relationship if he anticipated that marriage would rest too heavily on his shoulders.[29]

No letter in which Short directly confronted his indecision survives. Even if he knew his own mind, Short had become accustomed to concealing his relationship with Rosalie, as well as the emotions he invested in it, from personal friends such as John Rutledge and William Nelson, from his biological family, and from his adoptive father Thomas Jefferson. On William's instructions Rosalie destroyed most of his correspondence with her, yet surviving letters address one source of his unease indirectly by revealing his sensitivity concerning Rosalie's background and status. In 1794, he had been forced to offer James Monroe, the United States' minister to France, some explanation of his relationship with Rosalie in order to solicit Monroe's assistance in releasing her and Madame d'Enville from imprisonment. Short tried to confine the motivation behind his request to the terrains of masculine honor or gallantry: "I will simply inform you that I have a friend in Paris under misfortune in whose fate my happiness is entirely involved—this friend my dear Sir is a female." But, as Short elaborated for Monroe, he revealed his concern that such an attachment seemed redolent of a politically retrograde love of rank and luxury of almost exactly the kind that had led Jefferson to counsel young Americans from residing in France. It was Rosalie's "misfortune," Short insisted to Monroe, to have been born into the aristocracy. Her rank did not call into question her virtue, Madame d'Enville's, or his own. Short "pledged my life, my reputation, my all" that these "two helpless females" were no scheming counter-revolutionaries. He enlisted the testimony of no less a republican than Jefferson to convince Monroe on the point: Rosalie and "her family were known to Mr. Jefferson and myself from the time of our first arrival in France—they treated us both as friends and brothers because we were Americans and because they were always friends to that liberty and equality which existed in America." He insisted that he would "make use of every means of recovering that greatest of human blessings, liberty and the enjoyment of my natal air," which presumably entailed ending his involvement with Rosalie. With Jefferson, Short parsed the "particular circumstances" of Rosalie's background differently by suggesting that she would accompany him to America and presumably take up American ways. His efforts to surmount his doubts reflected the extent to which he had internalized Jeffersonian precepts. But it was Rosalie who finally forced William into a decision by making one last effort to convert William to her vision of a future together.[30]

———

In the summer of 1798, William finally acted on his oft-announced intention to make a trip to America to tend to his affairs. He booked passage from Le Havre, planning to sail in the company of Elbridge Gerry, one of three American commissioners sent to address Franco-American tensions but who found himself embroiled in a diplomatic incident, the XYZ affair, that further inflamed them. Though Short hated sea travel, the prospect of networking with Gerry during a transatlantic voyage made the prospect almost appealing. Short was eager to make himself useful to Gerry, hoping that he might serve as an honest broker, perhaps alongside Gerry, in a future peace commission. William left Paris on July 8, and, the next morning Rosalie wrote, from her bed, the first in a string of letters that expressed her pain at the prospect of separation but also a definitive understanding of their relationship.

For the first time she referred to William as "my tender husband," a spouse "taken momentarily away from me by important business." William's tears on departure had torn her heart but also softened its anguish. She planned to leave Paris to stay with Castellanes at Acosta, from where she would imagine his progress. He should have reached Rouen, he was probably sad and left alone with gloomy thoughts, as she was. She was sleeping in the bed he normally used. She was kissing the portrait of him that she had commissioned and cherishing the lock of his hair. Did he have everything he needed for the voyage? Was he looking after his health? When he returned they would love each other forever. He should think of her as his wife. The arrival of a letter from Le Havre, written by William the day before his scheduled departure, reawakened her tears but led her to reflect that, when two people loved one another as they did, they could never be unhappy. Later in July she returned to Paris, immersed in memories of their shared enjoyment of the familiar sights. She walked alone in the Champs Elysées, feeling the absence of the man most essential to her happiness and regretting the "little disagreements" that had sometimes arisen between them. For the first time she wondered whether he might abandon his trip and retrace his steps. She gave him a positive incentive to return. She was ready to marry him.

> You are my darling, I am your loving wife, nothing can prevent this sweet union anymore, your existence and mine are combining together and we can be but as one. . . . It pains me to wish you to leave Le Havre but it is so that you will come back sooner to me and then all our uncertainties, all our torments will find an ending in the most gentle and loving of unions.

The next day, writing in fear that William already had departed, she wondered how on earth she could have consented to this "awful separation." She had delayed "the only real happiness for two people who love each other and who know how to love." She need not have worried. William had decided to abandon his trip.[31]

Rosalie found it relatively easy to explain William's unexpected reappearance to friends and family. She simply told them that he had received new information from America. Elbridge Gerry found it easy to explain

Short's non-appearance to Jefferson. "Madame Ro—f—lt's irrisistible [sic] letters pursued him" to Le Havre. "I presume he is now in holy unison [sic] with her." The account of his change of heart Short offered Jefferson was more complicated. He claimed that Rosalie had initially "yielded" to the arguments he made in favor of the voyage on condition that he return to France within a year. But the prospect of even a short separation had caused such intolerable pain to "the future partner of my life" that he could not resist the "solicitation" "of a person whose desire has a right to be a law with me." Acknowledging his previous "reserve" on the subject of his relationship with Rosalie, Short reversed a device Jefferson used in his letters: had Jefferson been resident in France Short would certainly have "unbosomed" himself.[32]

In lengthy letters to Jefferson, Short preemptively addressed three interrelated criticisms of his behavior he felt his friend and father might level at him: that his life was being unduly controlled by a woman, that he had renounced his native country, and that his commitment to republicanism was unreliable. He assured Jefferson that he had not "consented" to renounce his native country; instead Rosalie had "consented" that their future residence would be in a location of Short's choosing. If the couple were to settle in the United States—the threat to Rosalie's fortune posed by calls from high Federalists that the property of non-citizens be subject to sequestration was prompting their current caution—then their residence would be, at least for part of the year, "in your neighborhood." The couple had been reading an advance copy of the Duke de La Rochefoucauld-Liancourt's *Voyage dan les États-Unis d'Amerique,* dwelling on those sections in which Rosalie's kinsman described his stay at Monticello and their host's connections with mutual friends in France. Rosalie had, so Short claimed, made residence in Albemarle County a condition of the couple settling in America. Not to be outdone by Rosalie, Short averred that "nobody can know better than I do . . . the happiness of forming part of your family."[33]

Jefferson did not comment on Short's intention to bring Rosalie to America. He had once indulged in the fantasy of bringing an exotic foreign mistress to Virginia. In the dialogue between head and heart he offered Maria Cosway, his heart had been sure that Maria would delight in visiting and drawing grand scenes such as the Natural Bridge, thus ensuring the couple's happiness. His head told him this was unlikely. Jefferson had later thought about offering Marguerite de Corny asylum at Monticello but he had concluded that she could not be happy in Virginia since its manners were so different from the society to which she was accustomed. He was not prepared

to encourage Short's dreams of a triumphant return to America with an aristocratic French wife through any form of invitation.

In his correspondence from this period, Short made explicit what had for
some time been implicit in the political commentary he offered his mentor
during the French Revolution. He believed that throughout Europe and now,
he feared, America, liberty was under threat. "If true liberty . . . not the meer
[sic] word but the substance contained in the security of property and of things
be lost in America, I shall give up all hopes of it ever existing permanently in
this world." This conservative definition of liberty potentially set Short's republicanism apart from Jefferson's more expansive vision. Convinced that security of property was under threat in the United States, Short issued detailed
instructions for the investment of his own money in safe assets. The actions
of the Adams administration demonstrated to Short's satisfaction the extent
to which America's "public mind" had been irretrievably poisoned by partisanship. "I really believed that a state of perfection in morals and government
existed" in America, Short told Jefferson, yet in recent years his countrymen
had disabused him of the notion; "for whilst each exalts his own party, [each]
assures me that for vile and base intrigue, avidity and corruption, the opposite party far surpass anything I can form an idea of from what I have seen in
the old countries of Europe." To condemn both main American parties was
to risk Jefferson's wrath. Although Jefferson decried partisanship, insofar as
parties collected and promoted the will of the people, they—or at least the
Democratic-Republicans—were a necessary evil. Jefferson did not attempt to
correct Short's views, which were in any case expressed diffusely. Suffering
under "the reign of witches" in America, he made no immediate comment of
Short's decision to remain in France or the reasoning behind it.[34]

He also continued to facilitate Short's residency abroad by managing
William's affairs in the United States and, by suggesting that his prolonged
absence from the United States had fatally damaged his career prospects and
by deflecting Short's requests that he should use his influence to revive that
career, implying that Short might be better off remaining in France with his
"amiable" friend. As President, Jefferson made sure to instruct the new minister to France, Robert Livingston, to avail himself of Short's connections and
local knowledge (while at the same time warning Livingston that Short's political views might be suspect). In 1802, he asked Short to assist in the purchase
of books for the embryonic Library of Congress from Parisian booksellers.
Meanwhile Short continued to make, and then break, plans to return to the
United States to sort out his affairs. He continued to feel a need to explain
postponements to Jefferson. His increasingly feeble excuses continued to

suggest that it was Rosalie, not William, who controlled the couple's domestic life. In 1801, he wrote wearily to Jefferson, "I have been prevailed upon . . . it would be useless to detail here why . . . I shall set out in two to three days for Auvergne where my friend has an estate."[35]

Between 1798 and 1802, William lived openly with Rosalie, accompanying her on trips to spa towns and annual visits to her estates. His letters to Jefferson attempted to suggest that he was living a life of affectionate domesticity, yet his underlying discomfort was evident from the frequency with which he insisted that he had never intended to permanently abandon his country or in the sketches of grand projects, among them the introduction of merino sheep to America, that he told correspondents he would undertake on his return. Visiting the Auvergne with Rosalie in 1801, he unconsciously laid bare for Jefferson the depth of his alienation and confusion in a description of the mountainous landscapes and views of the celebrated plain of Limagne he had encountered while touring the region with Rosalie. From a French mountain top,

> I pleased myself with forming a representation in Albemarle of what I had then under my view . . . to form one side of this, the situation of Monticello was perfectly adapted—I had only to increase the dimensions; and this costs nothing to the imagination—I gave therefore Monticello an elevation of more than three thousand feet, with a basis and circumference in proportion—Charlottesville became a city of twenty five thousand souls and the valley between you and the Blue Ridge representing the Limagne in situation and form, I had only to give it the proper fertility and culture—I thus transported myself to my native soil.

He was homesick, and it was clearly time to visit home. In 1802, Short finally sailed from Le Havre, embarking on what he had probably convinced himself would a temporary return to attend to his business and career prospects.[36]

———

No correspondence between William and Rosalie describing their feelings and expectations at the moment of William's departure for the United States survives. Nor does any correspondence between the couple written during what proved to be a seven-year separation. During that time Short procured for Jefferson a supply of Cahusac wine from Rosalie's estates, an indication of the existence of correspondence with her that likely covered more intimate terrain. William left his library in Rosalie's care, suggesting that he intended to return to France. He told his sister Jane, who visited him in Philadelphia, that he wished to return. Following this visit Jane wrote wishing that he would settle in "his own country" and suggesting that one of the women he had introduced her to in Philadelphia might make him happy. But at the same time she was "not so selfish" as to insist that he remain in America against his wishes and Rosalie's. Jane praised a background, the temple of Athena in Paestum in southern Italy, that William had chosen for a portrait of himself commissioned from Rembrandt Peale, but she wished it could have been "a view of the place you propose spending your summers whilst at France," namely La Roche-Guyon. She might then have placed her brother in some of the pleasing landscape he had obviously described to her. As it was, she was glad that William had posed for Peale in a waist-coat that Jane had altered and "your friend" Rosalie had embroidered. Jane asked her brother why, if Rosalie was all that was good and clever, as William had represented her, he did not "place her in a situation that I may respect and love her as a sister?" If William was bound and determined to Rosalie then he should marry her—with the Short family's blessing. But in the final version of the portrait the waistcoat was covered by a topcoat and the background remained Paestum, not La Roche-Guyon. In the image he presented to the world, he was his own man, but without identifiable roots in France or America.[37]

On the other side of the Atlantic, developments within Rosalie's family began to change the character of the life she sought to share with William. Following the return from exile of her brother Alexandre in 1800, Rosalie decided to take advantage of the softening of penal laws against émigres by sharing with him the estate she had inherited from Madame d'Enville. She ceded control and eventually title of La Roche-Guyon to Alexandre, and she moved to a smaller estate at Reuil. The relaxation of penal laws was part of a larger strategy to co-opt surviving members of the aristocracy to lend legitimacy to Napoleon's regime. The La Rochefoucauld-Liancourt dynasty and the imperial court aligned themselves when, in 1804, Rosalie's great-aunt Adélaïde Pyvart de Chastellué became *dame d'honneur* to Empress Josephine. Through Adélaïde, Rosalie struck up a friendly relationship with the Empress, which continued after Napoleon divorced her. Meanwhile Rosalie's cousin Fernand began an army career that saw him serve briefly as an aide-de-camp to the Emperor.

FIGURE 5.2 William Short by Rembrandt Peale, c. 1806. Oil on canvas. Gift of Mary Churchill Short, Fanny Short Butler, and William Short. © Muscarelle Museum of Art at William & Mary, Williamsburg, Virginia. Reproduced by permission.

Another realignment between old and new aristocracy involved Rosalie and William's mutual friend, Count Castellane. In 1802, Napoleon named Boniface Castellane prefect of the Lower Pyrenees, whose administrative center was Pau, a town she and William had enjoyed visiting. Rosalie continued to make the journey there after William's departure. Her visits acquired a fresh purpose from 1805, when the Count's wife Adélaïde died, leaving Boniface a widower with a seventeen-year-old son in whom Rosalie took a nurturing interest. Rosalie disliked Napoleon's pretentions, and she welcomed the collapse of his imperial regime. However, given the tensions between that regime and the Jefferson administration, Rosalie's friendship with an American, especially a man known to be an intimate of the President of the United States, became a matter of potential embarrassment to her and her extended family. Just as in the late 1790s William Short had struggled to imagine bringing Rosalie to a Francophobic America, so Rosalie had cause to ask whether a liaison with an American was feasible in imperial France.[38]

In 1808, Short returned to France at Jefferson's request, not Rosalie's. During what proved to be a short-lived and frustrating sojourn, Short visited Rosalie at her new country home in Reuil. She furnished him with introductions to the imperial court. He stayed in Paris, enjoying high society and reunions with old friends. His letters to Jefferson mentioned friends in common but made no mention of Rosalie, who, in February 1810, married Boniface Castellane. Short immediately made plans to leave France at the earliest opportunity.[39]

William's response to her marriage surprised and saddened Rosalie. After all, she had come as near as her pride would allow to asking William to marry her and stay in France and he had refused to act. But all that was now in the past. She had expected William to remain part of her life, and she subsequently explained to him that her new husband understood how affairs between them had once stood and so made no objection to a continuation of their correspondence. She asked him to write to her, as she would continue writing to him. How could he doubt her everlasting friendship? He would always be a special part of her little society. True to her word, Rosalie kept up a correspondence with William and tended to their relationship through small acts of consideration. She sent him a stewing kettle and a copy of the latest edition of *La Cuisiniere Bourgouise* so that back in America William's cook could make for him the ragouts he had enjoyed in France. She sent him a miniature of herself and, later, the bust of Condorcet that Madame d'Enville had consigned to the storerooms of La Roche-Guyon when Condorcet announced his conversion to republicanism. She met Alexandre-Marie Denis, the son of Lilite Royer, and, praising him to William, complimented his mentoring of the young man. Rosalie continued to seek a place in William's life, but he fended off her approaches.[40]

Short subsequently claimed to Jefferson that he had decided early on that he could not marry Rosalie and stay in France—it would not produce the happiness he sought—but that he could not break with her until "the same conviction could be wrought in the mind of each party." "This happily has been done by time and reflexion," he reported in the aftermath of Rosalie's marriage to Castellane. The "ties of a perfect and long-established friendship" between him and Rosalie remained "unimpaired." Yet Short saw Rosalie's second marriage as a kind of betrayal, not of shared emotions but of shared values. Rosalie's chatty accounts of her new life fueled William's bitterness. In August 1810, she offered William an account of the reception she and her husband had received in Pau and the Pyrennean spa town of Eaux-Bonnes which Short had previously visited with her. Greeting the newlyweds "royally," the "common people of the mountains" offered songs, food, and flattering expressions of their good will. Describing the engagement of her niece Adèle to a man fifteen years her senior and with the reputation of a Don Juan, Rosalie reported to William that "on the financial side of things it surpasses our hopes for her. He will have income of at least a hundred thousand livres." Short had once, he said, "taken an interest" in Adèle but, although he knew the realities of the marriage market as it bore on French women's choices, he claimed to find Rosalie's calculation vulgar. Such security and place in society as Castellane offered Rosalie was, Short explained to Jefferson, not only fragile but distasteful. Napoleon might have made the property of aristocrats more secure than it had been under the Directory, but only as a form of "bribe" to lend luster to a threadbare court. Those like Castellane and, Short now concluded, Rosalie, who put on the emperor's "livery," entered into a tawdry world of suspicion and envy. Napoleon would soon confirm Short's prejudices by removing Castellane from his prefecture precisely because Boniface had become too popular—though he subsequently prospered in other official positions.[41]

As he entered his fifties, Short became nostalgic for the liberal, aristocratic world of pre-revolutionary France and the friendships he had struck in the quirky society of the La Rochefoucauld family a generation earlier. The charms of that world had not been recreated in Napoleonic France; indeed, Short reflected, he scarcely recognized the country. For this reason, and not out of any strong desire to restore the monarchy, Short welcomed the destruction of the Napoleonic state. He treated the consequences for old friends, including Rosalie, of the military action necessary to destroy the imperial regime in detached tones reminiscent of Jefferson's commentary on the human cost of the destruction of the French monarchy. Short told Jefferson in 1814 that "poor Lafayette and his Merino [sheep] were on the very route by which" the allied armies invading France "passed and I much fear the Cossacks will have wolves in his fold. The country seat of M[adame] de La Rochefoucauld was also on the route . . . her house is the most visible object in the neighborhood and will without doubt have attracted their notice. She herself was not there at that season, she had no Merinos—but the furniture was valuable."

William kept a miniature of Rosalie in his pocketbook for the rest of his days but the image he carried was that of a younger woman, dressed in clothes of rustic simplicity. The living Countess Castellane, who could no longer read without glasses and busied herself in the affairs of her niece Adèle's young family, no longer interested Short. Admitting as much to Jefferson, Short advanced the inevitable waning of "exclusive attraction" as the reason why he would not pursue a marriage in America. In the absence of passion, marriage was a yoke. He ruefully cited the *Maximes* of the second Duke de La Rochefoucauld in support of his position: "there are good marriages, but no delightful ones."[42]

SIX

Money, Slaves, and Land

JEFFERSON'S TIES TO WILLIAM SHORT

IN 1795, JEFFERSON purchased for Short a one-thousand-acre estate within a day's ride of Monticello. He was acting on what could reasonably be regarded as Short's expressed wishes, and he used a power of attorney granted him by Short to complete the transaction using Short's money. Buying Indian Camp (now known as Morven) placed Jefferson's expressions of regard for Short's well-being, and Short's statements of respect for Jefferson, in a new light. Jefferson genuinely believed that Short's best interests would be served by leaving France, even at the cost of his relationship with Rosalie de La Rochefoucauld, to take up the life of a farmer in Albemarle. Like marriage, the notion of improvement, especially that provided by rational agriculture and enlightened plantation management, lay at the heart of Jefferson's republicanism. In addition to sharpening Jefferson's thinking, Short's indecision, his repeatedly delayed return to the United States, and then his disinclination to settle in Virginia on the estate Jefferson had chosen for him created a series of openings for Jefferson's further intervention in Short's financial affairs. Decisions Jefferson made on Short's behalf, and Short's reaction to them, in turn brought into play fundamental disagreements between the two men about land use, slavery, and Virginia's future. In these disagreements, Short began to identify and develop a political economy of his own. As much as Jefferson's actions had the appearance of establishing him as the dominant partner in their relationship, his indebtedness, which became woven into the pair's financial dealings, pushed Jefferson toward the position of a subordinate who was in no position to criticize Short's decisions.

Jefferson had hoped to sort out his financial affairs within a few months of his return to the United States in 1789, but instead resumed his protracted

Heir through Hope. Peter Thompson, Oxford University Press. © Peter Thompson 2023.
DOI: 10.1093/oso/9780197546833.003.0007

struggle with debt. Failing to find tenants to rent his lands for cash, he was thrown back on the sale of assets. In the spring of 1790, he sold a thousand acres of land in Cumberland County inherited from his father-in-law John Wayles's estate. He advertised his Elk Hill estate for sale. Finding little interest in a purchase among Virginians, he courted Frenchmen and refugee planters from St. Domingue before eventually mortgaging the land. While his financial situation worsened, his "periodical headache," migraines, returned. In November, he settled "a monstrous bill of freight" for the transport of his effects from France to Philadelphia. He had reached a settlement committing him to make regular payments to the Glasgow firm of Henderson, McCaul, and Company, and he was grappling with his portion of the debt owed to Wayles's creditors. Like many a Virginia planter, Jefferson met his obligations primarily through the sale of tobacco. Jefferson's estates produced 70,000 pounds of tobacco in 1790, with a portion of this total going to his overseers and managers. That spring Jefferson had realized twenty-six shillings a pound for his tobacco—a good price. By November the market was glutted. Jefferson hoped to use William Short in Paris and Alexander Donald, a Virginian based in London, to arrange sales of his tobacco in France, the only market in Europe that was not overstocked. This came to naught. While he eventually found an acceptable price for his tobacco in Philadelphia, returns generally remained low.[1]

Jefferson's estates also produced six hundred bushels of wheat, which Jefferson estimated to be worth four shillings and sixpence, Virginia currency, a bushel. In the summer of 1790, he hoped that he might be able to lay tobacco aside entirely in favor of wheat, relying on European war to drive up prices. Then came rains, "not seen since Noah's flood," which he believed had damaged his lands irreparably. Even so, as he left Monticello to take up his post as Secretary of State Jefferson instructed Nicholas Lewis, his estate manager, to support his daughter Patsy and son-in-law Thomas Mann Randolph with "whatever the plantations will furnish." In Philadelphia, with a precision suggestive of gallows humor, Jefferson calculated just how long he could make a pound of tea last and compared the cost to his budget of a cup of tea to a cup of coffee.[2]

Hard pressed for money, it was imperative for Jefferson that Short take charge of winding up his affairs in France. So, as Short tried to find a French buyer for Virginian tobacco, he was simultaneously tasked with finding a buyer for the horses, harnesses, and carriage that Jefferson had left in Paris. As Short began negotiating a loan to the United States of America, Jefferson, "begging pardon" for troubling him with the business, asked Short to chase up debts owed to him by their mutual friend Philip Mazzei. Jefferson's financial need drew both men into sensitive, secret, and potentially damaging terrain.[3]

French custom dictated that outgoing foreign ministers should thank two officials of the French court who dealt with the diplomatic corps with substantial leaving presents. Jefferson thought gold snuff boxes, valued at 1200 and 800 livres tournois, appropriate. But where could he find the money? Jefferson's solution was to offset his outlay against the leaving gift, customarily generous, offered to departing foreign ministers by the crown. Jefferson expected to receive from Louis XVI a portrait in a diamond-encrusted frame or perhaps a snuff box inlaid with diamonds. He had previously asked Short to explain to French Minister for Foreign Affairs Count Montmorin that he was forbidden by the US Constitution from accepting such a present. Eventually concluding that it would impolitic to insist on refusing the gift, and yet not wishing to ask permission of Congress to accept it, in January 1791, Jefferson asked Short to act in a manner that risked creating an international incident. Short was to remove the diamonds from the royal gift; sell them in Amsterdam; apply the proceeds to Jefferson's account with Van Staphorst and Willincks, where they would offset Jefferson's expenditures; and meanwhile return the remainder of the gift to Jefferson in America "sealed and unknown to the person who brings it." Short was to "above all things contrive that the conversion of the present into money be absolutely secret so as never to be expected at Court, much less find its way into an English newspaper." Short made the necessary arrangements. In commanding Short's assistance, Jefferson had to take Short's loyalty and discretion on trust. Short complied.[4]

Some of the ways in which Jefferson sought to sugar-coat such demands posed an even greater risk to Jefferson's political reputation than the affair of the diamonds. In March 1791, he offered Short advice that had the appearance of trading in market-sensitive information. "The excessive unpopularity of the excise and bank bills in the south," Jefferson wrote to Short, will "produce a stand against the federal government. In this case the public paper will tumble precipitately. I wish there was someone here authorized to take out yours." Warning Short that "particular reasons" prevented him from acting on Short's behalf, Jefferson nonetheless advised "you could not do better than subscribe into" stock in the new Bank of the United States "where you cannot receive less than six per cent and may perhaps receive ten." Short appointed James Brown of Richmond, who Jefferson also used and trusted, as his agent. Soon Short was asking Jefferson to "get over your scruples" and "direct Mr. Brown of Richmond confidentially what to do" with Short's money. Feeling pressure from Short, Brown in turn asked Jefferson's advice on continued investment in the Bank. Jefferson replied to Brown on Short's behalf, with as much de-tachment as possible, but risking the appearance of improper involvement.[5]

Despite the many other claims on Jefferson's attention in the 1790s, not least his own financial worries, Jefferson displayed a remarkable duty of care toward Short's financial well-being. Viewing Short's affairs in the round, in addition to offering Short investment advice, Jefferson eventually accepted a power of attorney over his financial estate and used it to direct agents of his choosing to maintain the value of Short's assets, such as his shares in the James River canal company.[6]

While Short remained in France Jefferson made two positive interventions in his financial affairs. Both were motivated by a quasi-familial understanding of their relationship and Jefferson's understanding of the dominant motif within in it: a desire to better orient the younger man toward true republican values. The purchase of Indian Camp, and Jefferson's willingness to manage it until such time as Short might return, clearly reflected Jefferson's estimation of the younger man's best interests. On the other side of the ledger, Jefferson diverted income from Short's estate into his Monticello nailery without prior permission. Since the outlay was substantial, was not immediately recouped, and could not be concealed from Short, this decision had the effect of making William Short a significant and undischarged creditor of Thomas Jefferson at the moment Jefferson assumed the presidency. This chapter demonstrates Jefferson's practical concern for Short's well-being but also highlights Jefferson the gambler, deriving a vicarious pleasure from making investment decisions with another person's money, decisions that his own straitened finances did not permit and that often had the effect of co-mingling his funds with Short's. Jefferson, the chronic debtor, drew Short, the "necessitous" investor, into his own affairs, adding further complexity to their relationship.

———

Short came from a relatively comfortable background but had always been keen to improve his financial status. Jefferson's offer to employ him as his sec-retary in Paris was made as William and his younger brother Peyton were set-tling their late father's estate. The settlement was not complete when William left. He pressed Peyton not to invest his remaining portion in western lands but to instead acquire on his behalf town lots in Norfolk, Virginia. The di-vision and sale of their father's slaves was another source of anxiety. While Short wanted a swift sale to facilitate the purchase of town lots and help fund his sojourn abroad, he fretted that enslaved families would be split to achieve it. Such financial decisions as Short was able to make as he prepared to leave the United States were as visionary as those Jefferson made on his return. Short sold an estate named Mush Island, in Halifax County, North Carolina to John Harvie, head of Virginia's land office. Harvie paid Short in a mixture of cash and land. The cash came in the form of interest-bearing certificates underwritten by the commonwealth of Virginia's military land grants. The land concerned was a two-thirds stake in a 15,000-acre tract in Kentucky, as well as the 1,000-acre Green Sea estate located in the region of the Great Dismal Swamp on the border between Virginia and North Carolina. Short was convinced that the economic potential of his Green Sea lands would be realized by a canal linking the area to Norfolk, where he hoped to purchase town lots. He instructed Harvie to deposit his land certificates with Benjamin Harrison, in Richmond, who would in turn, he hoped, organize regular remittances to France and invest any surpluses in purchases of military warrants for western lands.[7]

A neurotic hoarder of letters, bills, and receipts, Short fretted from a distance at what he took to be the casual treatment of certificates and deeds relating to his property by the men in whose care he entrusted them. He was soon criticizing Harrison's management of his affairs. Frustrated, Short placed his affairs in the hands of two men recommended by Jefferson: Alexander Donald, who ran a transatlantic trading house in partnership with Robert Burton based in London, and Donald's Richmond representative, James Brown.[8]

From 1790, Short began transferring deferred debt and interest-bearing debt certificates to Brown. Short's certificates were held in Brown's name to simplify the process of remitting interest to Short and, at the same time, so Short claimed, to guard him against the appearance of engaging in speculation while holding public office. When Short left France for Spain at the end of 1792, Brown held $30,000 in Short's name, and Brown, of his own volition, had begun transferring Short's holdings from state securities into federal funds. Short grudgingly accepted this shift in strategy as reflecting the wisdom of the man on the spot. He was pleased to learn that Jefferson had entered a "caveat" at the United States Treasury office, preventing Brown—a "good man," but a dealer in paper nonetheless—from selling bonds held on trust for Short. Nevertheless, Short continued to fret that "I am much more in" Brown's "power than I would wish to be." He sought Jefferson's assistance in transferring into his own name the funds held by Brown, and he offered Jefferson a formal power of attorney to enable him to manage this and other matters.[9]

Secretary of State Jefferson resisted accepting a power of attorney but he already had plans for Short's money. In March 1792, ignoring his previous advice that Short should buy bank stock, Jefferson, using the first-personal plural, asked Short to "judge what a slam you would have suffered if we had laid out your paper" for it. He "wished to God" that Short had some person who could, at a "judicious moment," sell Short's paper and reinvest it in Virginian lands. The value of good land was falling. Jefferson assured Short that he could acquire Edward Carter's land in the vicinity of Monticello for thirty shillings an acre. Although Jefferson maintained that he couldn't advise Brown to sell Short's securities without triggering further speculation, he undertook to purchase Carter's land on Short's behalf.[10]

Over the spring and summer of 1792, as Short repeated his grievances at being passed over for the post of minister to France, Jefferson withdrew himself from the oversight of Short's affairs on the grounds that, as he planned to resign the post of Secretary of State, he would in future lack advance information of developments endangering them. Short should make provision for someone else to guard his affairs. Then, in the winter of 1792–1793, the trading house of Donald and Burton failed, with their agent, James Brown, holding the bulk of Short's investments.[11]

Short, who had recently moved to his new post in Spain, learned of the failure before Jefferson. He immediately alerted Jefferson, complaining that he was "tortured from fear to anxiety and from anxiety to despair" by the prospect that his holdings would be sacrificed to the creditors of Donald and Burton. "If Mr. Browne is a man of honor or delicacy he will certainly have kept this deposit inviolate and sacred," Short reasoned. Yet both he and Jefferson recognized the tendency, as Jefferson put it in a phrase that would come back to haunt him, of otherwise good men to "avail themselves of the property of others in their power, to help themselves out of a present difficulty in an honest but delusive confidence that they will be able to repay." From Spain Short fired off a string of letters in which he requested sympathy, minute details, and assistance in equal measure. He asked Thomas Pinckney, the US ambassador to London, to call on Alexander Donald and enquire about his money, which Pinckney did. Donald told Pinckney that Short had no "just cause" for the "panic" that had seized him.[12]

By contrast Jefferson's response was swift, economical, and efficient. He immediately wrote to James Brown seeking assurance that Short's stock stood in Short's name and he asked his brother-in-law Henry Skipwith to travel to Richmond to secure confirmation from Brown. As Washington's fractious cabinet debated how best to respond to Citizen Genet's demand that the

United States speed up repayment of its debt to France, Secretary of State Jefferson took up Short's invitation to exercise a power of attorney over his financial affairs. By mid-July Jefferson was able to reassure Short that his holdings with James Brown were safe. Using his power of attorney, Jefferson had chased up interest on the money Short had left with Brown while at the same time tracking down a sum belonging to Short that Alexander Donald had entrusted to an associate, Patrick Kennan, in New York. The clerks of the United States Loan Office wrote to Short on April 29, 1793, to tell him that Brown had transferred the cache of securities held in Short's name to Short himself. Their value was $15,000 in 6 percent stock; $11,000 in 3 percent, $4,000 in deferred debt, and $1,000 dollars in 6 percent stock. Meanwhile the United States Dutch banking house held assets in Short's name including shares in the Bank of the United States and subscriptions to the loans taken out by the US government in 1791 and 1793. William Short was on his way to becoming a wealthy man, and Jefferson's involvement in Short's affairs had deepened further.[13]

Short was grateful for Jefferson's efforts on his behalf, taking them as proof of friendship. He asked for Jefferson's further advice and assistance in diversifying his holdings prior to a return to the United States. The failure of Donald and Burton had led him to conclude "too great a part of my estate is in paper." "Laying out a part of what I possess in lands when I return to America . . . to become a farmer and manufacturer perhaps—but certainly a farmer," one scheme Short had in contemplation, was music to Jefferson's ears. It held out the prospect that Short would join the "rational society" Jefferson hoped to found in Albemarle County. But Short was a cautious investor, willing to invest only a part of his funds in agricultural land. Seeking security in the aftermath of his financial scare, his thoughts turned first to purchasing lots in up-and-coming towns and cities that could be leased for ground rent when built on. He was interested in buying into Georgetown or other locations near the new federal capital. Jefferson promised to make enquiries about ground rents while at the same time counseling Short keep a quarter of his funds in stocks and undertaking to find Short a suitable broker on the Philadelphia market. Short's second preference, to invest in canal companies, was more to Jefferson's liking. Short was interested in both the James River and Potomac canal schemes. Here again, however Short's first thought was for his capital. He preferred to buy into a finished project, where the profit and interest on his investment could be predicted with a degree of certainty. The internal improvement of the country was a secondary concern. While in time Short made significant investments in both the James River, Virginia, and Schuylkill, Pennsylvania, canal companies, altruistic schemes of improvement, such as Jefferson's plan to raise a subscription to clear the Rivanna river of obstruction, did not tempt him.[14]

Buying land in Virginia was Short's third preference but fully engaged Jefferson's interests. "Could lands be tenanted in Virginia," Short wrote, "it would certainly be to me the most agreeable of all kinds of property." Jefferson had already suggested to Short that Virginian landowners could make a decent income from rents. Short replied that it would be "desirable" "if it were possible to vest my funds in lands yielding a clear rent of five per cent." From this point of agreement, Short's rambling and sometimes clumsily developed plans, sketched in miserable isolation in Spain and later from France, must have given Jefferson as much "pain" as Short's earlier reports on the progress of the French Revolution had given him. A first consideration for Short in the lands he proposed to purchase was location. "There was a time when my enthusiasm and inexperience of the affairs of this world was such that I would have preferred being settled on a few acres on the top of Montalto," overlooking Monticello, "to any other position," Short wrote, softening the past tense with an assurance that "even now" "being your neighbor" carried infinite weight with him. He liked the climate of Albemarle County but the "soil and position of any estate immediately around Monticello" wouldn't do for the type of "grazing, meadow" establishment Short had in mind. No part of Ned Carter's land, Short recalled, had an adequate water supply. The soil was "disagreeable" "stiffred [sic]" and "clayey." A house near Jefferson might do for a summer retreat but for a tenanted estate Short preferred a location in the Tidewater, on the Potomac, or even in Kentucky.[15]

Knowing that Short had chosen to buy land on the edge of the Great Dismal Swamp, Jefferson might have been reluctant to accept Short's assessment of Albemarle County. Yet he was in a poor position to disagree with it. In 1790, Jefferson specifically counseled his son-in-law Thomas Mann Randolph Jr, against buying land adjoining Monticello from Ned Carter. Carter's asking price was too high for land that was "naked." The top soil was thin and, resting on a bed of clay, was easily washed away. A settler arriving in the late 1790s recalled Albemarle as presenting "a scene of desolation that baffles description—farm after farm worn out, washed and gullied, so that scarcely an acre could be found in a place fit for cultivation." Jefferson insisted nevertheless that Short was quite wrong to assume that the "red lands of

Albemarle" were not "suitable for grass and grain." There were no highlands in America to equal them.[16]

Jefferson was sensitive to criticism of the fertility of Piedmont land because he was committed to its improvement. While he grudgingly acknowledged advances in agricultural practice promoted by Arthur Young, William Strickland, and other British writers, he craved discussion of agronomy with Virginians. Jefferson formed a bond with George Washington, for example, through exchanges of data and seeds. He discussed crop rotations with John Taylor. From observations of ploughing made during his tour of Holland and Germany in 1788, Jefferson designed an improved moldboard and, in time, a plowshare capable of penetrating the clay of Virginia's uplands to a depth that facilitated managed systems of crop rotation by improving the efficiency of planting. He was keen to share his thoughts, and son-in-law Thomas Mann Randolph, Jr. proved himself a willing ally in Jefferson's fight to reverse the effects of decades of wasteful farming. Randolph pioneered contour plowing techniques that mitigated against soil erosion. Although Jefferson did not necessarily follow Randolph's advice—continuing to plough "up and down hill" into the nineteenth century—the pair swapped detailed thoughts on crop rotation and their hopes for wheat production. Jefferson's correspondence with Randolph spoke of shared experience of floods, droughts, and the management of slaves and hired laborers.[17]

Jefferson may have shared his thoughts on soil and ploughs with Short during their shared time in France. Short was, after all, a Virginian who had expressed an interest in returning to his native lands. However, Short's father had tried and, so Short believed, failed to improve the quality of the soil on the family's Green Spring estate by seeding it with marl. That was that. Short was not inclined to join Jefferson in fighting to rejuvenate the fertility of the Piedmont. As with canals so with land, Short preferred to buy into proven returns. Jefferson in contrast was determined to take the "risk" of undertaking exemplary experiments in farming for the benefit of his neighbors.[18]

Those aspects of land management which Short most often discussed with Jefferson—tenancy and slavery—put the two men on a divergent course. Short did not choose to invest in an estate dependent on a slave workforce organized and disciplined in the manner that had become customary in Virginia. Western land attracted Short as an alternative investment because he believed it could be more easily let to cash-paying tenants or, the very least, sharecroppers. He was delighted to have his views confirmed by his brother's experiences in Kentucky. Tenants, he told his brother in 1800, were "far preferable to slaves." On each of the three occasions in the 1790s when Short

steeled himself to return to America he fretted about slavery. In a dialogue
with Jefferson conducted in the summer of 1793 and surrounding Short's first,
unfulfilled plan to return to the United States to organize his affairs in the
wake of the collapse of Donald and Burton, Short indicated a commitment to
reform the institution of slavery that he believed Jefferson shared.[19]

Short, recognizing the difficulty of attracting good tenant farmers to
Virginian land, favored the "humane and philanthropic system" of letting land
to slaves in a system of *metayer* or sharecropping. "Those who have the misfortune to own slaves," he mused, "should for the sake of humanity make the
experiment." When he returned to the United States, he told Jefferson in 1793,
he would purchase a small number of slaves to do just that. He granted that
some slaves—habituated to dependence by a lifetime of slavery—would lack
the foresight to care for themselves or their families. Nevertheless, he believed
that some of their children might be brought up into the condition of *metayers*
or even farmers. Were the slaves of "our southern states" to be converted to "free
tenants" then, so Short reasoned, those states would be to America's northern
states as Poland or Russia were to England or to France. That thought was, Short
told Jefferson, "one of the most pleasing reveries in which I indulge myself."[20]

Short knew that Jefferson had entertained similar thoughts. While resident in France, the pair had discussed the idea of improving land and people
through *metayage*, a system they observed during their respective tours of
southern Europe. In the winter of 1788–1789, Jefferson, who was in the process of contesting Condorcet's view that any observable inferiority in the
attainments of black slaves was a product of their servitude and not of their
race, was also called upon to field an inquiry from a New Englander based in
Paris, Edward Bancroft. Did Jefferson, Bancroft asked, have any more information on the experiment conducted by a Virginian who had freed his slaves
with the intention of converting them to wage laborers on his plantation?
Bancroft had heard that the experiment failed because slavery had rendered
the freedmen incapable of self-government and the industry necessary to
provide them with food and clothing. In response, Jefferson recollected that
the experiment had occurred some distance away from Monticello, which
indirectly strengthened the ascription of innate racial inferiority in his conclusion that the slaves in question had chosen to steal rather than work, became public nuisances, and were "in most instances reduced to slavery again."
Nevertheless Jefferson announced to Bancroft his intention to conduct an
extraordinary experiment of his own. On his return to the United States he
would endeavor to import to Albemarle County as many Germans as he had
slaves. Jefferson would "settle them and my slaves, on farms of 50 acres each,

intermingled, and place all of them on the footing of the Metayers of Europe." The children of the slaves, observing the Rhinelanders, would thereby be brought up "in habits of property and foresight and I have no doubt that they will be good citizens."[21]

Bancroft was a member of the Société des Amis du Noirs, as was Short. Jefferson was adept at deflecting critical scrutiny of his views on race and slavery by suggesting to correspondents, sometimes disingenuously, that he truly believed that the condition of slaves could be ameliorated. Yet it seems that the scheme Jefferson shared with Bancroft—and likely with Short, since Short would eventually propose a similar plan—was no smokescreen but rather an idea to which he had given serious consideration. Even before Jefferson visited the Rhineland, he had wondered how industrious German farmers might be attracted to America. During his visit to Holland in the first months of 1788, he continued inquiring about attracting Rhinelanders to America as *metayers*. Crossing the border from Holland to Germany, Jefferson thought he had identified a "push" factor encouraging such emigration. The transition from ease and opulence in Holland to extreme poverty in Germany was remarkable. The Dutch and the German territories shared the same soil; the key variable was their government. On the eastern side of the border, "alongside poverty, the fear also of slaves is visible in the faces of the Prussian subjects." That fear, the product of arbitrary government, would, Jefferson reasoned, encourage freedom-seeking Germans to take up lands in America, working for a period of years as tenants in order to pay their passage. Writing to Short from the Rhineland, Jefferson announced, "I have taken some measures . . . for realizing a project which I have wished to execute for twenty years past without knowing how to go about it. I am not sure but that you will enter into similar views when I can have the pleasure of explaining them to you at Paris."[22]

For a brief moment then, on the eve of his return to the United States, Jefferson entertained an uncharacteristically expansive vision of future race relations in which training in sustainable agriculture—through the visible example of innovative landlords, through sharecropping and, eventually, through land ownership itself—would lead to citizenship for some black Virginians. In Jefferson's scheme, the older slaves, those who did not learn from the example of the Germans around them, would, under good government, continue as sharecroppers, subsisting on the produce of their labor, save that "retained" by Jefferson as "a just equivalent for the use of the land" they worked and to defray other "necessary advances." The implication was that the younger slaves, those who had learned European lessons, might become independent landowners and hence citizens.[23]

However, following his return to the United States. the means by which "the idea of property" might be "excited" in the minds of slaves, a subject that continued to preoccupy Short in Europe, no longer claimed Jefferson's sustained attention. Short continued to maintain that the only consideration which made slave owning tolerable was the opportunity afforded the slave owner to encourage industry and an understanding of property among "these unfortunate people." He imagined a future in which some slaves achieved, through benign ownership and varieties of land tenancy, a recognition of their humanity and a provisional citizenship. Jefferson's thoughts had taken a radically different turn. Monticello's labor force would remain enslaved.

As he prepared for retirement in June 1793, Jefferson wrote to George Washington that he was determined to introduce good husbandry to the Piedmont. As a first step, he hoped to establish a model farm on five hundred acres of cleared land and, with a dozen laborers, abandon Indian corn and tobacco in favor of a planned rotation "of wheat, rye, potatoes, clover, with a mixture of some Indian corn with the potatoes, and to push the number of sheep." He was confident that under this regime exhausted lands would soon produce fifteen, even twenty bushels of corn per acre. But the laborers charged with the work of redemption would most likely be Virginians, not Germans; best practice would be supplied and enforced by an overseer recruited from outside Virginia but not from Europe; and slaves recruited to the model farm's workforce would not be embarking on apprenticeship to freedom. Jefferson had realized that using an enslaved labor force to work a model farm left the slave with time on his hands. He proposed to fill that time with artisanal activity. The paradoxical effect was that Jefferson's semi-skilled slaves would become more valuable, further delaying their freedom.[24]

There was another factor. The indebted Jefferson calculated that the likelihood of slaves bearing children who survived to adulthood amounted to a 4 percent return on investment. This was a powerful incentive to recognize and protect slave families. Return on investment was not a dominant consideration in Short's thinking about slavery. He sought to acknowledge the humanity of slaves and protect their family lives by converting Virginia into Poland and slaves into serfs. As their divergent definitions of humanitarianism became apparent, Jefferson took a series of decisions that placed his fully developed political economy in conflict with Short's diffuse thinking on land use, labor systems, and the prospect of a return to his native state.[25]

When Jefferson purchased Indian Camp for Short his enthusiasm for the life of an enlightened farmer was at its zenith. Letter-writing had become a "rainy day" activity as Jefferson lived on his horse "nearly the whole day" while directing the cultivation of his estate. "I am now the most ardent farmer in the state," he told the merchant Alexander Donald in May 1795. Jefferson had earlier offered to take charge of building a house on James Monroe's estate to induce Monroe to spend his retirement as Jefferson's neighbor. He now wrote to Short for the first time in over a year to announce that he had used his power of attorney to purchase on Short's behalf, and through the sale of Short's stock, a 1,334-acre tract on the northwest side of Carter's mountain known as the Indian Camp quarter. On survey the tract proved a little larger than advertised, although Jefferson assured Short that the purchase price of twenty-three shillings and sixpence an acre or $4,700 in total would represent a good return on investment and could easily be recovered if Short decided to sell.

For all his desire to see Short join the community of gentlemen farmers he was creating, the transfer of funds into his hands from Short's to cover the purchase of Indian Camp concerned Jefferson. Feeling some justification for his actions was necessary, he referred to Short's previous statements of "partiality" for "our neighbourhood," and he assured him that there that were no lands in the state of a lower price and equal fertility. He carefully detailed the current state of the tract, its existing tenancies, and the likely income. He undertook to manage the estate for Short until he returned or made his preferences known. Although he continued to buy canal shares and search for ground rents on Short's behalf, Jefferson could not suppress his excitement as he described to Short the improvement to be expected from clearing the tract's wooded uplands and the introduction of an annual field rotation: wheat, peas and potatoes, corn and potatoes, rye and two crops of red clover. He assured Short that "no land in the world" seems so "congenial to red clover as our red mountain land." Indian Camp bordered James Monroe's estate and lay within easy reach of Monticello. That the tract did not contain any kind of habitation for Short to stay in, should he choose to take up residence in Albemarle County, was a problem Jefferson repackaged as an opportunity: "I never saw a more fortunate position" for a house.[26]

Short had recently received a declaration of undying love from Rosalie de La Rochefoucauld and, with it, an invitation to remain in France. His first reaction to the purchase of Indian Camp was to express his pleasure to learn that it could be easily resold. He was agreeably surprised by Jefferson's estimates of the rental income. Short understood that an annual return on the purchase price of 6 percent might be possible if the tract could be tenanted with careful farmers (whom he implicitly accepted would be white). Were his estate to produce a reliable income from tenants, then Jefferson's decision to buy Indian Camp would indeed represent a "fine placement" of Short's capital, "much better than having slaves or anything else." There matters rested. Short did not write a single letter to Jefferson in 1796, while Jefferson did not write to Short until the spring of 1797, when he traveled to Philadelphia to take up the vice presidency.

In March 1797, Short announced an intention to return to the United States. Jefferson, who days earlier written that affairs at Indian Camp demanded Short's urgent attention, wrote again to encourage Short to make the voyage without delay, but Short did not come to Virginia in 1797. In a letter to Jefferson that survives only in summary, Short reiterated his desire to see Indian Camp tenanted if at all possible and noted "I do not intend to buy slaves." Short expected the "hurricanes that have been raging" in continental Europe would soon produce revolution in Britain. Were this to happen the better class of English farmer, their property seized or threatened, might consider renting lands in America. But would a British farmer, or a Rhinelander, or even an expatriated Virginia such as Short himself want to relocate to Virginia's slave society? What if Virginia were thrown back on its own human resources, black as well as white? Short had already contemplated the social change that sharecropping might bring about in a slave society. In February 1798, as he once again steeled himself to return to Virginia, Short developed his thoughts on slavery, race, and the future of Virginia at length in one of the most extraordinary letters Jefferson ever received.[27]

From Paris Short wondered whether Jefferson had been following the progress of the "philanthropic establishment" for emancipated and colonized slaves in Sierra Leone? If he had not, Short recommended that Jefferson read Carl Bernhard Wadstrom's *An Essay on Colonization, Particularly Applied to the West Coast of Africa*. Wadstrom, a Swede, lived in Paris from 1795 and was a prominent member of the Société des Amis des Noir. Even if Short had not met the *Essay*'s author, he was clearly familiar with the buzz created by Wadstrom's arguments: the "infinite good" of "turning the researches of Philosophes and of Philosophers toward the black inhabitants of Africa." What excited Short was the likelihood that such further research would confirm that Africans were "susceptible" to all the arts of civilization. He "hoped" therefore that future generations of Americans and Europeans would one day see "improved, populous and extensive nations of the black colour" formed into "powerful societies" in every respect equal to "whites under the same circumstances." Were this to occur, then force of example, operating through American law, would ultimately lead to a "restoration of the rights of citizenship of those blacks who inhabit the United States." Civilized Africans had been stripped of their rights; enlightened white Americans would restore them.[28]

As if this wasn't enough Short was led on to develop a powerful line of thought that particularly challenged Jefferson's racial thinking. If black Americans were the descendants of civilized Africans, if any degradation in their condition was a product of slavery and not of race, if they were capable of advancement, then any aversion "to the mixture of the two colours" could and should dissolve. Even if some thinkers Short left unnamed continued to believe that interbreeding between free whites and free blacks was an evil, it was a lesser evil than keeping 700,000 people in perpetual slavery or keeping the same number free but "separated from the rest of the community by a marked and impassable line." Jefferson had argued in *Notes on the State of Virginia* that America's slaves, when freed, should be decisively "removed beyond the reach of mixture" lest they stain the blood of the master. Short, contemplating a return to Virginia, advanced a suspicion of his own: the United States could not afford a sudden and thorough "expopulation" of its slaves comparable to expulsion of the Moors from Spain. African American labor was too valuable. Hence racial mixture, if it occurred, was an acceptable consequence of emancipation, and emancipation was itself a precondition of economic development.[29]

These thoughts led Short to challenge the presumption expressed by Jefferson in *Notes on the State of Virginia* that nature had assigned immutable distinctions of beauty to distinct races. Skin color, Short suggested, was not fixed but conditioned by climate. If an African family was transported to Sweden their skin tone would lighten with each passing generation. Virginia's African Africans were less black, he reasoned, than their ancestors. Moreover, even if "mixture [miscegenation] should change our hue and that of all our Southern inhabitants should advance to the middle ground between their present colour and the black" (a scenario of darkening that Short regarded as unlikely since whites greatly outnumbered blacks), the population of Virginia would be no darker than that found in several provinces of Spain. That "immoveable veil" of blackness that lay between Jefferson and a recognition of the full humanity of African American slaves was, in Short's mind, neither "eternal" nor "monotonous." Nor in Short's eyes did a mixture of African ancestry and European disfigure the "countenance" of all who possessed it. Short did not illustrate his point by reference to the allure of light-skinned, mixed-race women such as Sally Hemings. Pulling his punches, Short instead asked Jefferson whether he had ever seen Mrs. Frances Bland Randolph Tucker, a dark-skinned woman of European ancestry. There was no "country that might not be content to have its women like her," he concluded.[30]

Although elsewhere Short rehearsed positions shared in common with Jefferson—the need to prepare enslaved peoples for freedom, the supposed humanitarian objections to either swift emancipation or sudden colonization—Short had said enough in his extraordinary letter to put Jefferson in an impossible position. To agree with Short that an increased likelihood of interracial sex among free people was no barrier to emancipation was to disavow the views put forward in *Notes on the State of Virginia*. Meanwhile, in the personal context of his relationship with Sally Hemings, agreeing with Short's view that mixed-race children could be beautiful, or at least of comparable quality to children born of white parents, raised the question of why such children could not be acknowledged and freed. Jefferson received Short's letter on miscegenation in June 1798. He never directly replied. Indeed he did not write to Short again until March 1800.

Short's musings on miscegenation provided Jefferson with further testimony that Short was framing his thoughts on returning to take up the Indian Camp estate and join Jefferson's "rational society" from the perspective of his membership of Rosalie de La Rochefoucauld's "little society," that is, from the perspective of an outsider. Despite his protestations that he had not renounced his native country, Short's letters from this period gave Jefferson ample evidence that he was thinking like a Frenchman and one Frenchman in particular: Rosalie's kinsman Francois-Alexandre-Frédéric, Duke de La Rochefoucauld-Liancourt. His published account of a visit to Monticello in 1796 stressed his pleasure at being able to discuss mutual friends with Jefferson and his daughters. Such reportage implied an intimacy between the two men that made the remainder of the duke's comments on Virginia harder for Jefferson to bear.

La Rochefoucauld-Liancourt, for example, did not believe Thomas Jefferson was the best farmer in the state. That honor he accorded to Davies Randolph, owner-proprietor of Presqu'ile on the James River. Jefferson deserved credit for attempting enlightened agronomy but drew his agricultural practice from theoretical works and from conversation. "Knowledge thus acquired often misleads," the duke concluded loftily. He conceded that Jefferson's slaves were comparatively well-treated but his published account of his visit to Monticello contained an incendiary passage that cannot have escaped Jefferson's attention or Short's.

In Virginia [*quateron*] negroes are found in greater number than in Carolina and Georgia; and I have seen, especially at Mr. Jefferson's, slaves, who, neither in point of colour nor features, shewed the least trace of their original descent; but their mothers being slaves, they retain, of consequence, the same condition. This superior number of people of colour is owing to the superior antiquity of Virginia, and to the class of stewards or bailiffs, who are accused of producing this … breed. … But public opinion is so much against this intercourse between the white people and the black, that it is always by stealth, and transiently [that] the former satisfy their desires, as no white man is known to live regularly with a black woman.

La Rochefoucauld-Liancourt was not commenting on Jefferson's liaison with Sally Hemings. What struck him, as well as the French writer Volney, who visited Monticello that same year, was that Virginia's mixed-race population remained predominantly enslaved. Unlike the slave societies of the French Caribbean or Louisiana, Virginia's laws and its culture resisted the creation of a class of free people of color. Short's willingness to imagine and tolerate free citizens of color, equal to whites, in a post-emancipation Virginia was as foreign to Jefferson's thinking (and that of most Americans) as La Rochefoucauld-Liancourt's public references to the obvious transgression within America's slave societies of supposedly imperishable racial distinctions of status and beauty. Virginians didn't talk of such things. Yet, in the process of considering a return to Virginia—with his exotic partner—Short was drawn into a consideration of the mores of the society into which he was born but of which he was no longer a part.[31]

———

While Jefferson never directly answered Short's proposition that an increased likelihood of interracial sex among free people was no barrier to emancipation, he did, covertly, engage with the future that Short had reflected on through an extraordinary arrangement. In 1795, Jefferson mortgaged fifty-eight slaves to William Short to prevent their seizure and enforced sale by hostile creditors. He gave the mortgage-deed and a letter of explanation to Thomas Bell for safekeeping, later disingenuously suggesting that he had expected Bell to forward them to Short. Bell, a justice of the peace and successful store-keeper in Charlottesville, had leased Sally Hemings's enslaved sister Mary from the Monticello estate in 1787. Thomas and Mary had children, and, in 1792, at

Mary's request, Thomas Bell purchased—but did not free—his partner Mary and their new family from Jefferson. Thereafter, contradicting the social mores described by La Rochefoucauld-Liancourt and Short, Thomas, Mary, and their children lived together openly on Main Street, Charlottesville. In 1800, with Bell in ill health, Jefferson was forced to describe the mortgage arrangement to Short. He explained his decision to lodge the deed with Bell, rather than with accustomed agents like George Jefferson or John Barnes, by describing Bell as a "man remarkable for his integrity." In its narrowest sense, "integrity" here referenced the likelihood that Justice Bell would keep the deed safe and could be expected to prevent, if possible, the dispersal of enslaved families through sales forced by creditors. However, it is hard to imagine that Jefferson did not also mean to commend Bell's integrity in purchasing his enslaved partner and their enslaved children to protect them. That is, Bell's integrity was further manifested by his actions as a father.[32]

The parallels between Bell's situation and his own must have presented themselves to Jefferson. The two men each had a child-bearing relationship with enslaved women who were sisters and who remained enslaved. Would the parallel between Bell's life and Jefferson's have been apparent to Short? Short could claim some limited knowledge of a relationship between Thomas Jefferson and Sally Hemings in Paris. Had Thomas Bell not died in 1800, Short might well have picked up the mortgage deed from him in Charlottesville when he returned from France. Witnessing the Bell's household and their place in the community while referencing Jefferson's comment on Bell's "integrity" would have offered Short an insight into Jefferson's attitude toward racial mixture to set against the declarations first offered in *Notes on the State of Virginia* and subsequently maintained through Jefferson's silence. If Short had "come home" he might have been reminded that the lived experiences of race and slavery were more complex than they appeared when viewed from France. As it was, following his return to the United States, Short avoided Monticello. Short never met Thomas Bell and probably never met Mary Hemings or her children. Yet disagreements over slavery, land use, emancipation, and its consequences continued to hang in the air between the two men, even after Short returned to the United States, because Jefferson chose to further commingle Short's estate with his own.[33]

———

When Jefferson lost nearly the entirety of 1794's harvest to the blight Virginians called "rust" he calculated that it would take the proceeds of two future harvests to pay off his obligations. However, he thought he had a sure-fire means to alleviate his situation. In the summer of 1795, he announced to James Lyle, a patient creditor, that "a nailery I have established with my own negro boys now provides completely for the maintenance of my family, as we make from 8,000 to 10, 000 nails a day." This would free up the proceeds of his Bedford estate to pay his debts. But the summer of 1795 brought with it storms and poor harvests, and the winter was marked by extreme cold. Jefferson's tobacco crop was worthless, and he had overestimated the output of his new nail manufactory. He began mortgaging slaves to friendly creditors, among them William Short, in order to prevent their seizure by creditors pursuing claims against the estate of his father-in-law. In the spring of 1796, Jefferson put the Bedford estate on the market. That fall Jefferson admitted to Francis Willis that his lands were as yet "unreclaimed from the barbarous state in which the slovenly business of tobacco-making left them." The nailery was doing little better.[34]

Jefferson planned to expand production of nails, but he found merchants were pressuring local retailers to take imports. Forced to compete on price and with the price of nailrod rising, his profits were squeezed. Several years passed before Jefferson described to Short what happened next. Jefferson decided to use his power of attorney over Short's assets to "avail myself, for a while, of your interest, which was almost exactly the amount of my quarterly supplies of nail rod." After all, he reasoned, the nailery had made a profit and Jefferson was sure that it would in future, thereby recompensing Short. However, "the facility offered" Jefferson by his access to the interest on Short's investments "drew me on insensibly after the real necessity had ceased." The result "astonished me beyond anything which has ever happened to me in my life." Jefferson found he owed a debt to Short which made him "profoundly uneasy" because it had risen to a sum well beyond what he could promptly pay. The presidential election was on the horizon, and, with the "public mind" "agitated" through newspaper accounts of his debts and efforts to repay them, Jefferson needed to settle his affairs with a minimum of fuss. In the summer of 1800, Jefferson and Short agreed that the principal of the debt owed Short, exclusive of interest and taking no account of the reduction in capital available for other uses, was $9,607.97. On the eve of his return to the United States in 1802, Short applied "the usual principles" to a calculation of compensation for income lost and of interest due him. He estimated that Jefferson owed him $11,771. Jefferson accepted this revised total, roughly $250,000 in inflation-adjusted modern values, in the spring of 1803.[35]

The letter in which he first owned up to his debt to Short was one of a pair breaking a near two-year silence on Jefferson's part, and he packaged the announcement with noticeable care. He began by reminding Short that "it was your desire that your property here should be in various forms." The canal shares Short had asked Jefferson to purchase weren't doing so well. Short had previously expressed an interest in manufacturing. Why not a nailery? Diverting Short's income into the Monticello operation had been a good-faith effort to act in Short's best interest. Jefferson assured Short that he was no longer receiving interest on Short's paper, having appointed John Barnes as an agent in his place. Still, Jefferson owed Short a sum of money beyond his power to repay swiftly or in one transaction.

Announcing his determination to repay Short in installments, Jefferson offered security for the debt. He had altered his will to ensure that, in the event of his death, Short would be the first creditor satisfied. He had attached his lands in Bedford to his debt to Short. He also reminded Short that he held the deeds to "eighty" of Jefferson's slaves, whose swift sale would realize £4,000 Virginia currency for Short and thus make a considerable dent in the sum owed him by Jefferson. Selling slaves invariably meant splitting slave families. Both men knew this, though by lodging Short's claim to Jefferson's slaves with Thomas Bell, Jefferson ensured that Short would receive a stark confirmation of the complexity of slave families should he decide to recoup his debt through the sale of a mortgaged "asset." At the moment he admitted his indebtedness therefore, Jefferson offered Short a choice between acting on his clearly expressed monetary self-interest or his loosely expressed humanitarian concern.[36]

The implications of this choice resonated with Short as he considered how to respond to Jefferson. Soon after he received the letter, Short sent a long, angst-ridden screed to his brother Peyton, congratulating him on his success in finding white tenants for his Kentucky lands and full of concern for the slaves he had sold when he liquidated his holding in Mush Island sixteen years earlier. "The idea of these poor creatures being put up for public sale scattered abroad and separated husbands, wives and children torments me exceedingly," he wrote, as prelude to asking Peyton to make inquiries and purchase any of those slaves in North Carolina who had become the property of cruel masters. He assured Peyton that, were he in Virginia, he himself would purchase and free such of his former slaves as were "sufficiently industrious and intelligent to provide for themselves." The fate of a series of named slaves in specified relationships that he and his brother had sold from their father's estate in 1784 troubled him even more. Short begged Peyton for "detail on the subject of these poor creatures" and urged him to purchase or free those slaves who had been part of their father's "family" and hence deserved a family life of their own. He described to Jefferson his feelings of responsibility toward these slaves in the course of the letter in which he responded to the bombshell that Jefferson owed him a substantial sum. These feelings were so strong that, were his arrival in the United States to be delayed, Short had directed his brother to apply through Jefferson for funds to rectify through purchase the plight of these "unhappy," "dispersed" people "separated from their nearest affections, husbands, wives and children." On his return to Virginia, so Short told Jefferson, he would bind out the family's under-age slaves and free those repurchased adult slaves who were industrious.[37]

Of course, by choosing to stay in France with Rosalie, Short distanced himself from any purposeful scheme to ameliorate the condition of his own family's slaves or those that he had previously sold. He described practical limits to his humanitarianism in terms that might have been offered by any Virginian slaveowner. "I think I could render this scheme [of emancipation] not too heavy," Short told Jefferson, by allowing "all the able-bodied to hire themselves out and open an account with them so as to recover back the advances I should make for their purchase." Moreover, Short's response to Jefferson's admission that he had diverted funds to the Monticello nailery reconciled his concern for the lives of enslaved people with his preference for free over enslaved labor. Having followed the fortunes of the nailery and other workshops from afar, Short believed they would be profitable, and he praised Jefferson for finding occupations to which enslaved women and children were "susceptible." "How much better," he reasoned, "to see a poor creature in a state of pregnancy" laboring in one of Monticello's workshops than exposed to hard labor in a field of tobacco or corn. Short asked Jefferson not to even consider selling assets to satisfy his debt. Meanwhile he never considered selling the slaves Jefferson had mortgaged to him, and he offered Jefferson a truthful statement of his own wealth: "it is no kind of inconvenience to me that the sum should remain in your hands."[38]

———

When Jefferson purchased Indian Camp for Short the tract was partially seated. One tenant, Joseph Price, held a lifetime lease, while five other men rented land, for a fixed annual rent, payable in arrears, and in tobacco if cash was not available. Jefferson introduced Joseph Price to Short as a fine English farmer. After eight years of managing Indian Camp on Short's behalf

Jefferson revised this opinion; Price was "illiterate and slow" but "very steady."
The other original tenants were a cut above the marginal "little men from
whom nothing can be got and who cannot be kept within any rules of culture" who populated Jefferson's Shadwell estate. Jefferson estimated, in 1795,
that the Indian Camp estate as a whole would provide employment for "about
15 laborers and 20 horses," an indication of the resources required for its successful cultivation. Short's new tenants possessed resources. They were long-
term residents of the area and were likely to have at one time owned slaves
or land elsewhere. In 1803, one of them, John Durrett, made what Jefferson
regarded as a credible offer to buy four-fifths of the tract from Short at $8
an acre. Far from being marginal men, Short's new tenants were Virginian
yeomen of the sort that Jefferson, and at one time Short, hoped to harness to
the rejuvenation of the Piedmont. They could be relied upon to pay their rent
but, as Short would discover, they preferred to do so in their own time and on
their own terms.[39]

The estate's tenancies, Price's excepted, had imprecise boundaries, and each
tenant had barely enough cleared acreage to practice crop rotation techniques.
Some four-hundred and fifty acres of potentially viable arable land remained
uncleared. When Short declined to hire laborers to clear trees to increase the
estate's productive acreage Jefferson offered the tenants adjustments in rent as
an inducement. Jefferson's ultimate ambition was to consolidate all the arable
land on the tract into a large "farm," rented on a long-term lease to encourage
the practice of advanced agriculture. In the shorter term, Jefferson was keen
to establish a five-field crop rotation across the land that had been cleared. To
achieve this Jefferson needed to accurately survey and subdivide the estate
into tenements, prior to binding tenants to fixed leases that stipulated adher-
ence to the crop rotation.

In 1798, with no assistance from Short, Jefferson began subdividing the estate into tenements. In 1800, he personally conducted a partial survey of the estate and introduced the new leases under which the planting of soil-depleting
maize came under some control. However the tenants were permitted to raise
one tobacco crop on land they had cleared, and they insisted on retaining the
right to pay rent in tobacco and other produce. Jefferson struggled to find
tenants willing to commit to both a long lease and a cash rent. As two of
the better tenants left, they were replaced by men who eventually paid their
rent but were described by Jefferson as "very petty." In April 1802, Jefferson
wrote Short that he was struggling with Indian Camp. The remaining tenants
were scattered across the tract in "little distinct patches of clearing." The rental
income from the estate was minimal, amounting annually to approximately

a dollar an acre cultivated. In 1797, four tenancies returned a total of $146. Short wrote from France that he was agreeably surprised to receive any rent at all. Rent arrears mounted. Tenants offered "fowls, eggs, butter and droppings" in lieu of cash. Jefferson dropped a heavy hint to Short that he should consider selling the estate he had bought him.[40]

Despite Short's interest in investing in a "well tenanted" estate he offered his tenants no inducement to improve their lands and took no steps to attract better farmers. His earlier enthusiasm for populating an estate with *metayers* had been supplanted in his affections by schemes to introduce merino sheep to America's uplands—and he proposed to undertake that experiment in Pennsylvania or New Jersey. The one concrete decision concerning Indian Camp that Short did take, renegotiating tenancies with a view to facilitating a sale, alienated his renters and undermined Jefferson's previous efforts to establish sustainable agriculture.[41]

John Durrett's offer to buy a majority share of Indian Camp in 1803 was probably made in response to Short's demand that Durrett relinquish his lease on valuable bottom lands. Durrett was a good tenant who had undertaken some fencing work on his holding. He wanted two hundred acres of land of comparable quality and a four-year lease. Jefferson and Price took his side. Short let the matter drop. Another tenant prepared to make trouble was Charles Lively. Lively was aggrieved by Short's demand that rent be paid in cash, not tobacco, and he considered the rent Short was asking for, $50, too high. He had paid his rent regularly over several years, adding value to his tenement by planting a good orchard at his own expense. "I will make you what I consider a liberal offer," Lively wrote to Short: $40. Writing to Jefferson from Paris Short indicated that he was prepared to let Lively remain. Short was reluctant to accept that his tenants added value to the land—"small tenants in the manner of mine . . . do the land more injury than the value of the rent received"—yet it was he, who by demanding payment of rent in cash, encouraged soil erosion through excessive tobacco cultivation.[42]

While Short accepted that he should probably hire an overseer to manage Indian Camp, he relied, until the winter of 1803, on the voluntary services of Jefferson's overseer Gabriel Lilly and on Jefferson himself, who, even while president, continued to involve himself in the business of collecting Short's rent. Short finally hired his tenant Jacob Price to oversee the management of the estate. Jefferson thought Price was the best overseer Short was likely to find. He might have difficulty presenting his accounts to Short but he was honest and Short could be confident of receiving "every farthing" due him. Short, however, was dissatisfied when Price took the tenants' side by insisting that $40 per annum was the best rent he could expect and that his tenants would leave if pushed. Short requested Jefferson's help in finding him a replacement manager while continuing to use him as an intermediary in his dealings with Price.[43]

Later in life Short made successful investments in tenanted land in Ohio and New York. He even had a town named for him in the Gennesee country of upper New York state. But in his dealings with Indian Camp, Short revealed himself to Jefferson as a classic *rentier*. Taking a negative view of the productivity that could be expected from white tenants in a slave society, Short combined the worst attributes of an absentee landowner with an investor's desire to maximize return. As his long-suffering agent and bookkeeper George Jefferson warned him, "it doesn't answer for a person at a distance to hold such property, under ... management." Short eventually cut his losses in Virginia but in doing so rejected something elemental in Jefferson's thought.

By the time Short returned to the United States Jefferson had fully developed the celebration of cultivation he had first voiced in *Notes on the State of Virginia*. In 1803, he offered Short his "fixed opinion" "that land is the best form in which one can have property in this country." Land generally rose in value faster than inflation and was capable of generating a rental income of 5 or 6 percent. In contrast, inflation depreciated the value of interest and dividends from money held in stocks. Short could have been forgiven for treating these calculations as arguments justifying his absentee ownership. But Jefferson believed the active management of agricultural practice drove any increase in land values. "The spontaneous energies of the earth" were a "gift of nature" but they required the "labor of man to direct their operation." Agriculture, in Jefferson's mind, involved its manager in choices—what proportion of his capital should he employ in land and what in labor? Explaining his thoughts to Robert Livingston, Jefferson argued that the fundamental question facing the farmer was not how to make an acre of land yield the greatest possible quantity of any given crop but how to invest in land and labor to produce the greatest sustainable profit possible.[44]

The choices facing an enlightened farmer had to be made within the constraints of local labor supply and regional commodity prices and might be informed and mediated by regional agricultural societies or by neighborhood example and experience, but, ultimately, they rested with individuals. The capacity to make choices underpinned the farmer's citizenship. "I have no fear of a people, well-informed, easy in their circumstances, dispersed over their *farms*," Jefferson told Volney in the course of his attempts to persuade him to settle in Albemarle County. "I say *over their farms* because these constitute the body of our citizens, the inhabitants of towns are but zero in the scale." The concerns of capital were inflexibly and inhumanely expressed in the life of a city, but among "those who labor on the face of the earth" the demands of property and the concerns of capital were, despite slavery, flexibly, even imaginatively, lived out. Enlightened farming was a form of "sorcery." This was what Short was rejecting in favor of stocks and bonds. Despite his admission that "I find I am not fit to be a farmer with the kind of labor we have," Jefferson persevered with agricultural improvement because the monetary value of land ownership, which Jefferson clearly recognized and indeed relied upon, had to be seen in the context of the ethical value derived from managing and improving human and physical property. "You seem to think rent is the sole measure of the value of land here. . . . This is far from being the case," Jefferson reproved Short on the eve of his return from France.[45]

Jefferson revealed himself, notably through his entanglements with Short's financial affairs, as a romantic, dreaming of supplanting the constraining logics of indebtedness and slave-ownership whose grim operation, as he understood all too well, frustrated his aesthetic of land management. Ideally, Jefferson told Charles Willson Peale, the farmer should give "to his grounds" that "style of beauty which satisfies the eye of the amateur." Yet "we have so little labor in proportion to our land," beauty was seldom attained. The professional, the Virginian farmer, understood that he was playing a losing game but he played it out to its end. Short did not think the game worthwhile. The two land owners, potential neighbors, had established and justified divergent interests.[46]

Short never again addressed Jefferson on slavery and emancipation as directly as he did in February 1798. As he continued "germing" over a return to Virginia in 1800, he heard reports of a slave uprising in Virginia named for its leader Gabriel Prosser. He wrote Jefferson that he could never think of "those people" without "uneasiness," yet he was not sure from his position in France that "I see what is for the best." The legislatures of the southern states could not "with prudence abandon" consideration of slavery to "time and chance" but he did not press Jefferson to advocate even gradual emancipation. He expressed his disinclination to invest in an agricultural estate dependent on slave labor primarily through the consideration of return on capital while avoiding discussion of natural increase within an enslaved population or moral objections to slave owning. Jefferson's knowledge of the status of slaves as property within Short's financial portfolio, as well as Short's willingness to accept mortgaged slaves as security for debt, softened through implied hypocrisy any element of rebuke in Short's decision not to return to life in a slave state.[47]

Short still cared about slavery and Jefferson's views on the subject. In 1814, Short took trouble, and pleasure, in setting up a meeting at Monticello between Jefferson and Portuguese botanist Jose Correa da Serra. Correa, Short reported subsequently, had been enchanted with Monticello and very partial to Virginia: "but for the slave part he thinks it is the first of the States." But for the slave part. Short quoted Correa so clumsily to Jefferson because the visitor spoke for him. Short had read and probably heard Jefferson's opinion that slavery disfigured Virginia and so still held out hope that he and Jefferson agreed on slavery questions. In 1816, Short asked Jefferson to speak out publicly against a covert international slave trade conducted by "scoundrels living in Rhode Island." Jefferson effortlessly turned the request aside. In private correspondence, Jefferson addressed Short's concerns, albeit tangentially. "Our only blot," the eighty-year-old Jefferson told Short in 1823, "is becoming less offensive by the great improvement in the condition and civilization of" enslaved African Americans "who can now more advantageously compare their situation with that of the laborers of Europe. Still it is a hideous blot."[48]

Short was not an effectual abolitionist. He told Jefferson he planned to leave money in his will to emancipate female slaves, but he never took practical steps to prepare slaves for freedom. The everyday business of managing human property in slaves, above all the operation of even the internal slave trade and its corrosive effect on enslaved families, was the lightning rod for Short's antislavery sentiment. The amelioration of American slavery that Short most often proposed to Jefferson, to tie slaves to specific estates as serfs, was designed to protect slave families from forced sales. Short believed it better that slaves should be "attached" to the land rather than "kept in their present moveable state, by which as regular a slave trade is carried from Virginia to Louisiana as from Africa to the West Indies."[49]

Unlike James Madison's secretary and protégé Edward Coles, who had been to Russia and studied serfdom firsthand, Short did not justify his enthusiasm on the grounds that it would improve the condition of the slave by offering economic agency. Coles had argued, in the *Richmond Enquirer*, which Jefferson claimed was the only paper he read, that the situation of the Russian "vassal" or serf was "enviable" compared to that of even the most favored slave since serfs might labor for their own benefit. Short, in contrast, advocated serfdom to Jefferson precisely because of its resemblance to slavery. "In order not to alarm too much the sticklers for the rights of property," Short proposed that "a law should be made authorising every owner of land and slaves who should be so disposed to change the condition of his slaves into that of serfs attached to the [land] so that this should be forever hereafter their fixed and permanent condition." He wished he had a voice in the Virginia legislature to push the idea, although he believed the legislature was nearly incapable of enlightened action.[50]

In one of the last letters he wrote to Short, Jefferson effortlessly rehearsed themes he had already developed countless times in correspondence. "The plan of converting blacks into Serfs would certainly be better than keeping them in their present condition," he told Short in January 1826, "but I consider that of expatriation to the governments of the West Indies of their own colour as entirely practicable and greatly preferable to the mixture of color here, to this I have a great aversion." Short was inclined to agree. He was a member of the American Colonization Society (ACS), which believed that freed men might refuse to relocate to West Africa yet perhaps consent to emigrate to Haiti. Although Short stepped up his involvement with the ACS in later years, while Jefferson was alive Short never caused Jefferson to doubt, let alone amend, his convictions. To the contrary, Short's willingness to embrace fanciful schemes of serfdom or colonization complemented Jefferson's world-weary conviction that practical solutions to the problem of slavery were unattainable.[51]

Jefferson must have felt keenly both Short's disinclination to settle on the estate he had purchased for him and his insistence that he manage it for him in his absence. Short had to confront Jefferson's unauthorized use of his capital and delayed repayment of the debt owed him. Their relationship survived because Short renounced the "several theories" and "very sanguine hopes" he had formed, as Jefferson would have recognized, while living in a France that had imposed immediate, uncompensated emancipation on slaveowners abroad and granted citizenship to former slaves. Short's views no longer posed a serious threat to Jefferson's core beliefs on race and slavery. Equally, recognizing that Short was no "double or quits" commercial man of the kind Jefferson believed had no place in Virginia, Jefferson was able to tolerate Short's preference for stocks and bonds over farming. Yet he was never able to bend Short to his will by having him take up the life of an enlightened Virginia farmer. Short was born in Virginia, but a Virginia gentleman did not reside within him.[52]

SEVEN

A Serpent's Tooth

WILLIAM SHORT'S LATER LIFE RELATIONSHIP
WITH JEFFERSON

TAKING ADVANTAGE OF the Peace of Amiens of 1802, which briefly suspended France's war with Britain, Short finally redeemed his promise to return to Virginia. He had announced an intention to take charge of his affairs. He landed at Norfolk at the end of July. Jefferson immediately opened a line of credit for Short and invited him to make Monticello his home. To Jefferson's annoyance, Short instead traveled first to Georgetown, where he planned and failed to rendezvous with his brother but met his business agent John Barnes. He left Georgetown for Berkeley Springs in western Virginia and another planned rendezvous with his brother before finally committing to visit Jefferson.[1]

At this first meeting in seventeen years Short and Jefferson undoubtedly reminisced about old times and old friends but if plans for Indian Camp were discussed, no record survives. Indeed, there is no indication from subsequent correspondence that Short actually visited Indian Camp and his tenants then or at any other time. On the other hand, the two men did address the debt Jefferson owed Short. Their discussions were attended by tension. Short would discover a "small error" in Jefferson's account with him. No interest on the amount Jefferson owed, $11,700, had been paid in three years. Jefferson demanded that Short provide receipts proving that he had received documents relevant to the debt. Later, promising Jefferson an itemized account of how matters stood between them (an account of the sort he so often demanded from others), Short told the President that he was a bad hand at "business of this kind" and perhaps somebody else could do it better. At the same time, he suggested that Jefferson read carefully any statement he might

Heir through Hope. Peter Thompson, Oxford University Press. © Peter Thompson 2023.
DOI: 10.1093/oso/9780197546833.003.0008

produce because "experience shews how much mischief may grow out of un-settled affairs when the parties change and do not understand one another." Jefferson warned Short that he would not be able to repay him as swiftly as he had wished. Still, he hoped that he could clear his debt by March 1805. When the pair returned to Washington, Short declined to lodge in the Executive Mansion, choosing instead to stay with seventy-two-year-old John Barnes, who resided in a small house.[2]

Over the course of 1803, Jefferson managed to remit $3,500 to Short be-fore "heavy demands for wines" and the other expenses of an unusually long congressional session induced him to suspend repayment. He offered Short a bond for the outstanding sum secured by a lien on his estate. Payments resumed, with interruptions, in 1804, but the self-imposed deadline of March 1805 came and went with Jefferson still owing Short $7,910 and managing only intermittent payments. By June 1806, Jefferson had managed to get the principal down to $4,848. In the spring of 1807, he prioritized repayment, making a final payment of $793.93 to Short on June 14, 1807.[3]

Although Short apologized for the trouble he was causing Jefferson and thanked him profusely for the efforts he was making on his behalf, he was loathe to release Jefferson from the business of superintending Indian Camp, and, while he did not overtly pursue the debt Jefferson owed him, Short attempted, with varying degrees of success, to leverage his ties with Jefferson to safeguard his financial interests and advance his career. Although Jefferson had repeatedly vouched for the integrity of John Barnes—his agent as well as Short's—Short continued to fault Barnes for acting too slowly to invest his capital on the most advantageous terms. He asked Jefferson to provide instruction on investments to Barnes. Remarkably, Jefferson, risking censure, complied. The announcement of a cessation of hostilities between Britain and France in 1802 produced a fall in the value of stocks and bonds in New York. "I knew that peace would produce many bankruptcies," Jefferson disclosed. He not only displayed a detailed knowledge of how Barnes planned to take ad-vantage of this market on Short's behalf, but also personally directed Barnes to take further action. "I have advised him to invest your money" in US govern-ment 3 percent bonds, wrote President Jefferson to Short. Treasury Secretary Albert Gallatin was appropriating $7 million annually to the redemption of the US national debt, and, though this had not yet been confirmed by Senate, Jefferson expected these "threes" to rise in value on the news. "I should be glad to learn from yourself," the President asked his creditor William Short, "to what point of their possible rise you would prefer ["threes"] to other stock?"[4]

In contrast to his willingness to attend to Short's financial affairs Jefferson was reluctant to resurrect Short's diplomatic career. He doubted Short understood the nation he sought to represent. In 1801, Jefferson told him that neither the significance nor the result of the recent presidential election could be properly understood abroad, even, or perhaps especially, by William Short. The present character of the American nation was so different from the one Short had left years earlier that it would appear to be a foreign country. Short's initial reaction to Jefferson's election victory seemed to offer further proof that he had lost touch with American values. From Paris Short wrote that French and American alike assumed that Jefferson's "long habits of friendship and favour" toward him made it certain he would be appointed the United States' minister to France. "An appointment under you would give me real pleasure and satisfaction," Short wrote, seemingly oblivious to past disappointments or their causes. As President, Jefferson could fix things for Short, a perception that may have been focused by Short's status as a creditor.[5]

Where Secretary of State Jefferson had brusquely dismissed Short's claims to promotion, President Jefferson attempted to cushion the blow to Short's self-esteem caused by his decision not to offer preferment. Jefferson asked John Dawson, a "fellow collegian" and old friend of Short's, whom he had dispatched to Paris to assist Robert Livingston, to seek a meeting with Short to explain Jefferson's thinking on diplomatic appointments in general and Short's future in particular. When Short proved too obtuse to allow Dawson to explain, Jefferson was forced back on blunt statement. He had just terminated the diplomatic commission of Short's rival David Humphreys on the grounds that Humphreys had been away from the United States for eleven years in total; Short had been absent for seventeen uninterrupted years. In these circumstances, it was "impossible" that President Jefferson should push for Short to be appointed minister to France. Short appeared to have been genuinely surprised, as well as mortified, that anyone could think him a stranger to his own country.[6]

Jefferson had warned Short that he would find the experience of returning to America jarring: "we return like foreigners and like them require a considerable residence here to become Americanized." Short was en route to Monticello when, on September 1, 1802, James Thomson Callender published the first in a series of articles purporting to detail Jefferson's relationship with Sally Hemings. Ill at ease with the hyper-partisanship of popular democracy, Short soon realized the racial contradictions of his native land presented another minefield.[7]

One of Callender's barbs was that Jefferson had commenced his affair with Sally Hemings while minister to France and thus dishonored his country abroad. This aspect of Callender's attack posed a problem almost unique to Short, whose main means of reintroducing himself to Americans as a man of consequence—the fact that he had been Jefferson's secretary in Paris and had resided in France for fifteen years in total—not only established him as a stranger to his countrymen but invited unwanted and loaded questions. He could expect to be pressed on his knowledge of Jefferson in France in two settings he needed particularly to visit: the halls of Congress and Albemarle County. The *Richmond Recorder* claimed that there was not an individual in the neighborhood of Charlottesville who did not know the story of Thomas Jefferson and Sally Hemings. Since Jefferson had bought Short an estate without a dwelling, if Short wanted to visit Indian Camp he had either to stay with Jefferson at Monticello or finding lodgings in Milton or Charlottesville. The keeper of Charlottesville's main tavern had supplied Callender with damaging material on the Jefferson–Hemings relationship, while down the street Mary Hemings and her children by Thomas Bell lived adjacent to the town's main store. Short may have wished to defend Jefferson from Callender's charges, especially the argument that no white man could possibly find a woman with black blood attractive unless he were depraved or had been seduced, but Short could not express the tolerant attitudes toward interracial sex or the beauty of mixed-race women he had expressed in France without further damaging Jefferson's reputation or injuring his own.[8]

Meanwhile, Short had kept possession of Jefferson's "Adam and Eve" letter and others that laid out what political opponents and a partisan press would regard as evidence of the leveling, Jacobinical sympathies they believed the President secretly harbored. Any attempt by Short to publicly clarify his disagreements with Jefferson on the nature and outcome of the French Revolution risked landing his friend in hot water. Equally, despite their previous disagreements, Jefferson was loathe to publicly disavow his connection with Short. Short was less prominent and less vocal than another figure from the French Revolutionary past—Thomas Paine—who returned to America in 1802, and who Jefferson first sidelined and then shunned. Still, even in letters enlisting Jefferson's help with his affairs, Short sounded off on politics and the American condition with a clumsy freedom that must have caused Jefferson "pain" similar to that which Short's reports from France in 1792 had produced. The nature and conduct of politics in the United States had changed irrevocably, yet perceptions, even language, derived from his long sojourn in France continued to shape Short's view of American democracy. Failing to

see in the existence of America's two great parties any expression of fundamental distinctions of principle, Short argued, as he had done in France, that
government should be conducted by wise men who acted on honest counsel
and at one remove from the passions of the people as amplified through the
workings of popular democracy. That these errant views were expressed privately helped Jefferson tolerate them.[9]

Despite the many other claims on his understanding, sympathy, and time,
throughout his presidency Jefferson troubled himself on Short's behalf. In
contrast, Short, from his return to the United States, slowly and often clumsily, developed an independence of character which underpinned a new and
more nearly equal relationship with Jefferson. Especially after Jefferson re-
tired from politics, the two men found a way to disagree with one another
while strengthening emotional ties underpinned by their shared years in
France. Yet, for all this, Jefferson ended his life more nearly estranged from
Short than reconciled. Short would not venerate his chosen father.

Jefferson recognized the particular character of his continuing relationship
with Short through various small acts that began a process in which the
younger man returned to his orbit on new terms of comparative equality. In
1804, he invited Short to attend the official dinner offered in Washington to
the incoming British ambassador Sir Anthony Merry and his wife. The dinner
itself was the occasion of a diplomatic incident that reflected and in turn defined the style of Jefferson's presidency. Instead of escorting Sir Anthony
Merry's wife in to dinner, Jefferson led in Dolley Madison and seated her at
his side. James Madison led in Elizabeth Merry. Sir Anthony Merry was left
to seat himself. The affront was compounded by the fact that Jefferson had
also invited France's *chargé des affaires* Louis Pichon and his wife. Protocol
held that representatives of warring nations should not be invited to the same
function. The President's behavior led to charges in Federalist newspapers
that he had gratuitously insulted the British and brought the United States
into disrepute. Jefferson was needled by these attacks and drew Short into a
defense of his conduct. Forgetting who he was addressing, in a lengthy letter
to Short, Jefferson denounced the diplomatic corp's obsession with status and
precedence as a "pest to the peace of the world" and spoke of the pride he took
from dismissing half the United States' diplomats. It was, he said, his duty
to change practices and expectations which smacked of "anti-republicanism."
He asked Short, who was in "much in society," to set critics of his conduct

to rights, appointing him as his unofficial emissary to the "monied corps" of Philadelphia and the cities of the northeast. His mission was to reduce the "anti-civism" of the great trading towns. If Jefferson had hoped to mold Short into a party operative he would be disappointed. His attentions had the effect of feeding Short's self-regard and consequently his ambition. Short, so he chose to believe, was above the party fray and, from that vantage point, could give advice to Jefferson.[10]

Jefferson asked Short to spend the summer months of 1804 at Monticello. After tasking Jefferson with collecting rents from the tenants of Indian Camp, Short declined. He instead journeyed north to New England. En route, he dined at Alexander Hamilton's country house in company with John Trumbull, William Stephens Smith, and his wife Abigail. Trumbull and Smith had broken with Jefferson over his refusal to condemn the violence of the French Revolution, and antipathy between Hamilton and Jefferson was deep-seated and long established. This was unpromising terrain to act on Jefferson's injunction that he should go forth into society to contest "anti-republicanism." The dinner took place in early July 1804, just days before Hamilton was killed in his duel with Aaron Burr.[11]

Short spent the remainder of the summer in New England, from where he conveyed his impressions of prominent Federalists to Jefferson with enthusiasm and without artifice. He assured Jefferson that the better sort of Federalist decried the licentiousness of the press and attacks on the office of the First Magistrate. "Our country" would be happier, he reflected, if party spirit could "be kept in such bounds on all sides." He compounded the irritation Jefferson must have felt at the implied equivalence of Democratic-Republican and Federalist tribalism with the world-weary conclusion that an end to partisanship was "more than we can expect the baser passions of man will ever submit to." In reply, Jefferson agreed that party division was unpleasant but took the opportunity to state that High Federalists who had refused Jefferson's "conciliation" were to blame for its continuation.[12]

During his time in Boston, so Short told Jefferson, he had met two or three particularly "enlightened" Federalists, and they had candidly admitted to him that there was no more chance of the Federalists regaining the reins of power than of a river flowing uphill. The tide had turned "four years ago"; there was no going back. Federalism posed no credible threat. Short may have intended this as a compliment on Jefferson's final victory but drew a conclusion which must have riled Jefferson. "Judging from what I had observed in scenes passing under my own eyes in the early part of the French Revolution," Short considered that it would not be in the best interests of the Jeffersonian

Republican party for the Federalist party to cease to exist. Equally, the articulation of a one-party state, clumsily linked by Short to the political operation of the masses, who Jefferson believed were responsible for his election and who fully supported him in the necessary struggle against Federalism, was not in the best interests of the United States. To suggest that Jefferson's Republican party might come to resemble the Jacobins and that its hegemony threatened democracy was to suggest that Short was thinking like a Federalist.[13]

Some twenty years later Jefferson passionately condemned these latest heresies of Short's. But, in 1804, with his debt to Short still unpaid, Jefferson granted that there were some "men of candor" among the New England Federalists, men "who know me personally and who give a credit to my intentions which they may deny to my understanding." However, Jefferson urged Short to accept that "to the mass of that political sect" the expiration of his second presidential term "will be a day of Jubilee." He himself was not partisan. True, he had removed Federalist officeholders but, in an unconscious echo of his "Adam and Eve" letter, he justified his actions to Short as a necessary piece of political "drudgery" in which he was no more than the public's "executioner." The end, republican involvement in government, justified the means, a purge of Federalist placemen.[14]

In the immediate aftermath of Short's trip to New England, Jefferson redoubled his efforts to have Short make himself known to Congress. The terms in which Short turned Jefferson's invitations aside further demonstrated his new-found confidence. In February 1805, he contemplated the discomfort of a winter journey from Philadelphia to Washington and decided not to attempt it. It would be "amusing" but of no direct advantage to him to be "known in the circle of public characters." Moreover he feared that he would not be received in the Capitol as "I should have chosen." Even the language in which he expressed this thought to Jefferson highlighted his alienation from the country of his birth. "I apprehend that a private individual who has been so long placed *sous la remise*" (that is, under suspicion) "would be too much (in company with such characters at Washington) like a French Bourgeois (before the revolution) in the house of a *grand Seigneur* or a man of the privileged orders at least, to admit of its being agreeable to a person of my turn." On this occasion President Jefferson bit his tongue.[15]

Short appeared almost gratuitously clumsy—or downright rude—in this period. He was by any reasonable standards a wealthy man, as demonstrated by the lists of his assets which he drew up annually. The debt owed him by Jefferson was itemized in these lists alongside his canal shares, government bonds, and occasionally the library he had left with Rosalie. Short continued to involve the President of the United States of America in questions such as finding a manager for Indian Camp and yet he was in other respects an infrequent correspondent. From March 1805 until November 1807, dates marking the resumption of Jefferson's payments to Short and the eventual retirement of the debt, President Jefferson sent Short eighteen letters for which no answer survives, and, in most cases, none was apparently offered. Short caused Jefferson anxiety by neither accepting nor declining invitations to visit Washington or Monticello and by failing to promptly acknowledge payments made to him by Jefferson. Yet Jefferson continued to be agreeable and approachable, repeating his invitations to stay at Monticello, chatting of shared interests in wine and books, and recommending horse-back riding as a cure for Short's "loose bowels." He expressed his gratitude that Short had not forced him to sell property to meet his debt. It was with "extreme concern" that Jefferson learned that Short had formed the impression that Jefferson's attachment to him had lessened. "I shall not, on my part, permit a difference of view on a single subject, to efface the recollections and attachments of a whole life," Jefferson wrote graciously, if slightly defensively.[16]

With the debt owed him by Jefferson repaid, Short began lobbying once again for a diplomatic posting. He offered Jefferson his services as a negotiator with Spain to resolve disputes over the borders of West Florida and the United States, or as an emissary to Napoleon to negotiate a suspension of the United States' embargo on trade with France, or as a negotiator of loans from the Dutch money markets to provide for rearmament. In each case, he presumed that an appointment could be made without congressional approval or the support of Secretary of State James Madison. In an earlier letter rebutting Short's claim that he had not exerted himself on Short's behalf, either as Secretary of State or as President, Jefferson had warned Short that he had the reputation of a "counter-revolutionary" among Congressmen. Once again Jefferson urged Short to settle in Washington, acquire a knowledge of "our political machine," and "court the good opinion of our Congressmen."[17]

Jefferson had always wanted Short to make an effort to develop relationships with lawmakers on principle. Through acquaintance with members of Congress he might understand "the *real* character of our government." Confronting head-on Short's prejudice against politicians, Jefferson told him that Congress represented the nation "in abridgement." Given the difficulty of studying the nation at large, the persons, manner, sentiments, and spirits of Congress were worthy subjects of inspection and observation. Short's replies pushed his desire to be taken at his own estimation of his worth to new heights. He didn't want to appear as a supplicant before Congress.

Some Senators would never overlook his "original sin of Virginianism." Appeasing less implacable opponents ran the risk of offending the favorably disposed. More than this, Short did not believe the "Senatorial ordeal" was necessary. Had he been seeking political employment in America it would have been appropriate to make himself known to Congress. However, "for transacting any particular business with a foreign government," Short wrote, "it would seem to me more necessary to possess a knowledge of the characters and secret springs of that government." His qualifications in these areas were evident from the record, and, if Senators sought further clarification, they need look no further than Jefferson's good opinion of Short's past service.[18]

It is hard to imagine a more complete rejection of Jefferson's oft-stated advice or his understanding of the proper working of government. But this was a case where, for Short, the end justified the means. Writing days after Congress passed the Embargo Act outlawing all foreign trade and threatening to ruin America's mercantile interests, Short offered his services as someone who could bring about a suspension of Napoleon's Berlin Decree and hence a repeal of the embargo. "I do not mean to say that I hope to change this man's [Napoleon's] ideas, nobody aims at that in a direct way," but, Short continued, "there are two men of influence who approach him and who, I know, have confidence in me, and would communicate freely and unreservedly with me." What he was proposing was an "experiment," the creation of a back channel to Napoleon's court for the remainder of Jefferson's presidency. Short alone possessed the experience, connections, and language skills to accomplish this. For these reasons Short's kowtowing to ignorant and close-minded Senators was an inappropriate means of bringing about a desired outcome.[19]

———

Short began the year 1808 by pressing Jefferson to acknowledge receipt of his proposals for overseas service and complaining that "the state of his cavalry," specifically his lack of a suitable coach, was delaying his departure from "winter quarters" in Philadelphia for Washington. At some point in the first half of the year, Jefferson spoke with Short about the possibility of a mission to St. Petersburg before making, in strictest secrecy, a formal request for Short's services. By November Short was in Paris, preparing to set out overland to Russia on Jefferson's behalf to open a covert negotiation with Tsar Alexander I of Russia. Not the least extraordinary feature of this extraordinary scheme is the speed with which it came together. This, in turn, helps explain its failure.[20]

Only on the eve of Short's departure did it occur to Jefferson and Secretary of State Madison that they should have insisted on briefing him in person. Meanwhile, as he departed, Short artlessly admitted that he wished he had spent more time informing himself of the background to the mission by reading official dispatches. Jefferson and Madison gave into Short's demand that he should spend as little time at sea as possible, traveling to St. Petersburg overland from the west coast of France. Short, despite wrangling over pay and allowable expenses, agreed to make the journey in advance of the granting of formal diplomatic status. However, the ambiguity of Short's status made travel through Europe difficult and created problems when, by good fortune, Short encountered Count Romanzoff, a former Russian foreign minister, in Paris. Short revealed to Romanzoff that he was Jefferson's choice to serve as an emissary to Russia. Romanzoff, who left Paris ahead of Short, conveyed the news that the United States sought a formal exchange of ministers to the imperial court and implied that Short would soon receive formal diplomatic status. Yet while Short may have been Jefferson's choice, he hadn't been confirmed by the US Senate. When, on February 25, 1809, just days before his presidential term expired, Jefferson asked for confirmation of Short's status, the Senate refused: partly due to dislike of Jefferson's use of recess powers, partly due to disinclination to establish a permanent ministry in Russia, but mainly because the nominee was William Short. Representative Samuel Taggart, a Federalist Congressman from Massachusetts, explained the unprecedented decision to reject a presidential nominee by the fact that Short had resided for the principal part of the past twenty years in France and had, in consequence, become "a mere Frenchmen."[21]

Jefferson seems to have been surprised by the defeat of Short's nomination and angered by its apparent insult to his presidential service. "An unworthy intrigue defeated my wishes," he told Madame de Tessé. Yet Jefferson's surprise occasions another: that he had considered Short the best available man for the mission. Jefferson had some reason to believe that Tsar Alexander, and a coterie of progressive advisors within his court, admired him personally and the United States more generally. Translating this good will into the establishment of formal diplomatic relations between the two countries would have been an achievement. Yet Jefferson hoped for more. An exchange of ministers might serve as the prelude for Russia joining the United States in its attempts to force France and Great Britain to respect the rights of nonbelligerents. Concessions on the rights of neutrals, especially regarding trade, if extracted from France by Russia, would benefit the United States by isolating Britain, thereby rendering it tractable. The project of using Russia to extract concessions from Britain favorable to the United States was subtle to the point of incomprehensibility. Short's self-importance, and the crude pragmatism of the conclusions he drew from his conception of himself as a man of experience, not of party, made him an unlikely candidate to respect Jeffersonian principles, let alone act with Jeffersonian guile.[22]

Short had some ten years earlier written eloquently of his desire to protect the maritime rights of non-belligerents. Perhaps Jefferson had some recollection of this letter. While in France Short spoke of his desire to attach his name to a treaty that would "avert the evils of war from the US and to secure to them the rights of peace whilst others are warring." Yet his approach to this strategic objective was crude. Writing from France Short proposed lifting the US embargo on the participation of American ships in foreign trade. He would instead allow "commerce" to "calculate its own risks." The export of goods from the United States "would become still more a game of hazard . . . but the losses would fall first on the gamesters." "It may be further said," he told Jefferson, "that this would be a game of their own seeking, since they have been the most impatient under the embargo and the most hostile to the measures adopted by Government in consequence of it." Proposals of this kind reflected and promoted Short's self-conception as a man of "no party" unjustly assailed on all sides. "Some will consider me a monarchist and others a Jacobin," he reflected as his mission unraveled. "All that I wish for is the approbation of good men."[23]

While it lasted, Short enjoyed being the man on the spot, the insider, the wheeler-dealer in talks with the likes of Count Romanzoff. He later insisted mysteriously that "chance gave me whilst in France an opportunity of being admitted further into the secret cabinet of the leader or rather the driver there." If the incoming President James Madison knew what he knew about the French government then he would be "mortified," though Short had no plans to share his knowledge. Short's dreams of returning to the United States as the author of "Short's Treaty" were dashed. In his correspondence with Jefferson at the time, Short took his rejection in good spirit, writing that it was a good job the news of the Senate's decision had reached Paris before he set out for St. Petersburg. However, perhaps conscious of the use made of his letters in congressional debate over the Giles Resolutions in 1793, Short asked Jefferson to burn those of his letters he still retained since an "inspection" of Short's correspondence to Jefferson "must come" if "not prevented." When critical accounts of his mission published in American newspapers reached him Short was disturbed. "I see they represent me as wishing to put my country under the vassalage of a foreign power, which is . . . diametrically opposite to the truth." Forgetting who he was addressing, Short told Jefferson, "I was cautioning my government" against the influence of France "eighteen years ago," at a time when his critics "were perhaps drinking, carousing, and throwing their hats up in the air to celebrate the triumphs of that very power."[24]

———

It is not surprising that, soon after his return to the United States, Short contemplated selling the Indian Camp estate. What is surprising is Jefferson's role in the sale. Although Short dithered, he was essentially announcing through the sale that he would never settle permanently as a member of that "rational society" of acolytes centered on Monticello that Jefferson had invited him to join. Having purchased the estate for Short, Jefferson willingly guided him through the tortuous process of selling it.

Jefferson had boasted in 1802 "I could sell your Indian Camp tomorrow for double what it cost you," but he found it unexpectedly hard to find a purchaser. The prospective sale illuminated realities about Virginia's economy that affronted Jefferson's pride in his native state. Yes, Jefferson told Short, the estate was worth $10 an acre but Short should not expect to receive more than $8. To be sure there were "mere planters" who might offer a sum closer to Short's asking price, but they would borrow money to make the purchase, use profits from tobacco cultivation to pay interest, and, when they had ruined the land, oblige Short to pursue them through the courts for the principal owed. By advertising in regional newspapers Short might find a purchaser for the entire estate but small choice spots were more likely to sell—to a local buyer. Then again, things might improve. and, if Short were to hold onto the land, he could in time expect to receive $12 an acre for it. In 1806, Short's book-keeper George Jefferson restated the advice that Short was loathe to follow when it was offered by Thomas Jefferson. Short should come to Albemarle in person, subdivide his land up into lots, and sell it at public auction, even at a "considerable sacrifice." Short declined.[25]

In the spring of 1811, Jefferson once again assumed the role of Short's realtor. He discussed the interest in the estate expressed by a Mr. Bankhead and, in a detailed letter describing the current market in land, James Monroe. In the spring of 1812, Jefferson showed an agent acting on behalf of Mr. Bankhead around Indian Camp. This resulted in an offer—$7 an acre—that Jefferson advised Short to reject. Later that year David Higginbotham, a merchant in nearby Milton, made an offer through Jefferson that Short could entertain.

This was the pretext for a final, extraordinary instance of Jefferson's involvement in Short's affairs.[26]

Higginbotham offered $10 an acre for the estate, roughly $13,000 in total (more than double the purchase price and returning a profit that easily outstripped inflation). Since the land was tenanted, and the existing leases had another three years to run, Higginbotham proposed paying Short in three annual installments. He would not pay interest on the balance owed Short but would instead allow Short the proceeds of two years' rent from the estate's tenants. As security for his ability to pay, Higginbotham offered Short bonds on James Monroe amounting to two-thirds of the purchase price. Were he in Short's shoes, Jefferson suggested, he would accept Higginbotham's word as sufficient security for the remaining third. Higginbotham was a native Virginian, brought up to the counting house trade, and "so snug and cautious" that he had never bought a shilling's worth on speculation and hardly ever incurred a bad debt. But knowing Short as he did, Jefferson suspected something further would be needed to seal the deal. Jefferson owed Higginbotham roughly $5,000. He proposed converting that debt into a bond which Higginbotham could use to pay Short the otherwise unsecured third of the purchase price.[27]

Having freed himself from indebtedness to Short in 1807, in 1812, Jefferson placed himself back on the hook. Instead of owing Higginbotham, he owed Short and at a moment when his own financial affairs were no better than normal. Jefferson was just clearing an $8,000 loan from a bank in Richmond occasioned by financial "embarrassments" when leaving the presidency. He had further debts outstanding with John Barnes. His debt to Higginbotham was his largest remaining. As much for his own reassurance as for Short's, Jefferson once again listed his assets. This time he did so with a hint of sarcasm: Short had "been so long absent from this part of the country as to have lost sight" of Jefferson's progress in the cultivation of wheat, the production of cloth, and the milling of flour. He assured Short that he could count on annual income of at least $7,000 from the sale of flour alone.[28]

Once again Jefferson had overestimated his financial capabilities. In January 1814, he sat down to write Short another "painful" letter of the sort he had written in 1800. A prolonged drought and the British blockade of Chesapeake ports had combined to make 1813 the most calamitous year Piedmont farmers had experienced since 1755. Jefferson had not been able to get his flour to market before the blockade took effect and the drought had destroyed his wheat production. "The total failure" of his first payment to Short had "become unavoidable from disasters not within my control or foresight." He glossed this conclusion with a certain bravado. If the debt owed had been to a Virginia merchant it could have been deferred but in Short's case "I do not know that I can propose to you anything but to place this first payment on the footing of the public funds." Short's immediate reply to this news, which has not survived, was evidently accommodating. But Jefferson's pride was hurt.[29]

On the night of August 24, 1814, marauding British troops seized the federal capital, setting fire to Congress' library as well as the Executive Mansion. A month later Jefferson asked his friend and newly appointed Treasury Secretary Samuel H. Smith to sound out Congress on the possibility of buying his personal library for its own use. This was larger than that destroyed by the British and renowned as the finest in America. Soon after he wrote to Smith, Jefferson seems to have informed Short that he would use part of the proceeds to clear his debt. Writing from Philadelphia, Short congratulated Jefferson on the news that his library would not be dispersed. Congress, despite some Federalist opposition, agreed to purchase the collection in its entirety. Short supposed that Congress would pay Jefferson in Treasury notes. He assured Jefferson that he would accept them in repayment of his debt, after allowing for their depreciation in value. Jefferson paid Short $10,500 (roughly $175,000 in modern terms) on April 18, 1815. Their financial business was at an end.[30]

———

Short continued to offer Jefferson political commentary with little regard for the man he was addressing. Democracy left the world "under the management of fools" he told the former President, before urging him to return to public life. Although Short recognized "I have now but a small pecuniary interest remaining in Virginia," in 1816, he wrote to express his concern that Jefferson was secretly sponsoring "revolutionary" changes to Virginia's constitution such as suffrage without freehold and appointment to office at the pleasure of the legislature. He was particularly concerned that any change might be introduced by a Convention since the word carried "something in it most awful to my ear . . . this perhaps may proceed from my having once assisted at the birth of a monster of that name" in France, although he granted that "though the name be the same" in Virginia "the animal may be different." Years after his return to the United States, when he might have been expected to have acclimatized, Short had failed to come to terms with the participatory democracy that emerged from the American Revolution. History "teaches us," he lectured Jefferson, "that in Republics, danger originates much more often and much more naturally from the democratic principle" than from an overbearing executive.[31]

Short allowed that the democratic principle was useful when a "counter-actor to feudal institutions" but dangerous when uncontrolled. The party system was failing to secure two great objects of government: "security of persons and security of property." Short sold his shares in the James River canal company, albeit making a profit, because he feared the Virginia legislature would expropriate the company's dividend payments to shareholders. "I know that an hundred men together are never ashamed of any thing," Short told Jefferson and "therefore I always endeavour . . . not to place myself within the immediate grasp of an Assembly." "As a moderate man I shall . . . meerly [sic] look on whilst the country at large allows the spoils of power to be contended for by the active and ambitious," he claimed. Still, writing to Jefferson from the sidelines, Short bemoaned the decision of our "wise Congress" to destroy the Bank of the United States. In consequence, "there is really now no such thing as [a] uniform currency in the country." He blamed that disaster on narrow-minded, self-interested state legislators. "When you talk to these Gentlemen of a National bank," he assured Jefferson, "they have recourse to their pretended republican and constitutional objections and thus claim a merit for following . . . a base and corrupt motive, that is, their personal interest" in a "miserable" "hydra" of state and county banks. Meanwhile "ignorant" German legislators in Short's adopted state of Pennsylvania were blocking the passage of internal improvements that did not benefit their constituents. He encouraged Jefferson to agree with him that it was a dangerous policy to admit foreigners into "our political rights" and that "entry into this sanctuary" should be reserved to the native-born alone since "this Republic may be, as Rome was, lost by this kind of bastard amalgamation." He seemed to remember that Jefferson had said something of this kind in *Notes on the State of Virginia* but he had lost his copy and, typically, asked Jefferson to send him a replacement rather than acquire one himself.[32]

There were any number of reasons for the two men to go their separate ways after Jefferson had paid off his final debt to Short. Short's egregious political commentary, often accompanied by deferential requests for Jefferson's view, might have justified a split. Yet Jefferson kept up a correspondence with him, seldom offering stinging rebuttals. The continuation of this friendship, by letter and occasional in-person visit, speaks to the evolution of Jefferson's personality as well as Short's.

In his first Inaugural Address, Jefferson had recognized a difficulty inherent in the political culture taking shape in the United States, that of applying the "sacred principle, that though the will of the majority is in all cases to prevail, that will to be rightful must be reasonable." In 1813, he had mused to John Adams that a "natural aristocracy" of virtuous republicans might usefully filter unreasonable public opinion. In later life, Jefferson attempted to create such a cadre. Revising his position that young men should develop a republican moral compass independently, Jefferson addressed a wider disinclination on the part of younger generations to cleave to and therefore perpetuate the republicanism of his generation by founding a university that would provide young Virginian men, destined to become future legislators, with a politically sound education. Jefferson saw the University of Virginia in prescriptive, political terms. "It is in our seminary that the vestal flame is to kept alive," he told Madison. Although the will of Virginia's legislature was that the university hire a professor of theology and teach religion, this was an instance where majority opinion was not "reasonable." Jefferson was determined that the university would be secular.[33]

Short showed a limited and selected interest in Jefferson's university. He wrote at some length on the need to keep students from easily frequenting taverns and, in the aftermath of reports of disorder on campus, interested himself in regulations concerning the use of tobacco by students. Short offered books from his library to the university but he did not subscribe funds to it. He vouched, at length, for the character of Dr. Thomas Cooper, a potential professor to whose appointment Virginia's legislature and religious lobbyists took great exception. The struggle over Cooper's appointment confirmed Short's opinion of elected legislators. Legislative interference was of more interest to Short than the university's intellectual design, which he had difficulty describing to interlocutors in Philadelphia even after he had visited Jefferson. He hoped, in terms which suggest he did not expect, that the university would produce leaders who would restore Virginia to its former preeminence within the Union.[34]

On occasion Short's fears chimed with Jefferson's. In December 1819, Short gave Jefferson his opinion that the growing crisis over the admission of Missouri would break apart the Union. He urged Jefferson to speak out: "if anything could check Congress it would surely be your warning voice . . . which . . . they would consider as a voice from Heaven." Jefferson was flattered by this and replied some months later, writing on the day of his

seventy-seventh birthday. He began by once again urging Short to visit the
University of Virginia before agreeing with Short.

> I have been among the most sanguine in believing that our Union
> would be of long duration. I now doubt it much. . . . My only comfort
> and confidence is that I shall not live to see this: and I envy not the pre-
> sent generation the glory of throwing away the fruits of their fathers
> sacrifices of life and fortune, and of rendering desperate the experiment
> which was to decide ultimately whether man is capable of self govern-
> ment? This treason against human hope will signalize their epoch in
> future history, as the counterpart of the medal of their predecessors.

The terms he adopted here prefigured those he would use in a celebrated letter
to John Holmes just ten days later. As he reflected on the "treason" committed
by sons against their fathers' "hopes," Jefferson reflected on Short and made
one last attempt to reform his character.[35]

In 1819, Short learned, from a newspaper, that Jefferson was unwell. He wrote
to Jefferson expressing his "envy" that their mutual friend Portuguese botanist Correa would soon be visiting Monticello. Short, aged sixty, could not
make the journey. His "faculties of locomotion" had atrophied. Indulging his
growing indolence, Short had given up his daily exercise of riding. "I have so
far adopted the principles of Epicurus (who, after all I am inclined to believe
was the wisest of all the ancient Philosophers, as he is certainly the least understood) . . . as to consult my ease towards the attainment of happiness in
this poor world." "From habitual indulgence I have come to consider repose
as the summum bonum," he added.[36]

Jefferson, recovering from an acute "stricture" of the liver, his legs so
swollen that he could hardly walk (though he claimed he could still ride),
responded with one final letter of instruction. If it was true that Short was
"indulging indolence" then "I take the liberty of observing that you are
not a true disciple of our master Epicurus." "Your love of repose," Jefferson
warned, "will lead . . . to a suspension of healthy exercise, a relaxation of
mind, an indifference to every thing around you, and finally to a debility of
body and hebetude of mind." The well-regulated indulgences of Epicurus
would thereby become unobtainable. Fortitude, Jefferson reminded Short,
was one of Epicurus's four cardinal virtues. Difficulties should be met and

surmounted. Jefferson was writing at the conclusion of a year that had seen Monticello partially destroyed by fire, the beginnings of his irreversible descent into catastrophic indebtedness, and the prospect of the United States of America tearing itself apart over slavery. Writing as much to himself as to Short, Jefferson expanded his thoughts on Epicurus to take in the manner in which he might "rescue" the "true" teachings of Jesus from sectarians. In the process, he produced a summation of his rationalism. For Short himself the injunction was clear, "Weigh this matter well, brace yourself up . . . and come and see the finest portion of your country which, if you have not forgotten, you still do not know, because it is no longer the same as when you knew it."[37]

Short was delighted and, for once, appropriately grateful to receive Jefferson's letter. He could not sufficiently thank Jefferson for his "penetrating and able research into the whole system of Epicurus." He announced an intention to make it his "vade mecum." At the same time Short pressed Jefferson for a copy of his syllabus of the morals of Jesus. "I have long intended to commence the serious perusal and examination of both the old and the new testament," Short announced. "Few have remained so ignorant of them [for] so long as I have done. The syllabus of which you speak would be a torch to guide me in this labyrinth and would make me more willing to enter it." Jefferson eventually allowed his granddaughter, Ellen Wayles Randolph, to make a copy of the syllabus, which he sent to Short, who treasured it and vowed to keep it from critical eyes.[38]

For one last time Short presented himself humbly to Jefferson as a pupil seeking instruction. "My endeavour has been from the time of my earliest recollection to do what was right, or what appeared to me to be so," he told Jefferson. Short "certainly should have felt uneasy," in his passage through life, "if I had acted otherwise." Given that Jefferson had recently received Short's confession that he knew little of the Bible or Epicurus, Jefferson might have read a thread of dawning self-awareness in those letters in which Short puzzled away at the question of why men followed a morally correct path. Here Short referenced the factors that would, in Jefferson's eyes, have explained his failure to internalize a moral compass. Chief among them were the facts that Short had never married and never fathered children. On his return to the United States Short had justified his decision to make Philadelphia his "headquarters" on the grounds that "a city is necessary to a single man." He enjoyed the visit of Jefferson's granddaughter Ellen Wayles Randolph to Philadelphia and was struck by her likeness to her mother. He wished he "had a house with a Lady in it, in which I could have received and entertained and lodged Miss Randolph," Short reflected. Yet it was "doubtful whether I shall ever possess such a house" and, therefore, the "natural" pleasure of receiving any and all of Jefferson's family in Philadelphia was denied him.[39]

Jefferson hoped his "academical village" would furnish "the selected society of a great city separated from the dissipations and levities of its ephemeral insects." If Jefferson considered Short an archetype of the "ephemeral insect," Short considered networking a vital and valuable intellectual activity. He was proud of his membership in the American Philosophical Society, proud that he could present it with the bust of Condorcet from La Roche-Guyon, proud to furnish visiting Frenchmen with introductions in the city and beyond. For all his professed intention to make a serious study of the system of Epicurus or the morals of Jesus, Short derived as much if not more pleasure from being among the first Americans to read Madame de Staël's history of the French Revolution, particularly since he had known the author in Paris. So had Jefferson, and Short urged him to revise the opinion he had formed of her forty years earlier. For his part Short was prepared to admit that he had been mistaken to assume that the rallying cry "*la patrie* in danger" heard in 1792 had appealed solely to grog shop patriots in both France and the United States. (Jefferson in reply offered no revision of his previous views, unflinchingly restating the principle that the people would always support their nation over their monarchs.) Daniel Webster, who visited Monticello in 1824, noted, as did other visitors, the excellence of Jefferson's French wines and his fondness for reflecting on the years he had spent in Paris. Short was well placed to keep Jefferson up to date with news of mutual acquaintances from those years, as well as reflections on the events they had witnessed, and Jefferson derived pleasure from this aspect of their continuing relationship.[40]

Yet Jefferson couldn't help but have noticed the development of an increasingly unpleasant side to Short's character. Short's dislike of popular democracy and his disdain for the actions of elected assemblies peopled by "per diem" hacks had hardened beyond correction. A resident of Philadelphia, he stayed indoors every July 4 to avoid the parades and "bustle." In a letter written, appropriately enough, on that holiday, he complained of the "miserable, filthy and pestilential people" found crowding the Philadelphia's mayor's office. Meanwhile the lofty self-regard Short developed in the years surrounding his second sojourn in Europe was a factor preventing him from joining Madison and Monroe as members of the community centered on Monticello.[41]

Short made a series of catty remarks to Jefferson about both Madison and Monroe, thereby belying his suggestion that he was their equal as well as placing Jefferson in an awkward situation. Madison had irritated Short on his first return to the United States by contradicting Short's personal testimony about the true character of the French Directory. Short told Jefferson that he could not help smiling—in another account, sneering—at the simplicity and ignorance Madison displayed. In consequence, Madison "knit his brow and never again interrogated me as to France." Jefferson attempted to build bridges, urging Short on his final return to the United States following the collapse of the mission to Russia to offer Madison an appraisal of the latest situation in France. He offered to convey his thoughts to Madison personally if Short did not wish to meet the President. Short refused, although, as the War of 1812 drew to a close, he rejoiced that Providence had gifted Madison a victory. "I congratulate him on his happy escape, because we are saved with him." Monroe's offense, in Short's eyes, was a craving for "idolatory." Still, when Monroe assumed the presidency in 1816, Short reflected for Jefferson's benefit "he has had a hard apprenticeship" and that "must have matured his judgment—his heart was always good." Short feared "embarrassment" were he to visit Monticello since he had pledged never to see either Madison or Monroe again. In Short's eyes, both men had attained their presidencies "by means of those jeux . . . so often exhibited in elective Republics." Short admitted that "They may . . . laugh at my unfavourable disposition towards them . . . if they knew it." Still their "unexpected success" caused Short "melancholy." Jealousy was nearer the mark. Nonetheless, Jefferson continued his attempts to smooth relations between the three men and once again invited Short to Monticello in handsome terms: "come now, come then, or come when you please."[42]

———

Short paid a final visit to Monticello in September 1824. Far from occasioning a reconciliation this visit marked the beginning of a final separation. Following his visit Short can have been in no doubt that Jefferson's health was frail and that maintaining correspondence was a burden. Still, in a reversal of their situation in the winter of 1792, it was Short's turn to consider whether, knowing what he knew of Jefferson's situation, it was better to let some sleeping dogs lie. Back in Philadelphia, perhaps continuing a disagreement initiated during his visit, Short reasserted that Federalists had never been in essence monarchists, had certainly never sought to reimpose monarchy, and had never posed any threat, even of secession, after 1800. In a twelve-hundred-word letter that must have occasioned an enormous physical effort, Jefferson refuted Short point by point, claiming personal knowledge of monarchical statements made by Hamilton at his own dining table while Short was still in France. Short refused to back down. "I was in habits of great intimacy with Hamilton," he told Jefferson, referencing presumably his visit to Hamilton in July 1804. "I can truly say in all our conversations of the freest and easiest kind in a company where he was always the most unburthened, I never heard a word that would have led me to suppose that he thought a monarchy practicable or desirable in the US." Short had specifically questioned Hamilton about his belief that the President and Senate should serve for life, and Short was satisfied that it was without any view to establishing monarchy in the United States. "I should more think of blaming a man for differing from me in his opinions of government, than in his opinion of religion," Short concluded, pointedly leaving open the question of whether he was talking of Hamilton or Jefferson. Jefferson countered by sending Short an essay on the early history of parties that would set him straight. Short dismissed this, adding that James Madison's career illustrated the fact that politicians rarely maintained consistent positions. Jefferson was forced to let the matter drop.[43]

Short's defense of New England Federalists might have triggered incandescent rage of the kind Jefferson directed around the same time toward John Quincy Adams's program of internal improvement. Adams's attempt to "consolidate" federal power at the expense of states' rights was, so Jefferson assured William Branch Giles in December 1825, the next chapter in the Federalists' "book of history." It was an attempt driven by "younger recruits, who having nothing in them of the feelings or principles of '76 now look to a single and splendid government of an Aristocracy, founded on banking institutions and monied in corporations under the guise and cloak of their favored branches of manufactures, commerce and navigation, riding and ruling over the plundered ploughman and beggared yeomanry" to secure monarchy. He did not include Short among these "recruits," though Short's views were at odds with his own. In 1826, Short decried the "states rights mania" raging in Virginia "where such influential and in other respects such sound minds are infected and seem to give authority for the disease." He spared Jefferson this opinion at least.[44]

The crisis in Jefferson's financial affairs cannot have escaped Short's notice, although, during his final visit to Monticello, Jefferson did not offer Short a direct description or a plea for assistance. As a wealthy man who still harbored a sentimental affection to Jefferson's family, Short must have considered whether and how he might help its beggared head. The Marquis de Lafayette's indebtedness became a proxy for Short to discuss Jefferson's. In the spring of 1824, as plans for Lafayette to visit the United States began to take shape, Short asked Jefferson to lobby Congress to vote the enormous sum of $50,000 to Lafayette. Concerned that Lafayette's crippling debts might prevent him from traveling Short passed on to Jefferson what he admitted were mere rumors that Congress would not only "pay off" the Marquis but also grant him an honorary rank in the US Army. Short failed to connect his appreciation of Lafayette's plight to Jefferson's. Lafayette "has certainly paid his full quota of misfortune in pursuit of the liberty of his country. . . . He has certainly borne enough and more than enough in the hopeless task of procuring liberty" for France and the French. Jefferson, by implication, was a victim of his own success. Short did not accompany Lafayette on his trip to Monticello in early 1825.[45]

In his final letter to Jefferson, Short described how he had assisted Thomas Jefferson Randolph in organizing a public meeting held in Philadelphia to raise funds to relieve the family's indebtedness. Following the lead of other northern cities Philadelphia eventually raised $5,000 on Jefferson's behalf, although ironically the success of these efforts hastened the Virginia legislature's cancellation of a state-sponsored lottery designed to relieve Jefferson's crippling indebtedness. Short followed closely the political battle within Virginia over whether and how to assist Jefferson and his family and prevent the forced sale of Monticello. He was well aware of the objections that held up the passage of a bill authorizing a lottery: that lotteries were immoral, that "timid" friends of Jefferson feared his posthumous reputation would be ruined by public assistance, that legislators were disinclined to extend recognition of Jefferson's service to the protection of his family. Professing a reluctance to write in recognition that the topic was painful, Short was still determined to draw a political moral from his friend's situation. He did so as Jefferson had done in the "Adam and Eve" letter of 1793, without regard to his friend's emotional well-being. Since Short had never had confidence in the gratitude of republics he was not surprised by the legislature's parsimony. "In all cases of this kind our Republican gentlemen bring forward and place in the front rank what they call Principle," Short told Jefferson, "let it be a question of adding a few dollars to their own <u>per diem</u> and observe how they employ Principle then."[46]

There would be no happy ending in which the wealthy Short eased Jefferson's final days. Instead, Jefferson went to his grave expressing something like hatred for the values Short espoused while Short professed a patronizing pity for the man who had helped him so much. As Jefferson's grandson Thomas Jefferson Randolph remarked, "how wretched are those possessing large property and unfortunate in the vices and ingratitude of their children." In these final years, Short was, like King Lear's daughter Goneril, sharper than a serpent's tooth.[47]

Some weeks after Jefferson's death Short asked John Hartwell Cocke to imagine "what must have been" Jefferson's "reflexions when he saw the manner . . . in which the virtuous and enlightened representatives of the people (for the people, who are all wise, never choose other than virtuous and good men to represent them) . . . these true Republicans . . . received his petition" to be granted a lottery. In this letter, and those written to the declining Jefferson, Short suggested the depths of his suppressed desire to take Jefferson by the shoulders and shake him until he admitted that the world he had created was incapable of delivering the world he wished for. Equally, Short recognized the impossibility of securing from Jefferson a bed-ridden conversion to his view of politics and politicians. "It was most difficult to make him change an opinion," Short told Cocke in the tones of someone who had tried. He summarized the opinion he most wished he could have changed. "It has always been demonstrated to my mind that Mr. J's greatest illusions in politics have proceeded from a most amiable error on his part; having too favourable an opinion of the animal called Man, who in mass in my opinion forms only a many-headed monster." Jefferson had emerged from France with his belief in the existence and potential of democracy intact, Short had not.[48]

Short was sixty-seven when Jefferson died, a member of a successor generation that had itself been supplanted. He possessed the materialistic, capitalist mentality of new, younger democrats and yet he denounced their political culture because he, like the titans of the preceding generation, still dreamed of somehow imparting virtue and wisdom to the nation through the actions of disinterested men such as himself. If it had been put to Short that his views were anti-democratic and elitist he would have replied that they were formed by his experience of life outside the United States, outside a profession, and, above all, outside politics. Throughout his life Short presented these factors as testimonies to a meritorious independence and to a superior discernment born of it. Yet if even Alexander Hamilton, the ultimate accomplished outsider, could conclude of the early republic "this American world was not made for me," then what hope of finding influence in the democracy Jefferson had created could a committed but inconsequential contrarian such as Short possess? Congressman Samuel Taggart's charge that he was a mere Frenchman hurt. Jefferson's shrewd suspicion that Short had failed to fashion from his experiences any sort of moral compass, let alone one attuned to American republican sensibilities, hurt more—because it was true. Try as he might to apply himself to the teachings of Epicurus, or Jesus, or even to Jefferson's letters, Short possessed a soul that remained in suspended animation. He was the prodigal who never returned.[49]

Epilogue

JEFFERSON'S HOPES, AND SHORT'S FEARS

FOR ALL HIS personal knowledge of Jefferson and the letters he retained, for all that he claimed to "pass and repass" in his mind Jefferson's "way of thinking," William Short actively rejected crucial components of Jefferson's personal advice and political wisdom while claiming, implausibly to a modern eye, to venerate his friend and father's counsel. He did not relocate to Virginia, marry, father children, or seek elective office to serve his country. He questioned Jefferson's embrace of popular democracy. He seldom recognized Jefferson's personal generosity toward him or the intellectual generosity of Jefferson's approach to the generations growing up in the shadow of the Founders. As one who had known Jefferson longer and in a greater variety of contexts than all but a handful of men alive, and as the recipient of direct practical expressions of Jefferson's thought, Short was well-equipped to offer a public interpretation of Jefferson's worldview. When Jefferson brushed aside Short's offer to write an authorized biography, Short did not proceed with an unauthorized appraisal of the Jefferson he had known. Following Jefferson's death Short did not offer himself as a public memorialist or interpreter. By describing Jefferson, in a rare private posthumous assessment, as a "visionary" undone by his "amiable" conviction in the goodness of mankind, he ducked critical engagement with Jefferson's beliefs. Short did not identify himself in thought, deed, or public utterance as in any meaningful sense a "Jeffersonian."[1]

Short's disinclination to associate himself with Jefferson's way of thinking was rooted in his personality, as amplified through its interaction with Jefferson's. Since an inner Short is as hard to recover as an inner Jefferson, specific personal questions, such as why Short never acted on Jefferson's

Heir through Hope. Peter Thompson, Oxford University Press. © Peter Thompson 2023.
DOI: 10.1093/oso/9780197546833.003.0009

admonitions to marry and settle down to family life, are hard to answer definitively. However, larger questions can be addressed. Many other members of Short's generation, and its successors, apparently failed to recognize the reasoning behind Jefferson's system of thought and its inherent generosity, or, believing they understood Jefferson all too well, actively rejected his beliefs. Despite Jefferson's place within the national consciousness of the early republic, a Jeffersonian way of thinking failed to fully root itself in the nation's mind, not just in Short's. Placing the Jefferson–Short relationship within the context of a wider public construction of Jefferson's legacy helps reveal its significance and speaks to the wider politics of generational succession in the early republic.

How much of Jefferson's thought, much of it worked out in private, did William Short, Jefferson's peers, or members of successor generations actually know, let alone understand? Modern historians, with the privilege of access to the entirety of Jefferson's surviving papers, are in a position to present Jefferson's way of thinking as a series of interlocking propositions forming a more or less coherent whole, albeit one Jefferson constantly recalibrated. Short was not privy to correspondence with John Adams, James Madison, and countless others in which Jefferson tested and retested his core beliefs. Even a figure like Adams could not know the full nature and extent of Jefferson's private speculations with other correspondents. When, occasionally, contemporaries accused Jefferson of being two-faced, their complaints highlighted the problem that what they thought they knew about Jefferson's thinking was based on incomplete knowledge.

Short's peers were even less well placed to come to terms with the deeper thoughts Jefferson submerged beneath his privacy. The scores of visitors who descended on Jefferson during his retirement in search of insight into the man and his ideas generally came away well-dined but with few conclusions apart from that he was polite, generous, disciplined—and somehow set apart from them. Many visitors to Monticello believed they could trace in Jefferson's character and thought the influence of the years their host had spent abroad. New England bookseller Samuel Whitcomb, who visited Jefferson in 1824, came away convinced that his host talked like a Frenchman, shrugging his shoulders and speaking rapidly on varying subjects. Another New Englander, George Ticknor, commented more charitably on Jefferson's love of paradox, discursive manner, and frequent references to French history when in conversation. When invited to inspect their host's library, guests noted the prevalence and diversity of foreign-language texts. Most commonly guests referenced their host's fine cellar of French wine, his preferences in the manner of seating dinner guests, and the excellence of the often unfamiliar European dishes they were offered in order to describe and explain their host's distinctiveness. Yet visitors and strangers alike wanted to bridge the distance between Jefferson and themselves. They, like Short, sought to understand Jefferson's core beliefs. In later life, Jefferson received requests, from Short among others, to speak out plainly from a Founder's perspective on important issues of the day. Occasionally Jefferson responded by authorizing correspondents to make public sentiments he had expressed in private letters. Generally, scarred by the partisanship of the 1790s and bruised during his two presidential terms, Jefferson in retirement preferred to keep his thoughts on politics and morality private. Although admirers and detractors believed they could define in part or in whole the essence of Jefferson's thought, Jefferson did little to assist them.[2]

The wider public construction of a Jeffersonian legacy was rooted in public documents associated with him—and in particular the Declaration of Independence. An important aspect of the United States' post-revolutionary settlement, and the cornerstone of attempts to transmit that settlement across generational lines, was the self-conscious creation of a national "history culture" offering an approved understanding of the American Revolution. In an early example of the historicizing of national identity, Ezra Stiles praised Jefferson in 1783 for having "poured the soul of the continent" into the Declaration of Independence. The Declaration took on a sacral quality partly because Jefferson, by not publicly claiming it as his own unaided work (although acting behind the scenes to quash rival claims to primary authorship), enabled Americans to read it as a document transcending distinctions of party or section. During Jefferson's long retirement, the Declaration became central to the story the nation was learning to tell about itself. Celebrations of America's rising glory, or jeremiads on its future based around well-worn, formulaic fears of corruption were reinvigorated by references to the Declaration as the true north of the nation's moral compass.[3]

This process led to misgivings even on the part of some of its signatories. Writing to John Adams in 1808, sixty-three-year-old Benjamin Rush wished he could remove his signature from the Declaration. He believed it had encouraged the unprincipled licentiousness of a "be-dollared nation." The American people no longer possessed sufficient morality to properly judge the issues of the day—in this case the propriety of American neutrality or the merits of the Embargo. Rush was responding to Adam's recent lament that once "we loved Liberty better than money" but now Americans loved money better than liberty, a word that had come to signify, said Adams, nothing but

"electioneering tricks and libels." Yet Adams told Rush that he could not renounce the Declaration without renouncing "virtue itself." Americans might
bemoan the dilution of a "spirit of '76" but, thanks in large measure to public
oratory associated with the annual celebration of July 4, the idea of disowning
the crowning expression of that spirit became very nearly unthinkable. The
Declaration of Independence embedded itself in the national consciousness
as a foundational text. Years after Jefferson's death, Abraham Lincoln, lacking
any personal knowledge of the great man or access to his private correspondence, declared that the Declaration "contemplated the progressive improvement of the condition of all men everywhere." He claimed "I have never had
a feeling politically that did not spring from the sentiments embodied in the
Declaration of Independence."[4]

Both the rigor with which Jefferson applied himself to the task of
contemplating how the progressive improvement of mankind might be
achieved and his dissatisfaction with simplistic public oratory celebrating
the passing of a torch of liberty are striking. He was proud of his authorship of the Declaration of Independence and yet, late in life, he, almost
alone among the founding generation, came close to stating its irrele-
vance to the resolution of contemporary problems. In 1825, Jefferson told
Henry Lee that he and his peers had not set out at the nation's birth to
discover, justify, or disseminate new principles of government. Instead they
had intended the Declaration of Independence to express the state of the
American mind as it had existed in the year it was written. The Founders'
successors could not expect to fully recapture that mental moment, nor
should they try.

Jefferson sensed that the forces driving the search for an authorized
American history and an authoritative founding text—chiefly the need to
mask Americans' strong state or sectional attachments and the perceived
weakness of federal or national identity—risked undermining the Founders'
achievements. If read one way the Declaration offered a blueprint for perpetual revolution. The only function of a just government was to protect
certain inalienable rights. When "a people," a subsequent generation or perhaps an individual state, decided that their government was not protecting
their rights, then they had a duty to dissolve that government and institute
another of their own choosing. Prudence dictated that fundamental reform would not be undertaken lightly, but no justifiable law could prevent
it. The implications of such a reading, adopted during Jefferson's lifetime
by advocates of states' rights and black emancipation, were truly millennial,
and, during the Missouri Crisis of 1819, Jefferson denounced such exegesis as

treason. Yet, having expressed his fear that younger generations might undo their elders' work, Jefferson called upon them to complete it.[5]

Jefferson's definition of the task facing America's younger generations was shaped by conclusions drawn from his earlier assessment of the French Revolution and vehemently expressed even in later life. For many of Jefferson's contemporaries around the Atlantic world the history of the French Revolution—seemingly consisting of a journey from violent anarchy, to dictatorship, and ultimately a reversion to counter-revolutionary monarchical government—served as a terrible warning. It encouraged an uncritical reading of America's destiny by picturing the United States as an exceptional nation providentially isolated from Old World corruption. In an exchange with John Adams in 1823, Jefferson drew on experiences in France he now shared with just a handful of other living Americans to apply a notably generous and permissive moral to America's situation. Like his reading of the Declaration of Independence, it was radically at odds with America's "history culture." Adams had suggested that the French Revolution and its aftermath proved that idealism should play no part in national development. In response, Jefferson conceded that a first effort to establish self-government in France had been defeated by Robespierre, a second by Bonaparte, and a third by Louis XVIII. He accepted that Frenchmen could expect some further years of desolation and that rivers of blood might yet flow in their country. Nevertheless Jefferson defiantly insisted that a fourth, a fifth, or even a sixth French generation would surely realize the dreams of their revolutionary forefathers by establishing a functioning democracy capable of protecting the rights of man. This led him to offer Adams a powerful conclusion aimed at Americans—"the generation which commences a revolution rarely compleats it."[6]

Jefferson and his dwindling band of peers were naturally loathe to conclude that their generation had failed to achieve that which it had set out to do when they declared independence. They were also prone to doubt that successor generations might improve upon their work, let alone complete it, unless, that is, they were given specific guidance as to the essential character of the American Revolution. But since, unlike France, the United States at the moment of its creation already possessed in colonial assemblies and national congresses institutions of representative government, what was the American Revolution's animating spirit? If the Founders could not agree on an answer to this question, how might their successors recognize what more needed to be done? Believing that the work of identifying, passively venerating, or willfully appropriating foundational documents was futile and potentially

dangerous, Jefferson sidestepped definitional questions in favor of an evoca-
tion of progress achieved through a rigorous program of self-improvement. In
doing so, he combined political optimism and personal generosity. America's
revolution was not complete; there was a better world to be achieved and
work for the younger generation to do. On balance, Jefferson trusted them to
do right by their elders.

The personalized advice Jefferson gave Short, along with other younger
men, and the institutional realization of his desire to "develop the reasoning
faculties of our youth" in the intellectual design of the University of Virginia,
reflected Jefferson's cautious optimism. Since improvement lay within the
grasp of the "animal called man," younger generations had a duty to attend
to their moral development. They could and should identify, by their own
efforts, their role in furthering America's republican experiment. These
assumptions lay at the core of Jeffersonianism, and he was confident that
younger generations could acquire this aspect of his "way of thinking." Yet
Jefferson's fears—that younger generations would undo their elders' work—
and his hopes—that younger men might complete their revolution—clashed
in the minds of those who understood them, not least William Short.[7]

We might sympathize with Short's disinclination to take up the challenge
Jefferson laid down for him and his peers. Jefferson framed the task facing
them in ways that presumed a preexisting moral fiber and sense of duty. As experienced by men who, like Short, possessed less self-discipline than Jefferson,
his advice seemingly offered a regimen of correction, not a road to freedom.
He had asked Short to believe that the murder of mutual friends was justified
and should be forgiven. He had told Short that he could not advance his career and that the years Short had spent abroad had irreparably damaged his
standing at home. He had asked him to relocate to a mediocre plantation
that lacked even a house to stay in. Short was a wealthy man who in maturity
could afford to ignore Jefferson while paying lip service to his wisdom. Many
Americans ducked the inherent challenges of Jefferson's core beliefs with
scarcely a thought. To Jefferson's dismay students at the University of Virginia
behaved as though their presence in his "academical village" provided little
more than an opportunity to confirm unearned entitlement. Individuals like
John Adams's son John Quincy, who were prepared to pay more than rhetorical deference to the wisdom of the Founders by self-consciously working
through their perceived political legacy whatever the personal cost, were few
and far between.[8]

However, William Short is an example of a man who knew enough of
Jefferson's thinking to actively choose to reject the greater part of it and, at the

same time, cast his relationship to the revolutionary generation in largely negative terms. In the process, he established his own distance from the nation's
culture, and, like Jefferson, his distance from that culture was ultimately
grounded in his experience of living in revolutionary Europe.

In retirement, Jefferson had expressed an "earnest wish . . . to see the republican element of popular control pushed to the maximum to its practicable exercise" since the "full experiment" of a "democratical government"
was "and is still reserved for us." Abraham Lincoln later distilled this thought
in his Gettysburg Address, identifying popular democracy—government
of the people, by the people, for the people—as the central achievement of
America's revolution. If this was the legacy of America's Revolution in general
and Jefferson's thinking in particular, then Short wanted no part of it. He
loathed the political culture of participatory democracy. He would rather
stay indoors on July 4 than listen to populist celebrations of the values of the
Founders.[9]

Short's diatribes against popular democracy, often prompted by the
perceived threat to his financial assets posed by state and federal lawmakers,
might be taken as proof that his judgment had been corrupted by commerce.
If ever a man was, to use Benjamin Rush's term, "be-dollared," it was William
Short. Devoting himself to the careful management of his stocks and bonds,
making judicious land speculations, and benefiting from Jefferson's superin-
tendence of his affairs as well as the substantial loan made to him by Rosalie
de La Rochefoucauld, Short became a self-described millionaire and one of
the wealthiest men in Philadelphia. Yet Short's understanding of the threat
to his property posed by majoritarian democracy was grounded in personal
experiences shared with Jefferson but uncommon among his peers. Short lived
long enough to be among the last Americans to have seen at close hand the
rule of law, and with it the security of life, liberty, and property, overthrown in
France by revolutionary "furies." It could happen again, and it could happen in
the United States. He had shared his concerns with Jefferson, and his fears continued to influence him after Jefferson's death. Although he voted for Andrew
Jackson in 1828, he had come to believe that he was living in the shadow of a
"volcano" whose visible cone lay in celebrations of the common man. "Man,
proud vain man, has from all time been led by the noses, by some cabalistic
words—the present words with us are *Old Hickery*," Short concluded in 1832.
An eruption of deeper-lying forces could be expected. "God knows where it
will all end," he wrote, "we poor mortals only know that we must submit."[10]

Short's political outlook, as well as his disinclination to accept Jefferson's,
speaks to a debate regarding the character of American democracy

FIGURE E.1 William Short, engraving by J. Sartain, after a portrait by John Neagle, undated. Simon Gratz Autograph Collection [0250A], Case 2, Box 10, Historical Society of Pennsylvania, Philadelphia. Reproduced with permission from the Historical Society of Pennsylvania.

reinvigorated by Gordon Wood thirty years ago. In *The Radicalism of the American Revolution*, Wood characterized the popular democracy of the early national period as a suboptimal outcome. "Instead of creating a new order of benevolence and selflessness, enlightened republicanism" bred "social competitiveness and individualism." White males had taken too seriously the belief that they were free and equal with every right to pursue their happiness however they saw fit. New generations of Americans, Wood argued, were consequently prone to believe that America would discover its greatness by creating a prosperous free society belonging to obscure people with workaday concerns who pursued happiness by making money and getting ahead. "No doubt," Wood concluded, "the cost Americans paid for this democracy was high." Wood cited "vulgarity," "materialism," "rootlessness," and "anti-intellectualism." Influential critics of Wood's argument have contested its conclusion that democracy, then and now, brings together "a lot of elbowing competitors in a capitalist economy" without creating "participants in a public debate about what is natural, what is just, and what is true," as historian Joyce Appleby puts it. But the eloquent expressions of doubt, fear, even hatred of democracy offered in later life by Short and, very occasionally by Jefferson himself, illustrate the sense of aspirations forged in a transatlantic "Age of Revolution" and dashed in the American republic that grew out of it that Wood's argument draws upon. America's political culture and not the workings of its capitalist economy had, so Short's jeremiads assumed, set in motion a race to the bottom that made the task of completing America's revolution impossible and even irrelevant. There was little of political value to transmit across generational lines, that which was being transmitted meant things could only get worse, and Jefferson's optimism was misplaced.[11]

Short's active avoidance of the greater task of completing a revolution was accompanied by a personal, passive conviction that rigorous self-improvement was beyond him. Short in his maturity struck his contemporaries much as Short in his twenties had struck Jefferson. He remained rootless. After contemplating a return to France he finally adopted Philadelphia as his permanent place of residence, yet he flitted between dwellings, initially living in a hotel, later buying and selling properties, sometimes boarding with French landladies in the city capable of accommodating his preferences in housekeeping. Lodging with a French emigré he described as "the best educated woman I know" and charmed by her musically accomplished sixteen-year-old daughter, the elderly Short replicated the attempts at intrusive family management he had applied to the Royer family in the 1780s.

In his mid-fifties, Short presented acquaintances in Philadelphia with evidence of an immature approach to women and relationships of the sort that had earlier led Countess Castiglione in Paris to pity "poor in love Mr. Short." Never married, Short remained an eligible, if ageing, bachelor who enjoyed female attention but whose affairs with women risked making him an "oddity" of a type the author of a light-hearted piece in the Philadelphia journal

Lady's Book described in 1839. The author criticized confirmed bachelors as selfish and overly fastidious. Ending on a humorous note, the piece suggested levying an ad valorem tax on old bachelors before discounting the idea on the grounds that old bachelors had no value. Jefferson occasionally faced challenging questions concerning his disinclination to remarry. But Jefferson was a widower. Short might have explained or defended his unmarried status in Philadelphia or further afield by reference to a failed love affair with Rosalie de La Rochefoucauld, whose miniature he carried in his pocketbook until his death. He did not. He reflected ruefully that lacking a wife or a settled abode he had not been able to entertain Jefferson's granddaughter Ellen Wayles Randolph during her visit to Philadelphia in the manner he would have wished, but he had actively chosen his lifestyle. He seldom discussed in depth his inability to choose a wife and on just two occasions alluded to a consequence of his bachelor status: that he never fathered an acknowledged child.[12]

The terms in which Short justified his desire to write a biography of Jefferson glancingly suggested self-awareness. He thought that a memoir of Jefferson's life "might be invaluable to our country (I am sorry I cannot say to our posterity)." Jefferson made no comment on this implied equivalency and Short never directly raised the issue of his own childless status with Jefferson again. Short's correspondence with his family was more revealing. It laid bare debilitating levels of self-doubt behind a veneer of self-regard.[13]

William enjoyed painting his brother Peyton as the black sheep of the family. When Peyton lost most of his estate in an ill-fated land speculation William stepped in to furnish Peyton's son, John Cleves Short with enough money to allow him to complete his studies at Princeton. Yet William felt that, in light of Peyton's failure, he should say something more. He offered Peyton's sons the benefit of his own experience in a series of pompous reflections: "If I could make you see things and estimate them as I do it would be a great relief to your feelings—for you would then see that the inheriting [of] a fortune is much less desirable than acquiring it oneself." The fable of the tortoise and the hare recurred in his advice on how a fortune might be acquired. His nephews should shut their ears, as he claimed he had, to the "siren song" of get-rich-quick land speculations. Offering these admonitions led Short to ruminate "knowingly and feelingly" on the "fickleness" of the entire Short family and its inability, his own included, to persevere with anything. He considered this "family disorder" to be in his blood. In a letter written to John in 1836, he offered an extraordinary self-revelation. "You like myself are so fortunate as to be without the cares of [family]," the uncle told his nephew. "After my observation of the cause of things in this world I really think it fortunate for me at least, with my disposition, to be without them."[14]

To the extent that his own character traits were inherited rather than acquired William Short could be forgiven—and he seemingly did forgive himself—for his inability to follow Jefferson's advice. He just didn't have it in him. He recognized Jefferson's faith in man's innate moral rectitude, and, while he generally characterized that faith in dismissive terms, he was loathe to renounce the Jeffersonian project in its entirety. "If we could look forward with any hope to universal education and universal virtue, we might then look forward to the political millennium," he wrote in one of his last letters to Jefferson. Deep down Short retained a wish to be reborn as a better, more complete individual. In this at least, he was representative of the thousands of men and women across the nation who found spiritual fulfillment in religious revivals or moral uplift through campaigns for social reform.[15]

Jefferson's moral philosophy was its most pointed and political when addressed to young men and to Virginians in particular. These were his heirs. He expected to be understood by the likes of William Short, although his confidence must have been dented by the passage of time. He used the phrase "adoptive son" for Short alone. It reflected Jefferson's affection for the younger man but it was accompanied by a statement of purpose. Short had placed himself under Jefferson's direction. Setting the amiable Mr. Short straight was a project to which Jefferson was prepared to commit for the long haul. He remained invested in Short's future to the end of his days.

Short, in his own way, projected himself as forcefully as Jefferson. Overriding his inner doubt and insecurities he spent much of his life constructing and burnishing the self-image of a talented but overlooked outsider whose worth set him apart from social or political conformity. Ignoring Jefferson's advice and Rosalie de La Rochefoucauld's entreaties were almost necessary actions for a man who liked to project himself as a bachelor by choice. Although he had once been flattered by Alexander Hamilton's regard for him, Short was never inclined to search for a patron more willing than Jefferson to advance a career in public service since he regarded himself as being of no party and therefore above the wheeling and dealing of political preferment. Jefferson's earlier role in easing him out of formal diplomatic employment was ultimately of less importance to Short than Jefferson's later willingness to use executive power to appoint him a presidential envoy or to manage the affairs of Indian Camp. Jefferson's continuing regard was the manifestation of a special destiny, seemingly confirmed by great wealth, which Short attributed to his unique personality and not to Jefferson's generosity. Short's inclination to take his relationship with Jefferson more or less for granted while ignoring his advice complemented Jefferson's confidence that, through the force of his own personality, he could create and maintain friendships that transcended the "slipperiness of human reason."[16]

Both Jefferson and Short lived to advanced ages increasingly uncomfortable with the nation taking shape around them. Jefferson trembled for his country when he reflected that God was just and that his justice could not sleep for ever. But on the issue that gave rise to these thoughts, the institution of slavery, Jefferson could not bring himself to act. Short was similarly irresolute in areas of central concern to him. He believed marriage to be a harness while often bemoaning his solitary status. He believed his "disposition" rendered him unfit for family life and yet the idea of affective flesh and blood familial bonds was as important for Short as it was for Jefferson. Short sought a place in Jefferson's family circle, imposed himself on the Royer family, and had been offered membership through marriage of the La Rochefoucauld family; yet he failed to join any of them. He experienced family through fear and failure and, in the process, became that most modern of characters, the atomized individual, striking out on his own yet believing himself at the mercy of fate. If Short had the sensibility of an emergent modern age, Jefferson was a creature of the Enlightenment. As Henry Adams noted more than a century ago Jefferson believed in the manner of an Enlightenment thinker that moral progress could be achieved by challenging formal religious instruction or denominational faith. Received wisdom existed to be questioned, not passively accepted. Both men willfully changed their surroundings, moving from Virginia to France and back to the United States, remodeling houses, living in more than one location, and adopting unconventional personal lifestyles. Jefferson saw in such activity a process through which moral progress might be achieved. A change for the better in surroundings helped bring about a change for the better in the man. The restless William Short never swapped residence in Philadelphia for neighborliness in Albemarle County, and he never changed. His was a coming-of-age story lacking a final chapter. Despite his hopes Jefferson went to his grave without an heir and Short without a father.[17]

Notes

ABBREVIATIONS

APS   American Philosophical Society
Autobiography   *The Autobiography of Thomas Jefferson, 1743–1790*, ed. Paul Leicester
                    Ford. New Introduction by Michael Zuckerman (Philadelphia:
                    University of Pennsylvania Press, 2005)
Harsanyi *Lettres* Doina Pasca Harsanyi, ed., *Lettres de la duchesse de La Rochefoucauld
                    à William Short. Texte Inédit* (Paris: Mercure de France, 2001)
JHCP UVA   John Hartwell Cocke Papers, Special Collections, University of
                    Virginia
JQFL   *Jefferson Quotes and Family Letters* accessed via tjrs.monticello.org
LOC   Library of Congress
Monroe Papers   Daniel Preston and Marlena C. DeLong, eds., *The Papers of
                    James Monroe. Vol. 2 Selected Correspondence and Papers, 1776–
                    1794* (Westport, CT: Greenwood Press, for the James Monroe
                    Presidential Center, 2006)
PAHDE   *The Papers of Alexander Hamilton Digital Edition*, ed. Harold C.
                    Syrett (Charlottesville: University of Virginia Press, Rotunda, 2011)
PGWDEP   *The Papers of George Washington Digital Edition: Presidential Series*
                    (Charlottesville: University of Virginia Press, Rotunda, 2008)
Pinckney Papers   *The Papers of the Revolutionary Era Pinckney Statesmen of South
                    Carolina: A Digital Documentary Edition* (Charlottesville:
                    University of Virginia Press, Rotunda, 2019)
PJADE   *The Papers of John Adams Digital Edition* (Charlottesville:
                    University of Virginia Press, 2019)
PJMDE   *The Papers of James Madison Digital Edition,* J. C. A. Stagg, ed.
                    (Charlottesville: University of Virginia Press, Rotunda, 2010)

PTJDE   *The Papers of Thomas Jefferson Digital Edition,* ed. James P. McClure
             and J. Jefferson Looney (Charlottesville: University of Virginia
             Press, Rotunda, 2008–2022)

SHC UNC   Southern History Collection, Special Collections, University of
             North Carolina

TAPDE   *The Adams Papers Digital Edition,* ed. Sara Martin (Charlottesville:
             University of Virginia Press)

UVA   University of Virginia Special Collections

WPSP WM   William and Peyton Short Papers, Special Collections, College of
             William and Mary

INTRODUCTION

1. Jan Ellen Lewis, "The White Jeffersons," in Jan Ellen Lewis and Peter S.
   Onuf, eds., *Sally Hemings and Thomas Jefferson: History, Memory and Civic
   Culture* (Charlottesville: University of Virginia Press, 1999), 127–60, at 130;
   Annette Gordon-Reed, *The Hemingses of Monticello. An American Family*
   (New York: Norton, 2008). See also Sarah M. S. Pearsall, *Atlantic Families: Lives
   and Letters in the Later Eighteenth Century* (Oxford: Oxford University Press,
   2008); Sarah Maza, "Only Connect: Family Values in the Age of Sentiment,"
   Eighteenth-Century Studies, 30 (1997), 207–12, at 208. On patriarchy, see Lorri
   Glover, *Founders and Fathers: The Private Lives and Politics of the American
   Revolutionaries* (New Haven: Yale University Press, 2014), 6–35. William Byrd
   II to Charles Boyle, Earl of Orrery, July 5, 1726, in Marion Tinling, ed., *The
   Correspondence of the Three William Byrds of Westover, Virginia, 1684–1776*
   (Charlottesville: University of Virginia Press, 1977), 355. See also Michael
   Zuckerman, "The Family Life of William Byrd," *Perspectives in American History,*
   12 (1979), 253–311; Rhys Isaac, *Landon Carter's Uneasy Kingdom: Revolution and
   Rebellion on a Virginia Plantation* (New York: Oxford University Press, 2004). TJ
   to Angelica Schuyler Church, November 27, 1793, *PTJDE,* 27: 449–50, at 449. TJ
   to Edward Rutledge, November 30, 1795, *PTJDE,* 28: 541–2, at 541.

2. TJ to John Wayles Eppes, April 30 with postscript May 7, 1816, *PTJDE: Retirement
   Series,* [hereafter cited as *PTJDE: Retirement*] 9: 712–4, at 713. John Wayles Eppes
   to TJ, June 14, 1804, *PTJDE,* 43: 582–4, at 583; John Wayles Eppes to TJ, July 10,
   1809, *PTJDE: Retirement,* 336–8, at 337 and editorial notes. TJ to John Wayles
   Eppes, May 24, 1806, *Founders Online;* see also, TJ to John Wayles Eppes, May 28,
   1807. TJ to John Wayles Eppes, April 21, 1810, *PTJDE: Retirement,* 2: 340–1, at 341.
   TJ to John Wayles Eppes, April 30 with postscript May 7, 1816, *PTJDE: Retirement,*
   9: 712–4 at 713. TJ to John Wayles Eppes, July, 16, 1814, *PTJDE: Retirement,*
   7: 482–3, at 483.

3. TJ to Elbridge Gerry, June 11, 1812, *PTJDE: Retirement,* 5: 125–7, at 126. "Memoirs
   of Madison Hemings," rep. in Annette Gordon-Reed, *Thomas Jefferson and Sally*

Hemings: An American Controversy (Charlottesville: University of Virginia Press, 1997), 245–8, at 247.

4. Glover, *Founders and Fathers*, esp. 208. TJ to James Madison, September 6, 1789, *PTJDE*, 15: 392–7. A Bill for Establishing Religious Freedom and Epitaph [1826], in Merrill D. Peterson, ed., *Jefferson: Writings* (New York: Library of America, 1984), 346–8, 706. TJ to John Holmes, April 22, 1820, *PTJDE: Retirement*, 15: 550–1, at 550; see also TJ to Thomas Lomax, March 12, 1799, *PTJDE*, 31: 77–8.

5. Short was the nephew of Robert and Henry Skipwith. The Skipwith brothers were married to John Wayles's daughters Tabitha and Anne Wayles, respectively. See Gordon-Reed, *Hemingses of Monticello*, 159. Short to James Madison, August 1, 1787, *PJMDE: Congressional Series*, [hereafter cited as *PJMDE: Congressional*] 10: 121–23, at 123. TJ to Short, June 1, 1780, *PTJDE*, 15: [Supplementary Documents Down to the Year 1789], 586. Jefferson's Certification of William Short as an Attorney, September 30, 1781, *PTJDE*, 6: 122.

6. The editors of the Papers of Thomas Jefferson state that Short accompanied Jefferson's family on their flight from Monticello and was present during the subsequent stay at Poplar Forest, see Memorandum Book, 1781, *PTJDE: Second Series*, 512, n. 19 and entries made July 18, 20, 25, 26.

7. "The Flat Hat Club" *William and Mary Quarterly* [hereafter *WMQ*], 1 ser., 25 (January 1917), 161–4. "Original Records of Phi Beta Kappa," *WMQ*, 1 ser., 4 (April 1896), 213–41. TJ to John Harvie, January 14, 1760, *PTJDE*, 1: 3. For a description of Mount Valérien, see Marie Kimball, *Jefferson: The Scene of Europe 1784–1789* (New York: Coward-McCann, 1950), 120–1. G. S. Wilson, *Jefferson on Display: Attire, Etiquette, and the Art of Presentation* (Charlottesville: University of Virginia Press, 2018), 152, 227. TJ to Abigail Adams, September 25, 1785, *TAPDE: Adams Family Correspondence*, 6: 390–2, at 391.

8. TJ to Madison, September 30, 1781, *PTJDE*, 6:122. See also TJ to Thomas McKean, September 30, 1781, *PTJDE*, 6: 123; TJ to Richard Peters, September 30, 1781, *PTJDE*, 6: 124. TJ to Short, December 19, 1783, *PTJDE*, 6: 393; TJ to Short, March 1, 1784, *PTJDE*, 6: 569–70.

9. Short is the subject of one published biography, see George Green Shackelford, *Jefferson's Adoptive Son: The Life of William Short, 1759–1848* (Lexington: University of Kentucky Press, 1993). I correct Shackelford on several points of fact. I expand on his treatment in key areas, notably Short's relationship with Rosalie de La Rochefoucauld, the context in which Short became the recipient of Jefferson's letter justifying revolutionary terror, and Short's views on slavery. Examples of studies fusing the study of relationships with the examination of political thought include Jan Ellen Lewis, " 'The Blessings of Domestic Society': Thomas Jefferson's Family and the Transformation of American Politics," in Barry Bienstock, Annette Gordon-Reed, and Peter S. Onuf, eds., *Family, Slavery, and Love in the Early American Republic: The Essays of Jan Ellen Lewis* (Chapel Hill: University of North Carolina Press and Omohundro Institute of Early American History and Culture,

2021), 309–48; Joseph J. Ellis, *First Family: Abigail and John Adams* (New York: Knopf, 2010); Patrick Griffin, *The Townshend Moment: The Making of Empire and Revolution in the Eighteenth Century* (New Haven: Yale University Press, 2018); Julie Flavell, *The Howe Dynasty: The Untold Story of a Military Family and the Women Behind Britain's Wars for America* (New York: Liveright, 2021).

10. Thomas Jefferson, *Notes on the State of Virginia*, ed. William Peden (Chapel Hill: University of North Carolina Press, 1982), 162. TJ to Edward Coles, August 25, 1814, *PTJDE: Retirement*, 7: 603–5, at 604, 605.

11. Cynthia A. Kierner, *Martha Jefferson Randolph, Daughter of Monticello* (Chapel Hill: University of North Carolina Press, 2012), 64–5. "Memoirs of Madison Hemings" in Annette Gordon-Reed, *Thomas Jefferson and Sally Hemings*, 245–8, at 246. For Jefferson's consciousness of French manumission laws, see TJ to Paul Bentalou, August 25, 1786, *PTJDE*, 10: 296. TJ to John Trumbull, May 21, 1789, *PTJDE*, 15: 143–4.

12. TJ to John Trumbull, May 21, 1789, *PTJDE*, 15: 143–4; John Trumbull to TJ, May 26, 1789, *PTJDE*, 15: 151–2. When Trumbull objected that he sought instead the honor afforded artists in ancient Greece, his father replied "You appear to forget sir that Connecticut is not Athens," *Autobiography, Reminiscences and Letters of John Trumbull, 1756–1841* (New York, 1841), 89. TJ to John Trumbull, June 1, 1789, *PTJDE*, 15: 163–4.

13. For the planned series of miniatures, see John Trumbull to TJ, June 11, 1789, *PTJDE*, 15: 176–9, at 179. Jefferson recognized the dilemma he had created for himself; see TJ to Short, March 24, 1789, *PTJDE*, 14:694–7, at 695.

14. Short to TJ, April 3, 1789, *PTJDE*, 15: 27–31 at 29. TJ to Short, March 24, 1789, *PTJDE*, 14: 694–7, at 697.

15. Madame de Corny to TJ, November 25, 1789, *PTJDE*, 15: 554–5; See also Short to TJ, March 14, 1788, PTJDE 12: 667–8. Madame de Tessé to TJ, January 21, 1787, *PTJDE*, 11: 60; Madame de Tessé to TJ, March 11, 1787, *PTJDE*, 11: 206–7; Madame de Tessé to TJ, March 30, *PTJDE*, 11: 257–60, at 258. See also Madame de Bréhan to TJ, November 3, 1787, *PTJDE*, 12: 308–9; Madame de Bréhan to TJ, March 1, 1788, *PTJDE*, 12: 635–6. For Jefferson's affair with Maria Cosway, see Helen D. Bullock, *My Head and My Heart: A Little History of Thomas Jefferson and Maria Cosway* (New York: Putnams, 1945); Fawn M. Brodie, *Thomas Jefferson: An Intimate History* (New York: W. W. Norton, 1974), 204–26; John P. Kaminski, *Jefferson in Love: The Love Letters Between Thomas Jefferson and Maria Cosway* (Madison, WI: Madison House, 1999). Maria Cosway to TJ, April 29, 1788, *PTJDE* 13: 114–6, at 116; see also Maria Cosway to TJ, December 10, 1787, *PTJDE*, 12: 415. Maria Cosway to TJ, December 1, 1787, *PTJDE*, 12: 387. Maria Cosway to TJ, July 9, 1787, *PTJDE*, 11: 567–69, at 568; Maria Cosway to TJ, April 29, 1788, *PTJDE*, 13: 114–16. For Short's acquaintance with Patsy Jefferson's circle, see Short to TJ, April 24, 1787, *PTJDE*, 11: 315–18, at 315; Short to TJ, March 6, 1788, *PTJDE*, 12: 646–7; Short to TJ, March 17, 1788, *PTJDE*, 12: 676–7. Marie Jacinthe de Botidoux to

Martha Jefferson Randolph, February 6, 1810; Marie Jacinthe de Botidoux to Martha Jefferson Randolph, epistolary journal, entry made January 10, 1790, *JFQL*. See also Elizabeth Tufton to Martha Jefferson, October 23, 1790, *JFQL*.

16. Madame de Tessé to TJ, March 11, 1787, *PTJDE*, 11: 206–7; Madame de Tessé to TJ, March 30, *PTJDE*, 11: 257–60, at 258.

17. TJ to James Madison, September 6, 1789, *PTJDE*, 15: 392–97, at 392. Jefferson restated the proposition in TJ to John Wayles Eppes, June 24, 1813, *PTJDE: Retirement*, 6: 220–6. Jean M. Yarborough, *American Virtues: Thomas Jefferson on the Character of a Free People* (Lawrence: University of Kansas Press, 1998).

18. TJ to Thomas Jefferson Randolph, November 24, 1808, *Founders Online*. Kevin J. Hayes, *The Road to Monticello: The Life and Mind of Thomas Jefferson* (New York: Oxford University Press, 2008); Andrew Burstein, *The Inner Jefferson: Portrait of a Grieving Optimist* (Charlottesville: University of Virginia Press, 1996).

19. James Monroe to TJ, October 12, 1786, *PTJDE*, 10: 456–8, at 457; TJ to James Monroe, December 18, 1786, *PTJDE*, 10: 611–3, at 612. TJ to James Madison, February 20, 1784, *PTJDE*, 6: 544–51, at 450. For other invitations, see TJ to Alexander Donald, May 30, 1795, *PTJDE*, 28: 366–8, at 368; TJ to Volney, December 9, 1795, *PTJDE*, 28: 550–1, at 551; Jean Gaulmier, *Volney: Un Grand Témoin De La Révolution et De L'Empire* (Paris: Hachette, 1959), 210–3; TJ to Jean-Baptiste Say, March 2, 1815, *PTJDE: Retirement*, 8: 303–8, at 304. TJ to Short, March 25, 1815, *PTJDE: Retirement*, 8: 382–3, at 383. François Furstenberg, *When the United States Spoke French: Five Refugees Who Shaped a Nation* (New York: Penguin Books, 2014).

20. Jefferson cited in John Gilbert McCurdy, *Citizen Bachelors: Manhood and the Creation of the United States* (Ithaca: Cornell University Press, 2009), 183.

21. Short cited in Myrna Boyce, "The Diplomatic Career of William Short," *Journal of Modern History*, 15 (June, 1943), 97 n. 1. TJ to Short, January 3, 1793, *PTJDE*, 25: 14–7; TJ to Short, April 13, 1820, *PTJDE: Retirement,* 15: 538–41; on religious morality and epicureanism, see Short to TJ, October 21, 1819, *PTJDE: Retirement*, 15: 148–50; TJ to Short, October 31, 1819, *PTJDE: Retirement*, 5: 162–5; TJ to Short, August 4, 1820, *PTJDE: Retirement*, 16: 163–8. The surviving tranche of letters written by Jefferson to Short is roughly equivalent in number to Jefferson's extant correspondence with his son-in-law Thomas Mann Randolph. Short to TJ, December 1, 1819, *PTJDE: Retirement*, 15: 252–5.

22. TJ to Robert Walsh, April 5, 1823, *Founders Online*. See also TJ to Short, May 5, 1816, *PTJDE: Retirement*, 10: 9–11, at 11. On race relations, see Short to TJ, February 27, 1798, *PTJDE*, 30: 146–54.

23. For expressions of regret, see Short to TJ, December 23, 1790, *PTJDE*, 18: 355–59, at 356; Short to TJ, December 29, 1790, *PTJDE*, 18: 445–51, at 445. Short to TJ, October 3, 1790, *PTJDE*, 17: 558–60, at 560. On burning letters, see Short to TJ,

October 15, 1791, *PTJDE: Retirement*, 22: 215–7, at 217; Short to TJ, May 27, 1809, *PTJDE: Retirement*, 1: 234.

24. Burstein, *Inner Jefferson,* 116–49; Pearsall, *Atlantic Families.* For a brilliant analysis of "unbosoming," see Andrew S. Trees, *The Founding Fathers & the Politics of Character* (Princeton: Princeton University Press, 2004). TJ to Elbridge Gerry, January 26, 1799, *PTJDE,* 30: 645–51, at 650. Jefferson's and Gerry's views on the political function of friendship mirrored those of French Jacobins; see Marisa Linton, "Fatal Friendships: The Politics of Jacobin Friendship," *French Historical Studies* 31 (Winter, 2008), 51–76. TJ to Short, October 16, 1792, *PTJDE,* 24: 490–1. TJ to Short, January 3, 1793, *PTJDE,* 25: 14–17.

25. Short to TJ, May 27, 1809, *PTJDE: Retirement,* 1: 229–35, at 234. Short to TJ, October 24, 1814, *PTJDE: Retirement,* 8: 50–3, at 52.

26. TJ to Short, January 3, 1793, *PTJDE,* 25: 14–17.

27. TJ to Short, January 18, 1826, *Founders Online.*

CHAPTER ONE

1. TJ to James Monroe, May 20, 1782, *PTJDE,* 6: 184–7. *Travels in North America in the Years 1780, 1781 and 1782 by the Marquis de Chastellux,* ed., Howard C. Rice, Jr., 2 vols. (Chapel Hill: University of North Carolina Press, 1963), 2: 391. TJ to Marquis de Chastellux, November 26, 1782, *PJTDE,* 6: 203–4, at 203. Editorial Note: Jefferson's Contemplated Mission to Europe, [31 December 1782–24 January 1783], *PTJDE,* 6: 210–5; James Madison to Edmund Randolph, December 2, 1782, *PJMDE: Congressional,* 5: 343–4; TJ to James Madison, August 31, 1783, *PTJDE,* 6: 335–6, editorial note.

2. TJ to Robert Skipwith, With a List of Books for a Private Library, August 3, 1771, *PTJDE,* 1: 76–81, at 77, 76. Several Frenchmen and settings identified by Sterne achieved notoriety, Laurence Sterne, *A Sentimental Journey Through France and Italy and Other Writings* eds., Ian Jack and Tim Parnell (Oxford: Oxford University Press), note 7, 225. Passing through Calais, Jefferson himself recorded a payment to "the successor of Sterne's monk," Memorandum Book, 1786, *PTJDE: Second Series,* 624, entry made April 29. John and Abigail also referenced Sterne in travel descriptions of France; see John Adams to TJ, May 23, 1785, *PTJDE,* 8: 161; Abigail Adams to Lucy Cranch, September 5, 1784, *TAPDE: Adams Family Correspondence,* 5: 436–9. Lawrence S. Kaplan, *Jefferson and France* (New Haven: Yale University Press, 1967), 2; Robert Withington, "The Marquis de Chastellux on Language and Peace," *The New England Quarterly,* 16 (June 1943), 316–9. TJ to Robert Skipwith, With a List of Books for a Private Library, August 3, 1771, *PTJDE,* 1: 76–81. List of Books Sold to James Monroe, May 10, 1784, *PTJDE,* 7: 240–1, editorial note. *The American Wanderer, Through Various Parts of Europe, In A Series of Letters to a Lady (Interspersed with a Variety of Interesting Anecdotes). By a Virginian* (London, 1783).

On anglophone critiques of French culture, see David A. Bell, *Cult of the Nation in France* (Cambridge, MA: Harvard University Press, 2001).

3. Jefferson replied to Short's request in, TJ to Short, November 27, 1783 [summary], *PTJDE*, 6: 359. TJ to James Madison, May 7, 1783, *PTJDE*, 6: 266–7. TJ to Short, December 19, 1783, *PTJDE*, 6: 393, TJ to Short, March 1, 1784, *PTJDE*, 6: 569–70. Frank Landon Humphreys, *Life and Times of David Humphreys, Soldier Statesman, Poet*, 2 vols. (New York: G. P. Putnam, 1917), 1: 233–5. David Humphreys to George Washington, January 6, 1784, *PGWDE: Confederation Series*, 1: 13–17. Samuel Hardy explained that Washington's influence would always place Humphreys first in line for preferment in Europe; see Samuel Hardy to Short, June 14, 1785, WSP LOC.

4. *Autobiography*, 89, 90–1; TJ to Short, March 1, 1784, *PTJDE*, 6: 569–70, at 569; TJ to James Madison, February 20, 1784, *PTJDE*, 6: 544–50, at 548.

5. TJ to Short, April 30, 1784, *PJTDE*, 7: 148–9. Short to TJ, c. March 10, 1784, *PTJDE*, 7: 17–8, at 18. William Short to Peyton Short, October 3, 1783, WPSP WM.

6. TJ to Short (Extract), April 30, 1784, *PTJDE*, 7: 148–9; TJ to Short, May 7, 1784, *PTJDE*, 7: 229. Annette Gordon-Reed, *Hemingses of Monticello*, 156–60.

7. Short to TJ, May 14, 1784, *PTJDE*, 7: 253–5.

8. Short to TJ, May 14, 1784, *PJTDE*, 7: 253–6, at 254–5. Alexander's acquaintance with Franklin described in *The American Wanderer*, Letter 23.

9. TJ to James Monroe, May 21, 1784, *PTJDE*, 7: 279–81. On James Hemings' status in French law, see Gordon-Reed, *Hemingses of Monticello*, 156–60, 169–82; see also Jennifer L. Palmer, *Intimate Bonds: Family and Slavery in the French Atlantic* (Philadelphia: University of Pennsylvania Press, 2014).

10. TJ to James Monroe, May 21, 1784, *PTJDE*, 7: 279–1; James Monroe to TJ, June 1, 1784, *PTJDE*, 7: 299–300, at 300; James Madison to TJ, September 7, 1784, *PTJDE*, 7: 416–8, at 416. Short alluded to his fear of sea travel in several letters; see Short to John Banister, Jnr., March 21, 1787, Gilpin Collection, HSP; Short to TJ, June 7, 1791, *PTJDE*, 20: 541–46, at 543. Short to TJ, July 28, 1784, *PTJDE*, 7: 384–6, at 385. Short to TJ, May 14 [15th], 1784, *PTJDE*, 7: 256–8, at 257.

11. Short to TJ, June 28, 1784, *PJTDE*, 7: 321. Short to TJ, July 28, 1784, *PTJDE*, 7: 384–6, at 385.

12. TJ to James Madison, November 11, 1784, *PTJDE*, 7: 503–08, at 503. Valcoulon, who could speak little English, had traveled to Richmond in company with Albert Gallatin to recoup debts and invest in western lands; see Henry M. Dater, "Albert Gallatin—Land Speculator," *Mississippi Valley Historical Review*, 26 (1939), 21–38; Yvon Bizardel and Howard C. Rice, "'Poor in Love Mr. Short,'" *WMQ* 21 (October 1964), 516–33. Short to Savary de Valcoulon, [in French] July 20, 1786, WSP LOC ["*Je m'ont adopté comme leur fils*"]; Memorandum Book, 1784, *PTJDE: Second Series*, 571, entry made December 30; Preeson Bowdoin to Short, April 7, 1785, WSP LOC.

13. TJ to David Humphreys, July 4, 1784, *PTJDE*, 7: 363–4; Humphreys, *Life and Times of David Humphreys*, 1: 317. American Commissioners to De Souza,

September 9, 1784, *PTJDE*, 7: 419–20, editorial note; Marie Kimball, *Jefferson*, 17. David Humphreys to George Washington, May 10, 1785, *PGWDE: Confederation Series*, 2: 545–47, at 545. Jefferson turned Williamos out of his household for embezzlement; TJ to Charles Williamos, July 7, 1785, *PTJDE* 8: 269–73, editorial note. Crèvecoeur mentioned being informed of Jefferson's health by Williamos; Crèvecoeur to TJ, August 15, 1785, *PTJDE*, 8: 381. Abigail Adams to Elizabeth Cranch, March 8, 1785, *TAPDE: Adams Family Correspondence*, 6: 74–6.

14. Abigail Adams to Lucy Cranch, May 5, 1787, *TAPDE: Adams Family Correspondence*, 6: 120–3. William Short's Account Book, Gilpin Collection HSP. For Johns Adams learning French, see *TAPDE: Diary and Autobiography of John Adams*, 2: 352; 4: 354, 361, 370, 384, 4:79. Abigail Adams learned the same way; see Abigail Adams to Elizabeth Cranch, December 3, 1784, *TAPDE: Adams Family Correspondence*, 6: 3–10; Abigail Adams to Mercy Otis Warren, *TAPDE: Adams Family Correspondence*, 5: 446–53. John Adams cited in Paul M. Spurlin, "The Founding Fathers and the French Language," *The Modern Language Journal*, 60 (March 1976), 85–96. For Short's fragmentary dictionary of colloquialisms, see WSP LOC. Lewis Littlepage to John Jay, July 15, 1780 in *Letters, Being the Whole of the Correspondence between the Hon. John Jay, Esquire, and Mr. Lewis Littlepage* (Philadelphia, 1786), 6.

15. Madame de Tessé to TJ, September 29, 1786, *PTJDE*, 10: 413–4, at 414; Duchess Rosalie de La Rochefoucauld [hereafter Rosalie] to Short, January 6, 1791, in Harsanyi *Lettres*, 24. Jefferson expressed an awkwardness with written and spoken French, in TJ to Madame Plumard de Bellanger, April 25, 1794, *PTJDE*, 28: 58–60, at 60. See also TJ to Ferdinand Grand, October 10, 1788, *PTJDE*, 14: 7, editorial note. Spurlin, "Founding Fathers and French," 89, 93. Abigail Adams Jr. to Lucy Cranch, May 6, 1785, *TAPDE: Adams Family Correspondence*, 6: 127–29. TJ to Francis Eppes, August 30, 1785, *PTJDE*, 8: 451. TJ to Thomas Mann Randolph, Jr., July 6, 1787, *PTJDE*, 11: 556–59, at 557; TJ to Thomas Mann Randolph, Sr., August 11, 1787, *PTJDE*, 12: 20–3, at 22. TJ to Dugald Stewart, June 21, 1789, *PTJDE*, 15: 204–5, at 204.

16. TJ to Short, April 2, 1785, *PTJDE*, 8: 68. TJ to Short, April 30, 1785, *PTJDE*, 8: 132–3. TJ to Short, May 2, 1785, *PTJDE*, 8: 133–4; see also William Stephens Smith to TJ, February 13, 1786, *PTJDE*, 9: 281–2. TJ to Short, April 30, 1785, *PTJDE*, 8: 132–3. TJ to Philip Mazzei, May 12, 1785, *PTJDE*, 8: 152. Abigail Adams, Jr. to Lucy Cranch, May 6, 1785, *TAPDE: Adams Family Correspondence*, 6: 127–29. TJ to Short, June 28, 1785, *PTJDE*, 8: 257.

17. Jefferson first broached the subject of creating a rational society in TJ to James Madison, February 20, 1784, *PTJDE*, 6: 544–51, at 550. See also, TJ to James Monroe, May 11, 1785, *PTJDE*, 8: 148–150, at 150; TJ to James Monroe, December 18, 1786, *PTJDE*, 10: 611–13, at 612; TJ to Short, June 28, 1785, *PTJDE*, 8: 257.

18. American Commissioners to Short, July 27, 1785, *PTJDE*, 8: 313–15. For background, see American Commissioners to Baron De Thulemeier, May 26, 1785,

PTJDE, 8: 165–6. Baron De Thulemeier to American Commissioners, June 17, 1785, *PTJDE*, 8: 234; TJ to John Adams, June 22, 1785, *PTJDE*, 8: 246–7, at 246; TJ to John Adams, July 7, 1785, *PTJDE*, 8: 265–7. TJ to John Adams, July 28, 1785, *PTJDE*, 8: 315–17. TJ to Baron De Thulemeier, July 28, 1785, *PTJDE*, 8: 323–4. TJ to G. K. van Hogendorp, July 29, 1785, *PTJDE*, 8: 324. TJ to John Adams, 28 July 1785, *PTJDE*, 8: 315–17, at 316.

19. Abigail Adams to TJ, August 12, 1785, *TAPDE: Adams Family Correspondence*, 6: 262–6. Short to Sir Peyton Skipwith, cited in Shackelford, *Jefferson's Adoptive Son*, 29. John Adams described London during August as "dull, disgusting . . . unwholesome" and "deserted by Men of Business"; John Adams to William Stephens Smith, August 5, 1785, *PJADE*, 17: 301–2, at 301. Short to TJ, August 7, 1785, *PTJDE*, 8: 358–9, at 358. Short to TJ, August 23, 1785, *PTJDE*, 8: 431–4, editorial note. Short to John Adams, August 23, 1785, *PJADE*, 17: 352–3.

20. Proposed Changes in Translation of the Treaty with Prussia, c. March 1, 1785, *PTJDE*, 8: 9–10. See also TJ to John Adams and Benjamin Franklin, March 1, 1785, *PTJDE*, 8: 8–9; American Commissioners to Baron De Thulemeier, March 14, 1785, *PTJDE*, 8: 26–32; American Commissioners to John Jay, October 11, 1785, *PTJDE*, 8: 606. For Short's description of discrepancies and errata in and between the French and English iterations of the treaty, see Short to TJ, August 23, 1785, *PTJDE*, 8: 431–34; Short to John Adams, August 23, 1785, *PJADE*, 17: 352–3. Short described his tour in Short to TJ, August 28, 1785, *PTJDE*, 8: 446–48, at 448, 447. See also G. K. Van Hogendorp to Jefferson, September 8, 1785, *PTJDE*, 8: 501–05, at 502.

21. John Adams to Short and C. W. F. Dumas, September 11, 1785, *PJADE*, 17: 427–28. Short to TJ, September 11, 1785, *PTJDE*, 8: 515. TJ to John Adams, September 24, 1785, *PTJDE*, 8: 542–45, at 544. In a subsequent letter presenting the treaty to the French Minister for Foreign Affairs, Jefferson stressed that the two languages in which the treaty was expressed were deemed equal, TJ to Comte de Vergennes, October 20, 1786, *PTJDE*, 10: 472–3. American Commissioners to John Jay, October 11, 1785, *PTJDE*, 8: 606. TJ to Short, September 24, 1785, *PTJDE*, 8: 547. Jefferson instructed the banker Ferdinand Grand to pay Short "from time to time"; TJ to Ferdinand Grand, September 24, 1785, *PTJDE*, 8: 546. On Jefferson's prior determination to have a secretary, see TJ to John Jay, August 30, 1785, *PTJDE*, 8: 452–56, at 544; TJ to James Monroe, August 28, 1785, *PTJDE*, 8: 444–46, at 445. TJ to David Humphreys, December 4, 1785, *PTJDE*, 9: 77; TJ to Abigail Adams, December 27, 1785, *PTJDE*, 9: 126.

22. TJ to David Humphreys, January 5, 1786, *PTJDE*, 9: 152; see also William Stephens Smith to TJ, February 13, 1786, *PTJDE*, 9: 281–3, at 283.

23. William Stephens Smith to Short, June 3, 1787, WSP LOC.

24. For Short's interest in Henri-Raphael, see Le Ray de Chaumont to Short, February 22 and November 4, 1804, WSP LOC. Henri-Raphael corresponded with Short from New Orleans, see Henri-Raphael to Short, April 10, June 13, and September

28, 1806, WSP LOC. Short to George Taylor, September 10, 1808, WSP LOC. Bizardel and Rice, "'Poor in Love Mr. Short,'" 531–33; Rosalie de La Rochefoucauld to Short, March 23, 1811, APS; William Short to John Cleves Short and John Wilkins Short, September 27, 1836, WSP LOC.

25. TJ to Martha Jefferson, March 6, 1786, *PTJDE*, 9: 318. Short to TJ, April 2, 1786, *PTJDE*, 9: 367–8.

26. The death of Polly and Jefferson's resolve to bring her to Paris is discussed in Gordon-Reed, *Hemingses of Monticello*, 191–203. Short to TJ, August 7, 1785, *PTJDE*, 8: 358–9, at 358. TJ to Abigail Adams, December 21, 1786, *PTJDE*, 10: 621. Short to TJ, March 12, 1787, *PTJDE*, 11: 207–11, at 209; Martha Jefferson to TJ, April 9, 1787, *PTJDE*, 11: 281–2, at 281.TJ to Short, March 27, 1787, *PTJDE*, 11: 246–8, at 246. For Jefferson's uncertainty as to how to bring Polly to Paris, see TJ to Martha Jefferson, April 7, 1787, *PTJDE*, 11: 277–78; TJ to Martha Jefferson, June 1, 1787, *PTJDE*, 11: 394.

27. Abigail Adams to TJ, June 26, 1787, *PTJDE*, 11: 501–2. TJ to Elizabeth Wayles Eppes, July 28, 1787, *PTJDE*, 11: 634–5. Abigail Adams to TJ, July 6, 1787, *PTJDE*, 11: 550–2, at 551. TJ to Mary Jefferson Bolling, July 23, 1787, *PTJDE*, 11: 612–13, at 612.

28. Gordon-Reed, *Hemingses of Monticello*, 159.

29. David Humphreys to TJ, January 30, 1786, *PTJDE*, 9: 241–2; TJ to David Humphreys, March 14, 1786, *PTJDE*, 9: 328. Jefferson recommended Humphreys for further employment; see TJ to James Monroe, May 10, 1786, *PTJDE*, 9: 499–504, at 503. TJ to William Short, March 28, 1786, *PTJDE*, 9: 362–4. For Short's enquiry and Monroe's reply: James Monroe to Short, January 23, 1786, *Monroe Papers*, 2: 268. TJ to James Monroe, January 27, 1786, *PTJDE*, 9: 236–7, at 237; James Monroe to TJ, October 12, 1786, *PTJDE*, 10: 456–8, at 458. Short to TJ, March 19, 1786, *PTJDE*, 9: 347–8. Gordon-Reed, *Hemingses of Monticello*, 166–7. Philip Mazzei to TJ, April 17, 1787 [summary], *PTJDE*, 11: 297; TJ to Philip Mazzei, May 6, 1787, *PTJDE*, 11: 354–5.

30. TJ to John Trumbull, May 21, 1789, *PTJDE*, 15: 143–4, at 144. TJ to Short, March 29, 1787, *PTJDE*, 11: 253–5, at 253; Short to James Madison, March 23, 1787, *PJMDE: Congressional*, 9: 329–30. *Autobiography*, 98; Documents on the American Tobacco Trade [1787]: Editorial Note, *PTJDE*, 12: 76–8. Short to TJ, March 12, 1787, *PTJDE*, 11: 207–11, at 210. TJ to Short, March 27, 1787, *PTJDE*, 11: 246–7.

31. John Ledyard to TJ, August 16, 1786, *PTJDE*, 10: 258–60; Stephen D. Watrous, ed., *John Ledyard's Journey Through Russia and Siberia: The Journal and Selected Letters* (Madison: University of Wisconsin Press, 2011), 109. Notes on American Medals Struck in France, *PTJDE*, 16: 53–66; see also "Jefferson's Descriptions of the Medals," *PTJDE*, 16: 69–76; TJ to Short, April 30, 1790, *PTJDE*, 16: 395–6. TJ to Short, March 29, 1787, *PTJDE*, 11: 253–5; Short to John Jay, March 25,

1790, *PTJDE*, 16: 267–71. Short reported the loss in Short to TJ, March 25, 1790, *PTJDE*, 16: 271–4, at 272.

32. For a summary of Jefferson's efforts, see Merrill D. Peterson, *Thomas Jefferson and the New Nation: A Biography* (New York: Oxford University Press, 1970), 314–30. See also Jefferson's Observations on Calonne's Letter Concerning American Trade, October 1786, *PTJDE*, 539–42.

33. TJ to the Editor of the *Journal de Paris*, August 29, 1787, *PTJDE*, 12: 61–5, at 62. Editorial Note: The Article on the United States in the *Encyclopédie Méthodique*, *PTJDE*, 10: 3–65; TJ to George Washington, November 14, 1786, *PTJDE*, 10: 531–33, at 532. TJ to Mirabeau, August 21, 1786, *PTJDE*, 10: 283. TJ also engaged in a dialogue with François Soulés to correct errors in Soulés's *Histoire des Troubles de l'Amérique Anglaise*; see TJ to François Soulés, January 19, 1787, *PTJDE*, 11: 56; TJ to Soulés, February 2, 1787, *PTJDE*, 11: 110.

34. Shackelford, *Jefferson's Adoptive Son*, 28; Short to TJ, February 10, 1790, *PTJDE*, 16: 159–62, at 160; Richard J. Buel Jr., *Joel Barlow: American Citizen in a Revolutionary World* (Baltimore: Johns Hopkins University Press, 2011), 96–119. On the use of America made within French polemics, see Robert Darnton, "Trends in Radical Propaganda on the Eve of the French Revolution (1782–88)" (D. Phil. dissertation, University of Oxford, 1964), 155–61. TJ to Hector St. John de Crèvecoeur, December 8, 1786, *PTJDE*, 10: 583. Brissot de Warville, *Examen Critique des Voyages dans l'Amérique de Chastellux* (1786); [Chastellux] *Travels in North America*, ed. Rice. Kaplan, *Jefferson and France*, 29; Short criticized Chastellux's *Travels*; see Short to William Nelson, February 7, 1787, Gilpin Collection, HSP. TJ to Brissot de Warville, August 16, 1786, *PTJDE*, 10: 261–3; TJ to Brissot de Warville, February 11, 1788, *PTJDE*, 12: 577–8. TJ to James Madison, May 3, 1788, *PTJDE*, 13: 129–33, at 129.

35. Shackelford, *Jefferson's Adoptive Son*, 166 n. 41, 176 n. 53. Brissot de Warville to TJ, February 10, 1788, *PJTDE*, 12: 577; TJ to Brissot de Warville, February 11, 1788, *PTJDE*, 12: 577. For Short's introductions, see Short to William Nelson, May 5, 1788 WSP LOC; Short to Edward Carrington, May 26, 1788, Gilpin Collection, HSP; Short to William Stephens Smith, May 27, 1788, Gilpin Collection, HSP. Short discussed the "libel" aimed at the Société by the colonial lobby in Short to TJ, December 25, 1789, *PTJDE*, 16: 43–8, at 47.

36. Short believed the island's Assembly had mismanaged the colony; see Short to TJ, November 3, 1789, *PTJDE*, 15: 530–8, at 536; Short to TJ, October 3, 1790, *PTJDE*, 17: 555–8, at 558. See also, Short to TJ, December 25, 1789, *PTJDE*, 16: 43–8, at 46; Short to Alexander Hamilton, December 28, 1791, *PAHDE*, 10: 472–81, at 479. For Short's relationship with Condorcet, see Short to William Nelson, February 7, 1787, Gilpin Collection, HSP; Short to TJ, November 3, 1789, *PTJDE*, 15: 530; Short to TJ, March 30, 1791, *PTJDE*, 19: 633–8. Durand Echevarria, "Condorcet's 'The Influence of the American Revolution on Europe,'" *WMQ*, 25 (January 1968), 85–108, at 91. Jefferson's Notes from Condorcet on Slavery, *PTJDE*, 14: 494–98,

Jefferson was reluctant to let the matter drop; see TJ to Condorcet, August 30, 1791, *PTJDE*, 22: 98–9; TJ to Edward Bancroft, January 26, 1789, *PTJDE*, 14: 492–4, at 492.

37. TJ to G. K. Van Hogendorp, August 25, 1786, *PTJDE*, 10: 297–300. Short to William Nelson, July 20, 1786, WSP LOC. Memorandum Book, 1787, *PTJDE: Second Series*, 677, entry made August 2. On Mazzei's *Researches*, see Jean Nicolas Démeunier to TJ, February 11, 1788, *PTJDE* 11: 578–80; Alexander DeConde, *Entangling Alliance: Politics & Diplomacy under George Washington* (Westport, CT: Greenwood Press, 1974), 174, n. 28.

38. Short to William Nelson, February 7, 1787, Gilpin Collection, HSP. Jefferson made this remark of Buffon's *Histoire Naturelle*; see Thomas Jefferson, *Notes on the State of Virginia*, ed. Peden, 54.

39. Brodie, *Thomas Jefferson*, 200–3. For other accounts of the affair, see Kaminski, *Jefferson in Love*, 3–38; Gordon-Reed, *Hemingses of Monticello*, 275–81.

40. Maria Cosway to TJ, October 30, 1786, *PTJDE*, 10: 494–6, at 495. Maria Cosway to TJ, December 1, 1787, *PTJDE*, 12: 387. Maria Cosway to TJ, April 29, 1788, *PTJDE*, 13: 114–6. TJ to Maria Cosway, January 31, 1788, *PTJDE*, 12: 539–40. TJ to John Trumbull, February 23, 1787, *PTJDE*, 11:181. Maria Cosway to TJ, January 1, 1787, *PTJDE*, 11: 3–4. TJ to Maria Cosway, October 12, 1786, *PTJDE*, 10: 443–45.

41. Brodie, *Thomas Jefferson*, 207–8. TJ to Maria Cosway, October 12, 1786, *PTJDE*, 10: 443–455. For accounts of the ceremony, see Ethis de Corny to TJ, February 20, 1787, *PTJDE*, 11: 170–2, editorial notes; Rayvenal with Enclosure, September 30, 1786, *PTJDE*, 10: 414–16, editorial notes. Short to TJ, May 29, 1787, *PTJDE*, 11: 381–3, at 382. TJ to Short, June 1, 1787, *PTJDE*, 11: 395–6. John Jay to Short, July 5, 1787, *PTJDE*, 11: 549–550. Short to James Madison, May 7, 1787, *PJMDE: Congressional*, 9: 411–3; Short to James Madison, December 21, 1787, *PJMDE: Congressional*, 10: 342–4, at 344; Short to TJ, March 26, 1787, *PTJDE*, 11: 239–41, at 239.

42. Short to TJ, March 26, 1787, *PTJDE*, 11: 239–41, at 239; Short to TJ, April 6, 1787, *PTJDE*, 11: 274–77, at 275. Short to TJ, March 14, 1788, *PTJDE*, 12: 667–8, at 667.

43. TJ to Short, March 29, 1788, *PTJDE*, 12: 696–7, at 697. TJ to Martha Jefferson, March 6, 1786, *PTJDE*, 9: 318. Short to TJ, May 8, 1787, *PTJDE*, 11: 356–7, at 357; TJ to Short, June 1, 1787, *PTJDE*, 11: 395–6.

44. Short to TJ, March 26, 1787, *PTJDE*, 11: 239–41, at 240; Martha Jefferson to TJ, March 25, 1787, *PTJDE*, 11: 238, editorial note. Short to TJ, April 2, 1786, *PTJDE*, 9: 367–8. Short to TJ, April 24, 1787, *PTJDE*, 11: 315–18, at 315. Short to TJ, March 9, 1788, *PTJDE*, 12: 657–8, at 658; Short to TJ, March 17, 1788, *PTJDE*, 12: 676–7, at 676; Short to TJ, March 6, 1788, *PTJDE*, 12: 646–7; Short to TJ, April 6, 1787, *PTJDE*, 11: 274–7, at 276.

45. Caroline Tufton (Barham) to Martha Jefferson, August 13, 1789, *JQFL*. Elizabeth Tufton to Martha Jefferson, October 23, 1789, *JQFL*. Marie Jacinthe de Botidoux to

Martha Jefferson, epistolatory journal, entries made, January 10, 1790, January 20, 1790, May 7, 1790; May 9, 1790; November 4, 1789, *JQFL*.

46. Martha Jefferson to TJ, April 9, 1787, *PTJDE*, 11: 281–2, at 282. See also, Kierner, *Martha Jefferson Randolph*. Marie Jacinthe de Botidoux to Martha Jefferson Randolph, February 6, 1810, *JQFL*.

47. TJ to Francis Dal Verme, September 15, 1788, *PTJDE*, 13: 605. TJ to Short, January 22, 1789, *PTJDE*, 14: 481–3. Short to TJ, February 11, 1789, *PTJDE*, 14: 538–43, at 539. Short to TJ, September 24, 1788, *PTJDE*, 13: 634–7, at 637.

48. TJ to Short, April 27, 1790, *PTJDE*, 16: 387–9, at 387. TJ to Short, March 12, 1790, *PTJDE*, 16: 228–9, at 228. Short to TJ, October 8, 1789, *PTJDE*, 15: 510–13, at 512. Short to TJ, October 3, 1790, *PTJDE*, 17: 558–60, at 560.

49. Jefferson calculated the chances of Martha marrying a blockhead in TJ to François Marbois, December 5, 1783, *PTJDE*, 6: 373–4, at 374. TJ to Short, March 24, 1789, *PTJDE*, 14: 694–7, at 697. Martha Jefferson to TJ, April 9, 1787, *PTJDE*, 11: 281–82, at 282. Short to TJ, March 12, 1787, *PTJDE*, 11: 207–11, at 211; Short to William Stephens Smith, March 11, 1787, Gilpin Collection, HSP; Gouverneur Morris, *A Diary of the French Revolution*, ed. Beatrix Cary Davenport, 2 vols. (Boston: Houghton Mifflin, 1939), 1: 15, entry made March 19, 1789. Kierner, *Martha Jefferson Randolph*.

50. Short to TJ, April 3, 1789, *PTJDE*, 15: 27–30, at 27. Short to TJ, October 2, 1788, *PTJDE*, 13: 652–56, at 654; Short to TJ, October 28, 1788, *PTJDE*, 14: 41–4, at 43. William Short, Travel Journal, Gilpin Collection, HSP. Short to TJ, April 3, 1789, *PTJDE*, 15: 28.

51. TJ to John Jay, November 19, 1788, *PTJDE*, 14: 211–6, 216. TJ to Short, November 21, 1788, *PTJDE*, 14: 275–77, at 276. TJ to Short, March 24, 1789, *PTJDE*, 694–7, at 695.

52. Short to TJ, March 2, 1789, *PTJDE*, 14: 607–09, at 608. Short to TJ, April 3, 1789, *PTJDE*, 15: 27–30, at 28. Short to TJ, October 28, 1788, *PTJDE*, 14: 41–44, at 44.

CHAPTER TWO

1. Dumas Malone, *Jefferson and His Time; Volume Two: Jefferson and the Rights of Man* (Boston: Little, Brown, 1951), xv; Kaplan, *Jefferson and France*, 11, 14; William Howard Adams, *The Paris Years of Thomas Jefferson* (New Haven: Yale University Press, 1997), 37. These interpretations are discussed and critiqued in Brian Steele, "Thomas Jefferson's Gender Frontier," *Journal of American History* (June 2008), 17–42. Shackelford, *Jefferson's Adoptive Son*.

2. TJ to John Adams, July 28, 1785, Enclosure, *PTJDE*, 8: 317–19. For a discussion of French attitudes toward America's constitution, see Count de Moustier to TJ, April 26, 1791, *PTJDE*, 20: 263–5, at 263. Philipp Ziesche, *Cosmopolitan Patriots: Americans in Paris in the Age of Revolution* (Charlottesville: University of Virginia Press, 2010); Thomas Schlereth, *The Cosmopolitan Ideal in Enlightenment Thought: Its Form and*

Function in the Ideas of Franklin, Hume and Voltaire (Notre Dame: University of Notre Dame Press, 1977); Janet Polasky, *Revolutions Without Borders: The Call to Liberty in the Atlantic World* (New Haven: Yale University Press, 2015).

3. [Abigail Adams, Jr.,], *Journal and Correspondence of Miss Adams* (New York, 1841); [John Trumbull] *Autobiography, Reminiscences and Letters of John Trumbull, 1756–1841* (New York, 1841), 147.

4. Hector St. John de Crèvecoeur to TJ, July 15, 1784, *PTJDE*, 7: 376–7, at 376; Hector St. John de Crèvecoeur to TJ, September 1, 1784, *PTJDE*, 7: 413–5, at 414. Hector St. John de Crèvecoeur to TJ, July 15, 1784, *PTJDE*, 7: 376–7, at 376. Crèvecoeur hoped Jefferson might assist his efforts to persuade the Duke de La Rochefoucauld to invest in a utopian community in America, see Darnton, "Trends in Radical Propaganda on the Eve of the French Revolution," 121–2, esp. n. 41.

5. Arthur Young, *Travels During the Years 1787, 1788 and 1789: Undertaken More particularly with a View of Ascertaining the Cultivation Wealth, Resources and National Prosperity of the Kingdom of France* (London, 1792), 98–9. Diana Ketcham, *Le Désert de Retz: A Late Eighteenth-Century French Folly Garden* (Cambridge, MA: MIT Press, 1994); L. H. Butterfield and Howard C. Rice, "Jefferson's Earliest Note to Maria Cosway with Some Facts and Conjectures on his Broken Wrist," *WMQ* 3d ser. 5 (January 1948), 26–33, at 31–2.

6. Madame du Deffand, quoted in J. D. de La Rochefoucauld, C. Wolikow and G. Inki, *Le Duc de La Rochefoucauld- Liancourt 1747–1827* (Paris: Librarie Académique Perrin, 1980), 59. Solange Fasquelle, *Les La Rochefoucauld: Une Famille Dans l'Histoire de France* (Paris: Perrin, 1992). Young, *Travels*, 98. Daniel Vaugelade, *Le Salon Physiocratique des La Rochefoucald Animé Par Lousie Elisabeth de La Rochefoucauld Duchesse d'Enville (1716–1797)* (Paris: Publibook, 2001); Yvon Bizardel, "Un Américain à la découverte de l'Auverge en 1801," *Revue de la Haute-Auvergne* 38 (1963), 429–37. Philip Mazzei's Memoranda Regarding Persons and Affairs in Paris c. July 1784, *PTJDE*, 7: 386–91, at 386. Vaugelade, *Le Salon Physiocratique des La Rochefoucauld*, 169–202, 133–44; Michèle Crogriez Labarthe, *Correspondance de la duchesse d'Enville* (Paris: Les éditions del'oeil/ la bibliothèque fantôme, 2019). The life of a commoner taken up by Madame d'Enville, Marc-Antoine Jullien, who tutored her grandchildren, is described in Lindsay A. H. Parker, *Writing the Revolution: A French Woman's History in Letters* (New York: Oxford University Press, 2013). John Adams, *TAPDE: The Diary and Autobiography of John Adams*, 4: 42 entry made April 9, 1778.

7. Abigail Adams to Elizabeth Cranch, May 12, 1785, *TAPDE: Adams Family Correspondence* 6: 141–3. Abigail Adams to Royall Tyler, September 5, 1785, *TAPDE: Adams Family Correspondence*, 5: 445–6, at 445. Abigail Adams to Lucy Cranch, September 5, 1784, *TAPDE: Adams Family Correspondence*, 5: 436–9, at 438.

8. Adams's opinion summarized in Marie Kimball, *Jefferson*, 85. Thomas Clarkson, *The History of the Rise, Progress and Abolition of the African Slave Trade*, 2 vols.

(London, 1808). I: 492, II: 128–30; Daniel P. Resnick, "The *Société des Amis des Noirs* and the Abolition of Slavery," *French Historical Studies* 7 (Fall 1972), 558–69. Young, *Travels*, 98. Short to TJ, July 17, 1791, *PTJDE*, 20: 641–45, at 645. Louis-Alexandre de La Rochefoucauld, *Opinion de M. de La Rochefoucauld, député de Paris, sur la Proposition d'une émission nouvelle d'assignats-monnoies. 27 September 1790* (Paris, 1790). On fossils, Philip Mazzei to Thomas Jefferson, [ca. June 1784], *PTJDE*, 15 [Supplementary Documents Down to the Year 1789]: 613–5, at 613. Ferdinand Dreyfus, *Un Philanthrope d'Autrefois: La Rochefoucauld-Liancourt* (Paris, 1903); see also La Rochefoucauld-Liancourt to TJ, July 11, 1796, *PTJDE*, 29: 148–49, editorial note. [Gouverneur Morris] *A Diary of the French Revolution*, ed. Beatrix Cary Davenport, 2 vols. (Boston: Houghton, Mifflin, 1939), 1: 220–1, entry made September 17, 1789, 1: 253, entry made October 11, 1789.

9. Duchess Alexandrine-Charlotte-Sophie de Rohan-Chabot is hereafter referred to as "Rosalie." For Rosalie's family, see Rousse, *La Roche-Guyon*, 307–8, 343–7; Fasquelle, *Les La Rochefoucauld*. Young, *Travels*, 98–9. Rosalie's admiration for Rousseau was a theme in correspondence with Short; see Harsanyi, *Lettres*. For references to her island, see Rosalie to Short, November 5, 1791, Harsanyi *Lettres*, 62–3; Rosalie to Short, July 8, 1792, Harsanyi, *Lettres*, 115–7, at 115. TJ to Duchess La Rochefoucauld d'Enville, April 3, 1790, *PTJDE*, 16: 296–97, at 296. Puisieux, cited in Dena Goodman, "L'Ortografe des Dames: Gender and Language in the Old Regime," *French Historical Studies* 25 (2002), 191–223, at 196. Abbé Louis Barthelemy, who sought to teach French noblewomen to spell "correctly," was a habitué of the La Rochefoucauld circle. Rosalie to Short, December 1, 1792, Harsanyi, *Lettres*, 159–63, at 161. For Short's interest in Voltaire and Rosalie's recommendations, see Rosalie to Short, August 3, 1797, Harsanyi, *Lettres*, 210–12, at 211.

10. Madame de Tessé to TJ, July 6, 1790, *PTJDE*, 17: 8–9, at 8. Davenport, ed., *Diary of the French Revolution*, 1: 6, entry made March 5, 1789. Steven D. Kale, *French Salons: High Society and Political Sociability from the Old Regime to the Revolution of 1848* (Baltimore and London: Johns Hopkins University Press, 2004), 47.

11. TJ to Madame d'Enville, April 2, 1790, *PTJDE*, 16: 290–1, at 291. Madame d'Enville to TJ, July 27, 1790, *PTJDE*, 17: 286–7, at 287.

12. Cited in Burstein, *The Inner Jefferson*, 73. TJ to Charles Bellini, September 30, 1785, *PTJDE*, 8: 568–70, at 568. TJ to Eliza House Trist, December 15, 1786, *PTJDE*, 10: 599–601, at 600. TJ to Francis Eppes, December 11, 1785, *PTJDE*, 9: 91–3, at 92. TJ to Eliza House Trist, December 15, 1786, *PTJDE*, 10: 599–601, at 600.

13. James Madison warned Eliza House Trist against circulating a letter in which Jefferson praised aspects of the French character while bemoaning a lack of congressional funding; see James Madison to Eliza House Trist, March 14, 1786, *PJMDE: Congressional*, 8: 498–500, at 499. TJ to James Monroe, June 17, 1785, *PTJDE*, 8: 227–234, at 233. TJ to John Rutledge, August 6, 1787, *PTJDE*, 11: 700–1, at 701.

14. Abigail Adams to Mary Smith Cranch, February 20, 1785, *TAPDE: Adams Family Correspondence* 6: 67–71, at 67. Abigail Adams to Cotton Tufts, September 8, 1784, *TAPDE: Adams Family Correspondence*, 5: 456–9, at 457. Abigail Adams to Cotton Tufts, January 3, 1785, *TAPDE: Adams Family Correspondence*, 6: 41–4, at 44. TJ to Abigail Adams, June 21, 1785, *PTJDE*, 8: 239–42.

15. Cited in Adams, *The Paris Years*, 76. Abigail Adams to Royall Tyler, January 4, 1785, *TAPDE: Adams Family Correspondence*, 6: 45–9, at 48.

16. Walker Maury to TJ, April 20, 1785, *PTJDE*, 8: 101. Jefferson believed the study of Anglo-Saxon to be especially beneficial to young Americans; see Peter Thompson, "'Judicious Neology': The Imperative of Paternalism in Thomas Jefferson's Linguistic Studies," *Early American Studies. An Interdisciplinary Journal*, 1 (2003), 187–224. TJ to Walker Maury, August 19, 1785, *PTJDE*, 8: 409–10, at 409. Nabby Adams recalled Jefferson opining that no American under the age of thirty-five should travel to Europe without a guardian, Abigail Adams, Jr., to Lucy Cranch, *TAPDE: Adams Family Papers*, May 6, 1785, 6: 127–9, at 129. TJ to Peter Carr, August 10, 1787, *PTJDE*, 12: 14–19, at 17.

17. John Banister, Jr., to TJ, September 19, 1785 [summary], *PTJDE*, 8: 529. TJ to John Banister Jr., October 15, 1785, *PTJDE*, 8: 636–7. Philip Mazzei asked Short to look after Banister, advising him that Banister was likely to waste his money; Philip Mazzei to Short, December 8, 1784, WSP LOC. See also John Banister, Jr. to TJ, March 11, 1786, *PTJDE*, 9: 322–3; TJ to John Banister, Jr., June 16, 1785, *PTJDE*, 8: 211–2. Jefferson exempted Edinburgh from his strictures; see TJ to Thomas Mann Randolph, Jr., *PTJDE*, 9: 59–60, at 60.

18. William Nelson to Short, Richmond, May 13, 1785, WPSP WM. William Short to Peyton Short, n.d. December, 1792, WPSP WM. William Short to Peyton Short, July 28, 1800, WPSP WM.

19. Short to William Stephens Smith, August 5, 1786, WSP LOC. Short to William Stephens Smith, December 19, 1786, WSP LOC. Short to William Nelson, January 11, 1787, WPSP WM.

20. Davenport, ed., *Diary of the French Revolution*, 1: 250, entry made October 9, 1789, 1: 22; entry made March 28, 1789. [TJ] Notes of a Tour into the Southern Parts of France etc., *PTJDE*, 11: 415–64, at 446. [TJ] Notes of a Tour Through Holland and the Rhine Valley, 1788, *PTJDE*, 13: 8–36, at 28.

21. TJ to Charles Bellini, September 30, 1785, *PTJDE*, 8: 568–70, at 569. TJ to John Banister, Jr., October 15, 1785, *PTJDE*, 8: 635–8, at 636. Louis-Sébastian Mercier, *Paris in Miniature: Taken from the French Picture at Full Length, Entituled Tableau de Paris* (London 1782), citations at 71, 72–3. Jefferson purchased a second copy of Mercier's *Tableau de Paris* in 1787; see Memorandum Book, 1787, *PTJDE: Second Series*, 650, entry made January 5, also note 96. TJ to James Madison, August 2, 1787, *PTJDE*, 11: 662–5, at 663.

22. Abigail Adams to Mercy Otis Warren, September 5, 1784, *TAPDE: Adams Family Correspondence*, 5: 446–51, at 447. Abigail Adams to Royall Tyler, January 4, 1785,

TAPDE: Adams Family Correspondence, 6: 45–50 at 48. Abigail Adams to Mary Smith Cranch, April 15, 1785, *TAPDE: Adams Family Correspondence*, 6: 82–5, at 84. Abigail Adams to Mercy Otis Warren, May 10, 1785, *TAPDE: Adams Family Correspondence*, 6: 138–141, at 139. Abigail Adams to Mary Smith Cranch, December 9, 1784, *TAPDE: Adams Family Correspondence*, 6: 14–23, at 16.

23. Vaugelade, *Le Salon Physiocratique de La Rochefoucauld*, 15–19, and 301; Rousse, *La Roche-Guyon*, 250–54. See also Fasquelle, *Les La Rochfoucaulds*; La Rochefoucauld, Wolikow, Inki, *Le Duc de La Rochefoucauld- Liancourt*.

24. Abigail Adams to Royall Tyler, January 4, 1785, *TAPDE: Adams Family Correspondence*, 6: 45–50, at 49; see also, Abigail Adams to Mercy Otis Warren, September 5, 1784, *TAPDE: Adams Family Correspondence*, 5: 446–53, at 447. Mercier, *Paris in Miniature*, 72–3.

25. TJ to Eliza House Trist, August 18, 1785, *PTJDE*, 8: 403–5, at 404. TJ to Charles Bellini, September 30, 1785, *PTJDE*, 8: 568–70, at 569. TJ to Eliza House Trist, August 18, 1785, *PTJDE*, 8: 403–5, at 404. TJ to Caesar Augustus Rodney, October 8, 1807, *Founders Online*. TJ to Benjamin Hawkins, March 14, 1800, *PTJDE*, 31: 345–47, at 347.

26. TJ to Abigail Adams, November 20, 1785, *PTJDE*, 9: 47–8, at 48. Nabby Adams Smith's request that Jefferson procure her a pair of corsets from the staymaker she had used while in Paris also prompted a series of bantering letters, see Abigail Adams Smith to TJ, December 2, 1786, *PTJDE*, 10: 572–3; William Stephens Smith to TJ, December 5, 1786, *PTJDE*, 10: 578–9, at 578; TJ to Abigail Adams Smith, January 15, 1787, *PTJDE*, 11: 45–6. TJ to William Stephens Smith, July 9, 1786, *PTJDE*, 10: 115–7, at 116. TJ to William Stephens Smith, October 22, 1786, *PTJDE*, 10: 478–9, at 479. Gordon-Reed, *The Hemingses of Monticello*, 147; Kierner, *Martha Jefferson Randolph*, 24.

27. TJ to Angelica Schuyler Church, September 21, 1788, *PTJDE*, 13: 623–4, at 623. TJ to Madame de Tessé, August 27, 1789, *PTJDE*, 15: 363–4 and editorial note. On the eve of his departure for the United States, Madame de Tessé left a surprise gift for Jefferson in the form of a large marble pedestal inscribed with the sentiment that Jefferson's name would descend to posterity as a defender of American liberties; see TJ to Madame de Tessé, August 27, 1789, *PTJDE*, 15: 363–4. Madame de Tessé advised Short to kneel before this "altar"; Short to TJ, November 19, 1811, *PTJDE: Retirement*, 4: 268–74, at 269.

28. Brian Steele, *Thomas Jefferson and American Nationhood* (New York: Cambridge University Press, 2012), esp. 64–72. TJ to Martha Jefferson, March 28, 1787, *PTJDE*, 11: 250–2, at 251. Visiting Monticello in 1815, George Ticknor noted that Patsy Jefferson and her daughter Ellen were "accustomed" to join after dinner conversation "however high the topic may be"; see George Ticknor's Account of a Visit to Monticello, 4–7 February, 1815, *PTJDE: Retirement*, 8: 238–43, at 240. Jan Ellen Lewis, "Jefferson and Women" in Bienstock, Gordon-Reed, and Onuf, eds.

Family, Slavery, and Love in the Early American Republic, 292–308. TJ to Elizabeth Wayles Eppes, October 31, 1790, *PTJDE*, 17: 658.

29. Abigail Adams to Elizabeth Cranch, December 3, 1784, *TAPDE: Adams Family Correspondence*, 6: 3–10, at 6. TJ to Anne Willing Bingham, May 11, 1788, *PTJDE*, 13: 151–2, at 151. TJ to Anne Willing Bingham, February 7, 1787, *PTJDE*, 11: 122–4, at 123. TJ to Anne Willing Bingham, May 11, 1788, *PTJDE*, 13: 151–2, at 151.

30. Anne Willing Bingham to TJ, June 1, 1787, *PTJDE*, 11: 392–4, at 392, 393.

31. John Rutledge, Jr. Journal of a Visit to Paris 1787–88, Duke University Special Collections, 30. Short to Edward Sterrett, December 15, 1786, WSP LOC. Short to Thomas Lee Shippen, May 31, 1788, Gilpin Collection, HSP.

32. Thomas Rhett Smith to John Rutledge, Jr., December 26, 1790, SHC UNC. See also Howard P. Chudacoff, *The Age of the Bachelor: Creating an American Subculture* (Princeton: Princeton University Press, 1999).

33. TJ to Charles Thomson, November 11, 1784, *PTJDE*, 7: 518–9, at 519. TJ to John Banister Jr., October 15, 1785, *PTJDE*, 8: 635–8, at 636. TJ to James Madison, February 14, 1783, *PTJDE*, 6: 241–4, at 241.

34. Jefferson cited in [Mazzei] *Memoirs of the Life and Peregrinations of the Florentine Philip Mazzei, 1730–1816*, trans. Howard R. Marraro (New York: Columbia University Press, 1942), 284, 294; Jefferson to Anne Willing Bingham, May 11, 1788, *PTJDE*, 13: 151–2, at 151.

35. *The American Wanderer Through Various Parts of Europe*; William Nelson to Short, January 11, 1785, WSP LOC. Preeson Bowdoin to Short, April 11, 1785, copy, WSPS WM; Preeson Bowdoin to Short, April 7, 1785, WSP LOC.

36. "'Poor in Love Mr. Short,'" 526–9. Short to William Nelson, March 22, 1787, Gilpin Papers, HSP. For redirected mail, Short to Andre Limosin, May 14, 1787, WSP; Andre Limosin to Short, May 17, 1787, WSP. TJ to Madame de Tessé, February 28, 1787, *PTJDE* 11: 187. Short to TJ, March 22, 1787, *PTJDE*, 11: 232–35, at 235.

37. David Roberts, ed., *Lord Chesterfield's Letters* (Oxford: Oxford University Press, 1992), Letter 67, June 13, 1751, 234; Roberts, *Chesterfield's Letters*, Letter 66, May 16, 1751, 230–31.

38. James Currie to Short, August 5, 1785, WSP LOC. TJ to Short, April 30, 1785, *PTJDE*, 8: 132–3. Short to Thomas Lee Shippen, May 31, 1788, Gilpin Papers, HSP.

39. Pauline Castiglione to Short, n.d. March 1789, APS. Margaret Crosland, *Louise of Stolberg, Countess of Albany* (Edinburgh: Oliver and Boyd, 1962). Davenport, ed., *Diary of the French Revolution*, 2: 331, entry made December 23, 1791, 2: 331, 2: 329, entry made December 28, 1791. Gouverneur Morris to Countess of Albany, August 30, 1792, in Jared Sparks, *Life of Gouverneur Morris: With Selections from His Correspondence and Miscellaneous Papers*, 3 vols. (Boston, 1852), 3: 34–6. Pauline Castiglione to Short, August 22, 1788, APS. Pauline Castiglione to Short, June 16, 1789, APS. Pauline Castiglione to Short, August 22, 1788, APS. Short to William Stephen Smith, December 19, 1786, WSP LOC; Short to William Stephens Smith, May 20, 1787, WSP LOC.

40. William Nelson to Short, July 7 1787, WPSP WM; William Nelson to Short, July 12, 1788, WPSP WM. John Mayo to Short, February 1, 1785, WSP LOC. Davenport, ed., *Diary of the French Revolution*, entry made March 28, 1789, 1: 23.

    Abraham Bishop to Short, November 27, 1787, WSP LOC; Short to Abraham Bishop, December 2, 1787, WSP LOC; Abraham Bishop to Short, December 4, 1787, WSP LOC. Preeson Bowdoin to William Short, June 15, 1785, WPSP WM; Preeson Bowdoin to Short, May 26, 1785, WPSP WM; Preeson Bowdoin to Short, March 6, 1785, WSP LOC. Preeson Bowdoin to Short, April 7, 1785, WSP LOC.

41. Preeson Bowdoin to Short, March 6, 1785, WSP LOC. TJ to Short, May 21, 1787, *PTJDE*, 11: 371–3, at 372. [TJ] Notes of a Tour into the Southern Parts of France, 3 March–10 June, 1787, *PTJDE*, 11: 415–63. Short to TJ, May 29, 1787, *PTJDE*, 11: 381–3, at 382. Rutledge's father had introduced his son to Jefferson and asked for guidance on an itinerary; John Rutledge, Sr., to TJ, June 7, 1787, *PTJDE*, 11: 405–6; TJ to John Rutledge, Snr., August 6, 1787, *PTJDE*, 11: 700–1.

42. Short to John Rutledge, Jr., February 3, 1790, Gilpin Papers, HSP. See also John Brown Cutting to John Rutledge, Jr., September 21, 1789, SHC UNC; John Brown Cutting to John Rutledge, Jr., October 10, 1789, SHC UNC.

43. Short to John Mayo, n.d., early 1785, WSP LOC. Gouverneur Morris found himself explaining to an "incredulous" French libertine that "gallantry" was unknown in America; see Davenport, ed., *Diary of the French Revolution*, 1: 23, entry made March 28, 1789. William Nelson to Short, July 12, 1788, WPSP WM. Merit Moore Robinson to Short, January 10, 1808, WSP LOC.

44. Short to William Stephens Smith, December 19, 1786, WSP LOC. Short to William Nelson, July 6, 1788, Gilpin Papers, HSP. Short to William Nelson, March 19, 1788, Gilpin Papers, HSP. William Short Account Book, 1785–1792, Gilpin Papers, HSP. Short to William Nelson, July 6, 1788, Gilpin Papers, HSP. William Nelson to Short, July 12, 1788, WPSP WM.

45. William Short to John Rutledge, Jr., September 17, 1792, Gilpin Papers, HSP; Short to Edward Carrington, November 30, 1786, WSP LOC; William Nelson to Short, March 4, 1788, WPSP WM. Short to William Stephens Smith, December 19, 1786, WSP LOC.

46. Short to William Nelson, November 3, 1787, Gilpin Papers, HSP. For a biographical notice of Plunkett Chastellux, see Madame de Chastellux to TJ, May 6, 1795, *PTJDE*, 28: 343–4, editorial notes.

47. Margaret Darrow, "Popular Concepts of Marital Choice in Eighteenth Century France," *Journal of Social History* 19 (Winter 1985), 261–72; Margaret Darrow, "French Noblewomen and the New Domesticity, 1750–1850," *Feminist Studies* 5 (1979) 41–65. Short's involvement with the Société des Amis des Noirs would also have exposed him to the argument that, in societies with slavery, "the chaste enjoyments of conjugal union" should supplant those "vile sallies of debauchery by which the majesty of moral sentiment" was insulted; see Abbé Gregoire "Letter to the Citizens of Colour in the French West Indies, May 15, 1791" reprinted in

Marcus Rainsford, *An Historical Account of the Black Empire of Hayti*, eds. Paul
Youngquist and Grégory Pierrot (Durham: Duke University Press, 2013), 223.
Élisabeth Badinter and Robert Badinter, *Condorcet: Un Intellectuel en Politique*
(Paris: France Loisirs, 1988), 219; Fasquelle, *Les La Rochefoucauld*, 301. Rosalie de
La Rochefoucauld to Short, November 27, 1791, Harsanyi, *Lettres*, 76–7. See also
William Nelson to Short, March 4, 1788, WSP LOC.

48. Short boasted of his introduction to the Duchess d'Orléans in Short to John
    Rutledge, Jr., December 10, 1789, Gilpin Papers, HSP; Short to TJ, December 25,
    1789, *PTJDE*, 16: 43–8, at 47. Short to TJ, January 12, 1790, *PTJDE*, 16: 105–9,
    at 107.

49. Merit Moore Robinson to Short, January 10, 1808, WSP LOC.

50. TJ to Short, October 3, 1801, *PTJDE*, 35: 380–3, at 381.

CHAPTER THREE

1. John Adams to TJ, December 13, 1785, *PTJDE*, 9: 97–8, at 97. William Temple
   Franklin to TJ, December 17, 1789, *PTJDE*, 16: 36–37, at 37. TJ to James Monroe,
   July 5, 1785, *PTJDE*, 8: 261–2, at 262. TJ to William Temple Franklin, February 14,
   1790, *PTJDE*, 16: 180.

2. Short to TJ, June 14, 1790, *PTJDE*, 16: 496–503, at 498–9. Short to Edmund
   Randolph, cited in Myrna Boyce, "The Diplomatic Career of William Short,"
   Journal of Modern History, 15 (June 1943), 97–119, at 116; Short to TJ, May 22, 1794,
   PTJDE, 28: 78–83, esp. 82; Short to TJ, January 29, 1795, *PTJDE*, 28: 252–6, at 253.

3. Short to TJ, July 26, 1792, *PTJDE*, 24: 249–59, at 257. Short to Jane Edmunds,
   August 21, 1791, cited in Boyce, "The Diplomatic Career of William Short," 108.

4. TJ to Short, September 30, 1790, *PTJDE*, 17: 543–6, at 544, 543.

5. Alexander DeConde, *Entangling Alliance*, 166–9. TJ to William Stephens Smith,
   September 28, 1787, *PTJDE*, 12: 192–93, at 193.

6. Maclay cited in Plans and Estimates for the Diplomatic Establishment: Editorial
   Note, *PTJDE*, 17: 216–222, at 217. The Consular Convention of 1788: Editorial
   Note, *PTJDE*, 14: 67–92. [Benjamin Hawkins] Notes on Senate Debate, c. January
   3, 1792, *PTJDE*, 23: 11–14.

7. Short to TJ, June 14, 1790, *PTJDE*, 16: 496–503, at 498, 497. TJ to Short,
   September 30, 1790, *PTJDE*, 17: 543–46, at 543.

8. TJ to George Washington, December 15, 1789, *PTJDE*, 16: 34–5, at 34. TJ to John
   Paradise, July 5, 1789, *PTJDE*, 15: 242. TJ to Short, April 6, 1790, *PTJDE*, 16: 318–
   21, at 318.

9. Short to Alexander Hamilton, December 18, 1790, *PAHDE*, 7: 348–57, at 353.
   Short to TJ, June 6, 1791, *PTJDE*, 20: 528–36; see also Short to TJ, May 3, 1791,
   PTJDE, 20: 363–71. On entangling alliances, see Short to Edmund Randolph,
   March 3, 1795, WSP LOC. On the organization of the diplomatic corps, Short to
   TJ, September 15, 1792, *PTJDE*, 24: 374–83; Short to TJ, October 22, 1792, *PTJDE*,

24: 513–22, at 514–6. A notable detractor was the Countess of Sutherland, wife of the British ambassador to Paris; see Davenport, ed., *Diary of the French Revolution*, 2: 316–7, 2: 343, entries made November 28, 1791; January 17, 1792. Nabby Adams also disparaged Short, see Abigail Adams Smith to John Quincy Adams, July 3, 1792, *TAPDE: Adams Family Correspondence*, 9: 292–4, at 293.

10. Short to Alexander Hamilton, June 5, 1791, *PAHDE*, 8: 439. Short to John Rutledge, Jr., April 11, 1790, SHC UNC; Short to TJ, July 17, 1791, *PTJDE*, 20: 641–45, at 645. Short discussed at length the possibility of retaining a role for the monarchy in Short to TJ, September 18, 1792, *PTJDE*, 24: 390–401. TJ to James Madison, January 12, 1789, *PTJDE*, 14: 436–38, at 437; Zeische, *Cosmopolitan Patriots*, esp. 20–38. See also Gouverneur Morris, "Speech for the King of France" and "Notes on the Form of a Constitution for France," in J. Jackson Barlow, ed., *To Secure the Blessings of Liberty: Selected Writings of Gouverneur Morris* (Indianapolis: The Liberty Fund, 2012), 251, 269–84.

11. America's bankers confirmed this arrangement in Willink, Van Staphorst, and Hubbard to TJ, September 24, 1789, *PTJDE*, 15: 471–74, at 471. Alexander Hamilton to Short, October 7, 1789, *PAHDE*, 5: 429–30; Short to Alexander Hamilton, November 30, 1789, *PAHDE*, 5: 570–4.

12. TJ to Short, October 4, 1789, *PTJDE*, 15: 506. TJ to Short, December 14, 1789, *PTJDE*, 16: 24–8, at 28–9. Jefferson described his decision-making process in TJ to Philip Mazzei, April 5, 1790, *PTJDE*, 16: 307–08, at 307; TJ to Gouverneur Morris, November 7, 1792, *PTJDE*, 24: 494–5. [TJ] Statement on Accounts as Minister Plenipotentiary in France, March 8, 1796, *PTJDE*, 29: 13–22, at 21. James Madison to TJ, January 24, 1790, *PTJDE*, 16: 125–6, at 125.

13. Short to TJ, November 30, 1789, *PTJDE*, 15: 563–8, at 564. For Short's belief that Jefferson would return, see Short to TJ, November 19, 1789, *PTJDE*, 15: 547–551, at 549; Short to TJ, March 4, 1790, *PTJDE*, 16: 202–5, editorial note. On the title "Secretary," see John Brown Cutting cited in Short to TJ, November 19, 1789, *PTJDE*, 15: 547–51, editorial note. Short to John Jay, May 23, 1790, *PTJDE*, 16: 436–41, at 440; Short to John Jay, February 10, 1790, *PTJDE*, 16: 162–65, at 165; Short to John Jay, May 1, 1790, *PTJDE*, 6: 400–1. Short to John Jay, November 30, 1789, *PTJDE*, 16: 3–8, editorial note, at 7. For the first official letter Short addressed to TJ as Secretary of State, see Short to TJ, June 5, 1790, *PTJDE*, 16: 473–4. See also Short to John Jay, November 30, 1789, *PTJDE*, 16: 3–8, editorial note. Short to TJ, June 14, 1790, *PTJDE*, 16: 496–503, at 496–98. Short to TJ, June 14, 1790, *PTJDE*, 15: 496–503, at 497–8, 499. Short to John Brown Cutting, January 1790, cited in Short to TJ, March 4, 1790, *PTJDE*, 16: 202–5, editorial note.

14. Short's letters to TJ were also delayed; see TJ to Short, March 12, 1790, *PTJDE*, 16: 228–30 and editorial note. Jefferson announced his decision in TJ to Short, April 6, 1790, *PTJDE*, 16: 318–21, at 319. TJ to Short, March 12, 1790, *PTJDE*, 16: 228–9. "Jefferson's Instructions for Procuring Household Goods," April 6, 1790,

PTJDE, 16: 321–24. For the scale of the shipping arrangements, see Short to TJ, November 7, 1790, *PTJDE*, 18: 30–39.

15. Short to TJ, June 14, 1790, *PTJDE*, 16: 496–503, at 502. Short to TJ, October 25, 1790, *PTJDE*, 17: 631–5, at 633.

16. Short to TJ, July 11, 1790, *PTJDE*, 17: 27–9, at 29. TJ to Short, March 16, 1791, *PTJDE*, 19: 578–79, at 579. TJ to Short, January 24, 1791, *PTJDE*, 18: 600–03, at 602 and note 5. Short to TJ, October 25, 1790, *PTJDE*, 17: 631–5, at 633.

17. TJ to Short, March 16, 1791, *PTJDE*, 19: 578–9, at 579. Short to TJ, 7 July 1790, *PTJDE*, 17: 10–4, at 13. Short to John Rutledge, Jr., August 25, 1790, SHC UNC.

18. For a detailed accounting of the United States' foreign debt, see [Hamilton] Report Relative to a Provision for the Support of Public Credit, January 9, 1790, Schedule B, *PAHDE*, 6: 112–3; dollar equivalents are provided in Forrest McDonald, *Alexander Hamilton: A Biography* (New York: Norton, 1982), 145. See also Rafael A. Bayley, *The National Loans of the United States from July 4, 1776, to June 30, 1880* [Washington, 1882], 14; Samuel Flagg Bemis, "Payment of the French Loans to the United States, 1777–1795," *Current History*, 23 (March 1926), 824–31. Jefferson first discussed the sum owed the French officers in TJ to John Adams, January 12, 1786, *PTJDE*, 9: 165–66, at 165. TJ to Commissioners of the Treasury, May 7, 1786, 9: 471. TJ to James Madison, with Enclosure, August 2, 1787, *PTJDE*, 11: 662–68. TJ to John Adams, July 1, 1787, *PTJDE*, 11: 515–8, at 517. For the cessation of congressional business during the Constitutional Convention, see John Jay to Short, July 5, 1787, *PTJDE*, 11: 549–50, at 549; TJ to C. W. F. Dumas, August 9, 1787, *PTJDE*, 12: 10. TJ to John Adams, July 1, 1787, *PTJDE*, 11: 515–8, at 517; TJ to Benjamin Hawkins, August 4, 1787, *PTJDE*, 11: 683–4. John Adams to TJ, July 10, 1787, *PTJDE*, 11: 575.

19. Commissioners of the Treasury to TJ, May 9, 1786, *PTJDE*, 9: 479–81. The crisis was caused by a large claim made on Grand by Thomas Barclay; see Thomas Barclay to TJ, *PTJDE*, June 12, 1787, *PTJDE*, 11: 466–7; TJ to James Madison, June 20, 1787, *PTJDE*, 11: 480–4, at 483. TJ to John Adams, July 23, 1787, *PTJDE*, 11: 610–11, at 611; see also TJ to John Jay, September 19, 1789, *PTJDE*, 15: 454–61. [TJ] Explanation of Ferdinand Grand's Accounts, February 21, 1792, *PTJDE*, 23: 128–37.

20. At the conclusion of the crisis Short noted that Grand held 14,000 livres on Short's account: List of All Sums Rec'd on Acct of my Salary beginning September 25, 1785, LOC WSP. Short to TJ, May 29, 1787, *PTJDE*, 11: 381–3, at 382. TJ to Commissioners of the Treasury, June 17, 1787, *PTJDE*, 11: 474–5. TJ to William Stephens Smith, August 31, 1787, *PTJDE*, 12: 71–3, at 72. See also William Stephens Smith to TJ, September 18, 1787, *PTJDE*, 12: 145–48, at 147. TJ to William Carmichael, June 14, 1787, *PTJDE*, 11: 469–70, at 469; TJ to C. W. F. Dumas, June 14, 1787, *PTJDE*, 11: 471. C. W. F. Dumas to TJ, July 12, 1787, *PTJDE*, 11: 581, editorial note; C. W. F. Dumas to John Adams, July 10, 1787, *PJADE*, 112–4, at 113. For a description of Dumas' past service to the United States, see Matthjis Tobias Tieleman, "A Revolutionary Wave: Dutch and American Patriots in the

Eighteenth-Century Atlantic World" (PhD Dissertation, University of California Los Angeles, 2021), 164–7, 228. William Carmichael to TJ, *PTJDE*, July 9, 1787, 11: 565–7, at 565. TJ to William Carmichael, September 25, 1787, *PTJDE*, 12: 172–6, at 172. TJ to Commissioners of the Treasury, June 17, 1787, *PTJDE*, 11: 474–5, at 475. John Adams to TJ, July 10, 1787, *PTJDE*, 11: 575. Short to TJ, January 16, 1791, *PTJDE*, 18: 500–07, at 501.

21. TJ to John Jay, September 26, 1786, *PTJDE*, 10: 405–6, at 406; TJ to John Jay, with enclosure, November 12, 1786, *PTJDE*, 10: 519–23; TJ to C. W. F. Dumas, December 25, 1786, *PTJDE*, 10: 630–32, at 631; TJ to John Jay, February 1, 1787, *PTJDE*, 11: 99. Jefferson's enquiries later became the subject of partisan attack; see, TJ to George Washington, October 17, 1792, *PTJDE*, 24: 494–5; [TJ] Observations on the French Debt, October 17, 1792, *PTJDE*, 24: 496–8. TJ to James Madison, June 20, 1787, *PTJDE*, 11: 480–84, at 482; Gouverneur Morris noted TJ's desire to avoid involvement in detailed negotiations; see Davenport, ed., *Diary of the Revolution*, 1: 227, entry made September 24, 1789. John Adams to Abigail Adams, March 14, 1788, *TAPDE: Adams Family Correspondence*, 8: 244–45; John Adams to Abigail Adams, March 11, 1788, *TAPDE: Adams Family Correspondence*, 8: 243–4. John Adams to TJ, February 12, 1788, *PTJDE*, 12: 581–82, at 582. *Autobiography*, 124. TJ to James Madison, June 20, 1787, *PTJDE*, 11: 482.

22. [Hamilton] Report Relative to a Provision for the Support of Public Credit, January 9, 1790, Schedule B, *PAHDE*, 6: 112–3; Willink and Van Staphorst to TJ, with Enclosures, January 31, 1788, *PTJDE*, 12: 543–8. John Adams to TJ, February 12, 1788, *PTJDE*, 12: 581–82, at 582. Short first outlined the context of Necker's proposals in Short to TJ, November 19, 1789, *PTJDE*, 15: 547–51, at 549; Short to Alexander Hamilton, November 30, 1789, *PAHDE*, 5: 570–4.

23. Willinks, Van Staphorst, and Hubbard to Short, November 19, 1789, LOC WSP; Willinks, Van Staphorst, and Hubbard to Short, January 25, 1790, LOC WSP.

24. Willinks, Van Staphorst, and Hubbard to Alexander Hamilton, January 25, 1790, *PAHDE*, 6: 210–8, at 210–2.

25. Short to Gouverneur Morris, November 20, 1790, cited in Melanie Randolph Miller, *Envoy to the Terror: Gouverneur Morris and the French Revolution* (Washington DC: Potomac Books, 2006), 96; Short to TJ, October 25, 1790, *PTJDE*, 17: 631–5, at 634. Short to TJ, January 28, 1790, *PTJDE*, 16: 130–5, at 135. Jefferson's Opinion on Fiscal Policy, August 26, 1790, *PTJDE*, 17: 425–6. Alexander Hamilton to Short, August 29, 1790, *PAHDE*, 6: 585–86. Alexander Hamilton to Willink, Van Staphorst and Hubbard, May 7, 1790, *PAHDE*, 6: 409–10. Alexander Hamilton to Short, August 29, 1790, *PAHDE*, 6: 585–6.

26. Short to TJ, January 12, 1790, *PTJDE*, 16: 105–9, at 109; Short to TJ, January 28, 1790, *PTJDE*, 16: 130–5, at 132. Short to Alexander Hamilton, November 30. 1789, *PAHDE*, 5: 570–4; Short to Alexander Hamilton, January 28[–31], 1790, *PAHDE*, 6: 227–32. For a brief history of schemes to corner the US debt to France, see "The Debt to France: The Proposals of Schweitzer, Jeanneret & Cie,"

PTJDE, 20: 175–197. The speculation was extensively discussed by Gouverneur Morris; see Davenport, ed., *Diary of the French Revolution*; Gouverneur Morris to Alexander Hamilton, January 31, 1790, *PAHDE*, 6: 234–9; Etienne Clavière to TJ with Enclosure "Observations Sur le Tableau en deux Parties," July 9, 1788, *PTJDE*, 13: 320–323, at 322.

27. Davenport, ed., *Diary of the French Revolution*, 1: 14, entry made March 18, 1789. Gouverneur Morris to George Washington, May 27, 1791, *PGWDEP*, 8: 208–13, at 210.

28. TJ to Short, April 25, 1791. *PTJDE*, 20: 254–6, at 255. "The Debt to France: The Proposals of Schweitzer, Jeanneret & Cie," *PTJDE*, 20: 175–197; Short to Alexander Hamilton, December 18, 1790, with enclosures, *PAHDE*, 7: 348–357, at 356–7. Short to TJ, November 25, 1790, *PTJDE*, 18: 75–77, at 77.

29. Short to TJ, April 3, 1789, *PTJDE*, 15: 27–30, at 28. Short to TJ, February 29, 1792, *PTJDE*, 23:167–9, at 168. Morris cited in Miller, *Envoy to the Terror*, 75. John Adams warned Jefferson and, before that, America's Dutch bankers about Parker; see John Adams to TJ, February 12, 1788, *PTJDE*, 12: 581–2, at 582; John Adams to Willinks and Van Staphorst, August 19, 1785, *PJADE*, 17: 342. William Stephens Smith to Short, October 31, 1787 WSP LOC; Short to William Stephens Smith, November 15, 1787, WSP LOC. Short to TJ, May 2, 1791, *PTJDE*, 20: 345–352. The money was not lost; see Short to TJ, April 2, 1793, *PTJDE*, 25: 482–83, at 482. In later life, Short praised Parker's patriotism and commercial acumen; see Short to TJ, November 19, 1811, *PTJDE: Retirement*, 4: 268–74, at 273.

30. For Hamilton's efforts to shape foreign policy, see Samuel Flagg Bemis, "Thomas Jefferson" in Bemis, *The American Secretaries of State and Their Diplomacy* (New York: Knopf, 1927); Julian P. Boyd, *Number 7: Alexander Hamilton's Secret Attempts to Control American Foreign Policy* (Princeton: Princeton University Press, 1964). Memoranda on Candidates and Places for Consular Appointments, ca. June 1, 1790, *PTJDE*, 17: 249–55. Jefferson's Opinion on Fiscal Policy, August 26, 1790, *PTJDE*, 17: 425–30, at 425–6.

31. TJ to Short, August 31, 1790, *PTJDE*, 17: 477. Short to TJ, October 25, 1790, *PTJDE*, 17: 631–35, at 634. Short to TJ, April 5, 1793, *PTJDE*, 25: 494–510, at 494; see also, Short to TJ, May 22, 1794, *PTJDE*, 28: 78–83, at 79. TJ to Short, September 6, 1790, *PTJDE*, 17: 496–97, at 497. TJ to Short, September 30, 1790, *PTJDE*, 17: 543–6, at 543.

32. Alexander Hamilton to Short, September 1, 1790, *PAHDE*, 7: 6–14, at 12. Short to Alexander Hamilton, December 18, 1790, *PAHDE*, 7: 348–57; Short to Alexander Hamilton, December 2, 1790, *PAHDE*, 7: 175–85.

33. Short to Alexander Hamilton, February 17, 1791, *PAHDE*, 8: 51–7, at 54; Short to TJ, February 18, 1791, *PTJDE*, 19: 291–2. Short to Alexander Hamilton, April 9, 1791, *PAHDE*, 8: 260–4, at 263.

34. Alexander Hamilton to Short, April 13, 1791, *PAHDE*, 8: 280–83, at 281. Hamilton indicated his desire to lift restrictions in Alexander Hamilton to Short, May 9, 1791,

PAHDE, 8: 335–6, at 335; Alexander Hamilton to Short, May 24, 1791, *PAHDE*, 8: 356–7. Alexander Hamilton to George Washington, April 10, 1791, *PAHDE*, 8: 270–1. Alexander Hamilton to George Washington, July 29, 1791, *PAHDE*, 8: 587–8; George Washington to Alexander Hamilton, July 29, 1791; *PAHDE*, 8: 587–8, at 587; see also Short to TJ, April 8, 1791, *PTJDE*, 20: 170–3, editorial note. Alexander Hamilton to Short, August 1–2, 1791, *PAHDE*, 9: 1–3. Short to Alexander Hamilton, October 10, 1791, *PAHDE*, 9: 311–16, at 316.

35. TJ to Short, August 26, 1790, *PTJDE*, 17: 431–435, at 433. Alexander Hamilton to Short, April 13, 1791, *PAHDE*, 8: 280–2, at 281; Alexander Hamilton to Short, May 9, 1791, *PAHDE*, 8: 335–36, at 336. Short to Alexander Hamilton, June 3, 1791, *PAHDE*, 8: 412–425; Short to TJ, May 2, 1791, *PTJDE*, 20:345–52, at 349. Alexander Hamilton to Short, March 5, 1792, *PAHDE*, 11: 106–7, at 107. Hamilton asked Short to distinguish between temporary exchange rate fluctuations and underlying depreciation, and Short attempted to meet this objective; see Alexander Hamilton to Short, September 2, 1791, *PAHDE*, 9: 158–62; Short to TJ, April 5, 1793, *PTJDE*, 25: 494–510. TJ to Jean Baptiste Ternant, September 1, 1791, *PTJDE*, 22: 119–20.

36. Short to TJ, September 29, 1791, *PTJDE*, 22: 173–74, at 174. Short to TJ, June 7, 1791, *PTJDE*, 20: 541–6 at 542.

37. Short to TJ, May 2, 1791, *PTJDE*, 20: 345–352, at 348. See also Short to TJ, July 17, 1791, *PTJDE*, 20: 641–45, at 643. Davenport, ed., *Diary of the French Revolution*, 2: 212, entry made July 4, 1791. Short to Alexander Hamilton, August 23, 1791, *PAHDE*, 9: 97–103, at 102. Short to Duke de La Rochefoucauld, March 23, 1790, Gilpin Collection. HSP; Short to TJ, September 29, 1791, *PTJDE*, 22: 171–3. Short to Marquis de Lafayette, February 1, 1790, Gilpin Collection, HSP. Short to John Rutledge, May 17, 1790, SHC UNC. Davenport, ed., *Diary of the French Revolution*, 1: 116, entry made June 17, 1789, 1: 116, 2: 255–6.

38. Miller, *Envoy to the Terror*. For Morris's view of mobs, see Gouverneur Morris to John Penn, May 20, 1774, in Peter Force, *American Archives*, 4th ser. 1: 342–3.

39. Short to TJ, October 22, 1792, *PTJDE*, 24: 513–22, at 516, 518. Bizardel and Rice "'Poor in Love Mr. Short.'" Davenport, ed., *Diary of the French Revolution*. Gouverneur Morris to Countess of Albany, August 30, 1792, in Sparks, *Life of Gouverneur Morris*, 3: 34–6. Gouverneur Morris to George Washington, November 22, 1790, *PGWDEP*, 6: 683–9, at 686–7. Washington showed this letter to Jefferson.

40. Miller, *Envoy to the Terror*, 48–72. TJ to Gouverneur Morris, July 26, 1791, *PTJDE*, 20: 680; TJ to Gouverneur Morris, August 30, 1791, *PTJDE*, 22: 104–5.

41. Julian P. Boyd, *Number 7*; Commercial and Diplomatic Relations with Britain: Editorial Note, *PTJDE*, 18: 220–83. For Hamilton's defamatory comments, see [Hamilton] Conversation with George Beckwith, September 25–30, 1790, *PAHDE*, 7: 70–2, at 72; Michael Schwarz, "The de-Anglicization

of America: Jefferson, Madison, and U.S.-British Relations, 1783–95" (Ph.D. Dissertation, University of Kentucky, 2008), chap. five.

42. Short to TJ, October 6, 1791, *PTJDE*, 22: 189–95, at 194.

43. See TJ to Thomas Pinckney, November 6, 1791, *PTJDE*, 22: 261 and editorial note. Schwarz, "De-Anglicization of America," 163–69.

44. Benjamin Hawkins to TJ, Enclosure: Notes on Senate Debate, January 3, 1792, *PTJDE*, 23: 11–14; [TJ] Memorandum on Meeting with Senate Committee, January 4, 1792, *PTJDE*, 23:19–24; TJ to Short, January 3, 1792, *PTJDE*, 23: 16. James Monroe cited in, *Envoy to The Terror*, 94. James Monroe to TJ, January [11] 1792, *PTJDE*, 23: 35–6, at 35; TJ to James Madison, January 12, 1792, *PTJDE*, 23: 37.

45. TJ to Short, January 28, 1792, *PTJDE*, 23: 83–4. For hostility to the creation of further diplomatic posts, see [TJ] Memorandum on Meeting with Senate Committee, January 4, 1792, *PTJDE*, 23: 19–22.

46. Unknown to Short, while minister to France, Jefferson had resisted a temporary secondment to Madrid; see TJ to James Madison, June 20, 1787, *PTJDE*, 11: 480–4, at 481. Short to TJ, July 26, 1792, *PTJDE*, 24: 249–59, at 257.

47. Thomas Paine to TJ, February 13, 1792, *PTJDE*, 23: 115. Marquis de Lafayette to George Washington, March 15, 1792, *PGWDE*, 10: 116–7. Madame d'Enville to TJ, December 30, 1792, *PTJDE*, 24: 798–9, at 799. See also Madame d'Enville to TJ, February 13, 1792, *PTJDE*, 23: 112–3.

48. Short to TJ, February 29, 1792, *PTJDE*, 23: 167–9, at 167, 168, 169. Short described how he heard the news in Short to Alexander Hamilton, March 24, 1792, *PAHDE*, 11: 178–85, at 182; Short to TJ, May 15, 1792, *PTJDE*, 23: 5059, at 505; Short to TJ, July 26, 1792, *PTJDE*, 24: 249–59, at 251. Gouverneur Morris wrote to Short from London and under the impression that the Senate would reject his own nomination; see Davenport, ed., *Diary of the French Revolution*, 2: 363. For accounts relishing Short's discomfort, see James Swan to Gouverneur Morris, February 9, 1792, APS; Abigail Adams Smith to John Quincy Adams, July 3, 1792, *TAPDE: Adams Family Correspondence*, 9: 292–4. Short to TJ, May 15, 1792, *PTJDE*, 23: 505–09, at 507. Short to Alexander Hamilton, March 24, 1792, *PAHDE*, 11: 178–85, at 182; Short to Alexander Hamilton, May 11, 1793, *PAHDE*, 14: 432–9, at 436. See also Short to TJ, May 2, 1792, *PTJDE*, 23: 477–9; Short to TJ, July 26, 1792, *PTJDE*, 24: 249–59.

49. TJ to Short, October 16, 1792, *PTJDE*, 24: 490–1, at 491.

50. Short to TJ, July 26, 1792, *PTJDE*, 24: 249–59, at 253. Davenport, ed., *Diary of the French Revolution* 2: 426–7, entry made May 11, 1792. Pierre Lebrun to TJ, January 15, 1793, *PTJDE*, 25: 57–8 editorial note. See also [TJ] Notes on a Conversation with William Stephens Smith and George Washington, February 20, 1793, *PTJDE*, 25: 243–45. Short to TJ, July 26, 1792, *PTJDE*, 24: 249–59, at 253. Short to TJ, May 15, 1792, *PTJDE*, 23: 503–5, at 504. Short sought to establish Morris's future responsibility for debt repayments and criticize Morris's tardiness in Short to Alexander Hamilton, March 24, 1792, *PAHDE*, 11: 178–85, at 182.

51. Short to Alexander Hamilton, December 30, 1791, *PAHDE*, 10: 485–90, at 487. Short to Hamilton, December 28, 1791, *PAHDE*, 10: 472–80. Short anticipated a French request for an advance on the debt in Short to TJ, February 29, 1792, *PTJDE*, 23: 170–1, at 170. TJ to Gouverneur Morris, April 28, 1792, *PTJDE*, 23: 467–8. Short to Alexander Hamilton, March 24, 1792, *PAHDE*, 11: 178–85, at 179, 184; see also Short to Alexander Hamilton, May 11, 1793, *PAHDE*, 14: 432–39. Jefferson also believed Morris would assume responsibility; see TJ to Gouverneur Morris, March 10, 1792, *PTJDE*, 23: 248–50, at 249. See also Short to TJ, April 5, 1793, *PTJDE*, 25: 494–510; Short to TJ, May 22, 1794, *PTJDE*, 28: 78–83.

52. Alexander Hamilton to Short, June 14, 1792, *PAHDE*, 11: 519–20, at 519. Short to Alexander Hamilton, October 9, 1792, *PAHDE*, 12: 534–38, at 537. Short had previously denied responsibility for calculating depreciation in, Short to Alexander Hamilton, June 28, 1792, *PAHDE*, 11: 593–99. For his description and criticism of Morris's deal, see Short to Alexander Hamilton, September 25, 1792, *PAHDE*, 12: 469–80; Short to Alexander Hamilton, August 30, 1792, *PAHDE*, 12: 293–97; Short to Alexander Hamilton, October 27, 1792, *PAHDE*, 12: 624–8. For Short's compliance and specified receipt, see Short to Alexander Hamilton, October 27, 1792, *PAHDE*, 12: 624–28, 625, 624; also Short to Alexander Hamilton, May 11, 1793, *PAHDE*, 14: 432–39, at 434.

53. Short to TJ, November 9, 1792, *PTJDE*, 24: 601–3, at 602. Short to TJ, April 5, 1793, *PTJDE*, 25: 494–510, at 506. Gouverneur Morris to Alexander Hamilton, September 25, 1792, enclosure Gouverneur Morris to Short, September 20, 1792, *PAHDE*, 12: 425–6; Gouverneur Morris to TJ, August 22, 1792, *PTJDE*, 24: 313–5. Lebrun's complaint against Short was included as an enclosure in Gouverneur Morris to Alexander Hamilton, September 25, 1792, *PAHDE*, 12: 425–6. In the same letter, Morris refused to criticize Short. For Morris's criticism of Jefferson, see Gouverneur Morris to Alexander Hamilton, December 24, 1792, *PAHDE*, 13: 376–8, at 377. TJ to George Washington, February 20, 1793, Enclosure: Extracts of Letters concerning Gouverneur Morris and William Short, *PTJDE*, 25: 247–9. TJ to Gouverneur Morris, October 15, 1792, *PTJDE*, 24: 484–6; TJ to Gouverneur Morris, November 7, 1792, *PTJDE*, 24: 592–4, at 593; TJ to Gouverneur Morris, December 30, 1792, 24: 800–2, at 800. Alexander Hamilton to Short, October 1 [–15], 1792, *PAHDE*, 12: 513–4.

54. Hamilton described Jefferson's incursions into his brief in Alexander Hamilton to Edward Carrington, May 26, 1792, *PAHDE*, 11: 426–44, at 439. For an overview establishing Jefferson's involvement in framing the case against Hamilton, see Jefferson and the Giles Resolutions: Editorial Note, *PTJDE*, 25: 280–92. TJ to George Washington, October 17, 1792, *PTJDE*, 24: 494–5; [TJ] Observations on the French Debt, October 17, 1792, *PTJDE*, 24: 496–8. The charges are listed in House of Representatives, 2nd Congress, Second Session, *Annals of Congress*, 899. Jefferson and the Giles Resolutions: Editorial Note, c. February 27, 1793, *PTJDE*, 25: 280–92.

55. For discussion of the congressional debate, see McDonald, *Alexander Hamilton*, 259–61; Stanley Elkins and Eric McKitrick, *The Age of Federalism: The Early American Republic, 1788–1800* (New York: Oxford University Press, 1993), 295–302.

56. Hamilton, Speech to the House of Representatives, February 13, 1793, 2nd Congress, Second Session, *Annals of Congress*, 1216, 1221. Here Hamilton utilized analysis made in Short to Alexander Hamilton, December 18, 1790, *PAHDE*, 7: 348–57. Alexander Hamilton to Short, February 5, 1793, *PAHDE*, 14: 7. Short to Alexander Hamilton, May 11, 1793, *PAHDE*, 14: 432–9, at 432, 437.

57. See also, [TJ] Notes on Alexander Hamilton's Report on Foreign Loans, ca. February 20, 1793, *PTJDE*, 25: 239–243. TJ to James Monroe, January 14, 1793, *PTJDE*, 25: 50. TJ to Short, March 23, 1793, *PTJDE*, 25: 436–7, at 436.

58. Short to TJ, May 22, 1794, *PTJDE*, 28: 78–83, at 78–9, 82. Short to TJ, November 20, 1792, *PTJDE*, 24: 646–50, at 649.

59. TJ to Short, January 28, 1792, *PTJDE*, 23: 83–43; TJ to Short, March 18, 1792, *PTJDE*, 23: 317–8. See also TJ to Short, January 23, 1792, *PTJDE*, 23: 58–60. For Jefferson's confidential instruction, see, TJ to Short, March 18, 1792, *PTJDE*, 23: 318–9, at 318. Samuel Gwynn Coe, "The Mission of William Carmichael to Spain" (PhD Dissertation, Johns Hopkins University, 1926). William Stephens Smith to Short, June 3, 1787, WSP LOC. Short to TJ, July 26, 1792, *PTJDE*, 23: 249–58, at 258. For Morris's regard for William Carmichael, see Gouverneur Morris to George Washington, January 22, 1790, *PGWDEP*, 5: 37–40, at 38.

60. For Short's views on an Anglo-Spanish alliance, see Short to TJ, February 3, 1793, *PTJDE*, 25: 139–42, at 140–1; Short to TJ, November 13, 1793, *PTJDE*, 27: 356–8, at 357. On accreditation, see William Carmichael and Short to TJ, February 19, 1793, *PTJDE*, 25: 232–34; Short to TJ, March 6, 1793, *PTJDE*, 25: 321–28, at 322; Short to TJ, November 11, 1793, *PTJDE*, 27: 350–1. Shackelford, "William Short, Jefferson's Adopted Son" (PhD Dissertation, University of Virginia, 1955), 433, 435. Short to TJ, November 7, 1793, *PTJDE*, 27: 324–8, at 326; Short to TJ, November 13, 1793, *PTJDE*, 27: 356–8.

61. For background, see Samuel Flagg Bemis, *Pinckney's Treaty: America's Advantage from Europe's Distress, 1783–1800* (rep. New Haven: Yale University Press, 1965); William Carmichael and Short to TJ, April 18, 1793, *PTJDE*, 25: 554–62. Short to TJ, November 13, 1793, *PTJDE*, 27: 356–8, at 357. Short outlined his proposal in Short to Don Diego de Gardoqui, August 6, 1794, LOC WSP. Shackelford, *Jefferson's Adoptive Son*, 104–5; Shackelford, "William Short, Jefferson's Adopted Son," 436–9.

62. Bemis, *Pinckney's Treaty*, 195 n. 49, 209. Short to TJ, January 29, 1795, *PTJDE*, 28: 252–6, at 254.

63. Pinckney had praised Short's past service in Timothy Pickering to George Washington, October 5, 1794: Enclosure: Thomas Pinckney to Secretary of State, July 21, 1795, *PGWDEP*, 19: 19–24, at 22. For Short's opinion of Pinckney, see Short to TJ, January 29, 1795, *PTJDE*, 28: 252–6, at 254. Short to TJ, September 2,

1795, *PTJDE*, 28: 442–46, at 442. TJ to Short, March 12, 1797, *PTJDE*, 29: 316–8, at 316.

64. Madison's opinion of Morris cited in Editorial Note: The War Crisis of 1790, *PTJDE*, 17: 35–108, at 99. Short's competence and Carmichael's failings are discussed in Bemis, *Pinckney's Treaty*, esp. 250. On Monroe, Short to TJ, January 29, 1795, *PTJDE*, 28: 252–6, at 253. Robert R. Livingston to TJ, May 2, 1801, *PTJDE*, 34: 12–13; TJ to Short, October 3, 1801, *PTJDE*, 35: 380–3, at 383; Jon Kukla, *A Wilderness So Immense: The Louisiana Purchase and the Nation's Destiny* (New York: Anchor Books, 2004), 239.

CHAPTER FOUR

1. Jefferson praised Montmorin's integrity in TJ to James Madison, June 20, 1787, *PTJDE*, 11: 480–84, at 482.

2. Madame de Houdetot to TJ, September 3, 1790, *PTJDE*, 17: 485–6, at 486; TJ to Madame de Corny, October 14, 1789, *PTJDE*, 15: 520. TJ to Thomas Paine, October 14, 1789, *PTJDE*, 15: 522. See also TJ to James Monroe, August 9, 1788, *PTJDE*, 13: 488–90, at 489.

3. C. W. F. Dumas to TJ, September 12, 1786, *PTJDE*, 10: 354–6, at 354. TJ to C. W. F. Dumas, September 22, 1786, *PTJDE*, 10: 397–8, at 397. Jefferson eventually made representations on Dumas's behalf, TJ to John Jay, October 8 1787, *PTJDE*, 12: 214–7, at 217. For background, see Lawrence S. Kaplan, "The Founding Fathers and the Two Confederations: The United States of America and the United Provinces of the Netherlands, 1783–89," in Kaplan, *Entangling Alliances with None: American Foreign Policy in the Age of Jefferson* (Kent, OH: Kent State Press, 1987); Peter Nicolaisen, "John Adams, Thomas Jefferson, and the Dutch Patriots," in Leonard Sadosky, Peter Nicolaisen, Peter S. Onuf, and Andrew J. O'Shaughnessy, eds., *Old World, New World: America and Europe in the Age of Jefferson* (Charlottesville: University of Virginia Press, 2007), 105–130. Tieleman, "A Revolutionary Wave."

4. TJ to Edward Carrington, January 16, 1787, *PTJDE*, 11: 48–50, at 49. TJ to James Madison, January 30, 1787, *PTJDE*, 11: 92–7, at 93. TJ to Abigail Adams, February 22, 1787, *PTJDE*, 11: 174–5, at 174. TJ to William Stephens Smith, November 13, 1787, *PTJDE*, 12: 355–7, at 356. See also, TJ to David Hartley, July 2, 1787, *PTJDE*, 11: 525–6, at 526.

5. TJ to Maria Cosway, July 25, 1789, *PTJDE*, 15: 305–6, at 305. For a description of the events of July 22, see Simon Schama, *Citizens: A Chronicle of the French Revolution* (New York: Knopf, 1989), 405–6, 446; Davenport, ed., *Diary of the French Revolution*, 1: 159, entry made July 22, 1789, 1: 159; Zeische, *Cosmopolitan Patriots*, 29. TJ to James Madison, July 22, 1789, *PTJDE*, 15: 299–301, at 301. Barnave cited in Schama, *Citizens*, 406; TJ to Maria Cosway, July 25, 1789, *PTJDE*, 15: 305–6, at 305.

6. TJ to John Jay, July 23, 1789, *PTJDE*, 15: 301–2, at 301; TJ to James Madison, July 29, 1789, *PTJDE*, 15: 315–6, at 316. In an earlier letter, Jefferson referred to the

"severing" of Foulon's head but by a "mob" and then only after he had been hanged and in defiance of efforts by "the gardes Bourgeoises" to save him; see TJ to James Madison, July 22, 1789, *PTJDE*, 15: 299–301, at 301. For Lafayette's reaction, see Schama, *Citizens*, 447.

7. For an indictment of Jefferson, see Conor Cruise O'Brien, *The Long Affair: Thomas Jefferson and the French Revolution* (London: Sinclair-Stevenson, 1996); see also Sophie Wahnich, *In Defense of the Terror: Liberty or Death in the French Revolution*, trans. David Fernbach (London: Verso, 2012). TJ to Thomas Paine, July 23, 1789, *PTJDE*, 15: 302. TJ to John Jay, July 29, 1789, *PTJDE*, 15: 314. On the killing of de Launay, see Schama, *Citizens*, 399–405. TJ to John Jay, July 19, 1789, 15: 284–91, at 288; see also TJ to Count Jean Diodati, August 3, 1789, *PTJDE*, 15: 325–7, at 325.

8. Malone, *Thomas Jefferson and the Rights of Man*, 180. See also TJ to John Jay, June 24, 1789, *PTJDE*, 15: 205–10; TJ to John Jay, August 27, 1789, *PTJDE*, 15: 356–61, at 359. TJ learned of the detention of the Princess of Orange from C. W. F. Dumas to TJ, June 30, 1787 [summary], *PTJDE*, 11: 510, editorial note. For background, see Tieleman, "A Revolutionary Wave: Dutch and American Patriots in the Eighteenth-Century Atlantic World," 224–6. TJ to John Jay, October 8, 1787, *PTJDE*, 12: 217–8, at 218. TJ to John Jay, August 6, 1787, PTJDE, 11: 693–700, at 697. TJ to David Humphreys, August 14, 1787, *PTJDE*, 12: 32–3, at 33.

9. TJ to John Rutledge, August 6, 1787, *PTJDE*, 11: 700–1, at 701. TJ to John Adams, September 28, 1787, *PTJDE*, 12: 189–90, at 189. John Adams to TJ, October 9, 1787, *PTJDE*, 12: 220–1.

10. TJ to John Jay, June 17, 1789, *PTJDE*, 15: 187–191, at 188–9, 190. TJ to John Jay, May 9, 1789, *PTJDE*, 15: 110–3, at 112; TJ to John Jay, September 19, 1789, *PTJDE*, 15: 454–461, at 458, 460. Character of Monsieur Necker [June 1789], *PTJDE*, 15:191–3. For Jefferson's assessment of Louis XVI, see TJ to John Jay, April 23, 1786, *PTJDE*, 9:402–3, at 402; TJ to John Jay, October 8, 1787, *PTJDE*, 12: 217–8. Marie-Antoinette described in TJ to John Jay, September 19, 1789, *PTJDE*, 15: 454–461, at 460. "Objects for the Attention of an American," in Jefferson's Hints to Americans Travelling in Europe, June 19, 1788, *PJTDE*, 13: 264–75, at 269. On scarcity of bread, TJ to John Jay, July 29, 1789, *PTJDE*, 15: 314–5, at 314; TJ to John Jay, August 27, 1789, *PTJDE*, 15: 356–61, at 358. TJ to John Jay, May 9, 1789, *PTJDE*, 15:110–3, at 110–1; for background, see Schama, *Patriots*, 326–31. TJ to William Carmichael, May 8, 1789, *PTJDE*, 15: 103–5, at 104.

11. See, for example, Short's description of the march of the *poissardes*, Short to TJ, November 3, 1789, *PTJDE*, 15: 530–8. Short to TJ, November 3, 1791, *PTJDE*, 20: 672–5, at 673. Short to TJ, July 24, 1791, *PTJDE*, 20: 672–5, at 673. Short referenced pamphlet literature in Short to TJ, December 25, 1789, *PTJDE*, 16: 43–8, at 45–6; Short to TJ, January 12, 1790, *PTJDE*, 16: 105–9, at 107; see also Short to John Rutledge, Jr., August 8, 1789, SHC UNC. Davenport, ed., *Diary of the French Revolution*.

12. TJ to David Humphreys, March 18, 1789, *PTJDE*, 14: 676–9, at 676, 678; TJ to Thomas Lee Shippen, March 11, 1789, *PTJDE*, 14: 638–40, at 638. TJ to George Washington, December 4, 1788, *PTJDE*, 14: 328–32, at 330.

13. Short to TJ, January 28, 1790, *PTJDE*, 16: 130–5, at 133. On the Société des Quatre-Vingts, see Marisa Linton, *Choosing Terror: Virtue, Friendship and Authenticity in the French Revolution* (Oxford: Oxford University Press, 2013), 76–9; Zeische, *Cosmopolitan Patriots*, 41–3; Marquis de Lafayette to George Washington, August 23, 1790, *PGWDEP*, 6: 315–9, at 317. Lafayette's house and La Rochefoucauld's translation described in Adams, *The Paris Years of Thomas Jefferson*, 95–6, 10. TJ to the Reverend Charles Clay, January 27, 1790, *PTJDE*, 16: 129–30, at 129. Jefferson described Lafayette's character in TJ to James Madison, January 30, 1787, *PTJDE*, 11: 92–7, at 95. See also, TJ to James Madison, March 18, 1785, *PTJDE*, 8: 38–41, at 38. Lafayette praised Short's ability, zeal, and connections in Marquis de Lafayette to George Washington, August 23, 1790, *PGWDEP*, 6: 315–9, at 318. TJ to James Monroe, August 9, 1788, *PTJDE*, 13: 488–90, at 489. See also Short to John Jay, March 9, 1790, *PTJDE*, 16: 219–22, at 219–20.

14. [Jefferson] Draft of a Charter of Rights, June 3, 1789, *PTJDE*, 15: 167–8; Lafayette's Draft Declaration of Rights, June 1789, *PTJDE*, 15: 230–3. TJ to John Jay, September 19, 1789, *PTJDE*, 15: 454–61, at 458. TJ to Archbishop of Bordeaux, July 22, 1789, *PJTDE*, 15: 298.

15. Marquis de Lafayette to TJ, August 25, 1789, *PTJDE*, 15: 354. The dinner is described in Adams, *The Paris Years*, 9–13; TJ to John Jay, September 19, 1789, postscript September 23, 1789, *PTJDE*, 15: 454–61, 459; [TJ] "Notes on the French Revolution," January 15, 1793, *PTJDE*, 25:58. *Autobiography*, 154. Zeische, *Cosmopolitan Patriots*, 31. TJ to Thomas Paine, September 13, 1789, *PTJDE*, 15: 424. Thomas Jefferson to Count Jean Diodati, August 3, 1789, *PTJDE*, 15: 325–7, at 326.

16. Gouverneur Morris but not, apparently, Short attended the farewell dinner; see Davenport, ed., *Diary of the French Revolution*, 1: 220–1, entry made September 17, 1789. TJ to Marquis de Lafayette, April 2, 1790, *PTJDE*, 16: 292–3, at 293. TJ to Duke de La Rochefoucauld d'Enville, April 3, 1790, *PTJDE*, 16: 296–7, at 297. TJ to Madame d'Enville, April 2, 1790, PTJDE, 16: 290–1. Madame d'Enville to TJ, July 27, 1790, *PTJDE*, 17: 286–7, at 286.

17. Rosalie to Short, December 15, 1790, Harsanyi, *Lettres*, 20–1, at 20; Armand-Charles Juste de Rohan-Chabot to Short, n.d. December 1790, APS. Short to TJ, January 17, 1791, *PTJDE*, 18: 510–1, at 51. Short had just learnt that Jerome Pétion, a member of the Assembly, friend of Robespierre, and, from July 1791, mayor of Paris, had named him as a covert accomplice of the Duke de La Rochefoucauld; see Short to Rosalie, January 17, 1791, Harsanyi, *Lettres*, 26–7.

18. Short to TJ, June 26, 1791, *PTJDE*, 20: 573–79. Short to TJ, July 20, 1791, *PTJDE*, 20: 648–55, at 648–50; Short to TJ, June 29, 1791, *PTJDE*, 20: 584–8, at 585. Short to TJ, July 17, 1791, *PTJDE*, 20: 641–5, at 642.

19. Short to TJ, May 2, 1791, *PTJDE*, 20: 345. Short to TJ, July 20, 1791, *PTJDE*, 20: 648–55, at 648. Keith Michael Baker, *Condorcet: Raison et Politique* (Paris: Herman, 1975), esp. 371–2, 397. Short learned of the La Rochefoucaulds' dissatisfaction with Condorcet in Rosalie to Short, November 11, 1791 and November 27, 1791, Harsanyi, *Lettres* 67–8 n. 1; 76–7, at 77. Fasquelle, *Les La Rochefoucauld*, 301 and note. Short to TJ, June 29, 1791, *PTJDE*, 20: 584–8, at 584; Élisabeth Badinter and Robert Badinter, *Condorcet*, 329.

20. Short to TJ, April 26, 1791, *PTJDE*, 20: 265–6, at 266. TJ to Short, July 28, 1791, *PTJDE*, 20: 691–3, at 692.

21. On failings of the Assembly, see Short to TJ, April 8, 1791, *PTJDE*, 20: 170–3, at 170; Short to TJ, October 22, 1791, *PTJDE*, 22: 221–23, at 222. Short to TJ, July 17, 1791, *PTJDE*, 20: 641–45, at 645. TJ to Short, November 25, 1791, *PTJDE*, 22: 333–5, at 334. Zeische, *Cosmopolitan Patriots*, 40–1.

22. TJ to Philip Freneau, February 28, 1791, *PTJDE*, 19: 351. TJ to James Madison, June 29, 1792, *PTJDE*, 24: 133–4.

23. Short to TJ, July 26, 1792, *PTJDE*, 24: 249–57, at 250. Short to TJ, August 24, 1792 and postscript, *PTJDE*, 24: 322–5, at 325. Short to Alexander Hamilton, June 28, 1792, *PAHDE*, 11: 593–600, at 597. Gouverneur Morris to TJ, July 10, 1792, *PTJDE*, 24: 207–9, at 208. Gouverneur Morris to TJ, June 10, 1792, *PTJDE*, 24: 50–6, at 55.

24. Rosalie to Short, August 16, 1792 and August 29, 1792, Harsanyi, *Lettres*, 139–40; 144–5.

25. Davenport, ed., *Diary of the French Revolution*, 1: 220–1, entry made September 17, 1789, 1: 220–21, 1: 253, entry made October 11, 1789, 1: 253. Badinter and Bandinter, *Condorcet*, 478. Marie-Brigitte Plunkett Chastellux to William Short, August 25, 1792 [year supplied], APS.

26. Bouffard had been a regent of the ecclesiastical college of Vernon, the nearest town to La Roche-Guyon, Fasquelle, *Les La Rochefoucauld*, 276; Rousse, *La Roche-Guyon*, 370; Vaugelade, *Le Salon Physiocratique des La Rochefoucauld*, 281–6. For the sojourn in Forges, see Rosalie to Short, August 22, 1792, Harsanyi, *Lettres*, 141–2, and note 276; Unknown, [presumed Alexandre de La Rochefoucauld] to Short, August 18, 1792, APS. For the delayed decision to leave Forges, see Rosalie to Short, August 25, 1792 and September 1, 1792, Harsanyi, *Lettres*, 142–3; 145–7, at 146. Rousse, *La Roche-Guyon*, 370–4, 372; Madame d' Astorg to Short, September 28, 1792, APS.

27. Alexandre de La Rochefoucauld-Liancourt to Short, September 8, 1792, Harsanyi, *Lettres*, 148–9; Rosalie de La Rochefoucauld to Short, September 16, 1792, Harsanyi, *Lettres*, 149. Madame d'Enville to Short, September 25, 1792, APS; Madame d' Astorg to Short, September 28, 1792, APS. Short to John Rutledge, September 17, 1792, Gilpin Papers, HSP.

28. Short to TJ, August 15, 1792, *PTJDE*, 24: 298–9, at 298. Jefferson received this on October 31, 1792. Short to TJ, September 18, 1792, *PTJDE*, 24: 390–402, esp. 391.

Jefferson received this letter on January 23, 1793, by which time he had already dispatched his "Adam and Eve" letter discussed below.

29. Gouverneur Morris to TJ, September 10, 1792, *PTJDE*, 24: 364–5.

30. Short to TJ, January 15, 1793, *PTJDE*, 25: 60–1. Madame d'Enville to Thomas Jefferson, December 30, 1792, *PTJDE*, 24: 798–9, at 799.

31. Jefferson was referencing events on the Hurault de Gondrecourt plantation; see Laurent Dubois, *A Colony of Citizens: Revolution & Slave Emancipation in the French Caribbean, 1787–1804* (Chapel Hill: University of North Carolina Press, 2004), 129. TJ to Martha Jefferson Randolph, May 26, 1793, *PTJDE*, 26: 122–3, at 122. Jefferson wasn't even sure the victims were former acquaintances of Martha's. She "had so many –courts [as terminations of names] among her class mates."

32. Peterson, ed., *Jefferson: Writings*, 1003. TJ to Short, January 3, 1793, *PTJDE*, 25: 14–7, at 14. Short to TJ, May 15, 1792, *PTJDE*, 23: 503–5, at 504; Short to TJ, July 20, 1792, *PTJDE*, 24: 240–6, at 242. Jefferson received this letter October 6, 1792.

33. Short to TJ, October 12, 1792, *PTJDE*, 24: 474–6, at 475.

34. TJ to Short, January 3, 1793, *PTJDE*, 25: 14–7, at 14. Gouverneur Morris to TJ, September 10, 1792, *PTJDE*, 24: 364–5.

35. John Adams to Abigail Adams, February 3, 1793, *TAPDE: Adams Family Correspondence*, 9: 389. TJ to Short, January 3, 1793, *PTJDE*, 25: 14–7, at 15, 14.

36. TJ to James Madison, March 25, 1793, *PJMDE*, 15: 1–2, at 2. For American attitudes toward the French Revolution, see Charles Downer Hazen, *Contemporary American Opinion of the French Revolution* (Baltimore, 1897); Simon P. Newman, *Parades and the Politics of the Street: Festive Culture in the Early American Republic* (Philadelphia: University of Pennsylvania Press, 1997), 123; David Waldstreicher, *In the Midst of Perpetual Fetes: The Making of American Nationalism, 1776–1820* (Chapel Hill: University of North Carolina Press, 1997), 126–30; Susan Branson, *These Fiery Frenchified Dames: Women and Political Culture in Early National Philadelphia* (Philadelphia: University of Pennsylvania Press, 2001), 55–100; Zeische, *Cosmopolitan Patriots*. Alexander Hamilton to Short, February 5, 1793, *PAHDE*, 14: 7.

37. TJ to Short, January 3, 1793, *PTJDE*, 25: 14–7, at 15.

38. [TJ] "Notes of a Conversation with George Washington on French Affairs, December 27, 1792, *PTJDE*, 24: 793–4. George Washington to Gouverneur Morris, October 13, 1789, *PGWDEP*, 4: 176–79. Jefferson's criticism of Morris as channeled by Washington is contained in TJ to George Washington, January 28, 1792, with Enclosure: George Washington to Gouverneur Morris, *PTJDE*, 23: 85–6. Jefferson was in the habit of drafting foreign policy statements for Washington, see "Notes of a Conversation with George Washington," *PTJDE*, 24: 793, editorial note. Jefferson/Washington asked Morris to remember that he was representative of his country and should avoid the appearance of favoring aristocracy. Jefferson, in his own voice, asked Short to "consider yourself as the representative of your country" in TJ to Short, January 3, 1793, *PTJDE*, 25: 14–7, at 15. For background,

see George Washington to Gouverneur Morris, October 20, 1792, *PGWDEP*,
11: 244–6, at 245; see also Gouverneur Morris to George Washington, June 10,
1792, *PGWDEP*, 10: 449. Morris also wrote to Jefferson on June 10, painting an
even darker picture of events: Gouverneur Morris to TJ, June 10, 1792, *PJTDE*,
24: 50–6. This was received October 18 and may be the letter to which Washington,
at Jefferson's prompting, responded on October 20.

39. TJ to Short, January 3, 1793, *PTJDE*, 25: 14–7, at 15.

40. [TJ] Notes on Conversations with William Stephens Smith and George
Washington, February 20, 1793, *PTJDE*, 25: 243–4. See also List of Names from
Whence to Take a Minister to France, May 19, 1794, *PAHDE*, 16: 422–5; James
Monroe to TJ, May 26, 1794, *PTJDE*, 28: 85–6, at 85.

41. Short to TJ, November 9, 1792, *PTJDE*, 24: 601–3. [TJ] Notes on Conversations
with William Stephens Smith and George Washington, February 20, 1793, *PTJDE*,
25: 243–4. Short to TJ, March 6, 1793, *PTJDE*, 25: 321–331, at 325.

42. Short to TJ, April 5, 1793, *PTJDE*, 25: 494–509, at 508. Short later maintained that
had President Washington and others acted on his reports from France the United
States would have avoided "debasing difficulties" in its relations with France; Short
to TJ, August 24, 1798, *PTJDE*, 30: 487–97, at 488.

43. Short to TJ, March 30, 1797, *PTJDE*, 29: 332–3, at 333. Brigitte-Marie Plunkett
Chastellux to Thomas Jefferson, March 5, 1797, *PTJDE*, 29: 312–3. Jefferson re-
corded receipt of both letters on June 29, 1797. Chastellux had discussed the La
Rochefoucauld circle in a previous letter to Jefferson in which she informed him
that Madame d'Enville was in declining health; Madame de Chastellux to Thomas
Jefferson, May 6, 1795, *PTJDE*, 28: 343–4, at 344. TJ to Short, June 30, 1797,
PTJDE, 29: 463–5, at 435. Short to TJ, December 27, 1797 [summary], *PTJDE*,
29: 597–8.

44. TJ to Robert R. Livingston, October 3, 1801, *PTJDE*, 35: 377–8, at 378. TJ to Short,
May 1, 1798, *PTJDE*, 30: 317–20, at 320. TJ to Short, March 12, 1797, *PTJDE*,
29: 316–8, at 317.

45. TJ to Henry Remsen, October 30, 1794, *PTJDE*, 28: 183. TJ to Jean-Nicolas
Démeunier, April 29, 1795, *PTJDE*, 28: 340–2, at 340, 341; Jean-Nicholas
Démeunier to Thomas Jefferson, March 30, 1795, *PTJDE*, 28: 319–21, at 321. The
article on the United States in the *Encyclopédie Méthodique*, *PTJDE*, 10: 3–65, at
48–54. Jefferson found particular fault with Démeunier's treatment of the Society
of the Cincinatti.

46. TJ to Short, October 12, 1806, *Founders Online*.

47. TJ to Short, October 12, 1806, *Founders Online*.

48. TJ to John Jay, July 19, 1789, *PTJDE*, 15: 286; *Autobiography*, 143. In its account
of the storming of the Bastille, the *Autobiography* relied heavily on Jefferson's official dispatch to John Jay, repeating word for word "the decapitation of de Launai
worked powerfully thro' the night on the whole Aristocratical party," TJ to John
Jay, July 19, 1789, *PTJDE*, 15: 284–91, at 288; *Autobiography*, 146, 149. Lynn Hunt,

"The Many Bodies of Marie Antoinette: Political Pornography and the Problem of the Feminine in the French Revolution," in Hunt, ed., *Eroticism and the Body Politic* (Baltimore: Johns Hopkins University Press, 1991), 108–30. Visiting Monticello in 1814, George Ticknor was surprised to find Jefferson fueling his detestation of monarchy by re-reading works of "regal scandal" which he had had bound in a "Book of Kings"; see George Ticknor's Account of a Visit to Monticello, 4–7 February, 1815, *PTJDE: Retirement*, 8: 238–43, at 240. See also TJ to John Adams, 4 September 1823, *Founders Online*.

49. TJ to John Taylor, June 4, 1798, *PTJDE*, 30: 387–9, at 389.
50. Felice Harcourt, ed., *Memoirs of Madame de La Tour du Pin* (London: Century Books, 1985), 167–68; Miller, *Envoy to the Terror*, 211. Short to William Nelson, February 21, 1791, cited in Short to Thomas Jefferson, April 26, 1791, *PTJDE*, 20: 265–7, at 267; Short to Van Staphorst et al., May 24, 1793, WSP LOC.

CHAPTER FIVE

1. Unless otherwise indicated, all correspondence between Rosalie de La Rochefoucauld, her family, and William Short cited in this chapter is reprinted in Harsanyi, *Lettres*, and identified solely by date and page number. Rosalie to Short, November 20, 1794, 189–95 at 189–90. For use of the second-person informal, see Rosalie to Short, November 20, 1794. Rosalie to Short, November 28, 1794, 192; 195–6, at 195.
2. Short to Rosalie, July 28, 1795, 199–202, at 200–1. For Rosalie's meetings with James Monroe, see Rosalie to Short, November 28, 1794, 195–6, at 195. Rosalie to Short, December 11, 1795, 204–5, at 204. Rosalie to Short, June 12–13, 1796 and June 17, 1796, 205–7, 207–9. Marie Goebel Kimball and Alexandre de Liancourt, "William Short, Jefferson's Only 'Son'" *North American Review* 223 (September—November 1926), 471–86, at 471.
3. Interpretive examples include Daniel Vaugelade, *La Question Américaine au 18eme Siècle: Au Travers de la Correspondance du Louis Alexandre de La Rochefoucauld (1743–1792)* (Paris: Publibook, 2005), 314–5; Polasky, *Revolutions Without Borders*, 216–221. For Rosalie's knowledge of English, see Rosalie to Short, July 12, 1792, 117–9, at 119.
4. Rosalie denied any previous experience of "falseness" in Rosalie to Short, May 27, 1791, 45–7, at 46. For gossipy references to Short's absences, see Madame de Tessé to TJ, January 21, 1787, *PTJDE*, 60–1, at 61; Madame de Tott to TJ, March 4, 1787, *PTJDE*, 11: 198–9, at 199.
5. See Madame Pauline Castiglione to Short, n.d. March 1789, APS [referencing Countess "d'Al"]; Madame Pauline Castiglione to Short, June 16, 1789, APS. Gouverneur Morris was a frequent visitor to Countess of Albany's Parisian salon and corresponded with her in exile; see Davenport, ed., *Diary of the French Revolution*, 2: 329, entry made December 23, 1791, 2: 331, entry made December

28, 1791. On Madame Flahaut, see Davenport, ed., *Diary of the French Revolution*, 1: 238, entry made October 1, 1789.

6. The expectations of French marriage reformers are discussed in Suzanne Desan, *The Family on Trial in Revolutionary France* (Berkeley: University of California Press, 2004). For the United States, see McCurdy, *Citizen Bachelors*; Chudacoff, *The Age of the Bachelor*. See also Andrew R. L. Cayton, *Love in the Time of Revolution: Transatlantic Literary Radicalism and Historical Change, 1793–1818* (Chapel Hill: University of North Carolina Press, 2013).

7. Short to John Rutledge, Jr., April 27, 1790, SHC UNC.

8. Gouverneur Morris remarked with a hint of envy that Short was a great favorite of Madame de Tessé; Davenport, ed., *Diary of the French Revolution*, 1: 178, entry made May 14, 1789. Madame de Tessé made her fondness for Short known to Jefferson in Madame de Tessé to TJ, July 6, 1790, *PTJDE*, 17: 8–9; for her continuing regard, see Short to TJ, November 19, 1811, *PTJDE: Retirement*, 4: 269. On plants, see Short to TJ, June 14, 1790, *PTJDE*, 16: 496–503, at 503; Short to TJ, January 24, 1792, *PTJDE*, 23: 64–6, at 64. See also Short to TJ, July 17, 1791, *PTJDE*, 20: 641–45, at 645. Madame d'Enville to TJ, July 27, 1790, *PTJDE*, 17: 286–7, at 286.

9. Gifts to the Royer family detailed in William Short Account Book, Gilpin Papers, HSP. Short to Gouverneur Morris, July 27, 1790, reprinted in Davenport, ed., *Diary of the French Revolution*, 1: 565–7. For secondment to Holland, TJ to Short, August 31, 1790, *PTJDE*, 17: 477–8, at 478; Short to TJ, October 25, 1790, *PTJDE*, 17: 631–5. Rosalie to Short, October 22, 1790, 17–18, at 18. Davenport, ed., *Diary of the French Revolution*, 2: 58, entry made November 13, 1790. Short explained his delayed departure in Short to TJ, November 6, 1790, *PTJDE*, 18: 13–23. Duchess d'Enville to Short, May 31, 1791, 48–9, at 48. Rosalie to Short, June 1, 1791, 49–50, at 49; Rosalie to Short, letter fragment ca. January 1792, 93.

10. Rosalie to Short, December 15, 1790, and January 6, 1791, 20–1, 22–4.

11. Short to Rosalie, January 17, 1791, 25–8, at 25–6; see also Rosalie to Short, January 23, 1791, 28–30, at 29; Short to Rosalie, January 31, 1791, 31–4, at 32–3. Rosalie to Short, February 10, 1791, 35–7. Gouverneur Morris thought *Psyché* "prodigiously fine"; see Davenport, ed., *Diary of the French Revolution*, 2: 227, entry made July 25, 1791. For Jefferson's reading of Fénelon's *Telemachus*, see Hayes, *The Road to Monticello*, 277, 23–4. Short described reading *Émile* in Short to Brigitte-Marie Plunkett Chastellux, January 17, 1791, Gilpin Collection, HSP. Short to Rosalie, February 20, 1791, 37–40, at 40.

12. Rosalie to Short, May 27, 1791, as reproduced and translated in Goebel and Liancourt, "William Short," 474. See also Harsanyi, *Lettres*, 45–7.

13. Short to Rosalie, January 17, 1791, 25–8, at 25. Short to TJ, June 7, 1791, *PTJDE*, 20: 541–4, at 543. Duchesse d'Enville to Short, May 31, 1791, 48–9; Rosalie to Short, June 1, 1791, 49–50. William Short, Account Book, entry made June 25, 1791, Gilpin Papers, HSP. Rosalie to Short, September 22, 1791, 52–3, at 53. Rosalie

to Short, September 22, 1791, 52–3, at 53. Rosalie to Short, November 7, 1791, 63–5, at 64.

14. Rosalie to Short, October 1, 1791, 56–8, at 57–8. Rosalie to Short, October 11, 1791, 60–1, at 60. Rosalie to Short, November 17, 1791, 72–4, at 73. See also Rosalie to Short, January 4, 1792, 90–2, at 92. Acting on Short's expressed wish Rosalie destroyed very nearly all his letters to her.

15. On the act of writing, Rosalie to Short, November 5, 1791, 62–3, at 62. Rosalie to Short, August 2, 1792, 132–3. Rosalie to Short, July 29, 1792, 129–30. Rosalie to Short, June 1, 1791, 49–50. Jacques-Pierre Brissot de Warville, "Private Morals in the Towns and in the Country," in *Nouveau Voyage dans les États-Unis de l'Amérique Septentrionale: Fait en 1788* (Paris, 1790), Letter VI. For description of her island retreat, see Rosalie to Short, July 8, 1792, 115–7, at 115–6.

16. Rosalie to Short, November 17, 1791, 70–2, at 71. Rosalie to Short, June 20, 1793, 170–2, at 171. Rosalie to Short, June 28, 1792, 108–10, at 110. For Rosalie's suggestion that William write to her husband, see Rosalie to Short, August 9, 1792, 135–8, at 138. Rosalie to Short, July 1, 1792, 110–2, at 112. Rosalie to Short, November 20, 1794, 189–95, at 192.

17. William Short to Peyton Short, December 18, 1792, WPSP WM. Peyton relied on Jefferson to facilitate correspondence with William, see Peyton Short to TJ, August 31, 1791, *PTJDE*, 22: 112–3; Peyton Short to TJ, October 15, 1791, *PTJDE*, 22: 215; Peyton Short to TJ, December 10, 1792, *PTJDE*, 24: 721. TJ to Short, December 14, 1789, *PTJDE*, 16: 24–8, at 25. William Short to Peyton Short, December 18, 1792, WPSP WM.

18. Short to TJ, January 24, 1792, *PTJDE*, 23: 64–6, at 65. From Holland Short asked Gouverneur Morris to look after his books; see Short to Gouverneur Morris, November 9, 1792, WSP LOC. For his continuing interest in his library, see Short to James Monroe, September 10, 1795, *Monroe Papers*, 3: 444.

19. Rosalie to Short, September 23, 1792, 149–50, at 149. Rosalie to Short, August 29, 1792, with enclosure, 144–5, at 144. Rosalie to Short, December 1, 1792, 159–63 at 159, 162. Rosalie to Short, October 14, 1792, 151–2, at 152. Rosalie to Short, October 31, 1792, 153–4, 153. Gouverneur Morris to TJ, September 10, 1792, *PTJDE*, 24: 364–5. Short to TJ, September 15, 1792, *PTJDE*, 24: 374–82, at 375. TJ to Short, January 3, 1793, *PTJDE*, 25: 14–16. Short to TJ, October 19, 1792, *PTJDE*, 24: 502–4. See also Short to TJ, October 12, 1792, *PTJDE*, 24: 474–6.

20. Short to Van Staphorst and Hubbard, May 24, 1793, WSP LOC. Gouverneur Morris to Robert Morris, March 28, 1793, cited in Miller, *Envoy to The Terror*, 104, n. 46. The ownership of the plantations Short asked the Morrises to secure is unclear. They may have been those belonging to Madame d'Enville's sister, Adélaide de La Rochefoucauld, who was born on St. Domingue; see Harsanyi, *Lettres*, 253–4, n. 1. See also, Short to TJ, September 18, 1800, *PTJDE*, 147–160, at 157.

256   *Notes to pages 143–146*

21. Short denominated the debt in both francs and dollars and described its repayment in Short to John Cleves Short, July 12, 1836, WSP LOC; Short to Charles Wilkins Short, September 27, 1836, WSP LOC.

22. George Shackelford claims that Rosalie advanced the loan in the winter of 1792–1793 and "formalized" it in 1810; see Shackelford, *Jefferson's Adoptive Son*, 132, 185 n. 40. He provides no evidence for the date on which Rosalie first offered the loan. The basis of his claim that Rosalie confirmed the loan in 1810 rests on two letters, Rosalie to Short, February 21, 1810, 240–1 and Rosalie to Short, July 8, 1810, APS. The first of these, written immediately prior to Short's final departure from France, makes a passing reference to a business transaction initiated by her and involving an English bank. That the matter referenced was her loan to Short is supposition on Shackelford's part. The second letter does not offer direct confirmation.

    Rosalie and her two brothers inherited substantial sums of money following the death of her paternal great-uncle Louis-Marie-Bretagne de Rohan-Chabot, Duke de Rohan, in November 1791; see Rosalie to Short, December 10, 1791, 83–5 at 84. Rosalie described the loss of her fortune in Rosalie to Short, November 20, 1794, 189–95. For Rosalie's position as sole heir to the Duchess d'Enville following the exile and proscription of her sole surviving brother Alexandre, see Rousse, *La Roche-Guyon*, 402–5. Short suggested that he would soon have additional funds to invest in American land in Short to TJ, August 6, 1798, *PTJDE*, 30: 473–83, at 476; Short to TJ, August 24, 1798, *PTJDE*, 30: 487–92, at 492. Alexandre de La Rochefoucauld returned from exile in 1800, and, following the relaxation of penal legislation against émigres, Rosalie agreed and notarized a division of her inheritance with him, which might have precluded a loan to William; see Rousse, *La Roche-Guyon*, 402–5.

23. Short to TJ, October 7, 1793, *PTJDE*, 27: 201–11, at 204. On the purchase of Indian Camp, TJ to Short, May 25 1795, *PTJDE*, 28: 353–6, at 354; Short to TJ, September 2, 1795, *PTJDE*, 28: 444–5.

24. Short to Rosalie, March 30, 1794, 174–5; Short to Rosalie, July 23, 1794, 179–82, at 181. Rosalie to Short, June 21, 1796, APS. Short was amassing a library in this period; see Charles Pougens to Short, February 4 and February 18, 1797, WSP LOC. Rosalie to Short, June 17, 1796, 207–9, at 208.

25. Rosalie to Short, June 15, 1796, APS. Rosalie to Short, June 19, 1796, APS.

26. TJ to Short, March 12, 1797, *PTJDE*, 29: 316–18, at 318. Short to TJ, March 30, 1797, *PTJDE*, 332–3, at 333. TJ to Short, June 30, 1797, *PTJDE*, 29: 463–5, at 464.

27. Rosalie to Short, August 3, 1797, 210–12, at 212. Short to TJ, December 27, 1797, *PTJDE*, 29: 597–8, at 597. Short to Van Staphorst, May 12, 1797, WSP LOC. See also Short to TJ, November 1, 1810, *PTJDE: Retirement*, 3: 197–200, at 197.

28. Rosalie to Short, August 18, 1813, APS. On venereal disease, Short to John Rutledge, February 3, 1790, Gilpin Collection, HSP. TJ to Caesar Rodney, October 8, 1807, *Founders Online*.

29. Short's acquaintances were well aware of his relationship with Rosalie and some expected that he would marry her. See Thomas Pinckney to James Monroe, *Monroe Papers*, March 26, 1796; Short to TJ, August 6, 1798, *PTJDE*, 30: 473–83, at 474.

30. Short to James Monroe, August 26, 1794, Gilpin Collection HSP. Short to James Monroe, February 23 1795, *Monroe Papers*, 3: 345.

31. The hopes Short invested in a future professional relationship with Gerry are apparent from Short to TJ, August 24, 1798, *PTJDE*, 30: 487–96; Short to TJ, June 9, 1801, *PTJDE*, 34: 286–94, at 292–3. Rosalie to Short, July 9, 1798, 214–5, at 214 ["Oui, c'est à mon tendre époux que j'écris, à mon époux que des affaires importantes éloignent momentanément de moi"]. Rosalie to Short, July 28, 1798, 215–8, at 218. Rosalie to Short, July 30, 1798, 221–23. Rosalie to Short, August 3, 1798, 228–31, at 228. Rosalie to Short, August 4, 1798, 231–3. Rosalie to Short, August 5, 1798, 234–6, at 235; Rosalie to Short, August 6, 1798, 236–7.

32. Elbridge Gerry to TJ, November 12, 1798, *PTJDE*, 30: 577–8, at 577. Short to TJ, August 6, 1798, *PTJDE*, 30: 473–83, at 474, 480, 479.

33. Short to TJ, August 24, 1798, *PTJDE*, 30: 487–96, at 488, 489. For Liancourt's description of Monticello, see François-Alexandre-Frédéric La Rochefoucauld-Liancourt, *Voyage dans les États-Unis d'Amerique, Fait en 1795, 1796 et 1797* 8 vols. (Paris, 1799), 5: 41. La Rochefoucauld-Liancourt dedicated the work to his aunt, Madame d'Enville. Short doubted that a printing in eight volumes would be a commercial success, Short to TJ, August 24, 1798, *PTJDE*, 30: 487–96, at 488. The first English-language edition was printed in two volumes: Short to TJ, August 6, 1798, *PTJDE*, 30: 473–82, at 474.

34. Short to TJ, August 6, 1798, *PTJDE*, 30: 473–92, at 478, 479, 474, 480. For the phrase "reign of witches," see TJ to John Taylor, June 4, 1798, *PTJDE*, 30: 387–90, at 389. TJ to Elbridge Gerry, January 26, 1799, *PTJDE*, 30: 645–51, at 650.

35. TJ to Robert R. Livingston, October 3, 1801, *PTJDE*, 35: 377; TJ to Short, October 3 1801, *PTJDE* 35: 380–3, at 382. TJ to Short, July 16, 1802, *PTJDE*, 38: 86. Short to TJ, June 9, 1801, *PTJDE*, 34: 286–93, at 287.

36. Short to TJ, December 9, 1800, *PTJDE*, 32: 291–96, at 296. On sheep, Short to TJ, October 18, 1801, *PTJDE*, 35: 461–65, at 464; Short to TJ, November 1, 1810, *PTJDE: Retirement*, 3: 197–200. Short to Thomas Jefferson, October 18, 1801, *PTJDE*, 35: 462–3, at 462; Arthur Young described the fertility of the Limagne in *Travels*, 318.

37. TJ to Short, June 9, 1806, *Founders Online*; TJ to Short, March 7, 1806, *Founders Online*. William Short, "Statement of My Property, June 30, 1806," Article 4, WSP LOC. Jane Short Wilkins to Short, August 8, 1805, WSP LOC; Jane Wilkins Short to Short, March 27, 1806, WSP LOC. Jane Wilkins Short to Short, February 27, 1807, WSP LOC. Short discussed with Jefferson returning to Spain or France, or to Holland as a negotiator of loans in Short to TJ, November 6, 1807, *Founders Online*. Jane Short Wilkins to Short, February 23, 1807, WSP LOC. Rosalie to Short, June 12, 1796, 206–6, at 206; Rosalie to Short, June 17, 1796, 207–9, at 209.

38. Rouse, *La Roche-Guyon*, 402–5. Comtesse de Rémusat, *Memoires de Mde de Rémusat 1802–1803*, 3 vols. (Paris: Calmann Levy, 1880); Harsanyi, *Lettres*, 254 n. 1, 284 n. 3, 286 n. 1. Short praised the waters of Pau over those of Vichy in Short to Fulwar Skipwith, July 10, 1801, WSP LOC. Rosalie to Short, March 23, 1811, APS. Rosalie to Short, April 25, 1814, APS.

39. For background to Jefferson's request, see TJ to Short, June 12, 1807, *Founders Online*, Short to TJ, June 20, 1808, *Founders Online*. TJ to Short, July 6, 1805, *Founders Online*. Short to TJ, May 27, 1809, *PTJDE: Retirement*, 1: 229–5. Short to TJ, April. 10, 1809, *PTJDE: Retirement*, 1: 115–22. For the date of Rosalie's marriage, Harsanyi, *Lettres*, 286, n. 1. Short announced his intention leave France, although not his reasoning, in Short to James Madison, February 7, 1810, *PJMDE: Presidential Series* [hereafter cited as *PJMDE: Presidential*], 2: 222; Short to TJ, February 7, 1810 [summary], *PTJDE: Retirement*, 2: 200.

40. Rosalie to Short, August 25, 1810, 241–4, at 240. Rosalie to Short, August 27, 1812, APS. Rosalie to Short, May 12, 1811, APS. Rosalie to Short, February 8, 1812, APS.

41. Short to TJ, November 1, 1810, *PTJDE: Retirement*, 3: 197–200, at 197. Rosalie to Short, August 25, 1810, 241–4, at 241. Short to TJ, November 19, 1811, *PTJDE: Retirement*, 4: 268–74, at 269. Short to TJ, November 1, 1810, *PTJDE: Retirement*, 3: 197–200, at 197.

42. Short to TJ, June 9, 1814, *PTJDE: Retirement*, 7: 402–5, at 403.

CHAPTER SIX

1. TJ to Short, May 25, *PTJDE*, 28: 353–6. TJ to Nicholas Lewis, July 11, 1788, *PTJDE*, 13: 339–44, at 349, 342. On the sale of land in Cumberland County and Elk Hill, see TJ to Nicholas Lewis, March 7, 1790, *PTJDE*, 16: 210–2; Advertisement for the Sale of Elk Hill [after January 10, 1790], *PTJDE*, 17: 567. TJ to John Joseph de Barth, March 17, 1792, *PTJDE*, 23: 289; TJ to Daniel L. Hylton, March 17, 1792, *PTJDE*, 23: 290–1; Mortgage for Elk Hill [c. June 3, 1792], *PTJDE*, 24: 23. On migraine see, TJ to Mary Jefferson, May 23, 1790; 16: 435; TJ to Alexander Donald, June 13, 1790, *PTJDE*, 16: 488–9. On freight, see Memorandum Book, 1790, *PTJDE: Second Series*, entry made November 30; William Short to TJ, November 7, 1790, *PTJDE*, 18: 30–9, at 34 and editorial note. For debt settlement, see Memorandum Book, 1790, *PTJDE: Second Series*, entries made, March 4, March 6, 1790. For the background to TJ's debts, see Herbert E. Sloan, *Principal & Interest: Thomas Jefferson and the Problem of Debt* (Charlottesville: University of Virginia Press, 1995); TJ to Francis Eppes, October 8, 1790, *PTJDE*, 17: 581–2, at 581; TJ to James Lyle, November 3, 1790, *PTJDE*, 17: 674–6; Notes of an Account with Richard Harvie & Company, July 22, 1795, *PTJDE*, 28: 413–7. On tobacco, TJ to Nicholas Lewis, July 11, 1788, *PTJDE*, 13: 339–44, at 339–40. Memorandum Book, 1790, *PTJDE: Second Series*, entry made March 7, 1790; Alexander Donald to TJ, October 5, 1790, *PTJDE*, 17: 566–7; TJ to Alexander Donald, November 25, 1790, *PTJDE*, 18: 71–2. TJ to

Nicholas Lewis, April 4, 1791, *PTJDE*, 20: 102–4. TJ to Alexander Donald, May 13, 1791, *PTJDE*, 20: 404–5.

2. Estimate by Nicholas Lewis of Yield of Jefferson's Estate, 1790, *PTJDE*, 18: 109–10. TJ to Nicholas Lewis, July 4, 1790, *PTJDE*, 16: 599. Jefferson cited in Avery O. Craven, *Soil Exhaustion as a Factor in the Agricultural History of Virginia & Maryland, 1606–1860*, 28; see also TJ to Thomas Mann Randolph, August 18, 1795, *PTJDE*, 28: 438. Memorandum for Nicholas Lewis, c. November 7, 1790, *PTJDE*, 18: 29–30, at 29. Memorandum Book, 1791, *PTJDE: Second Series*, entries made March 8, March 18.

3. TJ to Short, April 6, 1790, *PTJDE*, 16: 318–20, at 320. TJ to Short, August 25, 1790, *PTJDE*, 17: 421–3, at 422. Jefferson's Diary of Philip Mazzei's Affairs, *PTJDE*, 16: 308–9; see also TJ to James Madison, March 16, 1784, *PTJDE*, 7: 30–2, at 30.

4. TJ to Short, April 6, 1790, *PTJDE*, 16: 318–20, at 318; TJ to Short, September 30, 1790, *PTJDE*, 17: 543–6, at 544. TJ to Short, January 24, 1791, *PTJDE*, 18: 600–2, at 601. Short to TJ, May 2, 1791, *PTJDE*, 20: 345–52, at 346; Short to TJ, July 17, 1791, *PTJDE*, 20: 641–5, at 641.

5. TJ to Short, March 16, 1791, *PTJDE*, 19: 578–9, at 579. For Jefferson's prior involvement with Brown, see James Brown to TJ, November 25, 1790, *PTJDE*, 18: 69; TJ to Short, April 27, 1790, *PTJDE*, 16: 387–9. Short to TJ, June 7, 1791, *PTJDE*, 20: 541–6, at 545. James Brown to TJ, October 21, 1791, *PTJDE*, 22: 221; TJ to Brown, November 13, 1791, *PTJDE*, 27: [Appendix], 806.

6. Jefferson was at his most patient and effective in what both men eventually dubbed the "affair of the $9,000." In circumstances disputed by all parties involved, Edmund Randolph, Secretary of State in 1794–1795, withheld Short's government salary while Short remained in Europe, keeping it in the United States until Short's return. Randolph invested, ostensibly on Short's behalf, a portion of the sum owed but kept the certificates. Jefferson expended considerable personal energy directing efforts to recover for Short the certificates, the sum owed, and interest on it. For major milestones in the development of the case, see Short to TJ, September 2, 1795, *PTJDE*, 28: 442–5, at 443; Short to TJ, September 3, 1795, *PTJDE*, 28: 446–7; Short to TJ, August 6, 1800, *PTJDE*, 32: 71–90, at 74–6; Short to TJ, December 18, 1801, *PTJDE*, 36: 158–61; TJ to John Minor, March 10, 1802, *PTJDE*, 37: 50–1. TJ to John Barnes, January 28, 1797, *PTJDE*, 29: 277–8. John Barnes to TJ, April 2, 1799, *PTJDE*, 31: 87–8, at 87.

7. Short to TJ, April 3, 1789, *PTJDE*, 15: 27–30, at 28. Short to Peyton Short, September 17, 1784, WPSP WM; Short to Peyton Short, February 5, 1787, Gilpin Collection, HSP. Short detailed his concerns regarding the well-being of slave families in Short to Peyton Short, July 28, 1800, WPSP WM. Short to Peyton Short, November 26, 1785, WPSP WM; Short to Fulwar Skipwith, August 30, 1786, WSP LOC; Short to Peyton Short, December 18, 1792, WPSP WM. Charles Royster, *The Fabulous History of the Dismal Swamp Company: A Story of George Washington's Times* (New York: Vintage Books, 1999), 334–5; Shackelford, *Jefferson's Adoptive Son*, 15.

8. Short to TJ, June 7, 1791, *PTJDE*, 20: 545–6. Short to Alexander Donald, October 8, 1789, WPSP WM. Short began transferring his business in October 1790; see Alexander Donald to TJ, October 25, 1790, *PTJDE*, 17: 566–7; TJ to Short, November 25, 1790, *PTJDE* 18: 74; TJ to Alexander Donald, May 30, 1795, *PTJDE*, 28: 366–8. Jefferson also did business with James Brown; see James Brown to TJ, November 25, 1790, *PTJDE*, 18: 69; TJ to Short, April 27, 1790, *PTJDE*, 16: 387–9. See also, Short to TJ, August 6, 1800, *PTJDE*, 32: 71–90, at 76–81.

9. Short described the history of his relationship with Brown in Short to TJ, November 30, 1792, *PTJDE*, 24: 679–82, at 680; Short to TJ, December 18, 1792, *PTJDE*, 24: 752–5, at 752–3; Short to Thomas Pinckney, April 8, 1793, WSP LOC. Short reacted to Brown's transfer in Short to TJ, July 17, 1791, *PTJDE*, 20: 641–5, at 644; TJ to Short, April 24, 1792, *PTJDE*, 23:458–60, at 459. Short to TJ, November 30, 1792, *PTJDE*, 24: 679–82, at 680.

10. TJ to Short, March 18, 1792, *PTJDE*, 23: 318–9, at 319.

11. Short to TJ, January 24, 1792, *PTJDE*, 23: 64–6, at 66; Short to TJ, February 29, 1792, *PTJDE*, 23: 167–9, at 167. TJ to Short, October 16, 1792, *PTJDE*, 24: 490–1, at 490. TJ to Short, January 28, 1792, *PTJDE*, 23: 83–4, at 84. Alexander Donald to TJ, March 10, 1793, *PTJDE*, 25: 351–2.

12. Short to TJ, April 2, 1793, *PTJDE*, 25: 479–82, at 481. TJ to Short, April 24, 1792, *PTJDE*, 23: 458–60, at 459. Short to Alexander Donald, May 24, May 27, July 31, 1793, WSP LOC. Short to Thomas Pinckney, May 12, 1793, WSP LOC; Short to Thomas Pinckney, October 12–13, 1793, *Pinckney Papers*; Alexander Donald to Thomas Pinckney, June 10, 1793, enclosed in Thomas Pinckney to Short, June 12, 1793, *Pinckney Papers*; see also, Van Staphorst to Short, May 14, 1793, WSP LOC.

13. TJ to James Brown, April 10, 1793, *PTJDE*, 25: 524–5; TJ to James Brown, May 23, 1793, *PTJDE*, 26: 92–3, at 93; James Brown to TJ, April 15, 1793, *PTJDE*, 25: 549. TJ to Henry Skipwith, April 10, 1793, *PTJDE*, 25: 527–8. Short forwarded a blank power of attorney to Jefferson in Short to TJ, November 30, 1792, *PTJDE*, 24: 679–82, at 680. A letter from Jefferson delegating his authority to receive monies for Short establishes that TJ was acting as Short's attorney from April 1793; TJ to John Ross [Enclosure] January 2, 1794, *PTJDE*, 28: 4. TJ to Short, July 11, 1793, *PTJDE*, 26: 472–3, at 472. Alexander Hamilton to TJ, July 26, 1793, *PTJDE*, 26: 571; TJ to John Hopkins, October 10, 1793, *PTJDE*, 27: 225. TJ to Patrick Kennan, September 13, 1793, *PTJDE*, 27: 108; Patrick Kennan to TJ, September 19, 1793, *PTJDE*, 27: 137. Van Staphorst and Hubbard to William Short, August 22, 1793, WSP LOC.

14. Short to TJ, November 30, 1792, *PTJDE*, 24: 679–82, at 681. Short to TJ, October 7, 1793, *PTJDE*, 27: 201–18. TJ to Short, March 24, 1789, *PTJDE*, 14: 694–7, at 695. Short to TJ, October 7, 1793, *PTJDE*, 27: 201–18. TJ to Short, December 23, 1793, *PTJDE*, 27: 614–6, at 615; TJ to Short, May 25, 1795, *PTJDE*, 28: 353–6. Several extant lists of Short's assets, the first drawn up by John Barnes, detail Short's canal shares, "Memorandum for Mr. Short, November 1798," WSP LOC. [TJ] Project

for Making the Rivanna River Navigable, 1771 [?], *PTJDE*, 1: 87; Subscription for Extending the Navigation of the Rivanna [before November 8, 1790], *PTJDE*, 18: 39–41.

15. Short to TJ, October 7, 1793, *PTJDE*, 27: 201–18, at 204. See also Short to TJ, November 30, 1792, *PTJDE*, 24: 679–82, at 681. For Jefferson's estimates of rental income, TJ to Short, July 11, 1793, *PTJDE*, 26: 472–3, at 472; TJ to J. P. P. Derieux, March 10, 1793, *PTJDE*, 25: 356. Short to TJ, October 7, 1793, *PTJDE*, 27: 201–18, at 205.

16. TJ to Thomas Mann Randolph, Jr., October 22, 1790, *PTJDE*, 17: 622. Description cited in Roger G. Kennedy, *Mr. Jefferson's Lost Cause: Land, Farmers, Slavery and the Louisiana Purchase* (New York: Oxford University Press, 2003), 8. John H. Craven, cited in Lucia Stanton, "Thomas Jefferson: Planter and Farmer," in Frank Cogliano, ed., *A Companion to Thomas Jefferson* (Oxford: Wiley-Blackwell, 2012), 261. TJ to Short, December 23, 1793, *PTJDE*, 27: 613–4, at 614.

17. George Washington to TJ, May 13, 1793, Enclosure: Extracts from Arthur Young to George Washington, January 17, 1793, *PTJDE*, 26: 28, ibid., 26: 29–31. See also [TJ] Notes on Arthur Young's Letter to George Washington, June 18, 1792, *PTJDE*, 24: 95–98. TJ to John Taylor, December 29, 1794, *PTJDE*, 28: 230–4, at 233. [TJ] Notes of a Tour of the Rhineland, *PTJDE*, 13: 8–35, 27; TJ to Jonathan Williams, July 3, 1796, *PTJDE*, 29: 139–41, at 140; Lucia Stanton, "Better Tools for a New and Better World: Jefferson Prefects the Plow," in Sadosky, Onuf, Nicolaisen, and O'Shaughnessy, eds., *Old World, New World*, 200–22. TJ to Thomas Mann Randolph, Jr., April 11, 1796, *PTJDE*, 29: 63–4; TJ to Thomas Mann Randolph, Jr., February 18, 1793, *PTJDE*, 25: 230; TJ to Thomas Mann Randolph, Jr., January 23, 1801, *PTJDE*, 32: 499–500. On contour plowing, see TJ to Tristam Dalton, [enclosure: Model of Thomas Mann Randolph's Plow] May 2, 1817, *PTJDE: Retirement*, 11: 308–11; TJ to George Washington Jeffreys, March 3, 1817, *PTJDE: Retirement*, 11: 162–4. Thomas Mann Randolph, Jr., to TJ, July 11, 1793, *PTJDE*, 26: 470. An English visitor remarked on the "gullying" of Jefferson's estate, see Richard Beale Davis, ed., *Jeffersonian America: Notes by Sir Augustus John Foster* (San Marino: The Huntington Library, 1954), 147–8.

18. William Short, Snr. cited in Edward Ruffin, *An Essay on Calcareous Manures* (1852), 81–2. Craven, *Soil Exhaustion*, 93–4. See also [TJ] Notes on Potash and Pearl Ash, February 19, 1795, *PTJDE*, 28: 271–2. TJ to Ferdinando Fairfax, April 25, 1794, *PTJDE*, 28: 58.

19. Short to Peyton Short, July 28, 1800, WPSP WM. TJ to Short, July 11, 1793, *PTJDE*, 26: 472–3; Short to TJ, October 7, 1793, *PTJDE*, 27: 201–18.

20. Short to TJ, October 7, 1793, *PTJDE*, 27: 201–18, at 204, 205.

21. William Short, Travel Journal, Gilpin Papers, HSP; Short to TJ, October 2, 1788, *PTJDE*, 13: 652–6, at 654. [TJ] Notes of a Tour Into the Southern Parts of France, 1787, *PTJDE*, 11: 415–64, esp. 419 See also, TJ to Short, April 7, 1787, *PTJDE*,

11: 280–1, at 281. Edward Bancroft to TJ, September 16, 1788, *PTJDE*, 13: 606–8, at 607. TJ to Edward Bancroft, January 26, 1789, *PTJDE*, 14: 492–4, at 492.

22. [TJ] Notes of a Tour through Holland and the Rhine Valley [March 3, 1788], *PTJDE*, 13: 8–36, at 13. Jefferson referenced enquiries about procuring Rhinelanders he had made at this time in TJ to Van Staphorst and Hubbard, June 9, 1792, *PTJDE*, 24: 47. TJ to Short, April 9, 1788, *PTJDE*, 13: 48–9.

23. TJ to Edward Bancroft, January 26, 1789, *PTJDE*, 14: 492–4, at 493. See also Cara J. Rogers, "The French Experiment: Thomas Jefferson and William Short Debate Slavery," *American Political Thought* 10 (2021), 327–62.

24. Short to TJ, October 7, 1793, *PTJDE*, 27: 201–18, at 204. Short to TJ, August 6, 1800, *PTJDE*, 32: 71–90, at 84–5. TJ to George Washington, June 28, 1793, *PTJDE*, 26: 396–7. On Jefferson's search for an enlightened overseer, see TJ to Samuel Biddle, December 12, 1792, *PTJDE*, 24: 724–6; TJ to Thomas Mann Randolph, Jr., June 24, 1793, *PTJDE*, 26: 355–6, at 355.

25. [TJ] Notes on Arthur Young's Letter to George Washington, June 18, 1792, *PTJDE*, 24: 95–8, at 98. See also TJ to John Wayles Eppes, July 29, 1820, *PTJDE: Retirement*, 16: 148–50, at 149.

26. TJ to John Adams, April 25, 1794, *PTJDE*, 28: 57; TJ to Ferdinando Fairfax, April 25, 1794, *PTJDE*, 28: 58; TJ to Alexander Donald, May 30, 1795, *PTJDE*, 28: 366–8, at 366. TJ to James Monroe, May 26, 1795, *PTJDE*, 28: 359–62, at 361. TJ to Short, May 25, 1795, *PTJDE*, 28: 353–6, at 355. TJ to John Barnes, June 24, 1795, *PTJDE*, 28: 390. See also Articles of Agreement of Agreement with William Champe Carter, April 20, 1795, *PTJDE*, 28: 332–4; TJ to William Champe Carter, June 3, 1795, *PTJDE*, 28: 379. [Short] Debits of Mr. Jefferson's Acct. connected with his letter of April 18, 1800, WSP LOC. Here Short recorded the purchase price as $5224.83.

27. Short to TJ, September 2, 1795, *PTJDE*, 28: 442–6, at 444, 445. TJ to Short, March 12, 1797, *PTJDE*, 29: 316–18. Short to TJ, March 30, 1797, *PTJDE*, 29: 332–33. TJ to Short, June 30, 1797, *PTJDE*, 29: 463–5. Short to TJ, December 27, 1797, *PTJDE*, 29: 597–8. Short to TJ, February 27, 1798, *PTJDE*, 30: 146–54, at 148.

28. Short to TJ, February 27, 1798, *PTJDE*, 30: 146–54, at 148–53. Short purchased a further volume on Sierra Leone from Parisian bookseller Charles Pougens in the spring of 1798, [Pougens] Articles de Librairie, July 8, 1798, WSP LOC.

29. Short to TJ, February 27, 1798, *PTJDE*, 30: 146–54, at 148–53. Short to TJ, September 18, 1800, *PTJDE*, 32: 147–60, at 154–7. Peden, ed., *Notes on the State of Virginia*, 143.

30. Short to TJ, February 27, 1798, *PTJDE*, 30: 146–54, at 151. Gordon-Reed, *Hemingses of Monticello*, 537; Rogers, "The French Experiment," 354–5.

31. La Rochefoucauld-Liancourt described the mixed-race slaves he saw as "quaterons." Francois-Alexandre-Frédéric La Rochefoucauld-Liancourt, *Voyage dans l'États-Unis d'Amérique*, 8 vols. (Paris: Du Pont, 1799) 5: 35. Jefferson had a copy of the English language translation published in London. Here "quateron" was rendered as

"mongrel negroes"; see [La Rochefoucauld-Liancourt], *Travels Through the United States of North America, the Country of the Iroquois, and Upper Canada in the Years 1795, 1796, and 1797* (London, 1799), 2: 82. Short to TJ, August 24, 1798, *PTJDE*, 30: 487–96, at 488. Short maintained an acquaintance with Rochefoucauld-Liancourt, see Short to TJ, August 6, 1800, *PTJDE*, 32: 71–90, at 85.

32. Jefferson explained his actions in TJ to Short, April 13, 1800, *PTJDE*, 31: 501–11 at 503. For the number of slaves mortgaged, see Deed of Mortgage of Slaves to Van Staphorst & Hubbard, November 21, 1796, *PTJDE*, 29: 209. Justice Thomas Bell also witnessed the power of attorney with John Barnes that Jefferson drew up on Short's behalf; see TJ to John Barnes, Enclosure: Power of Attorney to John Barnes for William Short, December 10, 1796, *PTJDE*, 29: 219. Kirt Von Daacke, *Freedom Has a Face: Race, Identity, and Community in Jefferson's Virginia* (Charlottesville: University of Virginia Press, 2012), 176. See also Gordon-Reed, *The Hemingses of Monticello,* 407–8; to Annette Gordon-Reed, " 'The Memories of a Few Negroes': Rescuing America's Future at Monticello," in Lewis and Onuf, eds., *Sally Hemings and Thomas Jefferson,* 236–54, esp. 250; Henry Wiencek, *Master of the Mountain: Thomas Jefferson and His Slaves* (New York: Farrar, Strauss, Giroux, 2012), esp. 169–72.

33. Short to TJ, August 6, 1800, *PTJDE*, 32: 71–89, at 73. Short to TJ, December 9, 1800, *PTJDE*, 32: 291–97, at 295. Short to TJ, October 9, 1823, *Founders Online.*

34. TJ to James Lyle, July 10, 1795, *PTJDE*, 28: 405–6, at 405. TJ to Thomas Mann Randolph, August 11, 1795, *PTJDE*, 28: 434–5, at 434; TJ to John Barnes, December 11, 1795, *PTJDE*, 28: 552. TJ to Thomas Mann Randolph, February 7, 1796, *PTJDE*, 28: 607–9, at 608. For the sale of Bedford, TJ to James Lyle, May 1, 1796, *PTJDE*, 29: 93. Notes of Account with Richard Harvie and Company, July 22, 1795, *PTJDE*, 28: 413–17. Deed of Mortgage of Slaves to Van Staphorst & Hubbard, November 21, 1796, *PTJDE*, 29: 209. See also TJ to James Lyle, May 12, 1796, *PTJDE*, 29: 96 and editorial note. TJ to Francis Willis, July 15, 1796, *PTJDE*, 29: 153–4, at 153.

35. TJ to Caleb Lownes, December 18, 1793, *PTJDE*, 27: 586–7; TJ to Henry Remsen. October 30, 1794, *PTJDE*, 28: 183; TJ to Henry Remsen, March 11, 1795, *PTJDE*, 28: 304–5; TJ to Henry Remsen, June 18, 1795, *PTJDE*, 28: 388. On competition from imports, TJ to Archibald Stuart, January 3, 1796, *PTJDE*, 28: 572–4, at 573. TJ to Thomas Mann Randolph, Jnr., January 11, 1796, *PTJDE*, 28: 579–80; TJ to Sir Peyton Skipwith, December 24, 1795, *PTJDE*, 28: 560. Jefferson explained his diversion of Short's monies in TJ to Short, April 13, 1800, *PTJDE*, 31: 501–11, 502–3. For indebtedness as an election issue see, [TJ] Statement for the Aurora, March 25, 1800, *PTJDE*, 31: 457–60; TJ to Short, March 26, 1800, *PTJDE*, 31: 463–6, at 464. Short, Observations Respecting My Affairs in Virginia, August 1800, WSP LOC. For the adjusted current value of the loan www.officialdata.org/us/inflation consulted August 28, 2020. Short, Statement of My Property As Far As Is Known

to Me at This Time, March 1802, WSP LOC. TJ to Short, March 23, 1803, *PTJDE*, 40: 106–7.

36. TJ to Short, April 13, 1800, *PTJDE*, 31: 501–11, at 502–3; [Short] List of the Certificates of Stock as now standing in my name, 1803[?], WSP LOC.

37. Short to Peyton Short, July 28, 1800, WSPS WM. Short to TJ, August 6, 1800, *PTJDE*, 32: 71–90, at 81.

38. Short to TJ, August 6, 1800, PTJDE 32: 71–90, at 81, 87; Short to TJ, September 18, 1800, *PTJDE*, 32: 147–60, at 157.

39. TJ to William Short, May 25, 1795, *PTJDE*, 28: 353–356, at 354, 355. TJ to Short, April 19, 1802, *PTJDE*, 37: 287–91, at 289. TJ to William Short, January 12, 1804, *PTJDE*, 42: 267–69. On Durrett, see TJ to Short, March 23, 1803, *PTJDE*, 40: 106–7. See also TJ to Philip Mazzei, April 24, 1796, *PTJDE*, 29: 81–83 and editorial notes. Laura Voisin George, "Tenant Farmers at 'Indian Camp' in Albemarle County, Virginia, 1796–1813," unpublished paper, University of Virginia.

40. TJ to William Short, May 25, 1795, *PTJDE*, 28: 353–356, at 354–55. TJ to Short, May 1, 1798, *PTJDE*, 30: 317–20, at 318. TJ to Short, April 13, 1800, *PTJDE*, 31: 501–11, at 506. Form of Lease, ca. 13 April–May 1800, *PTJDE*, 31: 518. On maize, see TJ to Short, January 12, 1804, *PTJDE*, 42: 267–9, at 268. TJ to Short, April 19, 1802, *PTJDE*, 37: 287–91, at 289. TJ to Short, January 12, 1804, *PTJDE*, 42: 267–69. TJ "The Following Rents were Accounted for to Mr. Short, November 21, 1799" [January 12, 1804], WSP LOC; TJ to Short, January 12, 1804, *PTJDE*, 42: 267–9, at 267. For Short's "pleasure" with the returns from Indian Camp, see Short to TJ, *PTJDE*, 32: 71–90, at 82. See also [TJ] Statement of William Short's Tenements, May 17, 1802, *PTJDE*, 37: 472–3; Statement of William Short's Tenements, May 26, 1802, *PTJDE*, 37: 503. TJ to Short, April 19, 1802, *PTJDE*, 37: 287–91, at 289.

41. Short to TJ, December 18, 1801, *PTJDE*, 36: 158–62, at 160–1; see also Short to TJ, September 18, 1800, *PTJDE*, 32: 147–60, at 152–3. On merino sheep, Short to TJ, September 18, 1800, *PTJDE*, 32: 147–60, at 147–9; Short to TJ, October 18, 1801, *PTJDE*, 35: 461–5, at 463–4; Short to TJ, November 1, 1810, *PTJDE: Retirement*, 3: 197–200, at 198; Short to TJ, November 19, 1811, *PTJDE: Retirement*, 4: 268–74, at 268.

42. Short to TJ, April 2, 1803 [summary], *PTJDE*, 40: 124; Short to TJ, February 15, 1804 [summary], *PTJDE*, 42: 480 and editorial note; TJ to Short, September 20, 1804, *PTJDE*, 44: 415–6; Joseph Price to Short, January 13, 1804, WSP LOC; George Jefferson to Short, November 24, 1804, WSP LOC. Charles Lively to Short, August 27, 1808, WSP LOC; Short to TJ, May 27, 1809, *PTJDE: Retirement*, 1: 229–235, at 234. Short to TJ, November 6, 1807, *Founders Online*.

43. Short to TJ, December 18, 1801, *PTJDE*, 36: 158–63, at 159. For Jefferson's involvement in the collection of rent, TJ to Short, January 12, 1804, *PTJDE*, 42: 267–69; TJ to Short, September 20, 1804, *PTJDE*, 44: 415–7. Short to TJ, November 10, 1803, *PTJDE*, 41: 695. TJ to Short, June 12, 1807, *Founders Online*. See also TJ to Short, November 15, 1807, *Founders Online*. Jacob Price to Short, August 27, 1808,

WSP LOC. For Short's doubts about Price, see George Jefferson to Short, April 11, 1806, WSP LOC; TJ to Short, May 19, 1807, *Founders Online*. Jefferson undertook to find a replacement in TJ to Short, June 12, 1807, *Founders Online*. For Jefferson as an intermediary, see Short to TJ, December 31, 1810, *PTJDE: Retirement*, 3: 272–5; TJ to Short, March 8, 1811, *PTJDE: Retirement*, 3: 438.

44. Shackelford, *Jefferson's Adoptive Son*, 178–85. George Jefferson to Short, April 11, 1806, WSP LOC. Peden, ed., *Notes on the State of Virginia*, 164–5. TJ to Charles Willson Peale, April 17, 1813, *PTJDE: Retirement*, 6: 68–70, at 69. TJ to Short, November 6, 1803, *PTJDE*, 41: 678–9. TJ to Robert R. Livingston, September 2, 1800, *PTJDE*, 32: 120–22.

45. TJ to Volney, December 9, 1795, *PTJDE*, 28: 550–1, at 551. TJ to Charles Willson Peale, April 17, 1813, *PTJDE: Retirement*, 6: 68–70, at 69. TJ to Stevens Thomson Mason, October 27, 1799, *PTJDE*, 31: 222–3, at 222. TJ to Short, April 19, 1802, *PTJDE*, 37: 287–91, at 289.

46. TJ to Charles Willson Peale, August 20, 1811, *PTJDE: Retirement*, 4: 93–94. See also Susan A. Dunn, *Dominion of Memories: Jefferson, Madison and the Death of Virginia* (New York, Basic Books, 2007).

47. Short to TJ, August 6, 1800, *PTJDE*, 32: 71–90, at 73. Short to TJ, December 9, 1800, *PTJDE*, 32: 291–97, at 295.

48. Short to TJ, January 18, 1814, *PTJDE: Retirement*, 7: 135–39, at 139. Short to TJ, July 18, 1816, *PTJDE: Retirement*, 10: 253–5, at 255; TJ to Short, August 10, 1816, *PTJDE: Retirement*, 10: 314–5, at 315. TJ to Short, September 8, 1823, *Founders Online*.

49. Short to TJ, October 9, 1823, *Founders Online*. Short to TJ, December 14, 1825, *Founders Online*. Short to TJ, January 11, 1826, *Founders Online*.

50. For the views on serfdom Coles published in the *Enquirer*, see Scott Taylor Morris, "Southern Enlightenment: Reform and Progress in Jefferson's Virginia" (PhD Dissertation: Washington University in St. Louis, 2014), 183. Jefferson praised the *Richmond Enquirer*, in TJ to Nathaniel Macon, January 12, 1819, *PTJDE: Retirement*, 13: 571–2, at 571; TJ to Short, September 8, 1823, *Founders Online*. Short to TJ, January 11, 1826, *Founders Online*.

51. TJ to Short, January 18, 1826, *Founders Online*. Short to TJ, July 4, 1817, *PTJDE: Retirement*, 11: 500–3, at 501. For Short's later life involvement in the ACS, see Nicholas Guyatt, *Bind Us Apart: How Enlightened Americans Invented Racial Segregation* (New York: Basic Books, 2016).

52. Short to TJ, October 9, 1823, *Founders Online*. For a late life expression of Jefferson's core beliefs, TJ to Short, September 8, 1823, *Founders Online*. TJ to Short, March 8, 1811, *PTJDE: Retirement*, 3: 348.

CHAPTER SEVEN

1. For the date of Short's arrival and offer of credit, see TJ to George Jefferson, August 5, 1802, *PTJDE*, 38: 161. TJ to Short, August 12, 1802, *PTJDE*, 38: 205. John Barnes to TJ, August 16, 1802, *PTJDE*, 38: 225–6, at 225. TJ referenced the "rapidity" of Short's movements in TJ to Short, August 12, 1802, *PTJDE*, 38: 205. TJ to Short, October 9, 1802, *PTJDE*, 38: 468–9, at 468.

2. Madame de Tessé wished Short to update Jefferson on her condition; Madame de Tessé to TJ, May 21, 1802, *PTJDE*, 37: 480. Short to TJ, March 10, 1803 [summary], *PTJDE*, 40: 28; TJ to Short, October 18, 1802, *PTJDE*, 38: 517; TJ to Short, March 23, 1803, *PTJDE*, 40: 106–7. Short to TJ, February 14, 1805, *Founders Online*. TJ to Short, April 15, 1803, *PTJDE*, 40: 218–20, at 219. Short's servant stayed at the Executive Mansion even though Short did not; TJ to Short, October 9, 1803, *PTJDE*, 38: 468–9. For a biographical notice of Barnes, see Cordelia Jackson, "John Barnes, A Forgotten Philanthropist of Georgetown," *Records of the Columbia Historical Society*, VII (1904), 39–48. Planning a subsequent meeting, Jefferson instructed Short to stay at the presidential house since John Barnes had not room for a guest, TJ to Short, November 6, 1803, *PTJDE*, 41: 678–9, at 679.

3. TJ to Short, January 12, 1804, *PTJDE*, 42: 267–9, at 268; TJ to Short, February 8, 1805, *Founders Online*. Statement of Account with George Taylor, 1804 WSP LOC. TJ to Short, May 4, 1805, *Founders Online*. [Short] Statement of Property June 23, 1806, WSP. TJ to Short, April 6, 1807, *Founders Online*; TJ to Short, May, 19, 1807, *Founders Online*. TJ to Short, June 14, 1807, *Founders Online*. See also Memorandum Book, 1807, *PTJDE: Second Series*, entry made July 6, 1206, where the final payment is noted at $797.11.

4. For Short's apologies, see Short to TJ, December 18, 1801, *PTJDE*, 36: 158–63, at 159; Short to TJ, June 9, 1801, *PTJDE*, 34: 286–93, at 292. Short expressed his preference for the management of his affairs to remain unchanged in Short to TJ, June 9, 1801, *PTJDE*, 34: 286–94, at 293, 287–8. TJ to Short, April 13, 1800, *PTJDE*, 31: 501–11, at 503. Barnes had been receiving interest due Short since 1796; see TJ to John Barnes, December 11, 1796, *PTJDE*, 29: 219 and Enclosure; Short to TJ, September 18, postscript September 29, 1800, *PTJDE*, 32: 147–60, at 153–4; John Barnes's Memorandum on William Short's Account, June 22, 1802, *PTJDE*, 37: 652. Jefferson vouched for Barnes in TJ to Short, March 17, 1801, *PTJDE*, 33: 337–9, at 338; Short found fault with Barnes in Short to TJ, January 23, 1802, *PTJDE*, 36: 423–4. TJ to Short, April 19, 1802, *PTJDE*, 37: 287–91, at 287, 288. TJ to Short, July 19, 1802, *PTJDE*, 38: 105. See also TJ to Short, March 17, 1801, *PTJDE*, 33: 337–9.

5. TJ to Short, March 17, 1801, *PTJDE*, 33: 337–9, at 338. Jefferson expressed similar thoughts on the changed character of America to Philip Mazzei; see TJ to Mazzei, June 13, 1806, *Founders Online*. Short to TJ, April 19, 1801, *PTJDE*, 33: 615–8, at 616, 615. Short to TJ, August 6, 1800, *PTJDE*, 32: 71–90, at 74.

6. TJ to Short, March 17, 1801, *PTJDE*, 33: 337–9, at 337; TJ to John Dawson, March 12, 1801, *PTJDE*, 33: 253. Short to TJ, June 9, 1801, *PTJDE*, 34: 286–93, at 292. TJ to Short, October 3, 1801, *PTJDE*, 35: 380–3, at 381, 382. TJ to David Humphreys with Levi Lincoln, March 17, 1801, *PTJDE*, 33: 321–33, at 322; TJ to Robert Livingston, May 8, 1801, *PTJDE*, 34: 62–4, at 63. TJ to Short, October 3, 1801, *PTJDE*, 35: 380–3, at 382, 381. Short to TJ, June 9, 1801, *PTJDE*, 34: 286–93, 287.

7. TJ to Short, October 3, 1801, *PTJDE*, 35: 380–3 at 381. John Barnes to TJ, August 16, 1802, *PTJDE*, 38: 225–6, at 225. Callender's first article in the *Richmond Recorder* is reproduced in John Barnes to TJ, August 31, 1802, *PTJDE*, 38: 323 editorial note. Annette Gordon-Reed, *Thomas Jefferson and Sally Hemings*, 59–62.

8. Annette Gordon-Reed, *Thomas Jefferson and Sally Hemings*, 59–62. TJ to Short, October 3, 1801, *PTJDE*, 35: 380–3 at 381. Joshua D. Rothman, "James Callender and Social Knowledge of Interracial Sex in Antebellum Virginia," in Lewis and Onuf, eds., *Sally Hemings and Thomas Jefferson*, 87–113, esp. 98–99. For a discussion of the theme of depravity in readings of white-male, black-female sexual encounters, see Annette Gordon-Reed, "Engaging Jefferson: Blacks and the Founding Father," *WMQ*, 57 (January 2000), 171–182, at 180–1.

9. On Paine's relationship with Jefferson after 1802, see Seth Cotlar, *Tom Paine's America: The Rise and Fall of Transatlantic Radicalism in the Early Republic* (Charlottesville: University of Virginia Press, 2011), 211–4. Short to TJ, February 14, 1805, *Founders Online*; Short to TJ, December 31, 1810, *PTJDE: Retirement*, 3: 272–5, at 273.

10. For Short's presence at the dinner, see TJ to Short, January 23, 1804, *PTJDE*, 42: 331–4, at 331. The event and its consequences are described in James Madison to James Monroe, January 19, 1804, *PJMDE: Secretary of State Series*, 6: 361–6; Canons of Official Etiquette: Editorial Note, *PTJDE*, 42: 154–7; Catherine Allgor, *Parlor Politics: In Which the Ladies of Washington Help Build a City and a Government* (Charlottesville: University of Virginia Press, 2000), 36–47; G. S. Wilson, *Jefferson On Display*, 142–6. TJ to Short, January 23, 1804, *PTJDE*, 42: 331–4, at 333–4.

11. TJ to Short, September 20, 1804, *PTJDE*, 44: 415–7. Alexander Hamilton to Short, July 3, 1804, *PAHDE*, 26: 292. For Trumbull's attitudes toward the French Revolution, see *Autobiography, Reminiscences and Letters of John Trumbull* (New York, 1841), 167–9, 245–6; for cooling of his relationship with Jefferson, 170–2, 352. Short likely mentioned the dinner in a letter to Jefferson written on July 19, apparently received, but no longer extant.

12. Short to TJ, November 5, 1804, *PTJDE*, 44: 646–8, at 647. TJ to Short, November 10, 1804, *PTJDE*, 4: 707–8, at 707.

13. Short to TJ, November 21, 1804, *PTJDE*, 44: 55–6. Short maintained this view into old age; see Short to TJ, December 18, 1824, *Founders Online*.

14. TJ to Short, January 8, 1825, *Founders Online*. TJ to Short, May 19, 1807, *Founders Online*. C. E. Prince, "The Passing of the Aristocracy: Jefferson's Removal of the Federalists, 1801–1805," *Journal of American History*, 57/3 (1970), 565–8.

15. TJ to Short, February 8, 1805, *PTJDE*, 45: 471–2. Short to TJ, February 14, 1805, *PTJDE*, 45: 508–10, at 508–9.

16. TJ to Short, January 5, 1807, *Founders Online*; TJ to Short, May 19, 1807, *Founders Online*; TJ to Short, June 12, 1807, *Founders Online*. For invitations to stay at Monticello, see TJ to Short, May 4, 1805, June 14, 1805, June 9, 1806, *Founders Online*. For discussion of wine, see TJ to Short, June 9 1806, June 13, 1806, August 30, 1806, June 14, 1807, *Founders Online*. For books, December 12, 1806, *Founders Online*. On loose bowels, TJ to Short, August 30, 1806, *Founders Online*. TJ to Short, April 6, 1807, *Founders Online*. TJ to Short, June 12, 1807, *Founders Online*.

17. TJ to Short, November 6, 1807, *Founders Online*. TJ to Short, October 12, 1806, *Founders Online*. TJ to Short, November 15, 1807, *Founders Online*.

18. TJ to Short, January 27, 1806, *Founders Online*. TJ to Short, October 12, 1806, *Founders Online*. Short to TJ, November 25, 1807, *Founders Online*.

19. Short to TJ, December 29, 1807, *Founders Online*.

20. Short to TJ, January 27, 1808, *Founders Online*. TJ to Short, July 6, 1808, *Founders Online*.

21. TJ to Short, August 29, 1808, *Founders Online*. For Short's regret, Short to TJ, April 10, 1809, *PTJDE: Retirement*, 1: 115–22, at 118. See Short's subsequent account of the mission, Short to TJ, May 27, 1809, *PTJDE: Retirement*, 1: 229–35. Jefferson conveyed news of the rejection in TJ to Short, March 8, 1809, *PTJDE: Retirement*, 1: 38–9. See also Short to TJ, May 27, 1809, *PTJDE: Retirement*, 1: 229–35; Short to TJ, April 10, 1809, *PTJDE: Retirement*, 1: 115–22. Samuel Taggart, "Letters of Samuel Taggart, Representative in Congress, 1803–1814," *Proceedings of the American Antiquarian Society*, 33 part 2 (October 1923), 297–438, citation at 335. Madison explained the Senate's vote endorsing John Quincy Adams as an objection to Short and not to the mission itself in James Madison to John Quincy Adams, March 6, 1809, *PJMDE: Presidential*, 1: 21, editorial note.

22. TJ to Madame de Tessé, March 27, 1811, *PTJDE: Retirement*, 3: 503–4, at 504. See Tsar Alexander I to TJ, August 20, 1805, *Founders Online*; TJ to Tsar Alexander I, April 19, 1806, *Founders Online*. See also TJ to William Duane, July 20, 1807, *Founders Online*. Shackleford, *Jefferson's Adoptive Son*, 145–55.

23. Short to TJ, December 9, 1800, *PTJDE*, 32: 291–7; Short to TJ, May 27, 1809, *PTJDE: Retirement*, 1: 229–35, at 230. Short to TJ, April 10, 1809, *PTJDE: Retirement*, 1: 115–22, at 119. Short to TJ, May 29, 1809, *PTJDE: Retirement*, 1: 229–35, at 232.

24. Short to TJ, April 10, 1809, *PTJDE: Retirement*, 1: 115–22, at 116; Short to TJ, November 19, 1811, *PTJDE: Retirement*, 4: 268–74, at 269. Short to TJ, June 19, 1810, *PTJDE: Retirement*, 2: 475–9, at 477. Short to TJ, October 25, 1820, *Founders Online*. Short to TJ, May 27, 1809, *PTJDE: Retirement*, 1: 229–35, at 229, 235. Short to TJ, June 19, 1810, *PTJDE: Retirement*, 2: 475–9, at 476.

25. TJ to Short, April 19, 1802, *PTJDE*, 37: 287–91, at 289–90. TJ to Short, May 17, 1811, *PTJDE: Retirement*, 3: 621–3. TJ to Short, July 26, 1811, *PTJDE: Retirement*, 4: 59–61. TJ to Short, April 26, 1812, *PTJDE: Retirement*, 4: 674–6. For the

difficulties of absentee ownership, see George Jefferson to Short, April 11, 1806, WSP LOC.

26. TJ to Short, May 17, 1811, *PTJDE: Retirement*, 3: 621–3. TJ to Short, July 26, 1811, *PTJDE: Retirement*, 4: 59–61. See also TJ to Short, April 26, 1812, *PTJDE: Retirement*, 4: 674–6. TJ to Short, September 30, 1812, *PTJDE: Retirement*, 5: 362–64.

27. TJ to Short, September 30, 1812, *PTJDE: Retirement*, 5: 362–64; TJ to Short, October 17, 1812, *PTJDE: Retirement*, 5: 399–402. See also William Minor Dabney, "Jefferson's Albemarle: History of Albemarle County, Virginia, 1727–1819" (PhD dissertation: University of Virginia, 1951), 84. [TJ] Notes on Account with David Higginbotham, ca. February 3, 1814, *PTJDE: Retirement*, 7: 180–1.

28. TJ to Short, October 17, 1812, *PTJDE: Retirement*, 5: 399–402, at 400. For Jefferson's "embarrassments," see TJ to John Barnes, January 27, 1812, *PTJDE: Retirement*, 4: 462–3. TJ to Short, October 17, 1812, *PTJDE: Retirement*, 5: 399–402, at 400–1. See also TJ to Short, February 10, 1813, *PTJDE: Retirement*, 5: 622–4. TJ to Short, October 17, 1812, *PTJDE: Retirement*, 5: 399–402, at 400–1.

29. TJ to Short, January 28, 1814, *PTJDE: Retirement*, 7: 166–9, at 166–7. Jefferson registered receipt of a reply; see TJ to Short, February 23, 1814, *PTJDE: Retirement*, 7: 212–3, at 212 and editorial notes. See also TJ to Short, November 9, 1813, *PTJDE: Retirement*, 6: 604–6, at 605.

30. TJ to Samuel Harrison Smith, September 21, 1814, *PTJDE: Retirement*, 7: 681. For a measure of the fame of Jefferson's library, see "From Anonymous" to TJ, November 19, 1814, *PTJDE: Retirement*, 8: 94; Notes on Thomas Jefferson's Library at the Time of Sale [by April 18, 1815], *PTJDE: Retirement*, 8: 428. TJ to Samuel H. Smith, October 29, 1814, *PTJDE: Retirement*, 8: 55–7. Short to TJ, March 11, 1815, *PTJDE: Retirement*, 8: 330–32, at 331. TJ to Alexander J. Dallas, April 18, 1815, *PTJDE: Retirement*, 8: 428–9. On treasury notes and depreciation, see Short to TJ, March 11, 1815, *PTJDE: Retirement*, 8: 330–32, at 331; TJ to Short, March 25, 1815, *PTJDE: Retirement*, 8: 382–3, at 382. Jefferson also repaid John Barnes the sum of $4,870; TJ to John Barnes, April 18, 1815, *PTJDE: Retirement*, 8: 425–6.

31. Short to TJ, December 31, 1810, *PTJDE: Retirement*, 3: 272–5, at 273; see also TJ to Short, May 5, 1816, *PTJDE: Retirement*, 10: 9–11, at 11. Short to TJ, November 16, 1816, *PTJDE: Retirement*, 10: 529–31, at 529–30. Short to TJ, April 23, 1816, *PTJDE: Retirement*, 9: 693–6, at 696.

32. Short to TJ, November 16, 1816, *PTJDE: Retirement Series*, 10: 529–31, at 530. Short to TJ, June 19, 1810, *PTJDE: Retirement*, 2: 475–9, at 476. On the sale of canal shares, Short to TJ, December 12, 1818, *PTJDE: Retirement*, 13: 487–9, at 488. Short to TJ, June 19, 1810, *PTJDE: Retirement*, 2: 475–9, at 476. Short to TJ, June 21, 1815, *PTJDE: Retirement*, 8: 556–7, at 556, 557. Short to TJ, March 27, 1820, *Founders Online*; see also Short to John Hartwell Cocke, April 18, 1832, JHCP UVA. Short to TJ, July 18, 1816, *PTJDE: Retirement Series*, 10: 253–5, at 254. Short's recollection was correct: Jefferson discussed the potential for the foreign-born to

introduce "unbridled licentiousness" into the American political system in Query VIII (Population) of *Notes on the State of Virginia*. Short finally bought a fresh copy of *Notes*, Short to TJ, July 4, 1817, *PTJDE: Retirement*, 11: 500–3, at 503.

33. [TJ], First Inaugural Address, March 4, 1801, *PTJDE*, 33: 148–52, at 149. TJ to John Adams, October 28, 1813, *PTJDE: Retirement*, 6: 562–6, at 563. TJ to James Madison, February 17, 1825, *Founders Online*.

34. Short to TJ, November 17, 1818, *PTJDE: Retirement*, 13: 395–7, at 396. Short to TJ, October 4, 1825, *Founders Online*. Short to TJ, June 27, 1825, *Founders Online*. On Cooper, see Short to TJ, May 25, 1819, *PTJDE: Retirement*, 14: 321–5, at 322; Short to John Hartwell Cocke, March 16, 1819, JCHP UVA. On religious opposition, see Short to TJ, March 27, 1820, *PTJDE: Retirement*, 15: 491–4, at 491; Short to TJ, April 17, 1824, *Founders Online*. Short to TJ, December 12, 1818, *PTJDE: Retirement*, 13: 487–9, at 488; Short to TJ, November 2, 1824, *Founders Online*. See also TJ to Short, April 27, 1825, *Founders Online*.

35. Short to TJ, December 1, 1819, *PTJDE: Retirement*, 15: 252–55, at 254; see also Short to TJ, March 27, 1820, *PTJDE: Retirement*, 15: 491–4, at 492. Short to TJ, May 2, 1820, *PTJDE: Retirement*, 15: 562–5, at 564. TJ to Short, April 13, 1820, *PTJDE: Retirement*, 15: 538–41, at 540. TJ to John Holmes, April 22, 1820, *PTJDE: Retirement*, 15: 550–1, at 550.

36. Short had spoken of his growing indolence in Short to John Hartwell Cocke, March 16, 1819, JHCP UVA. Short to TJ, October 21, 1819, *PTJDE: Retirement*, 15: 148–50, at 148.

37. TJ to Short, October 31, 1819, *PTJDE: Retirement*, 15: 162–5, at 164.

38. Short to TJ, December 1, 1819, *PTJDE: Retirement*, 15: 252–5, at 252–3. Jefferson composed his Doctrines of Jesus Compared with Others for Benjamin Rush; see TJ to Benjamin Rush, April 21, 1803, *PTJDE*, 40: 251–2 and enclosure 253–5; TJ to Joseph Priestley, April 9, 1803, *PTJDE*, 40: 157–9. Short had struck up a friendship with Ellen Wayles Randolph on her visit to Philadelphia; see Short to TJ, April 23, 1816, *PTJDE: Retirement*, 9: 693–5, at 694. Short to TJ, March 27, 1820, *PTJDE: Retirement*, 15: 491–4, at 491 TJ to Short, April 13, 1820, *PTJDE: Retirement*, 15: 538–41, at 538–9; see also TJ to Short, August 4, 1820, *PTJDE: Retirement*, 16: 163. Short to TJ, May 2, 1820, *PTJDE: Retirement*, 15: 562–5, at 562.

39. Short to TJ, October 25, 1820, *PTJDE: Retirement*, 16: 370–3, at 371. Short to TJ, November 1, 1810, *PTJDE: Retirement*, 3: 197–200, at 197. Short to TJ, November 16, 1816, *PTJDE: Retirement*, 10: 529–31, at 530. Short to TJ, April 23, 1816, *PTJDE: Retirement*, 9: 693–5, at 694. Jefferson discussed Ellen's visit in TJ to Short, May 5, 1816, *PTJDE: Retirement*, 10: 9–11, at 11.

40. TJ to Short, October 31, 1819, *PTJDE: Retirement*, 15: 162–5, at 165. On making introductions and travel arrangements, see Short to TJ, July 18, 1816, *PTJDE: Retirement*, 10: 253–5; Short to TJ, November 17, 1818, *PTJDE: Retirement*, 13: 395–7, at 396–7. On Madame de Staël, see Short to TJ, December 12, 1818,

PTJDE: Retirement Series, 13: 487–9. Short to TJ, March 17, 1823, *Founders Online*. TJ to Short, March 28, 1823, *Founders Online*. For Webster's visit, see Henry S. Randall, *The Life of Thomas Jefferson*, 3 vols. (Philadelphia, 1871. rep. London: Forgotten Books, 2019), 3: 506.

41. Short to TJ, May 10, 1824, *Founders Online*. Short to TJ, April 17, 1824, *Founders Online*. Short to TJ, July 4, 1817, *PTJDE: Retirement*, 11: 500–3, at 500.

42. Short to TJ, March 11, 1815, *PTJDE: Retirement*, 8: 330–2, at 331; Short to TJ, May 7, 1816, *PTJDE: Retirement*, 10: 21–2, at 22. TJ to Short, September 21, 1810, *PTJDE: Retirement*, 3: 106–7, at 107. Short to TJ, March 11, 1815, *PTJDE: Retirement*, 8: 330–2, at 331. Short to TJ, July 4, 1817, *PTJDE: Retirement*, 11: 500–3, at 502. Short to TJ, April 23, 1816, *PTJDE: Retirement*, 9: 693–6, at 693. Short to TJ, June 29, 1820, *PTJDE: Retirement*, 16: 61–4, at 63; see also Short to TJ, October 25, 1820, *PTJDE: Retirement*, 16: 370–3, at 372. TJ to Short, August 4, 1820, *PTJDE: Retirement*, 16: 163–8, at 168.

43. The elaborate preparations he made to ensure a comfortable journey suggest some of the factors that might previously have deterred Short from visiting; Short to TJ, March 29, 1824, *Founders Online*; see also Short to TJ, April 17, 1824, *Founders Online*. Short's presence is established in Short to John Hartwell Cocke, September 12, 1824, JHCP UVA; Short to TJ, November 2, 1824, *Founders Online*. Short to TJ, December 18, 1824, *Founders Online;* Short to TJ, December 23, 1824, *Founders Online*. TJ to Short, January 8, 1825, *Founders Online*. Short to TJ, January 19, 1825, *Founders Online*. TJ to Short, April 4, 1825, *Founders Online*. Short to TJ, April 27, 1825, *Founders Online*.

44. TJ to William Branch Giles, December 26, 1825, *Founders Online*. Short to John Hartwell Cocke, April 5, 1826, JHCP UVA.

45. Short to TJ, May 10, 1824, *Founders Online*. Short was unaware that Jefferson had already been making efforts on Lafayette's behalf, presciently noting that a gift of land stood a better chance of passing Congress than a gift of money because it would be of less obvious benefit to Lafayette's family; TJ to Short, May 17, 1824, *Founders Online*. Short to TJ, November 2, 1824, *Founders Online*. For Short's involvement in arrangements for Lafayette's visit, Short to TJ, May 10, 1824, *Founders Online*; Short to TJ, July 19, 1824, *Founders Online*.

46. Short to TJ, May 6, 1826, *Founders Online*; see also Short to John Hartwell Cocke, April 5, 1826, JHCP UVA. Thomas Jefferson Randolph to TJ, February 3, 1826, *Founders Online*. Jefferson had previously opposed lotteries; see Alan Pell Crawford, *Twilight at Monticello: The Final Years of Thomas Jefferson* (New York: Random House, 2009), 224. For Jefferson's change of mind, see Thomas Jefferson's Thoughts on Lotteries, ca. January 1826, *Founders Online*. The lottery bill passed the Virginia legislature on February 20, 1826, with the proviso that Monticello be included in the prize. Short to TJ, March 4, 1826, *Founders Online*.

47. Thomas Jefferson Randolph to TJ, February 17, 1826, *Founders Online*.

48. Short to John Hartwell Cocke, August 12, 1826, JHCP UVA.

49. Alexander Hamilton to Gouverneur Morris, February 29, 1802, *PAHDE*, 25: 544–5, at 544. "Letters of Samuel Taggart," 335.

EPILOGUE

1. Short to TJ, October 24, 1814, *PTJDE: Retirement*, 8: 50–3, at 52. Short expressed a desire to write a biography of Jefferson in, Short to TJ, December 1, 1819, *PTJDE: Retirement*, 15: 252–5. Short to John Hartwell Cocke, August 12, 1826, JHCP UVA.

2. William Peden, "A Bookseller Invades Monticello," *WMQ*, 3d ser. 6 (October, 1949), 631–6, at 635. George Ticknor's Account of a Visit to Monticello [February 4–7, 1815], *PTJDE: Retirement*, 8: 238–43, at 239–40, 242. Margaret Bayard Smith's Account of a Visit to Monticello [29 July–2 August, 1809], *PTJDE: Retirement*, 1: 386–401. Short to TJ, April 23, 1816, *PTDE: Retirement*, 9: 693–6, at 695. Short encouraged TJ to speak out on the slave trade in Short to TJ, May 5, 1816, *PTJDE: Retirement*, 10: 9–11, at 11; Short to TJ, November 16, 1816, *PTJDE: Retirement*, 10: 529–31. See also Edmund Coles to TJ, July 31, 1814, *PTJDE: Retirement*, 7: 503–4. For examples of TJ encouraging correspondents to disseminate views expressed in private correspondence, see TJ to Martin Van Buren, June 29, 1824, *Founders Online*; TJ to John Holmes, April 22, 1820, *PTJDE: Retirement*, 15: 550–1.

3. See Michael D. Hattem, *Past and Prologue: Politics and Memory in the American Revolution* (New Haven: Yale University Press, 2020). See also Kariann Akemi Yokota, *Unbecoming British: How Revolutionary America Became a Postcolonial Nation* (New York: Oxford University Press, 2010). Samuel W. Haynes, *Unfinished Revolution: The Early American Republic in a British World* (Charlottesville: University of Virginia Press, 2010).

4. Stiles cited in Robert M. S. McDonald, *Confounding Father: Thomas Jefferson's Image in His Own Time* (Charlottesville: University of Virginia Press, 2016), 19, 13–20. Benjamin Rush to John Adams, June 13, 1808. *Founders Online*; John Adams to Benjamin Rush, February 25, 1808, *Founders Online*. John Adams to Benjamin Rush, June 20, 1808, *Founders Online*; John Adams to Benjamin Rush, April 18, 1808, postscript, *Founders Online*. Pauline Maier, *American Scripture: Making the Declaration of Independence* (New York: Knopf, 1997); Len Travers, *Celebrating the Fourth: Independence Day and the Rites of Nationalism in the Early Republic* (Amherst: University of Massachusetts Press, 1997). See also Mark Hulliung, *The Social Contract in America. From the Revolution to the Present Age* (Lawrence: University of Kansas Press, 2007), 141–72, at 156. Abraham Lincoln, Speech in Independence Hall Philadelphia, February 23, 1861, cited in Ronald L. Hatzenbuehler, "Abraham Lincoln's Evolving Appreciation of the Declaration of Independence," *American Nineteenth Century History*, 21 (2020), 171–86.

5. TJ to Henry Lee, May 8, 1825, *Founders Online*. See also TJ to Dr. James Mease, September 16, 1825, *Founders Online*. Peter Thompson, "David Walker's

Nationalism—and Thomas Jefferson's," *Journal of the Early Republic*, 37 (2017), 47–80.

6. John Adams to TJ, August 15, 1823, *Founders Online*. TJ to John Adams, September 4, 1823, *Founders Online*.

7. Rockfish Gap Report of the University of Virginia Commissioners, August 4, 1818, *PTJDE: Retirement*, 13: 209–223, at 221. Andrew J. O'Shaughnessy, *The Illimitable Freedom of the Human Mind: Thomas Jefferson's Idea of a University* (Charlottesville: University of Virginia Press, 2021).

8. Nancy Isenberg and Andrew Burstein, *The Problem of Democracy: The Presidents Adams Confront the Cult of Personality* (New York: Viking, 2019).

9. TJ to Isaac Tiffany, August 26, 1816. *PTJDE: Retirement*, 10: 349. Jefferson's empathetic understanding of the relationship between his generation and its successors has been extensively explored by Peter Onuf. For a brief summary, see "Priestcraft, Enlightenment, and the Republican Revolution" in Peter S. Onuf, *The Mind of Thomas Jefferson* (Charlottesville: University of Virginia Press, 2007), 139–68, esp. 153–4. Short to John Hartwell Cocke, December 3, 1833, JHCP UVA. Short was not alone in expressing distaste for the manner in which Philadelphians celebrated the Fourth, see Travers, *Celebrating the Fourth*, 211–3. Short to John Hartwell Cocke, December 3, 1833, JHCP UVA.

10. Shackelford, "William Short," 531. Short to John Hartwell Cocke, March 3, 1832, JHCP UVA. Short to John Hartwell Cocke, December 3, 1833, JHCP UVA.

11. Gordon S. Wood, *The Radicalism of the American Revolution* (New York: Vintage Books, 1993), 179, 368, 369. Joyce Appleby, "The Radical Recreation of the American Republic," *WMQ*, 3d ser., 51 (October 1994), 679–83, at 683. See also Sean Wilentz, *The Rise of American Democracy: Jefferson to Lincoln* (New York: Norton, 2005).

12. Short to TJ, June 9, 1814, *PTJDE: Retirement*, 7: 402–5, at 403. Short to John Hartwell Cocke, August 3, 1825, JHCP UVA. [William Short] Agreement with Charles Kuhn, August 7, 1835, WSP LOC. Short to John Hartwell Cocke, April 5, 1826, JHCP UVA. John Barnes to TJ, July 13, 1814, *PTJDE: Retirement*, 7: 469–70, 470–2. *Lady's Book*, August, 1839, 53. Gordon-Reed and Onuf, *Most Blessed of Patriarchs*, 127–8. Short routinely carried a miniature of Rosalie de La Rochefoucauld made by Jean Marchand; see Lucille Mowane Watson, "Our First Career Diplomat and the Duchess. Or, 'Uncle Willie's Wallet' and the Lady Inside," unpub. article WPSP WM; Howard C. Rice to Lucille Mowane Watson, November 22, 1976, WPSP WM. Short to TJ, April 23, 1816, *PTJDE: Retirement*, 9: 693–5, at 694. TJ to Short, May 5, 1816, *PTJDE: Retirement*, 10: 9–11, at 11.

13. Short to TJ, November 16, 1816, *PTJDE: Retirement*, 10: 529–31, at 530.

14. Short to John Cleves Short, April 6, 1811, WSP LOC. Short to John Cleves Short, November 15, 1812, WSP LOC. Short to John Cleves Short, September 3, 1836, WSP LOC.

15. Short to John Hartwell Cocke, August 12, 1826, JHCP UVA. Short to TJ, January 19, 1825, *Founders Online*.

16. TJ to Elbridge Gerry, January 26, 1799, *PTJDE*, 30: 645–51, at 650.

17. Adams cited in Richard Samuelson, "Painting with a Fine Pencil: Henry Adams' Jefferson," in Robert M. S. McDonald, ed., *Thomas Jefferson's Lives: Biographers and the Battle for History* (Charlottesville: University of Virginia Press, 2019), 106–24, at 111.

Index

For the benefit of digital users, indexed terms that span two pages (e.g., 52–53) may, on occasion, appear on only one of those pages.

Adam and Eve letter (Jefferson, 1793)
  revolutionary violence justified in, 5,
    14–15, 16–17, 118, 119–21, 127
  September massacres (1792) and, 119
  Short's refusal to publicize,
    128, 187–88
  Short's response to, 123–24
  US domestic politics and, 122
Adams, Abigail
  on American culture's virtues, 51
  Bingham and, 58–59
  Enville and, 47–48
  French culture as experienced by, 47–
    48, 51, 55
  Jefferson (Polly) and, 30, 51–52
  Jefferson (Thomas) and, 51–52, 103–4
  Short and, 24–28, 30
Adams, Abigail "Nabby" (daughter of
    John and Abigail Adams), 25, 26–
    27, 45, 51–52, 56–57, 90
Adams, Henry, 218
Adams, John
  as ambassador to Great Britain, 26–
    27, 45, 72
  on American culture's virtues,
    45, 51–52

on Americans' prizing money over
    liberty, 209–10
*Defense of the Constitutions of
    Government of the United States of
    America* written by, 34–35, 37
Dutch civil war (1780s) and, 106–7
Enville and, 47–48
French culture as experienced by, 51–52
French language abilities of, 24–25
French Revolution and, 120, 211
Jefferson's correspondence with, 12–13,
    26–27, 51–52, 72, 80–81, 106–7,
    208, 211
La Rochefoucauld (Louis-Alexandre
    de) and, 48–49
as minister to Holland, 80–81
monarchical title for presidency
    considered by, 105
as peace commissioner in Paris, 20,
    24–25, 26, 44, 45
presidency of, 150
Prussia's treaty with United States
    (1785) and, 27–28
return to the United States by, 45
Short and, 26–27, 30
US debt to France, 78–81

Adams, John Quincy, 47–48, 51–52, 112, 204, 212

The Adventures of Telemachus (Fénelon), 137

Albemarle County (Virginia). *See also* Indian Camp estate; Monticello

Jefferson's attempts to get Short to settle in, 16–17, 26, 41, 157, 164–65, 169, 212, 218

Jefferson's desire for patriarchal community in, 12, 56–57, 163–64, 180–81

Jefferson's plan for *metayer* experiment in, 166–67

knowledge of Jefferson-Hemings relationship in, 187

Madison's settlement in, 26, 202

Monroe's settlement in, 12, 26, 169, 202

Short's discussion of settling in, 149, 151, 164

Alexander, William, 21–22, 31–32

Alexander I (tsar of Russia), 192–94

Alfieiri, Vittorio, 64

American Colonization Society (ACS), 183

American Revolution

commemorative medals project in Europe for, 31–32

Founders' conclusions about the animating spirit of, 211–12, 213

French Revolution compared to, 102–3

pensions to French soldiers who fought in, 78–79

The American Wanderer, 18–19, 21, 62, 65–66

Amiens, peace (1802) of, 184, 185

Appleby, Joyce, 213–15

Astorg, Madame d', 115, 116

Autobiography (Jefferson), 13–14, 19–20, 31, 110, 127–28

Bancroft, Edward, 166–67

Banister, Jr., John, 51–53

Bank of the United States, 95, 159–60, 162–63, 198

Barlow, Joel, 33

Barnave, Antoine, 104–5

Barnes, John, 173–74, 176, 184–85, 196

Bastille attack (Paris, 1789), 7, 105–6, 127–28

Bell, Thomas, 173–74, 176, 187

Bellini, Charles, 50

Berlin Decree (Napoleon), 192

Bertier de Sauvigny, Louis Bénigne François, 104–5

Bill for Establishing Religious Freedom (Virginia), 2–3, 32–33

Bingham, Anne Willing, 58–60

Bishop, Abraham, 64–65

Blot, Mademoiselle du, 63

Bolling v. Bolling, 3

Boswell, James, 35–36

Botidoux, Marie-Jacinthe ("Bot"), 9–10, 39–40

Bouffard, Jean-Baptiste, 115–16

Bowdoin, Preeson, 61–62, 64–66

Brissot de Warville, Jacques-Pierre, 32–34, 82–83, 139–40

Brissotins, 125–26

Brown, James, 159–63

Burke, Edmund, 75

Burr, Aaron, 189

Burton, Robert, 161. *See also* Donald and Burton Trading House

Byrd, Abby, 68

Byrd II, William, 1

Callender, James Thomson, 186–87

Calonne, Charles-Alexandre de, 31

Carmichael, William, 80, 90–91, 97–98, 99–100

Carr, Peter, 52

Carrington, Edward, 103–4

Carter, Edward (Ned), 162, 164–65

Castellane, Boniface Louis André, Count de, 144–45, 148, 153–55
Castiglione, Pauline, 64, 215–16
Charlottesville (Virginia), 151, 187
Chastellux, Marquis de, 18, 33, 69–70
Chesterfield, Earl of, 63–65
Clarkson, Thomas, 48–49
Clavière, Etienne, 82–83
Coles, Edward, 182–83
Coles, John, 3–4
Condorcet, Marquis de
    accounts of American life for a French audience by, 32, 34
    anti-slavery views of, 33–34, 166–67
    Enville and, 47, 69–70, 112
    Jacobins and, 112
    Jefferson and, 34
    La Rochefoucauld family and, 49–50, 69–70, 112, 154
    marriage to Grouchy of, 69–70
    Mazzei and, 34–35
    republicanism of, 49–50
    Short and, 34, 35, 69–70, 75, 202
Confederation Congress, 78–79
Congress of the United States
    Commission for Negotiating Foreign Treaties of Amity and Commerce and, 20, 21–22
    diplomatic relationships with European countries and, 73–74, 193
    funding for US delegation in France and, 4–5, 31, 74
    Jefferson on the importance of cultivating, 191–92
    Library of Congress and, 150–51, 197
    US debt to France and, 81, 82, 84–85, 93–94
Constitutional Convention (1787), 78–79, 88
Constitution of the United States, 108
Cooper, Thomas, 199
Corny, Louis de, 105–6
Corny, Marguerite de, 9–10, 36–38, 57–58, 128–29, 149–50

Correa da Serra, Jose, 182, 200
Cosway, Maria
    Jefferson's affair with, 9–10, 35–38, 57–58, 149–50
    Jefferson's correspondence with, 104–5
    marriage of, 35–36
    physical appearance of, 35–36
    Short and, 9–10, 36–37, 43
Cosway, Richard, 35–36
Crèvecoeur, Hector St. Jean de, 32–33, 46
crop rotation, 165, 169, 178
Currie, James, 29–30, 63–64

Dauphin of France. *See* Louis XVIII (king of France)
Dawson, John, 186
Declaration of Independence, 32–33, 34, 108–9, 133–34, 209–11
Declaration of the Rights of Man and Citizen, 109, 114–15
Defense of the Constitutions of Government of the United States of America (John Adams), 34–35, 37
Deffand, Madame du, 47
De la France et des États-Unis (Brissot de Warville), 33
Démeunier, Jean-Nicolas, 32–33, 125–26
Democratic-Republicans, 95, 150, 189
Denis, Alexandre, 29, 62
Denis, Henri, 154
Désert de Retz, 46–47
Dickinson, John, 32–33
Dolomieu, Déodat Gratet de, 115
Donald, Alexander, 157–58, 161, 162–63
Donald and Burton Trading House, 141–42, 162–64, 165–66
Dumas, Charles William Frederick, 80–81, 103
Dupin, Madame, 63
Durrett, John, 177–78, 179

École des Arts et Métiers, 48–49

Émile (Rousseau), 137
Encyclopédie Méthodique, 32–33, 125–26
Enville, Élisabeth d'
　Adams family and, 47–48
　Condorcet and, 47, 69–70, 112
　death of, 124, 143, 145–46
　French Revolution and, 50, 110, 115–
　　17, 128–29
　imprisonment of, 115–16, 128–29,
　　130, 146–47
　Jefferson and, 37–38, 46, 47, 50, 57–58,
　　110, 117, 124, 135–36
　La Rochefoucauld family dynastic
　　considerations and, 55–56
　La Roche-Guyon chateau and, 46–47
　manners and clothing of, 47–48
　marriage and widowhood of, 55–56
　Morris's appointment as minister to
　　France and, 92
　September massacres (1792) and killing
　　of son of, 115–17, 124, 134, 141–42
　Short and, 37–38, 46, 110, 112–13, 117,
　　124, 131, 133, 135–36, 138, 144–45
Epicurus, 200–2, 206
Eppes, Elizabeth, 22–23, 29–30
Eppes, Francis, 1–2, 22–23, 29–30
Eppes, John Wayles, 1–2
Estates General meeting (1789), 47, 103–
　4, 108

Fauquier, Francis, 18–19
Federalists, 126, 149, 188–90, 203–4
Fénelon, François, 137
Ferdinand Grand banking house, 79–80
Fitzgerald, Robert, 41
Fitzhugh, William, 27–28
Flahaut, Adèle de, 88–89, 133
Foreign Intercourse Act (1790), 74
Foulon, Joseph-François, 104–5
France. *See also* French Revolution; US
　　debt to France
　Congress's funding of US diplomatic
　　presence in, 4–5, 31, 74
　financial crisis (1780s) in, 78–79, 81,
　　83–84, 85–87
　Jefferson's experience of the culture of,
　　44–46, 50–51, 54–55, 56–57, 58–59,
　　70–71, 108, 202
　marriage in, 28, 45–46, 54–56, 58, 62,
　　69–70, 133–34, 138
　Short's experience of the culture of,
　　44–46, 50, 53, 60, 63–64, 70–71,
　　78, 100
　women's roles in the culture of, 54–55,
　　56, 57–60, 61–62, 63, 64–65, 108
Francois-Alexandre-Frédéric. *See* La
　　Rochefoucauld-Liancourt, Duke de
Francois VI, Duke de La
　　Rochefoucauld, 47
Franklin, Benjamin, 20, 24, 45, 99–
　　100, 136
Franks, David Salisbury, 61
French Revolution
　American Revolution compared
　　to, 102–3
　Bastille attack (1789) and, 7, 105–
　　6, 127–28
　Battle of Valmy (1792) and, 120–21
　Estates General meeting (1789) and,
　　47, 103–4, 108
　execution of Louis XVI (1793) and,
　　120–21, 123, 127–28
　Jefferson and, 50, 94–95, 101–6, 107–
　　14, 116–29, 141–42, 189, 211
　La Rochefoucauld family and, 50, 110–
　　12, 113–18, 124, 128–29, 141–42
　March of the *Poissardes* to Versailles
　　(1789) and, 102–3
　Morris and, 88–89, 91, 94–95, 96–97,
　　101–2, 104–5, 107–8, 113–15, 116–17,
　　119, 122–23
　Napoleonic Wars and, 188–89, 191–
　　92, 193–94
　Prussian invasion of France (1792)
　　and, 115, 116, 118
　republicanism and, 109, 111–13, 121, 122

royal family's flight to Varennes (1791)
and, 111–12
September massacres (1792) and, 115–
17, 119, 124, 134, 141–42
Short and, 5–6, 16, 87–89, 91, 92–93, 94–
95, 96–97, 101–2, 107–9, 111–14, 116–
24, 126–29, 141–42, 189, 202, 203–4, 213
The Terror (1793-94) and, 16–17, 50,
101–3, 122, 125–26
Tuileries Palace attack (1792) and,
49–50, 113–15
US debt to France and, 94–95,
123, 162–63
US popular reaction to, 120–21
French West Indies, 86–87
Freneau, Philip, 113

Gallatin, Albert, 185
Gardel, Pierre, 137
Gardoqui, Don Diego de, 75, 97–98
Gênet affair, 128, 162–63
Georgetown (Maryland), 163–64
Gerry, Elbridge, 2, 147–49
"Gettysburg Address" (Lincoln), 213
Giles Resolutions (1793), 95–96, 194–95
Godoy, Manuel, 97–98
Grayson, William, 77, 85
Great Britain
Adams as ambassador to, 26–27, 45, 72
Napoleonic Wars and, 184, 185, 188–
89, 193–94
Spain's alliance with, 97–98
US treaty (1794) with, 99
War of 1812 and, 196–97
Green Spring estate, 160–61, 165
Grouchy, Sophie de, 69–70

Haiti. *See* St. Domingue
Hamilton, Alexander
Bank of the United States and, 95
Burr's killing of, 189
French Revolution and, 120–21, 126–27
Giles Resolutions (1793) and, 95–96

Great Britain's relations with the
United States and, 89
Jefferson and, 84–87, 95, 96, 126–27,
189, 203–4
Morris and, 89, 94–95, 96–97
Short and, 75–76, 82, 83–84, 85–88,
91, 92, 94–97, 113–14, 126–27, 189,
203–4, 217–18
US debt to France and, 82–87, 94, 95
US national debt consolidation
and, 95
Harrison, Benjamin, 160–61
Harvie, John, 160–61
Hemings, Harriet, 2
Hemings, James, 20, 21–22, 30
Hemings, James Madison ("Madison"), 2
Hemings, Mary, 173–74, 187
Hemings, Sally
children Thomas Jefferson fathered
with, 2, 7, 9–10, 172, 174
in France with Jefferson, 7, 174, 187
Jefferson's affair with, 37–38, 104–5,
172, 174, 186–87
mixed race ancestry of, 171–72
Patsy's social interactions with, 9–10
Short's social interactions with, 9–
10, 30, 43
travel to London (1787) by, 30
Hemings, Thomas Eston, 2
Hemings, William Beverley, 2
Higginbotham, David, 195–96
Hocquetot, Countess d', 50
Holland
civil war (1780s) in, 103, 106–7
Congress's funding of US diplomatic
presence in, 74
Short's diplomatic meeting (1785)
in, 26–28
Short's tenure as resident minister to,
16, 75, 85, 90–94, 136, 139–40
US loans from banks in, 16, 78–79,
80–83, 84–87, 93–95, 103, 191
Houdetot, Sophie de, 102–3

Humphreys, David
  as *chargé des affaires* in Lisbon, 91
  end of diplomatic commission of, 186
  French language abilities of, 25
  Jefferson and, 20, 25, 106–7, 108
  return to the United States from
    France (1786) of, 31
  as secretary to Peace Commission in
    Paris, 19, 24, 25, 26, 31
  Short and, 91
  Washington and, 19, 91, 99–100

Indian Camp estate (Virginia)
  Durrett's offer (1803) to buy majority
    share of, 179
  Jefferson's assistance in managing, 16–
    17, 145, 160, 177–80, 183, 185, 189,
    190–91, 195–96, 217–18
  Lilly as overseer at, 179–80
  Short's purchase through Jefferson
    (1795) of, 16–17, 131, 143–44, 157,
    160, 169–70, 177–78
  Short's role in managing, 178–79
  Short's sale (1812) of, 195–96
  tenants on and rental income from,
    169–70, 177–80, 189, 196
  tobacco crops at, 178–79
infidelity
  Chastellux and, 69–70
  Jefferson's affair with Maria Cosway
    and, 9–10, 35–38, 57–58, 149–50
  Jefferson's affair with Sally Hemings
    and, 37–38, 104–5, 172, 174, 186–87
  liaisons de coeurs and, 69, 70
  Morris's affair with Flauhaut and,
    88–89, 133
  Short's affair with Rosalie and, 16–17,
    130–34, 136–49, 150–51, 153–55, 157,
    169–70, 177, 215–16
  Short's unconsummated affair with
    Lilite and, 10, 23–24, 28–29, 36–37,
    41, 62–64, 133, 136

*The Influence of the American Revolution
  in Europe* (Condorcet), 34

Jackson, Andrew, 213
Jacobins
  Brissotin faction and, 125–26
  Condorcet and, 112
  Jefferson and, 113, 119, 123–24
  September massacres (1792)
    and, 117–18
  Short and, 111–12, 118, 123–24, 189
James River canal company, 160, 163–
  64, 198
Jay, John
  as Confederation Congress's Secretary
    of Foreign Affairs, 37, 76–77
  Jefferson and, 105–8, 110, 127–28
  Short and, 31–32, 42, 76–77
  treaty with Great Britain (1794)
    negotiated by, 99
Jefferson, George, 173–74, 180, 195
Jefferson, Lucy, 22–23, 29–30
Jefferson, Martha (daughter of Thomas
  Jefferson). *See* Patsy
Jefferson, Martha Wayles (wife of
  Thomas Jefferson)
  death of, 11, 18, 56–57
  Jefferson's children with, 1–2, 57
  Jefferson's destruction of his
    correspondence with, 14
  Short's kinship ties with, 3
Jefferson, Mary ("Polly"). *See* Polly
Jefferson, Thomas. *See also* Jefferson-
  Short correspondence
  agricultural innovations promoted by,
    165, 168, 169, 180–81
  on American culture's virtues, 45, 50–
    51, 52–53, 56–59
  Bank of the United States and,
    95, 159–60
  Bill for Establishing Religious
    Freedom (Virginia) and, 2–3, 32–33

Bingham and, 58–59
children fathered with Martha
    Jefferson by, 1–2, 57
children fathered with Sally Hemings
    by, 2, 7, 9–10, 172, 174
College of William and Mary and, 3
Condorcet and, 34
as Confederation Congress
    delegate, 19–20
on Congressional oversight of the
    State Department, 74
Continental Congress seat of,
    18, 19–20
Corny and, 9–10, 36–38, 57–
    58, 149–50
Cosway's affair with, 9–10, 35–38, 57–
    58, 149–50
on dangers of young American men
    developing romantic relationships
    in Paris, 61
death of, 205–6, 207
Declaration of the Rights of Man and
    Citizen and, 109
Democratic-Republicans and, 150, 189
departure for Paris (1784) by, 22–23
departure from Paris (1789) by, 102–3,
    104–5, 107–8, 109–10
diplomatic appointments during
    Secretary of State tenure of, 72, 73–
    74, 76–78, 89–91, 92–93, 97
Enville and, 37–38, 46, 47, 50, 57–58,
    110, 117, 124, 135–36
on expanding popular democracy, 213
Federalist officeholders removed
    by, 190
financial difficulties faced by, 7, 16–17,
    157–60, 168, 174–75, 185, 196–97,
    200–1, 204–5
French culture as experienced by,
    44–46, 50–51, 54–55, 56–57, 58–59,
    70–71, 108, 202
French language abilities of, 25

French Revolution and, 50, 94–95,
    101–6, 107–14, 116–29, 141–42,
    189, 211
gender expectations expressed by, 54,
    56, 57–59, 108
Giles Resolutions (1793) and,
    96, 194–95
Hamilton and, 84–87, 95, 96, 126–27,
    189, 203–4
Hemings' affair with, 37–38, 104–5,
    172, 174, 186–87
Holland civil war (1780s) and,
    103, 106–7
Humphreys and, 20, 25, 106–7, 108
Indian Camp estate and, 16–17, 145,
    160, 177–80, 183, 185, 189, 190–91,
    195–96, 217–18
Jacobins and, 113, 119, 123–24
lack of white male heir of, 1–2, 11
Lafayette and, 31, 108–10
La Rochefoucauld (Louis-Alexandre
    de) and, 46, 48, 108–9, 110, 113
La Rochefoucauld family and, 47, 50,
    112–13, 141–42, 146–47, 149
Library of Congress and, 150–51, 197
Madison and, 12–13, 54–55, 61, 78–79,
    80–81, 90, 103–4, 105, 113, 188–89,
    193, 208
mentors of, 11
as minister to France (1785–89), 4–5, 7,
    18, 25, 26, 32, 44
Morris and, 89–90, 93–95, 113–14,
    117, 121–23
Paine and, 102–3, 105, 112–13, 187–88
patriarchal nature of relationship
    between Short and, 5, 6–8, 10, 12,
    14–15, 23, 37–38, 42–43, 45–46,
    96–97, 133, 217
as patriarch at Monticello, 1, 11, 26, 58,
    139–40, 195
as peace commissioner in Paris (1784-
    85), 19–20, 24, 25

Jefferson, Thomas (*cont.*)
  Poplar Forest retreat home of, 4
  as president, 126–27, 150–51, 160, 184–
    86, 188–89, 190, 193–94, 199
  proposal to convert slavery into
    serfdom offered by, 166–67
  Prussia's treaty with United States
    (1785) and, 27–28
  racial views of, 33–34, 166–67, 171–
    72, 174
  return to Virginia from France (1789)
    of, 39, 41, 76, 157–59, 168
  revolutionary violence endorsed by,
    5, 14–15, 16–17, 101, 103–6, 118–21,
    125–26, 127–28, 189
  Rosalie's interactions with, 10, 49–50,
    110, 124, 145, 146–47
  September massacres (1792) and, 116–
    18, 119, 124, 141–42
  Short as private secretary in Paris to,
    4–5, 7–8, 15–16, 23–24, 27–28, 31–
    32, 35, 37, 160–61, 187
  Short's financial dealings with, 3–4, 5,
    10, 16–17, 23–24, 157–60, 162–65,
    169–70, 173–77, 181, 183, 184–86,
    190–91, 195–97, 205
  slavery views of, 166–67, 168, 182, 218
  slaves owned by, 1, 11, 20, 21–22, 166–
    67, 168, 172–75, 177
  Smith (William Stephens) and, 56–57,
    90, 91, 103–4
  successor generation's understanding
    of, 208–9, 212–13
  Madame de Tessé's friendship with,
    9–10, 28, 37–38, 49–50, 57–58
  tobacco cultivation and sales by, 157–
    59, 174–75
  travels to Holland and Rhineland
    (1788) by, 38–39, 40, 54, 165, 167
  travels to southern France and Italy
    (1787) of, 37–38, 40, 54
  University of Virginia and, 199, 212

  US debt to France and, 32, 78–87,
    93–95, 100
  US trade policy and, 32
  as vice-president, 99
  on vices of French and European
    culture, 52–53
  Virginia legislature seat of, 18
  Washington and, 74, 76, 108, 165, 168
  on younger generations' right to
    rebel against older generations'
    conventions, 10–11, 58
Jefferson-Short correspondence. *See also*
    Jefferson, Thomas; Short, William
  Adam and Eve letter by Jefferson and,
    5, 12–13, 14–15, 16, 118–22, 123–24,
    127–28, 187–88, 190, 205
  diplomatic protocol as topic
    in, 188–89
  Epicureanism as topic in, 12–13, 200–2
  French Revolution as topic in, 94–95,
    101–2, 111–14, 116–24, 126–27, 128–
    29, 141–42, 203–4
  Giles Resolutions (1793) and,
    96, 194–95
  Jefferson's career advice to Short in, 6,
    7, 20, 73, 74, 85, 91, 92, 97, 126–27,
    128–29, 150–51, 212
  Jefferson's moral and personal advice
    to Short in, 6, 8, 10, 11, 12, 61–62,
    65–66, 133–34, 200–2, 207–8,
    212, 217–18
  Jefferson's preservation of, 13–15
  letters written in support of Short and,
    4–5, 19–20, 26, 40–41, 42
  Missouri Crisis as topic in, 12–13,
    199–200
  Morris as topic in, 89–90, 92–
    93, 123–24
  Patsy as a subject in, 38–39, 40–41
  re-acclimation to life in the United
    States as topic in, 70–71
  Rosalie as topic in, 148–51, 154–55

Short family as topic in, 140–41
Short's appointments to diplomatic positions as topic in, 76–78, 91, 126–27, 128–29, 138, 186, 191–92, 194–95, 217–18
Short's plans to return to the United States as topic in, 42, 43
Short's preservation of, 12–13, 15
slavery and emancipation as topics in, 13–14, 165–66, 167, 177, 181–83
"unbosoming" and, 14–15, 43, 92
University of Virginia as topic in, 199
US debt to France as topic in, 87
US domestic politics as topic in, 150, 189–92, 198–99, 202–4
winding down of Jefferson's tenure in Paris (1789) and, 77, 158–59
Jones, John Paul, 79

Kant, Immanuel, 10–11
Kennan, Patrick, 162–63

Lafayette, Marquis de
Declaration of Independence and, 108–9
Declaration of the Rights of Man and Citizen, 109
financial difficulties faced by, 204–5
French Revolution and, 105, 114–15, 128–29
Jefferson and, 31, 108–10
Monticello visit (1825) by, 204–5
Morris's appointment as minister to France and, 92
Napoleonic Wars and, 155–56
Revolutionary War military service by, 78–79
Short and, 37, 89, 108–9, 128–29
US gift to Paris of bust of, 37
wife of, 55
La Rochefoucauld, Louis-Alexandre de
accounts of American life for a French audience by, 32

Adams (John) and, 48–49
Declaration of the Rights of Man and, 114–15
first marriage of, 55–56
French Revolution and, 101, 110, 113, 114–18, 119–20, 124, 128–29, 134, 141–42
as heir of La Rochefoucauld family, 55–56
intellectual interests of, 48–49
Jefferson and, 46, 48, 108–9, 110, 113
Morris and, 48–49
Rosalie as second wife of, 49, 55–56, 131–32
September massacres (1792) and mob killing of, 101, 115–18, 119–20, 124, 128–29, 134, 141–42
Short and, 46, 108–9, 112–13
Société de Quatre Vingt Neuf and, 108–9
Société des Amis des Noirs and, 48–49
La Rochefoucauld, Rosalie de. *See* Rosalie
La Rochefoucauld family. *See also specific individuals*
Condorcet and, 49–50, 69–70, 112, 154
Estates General representatives from, 47
French Revolution and, 50, 110–12, 113–18, 124, 128–29, 141–42
Jefferson and, 47, 50, 112–13, 141–42, 146–47, 149
La Roche-Guyon chateau and, 46–47, 112, 115, 134–35, 152
Liancourt family and, 46–47
September massacres (1792) and, 115–18, 124, 128–29, 141–42
Short and, 47, 74, 78, 100, 101–2, 110–12, 117–18, 134–36, 140, 141–42, 144–45, 146–47, 155–56, 218
St. Domingue holdings of, 142
The Terror's impact on, 16–17, 50, 101

La Rochefoucauld-Liancourt, Duke de, 48–49, 149, 172–73
Launay, Marquis de, 105–6
Lebrun, Pierre, 92–95
Ledyard, John, 31–32
Letters of An American Farmer (Crèvecoeur), 33
Lettres d'un Bourgeois de New-Haven (Condorcet), 34–35
Lewis, Nicholas, 158
Liancourt family, 46–47
Library of Congress, 150–51, 197
Lilite (Anne-Hipolyte-Louise Royer)
    children of, 62, 133, 154
    marriage to Alexandre Denis of, 29, 62, 63–64, 133
    Short's unconsummated affair with, 10, 23–24, 28–29, 36–37, 41, 62–64, 133, 136
Lilly, Gabriel, 179–80
Limagne plain (France), 151
Lincoln, Abraham, 209–10, 213
Lively, Charles, 179
Livingston, Robert, 18, 99–100, 150–51, 186
Louis XVI (king of France)
    Estates-General and, 47
    execution (1793) of, 120–21, 123, 127–28
    flight from Paris to Varennes by (1791), 111–12, 114
    Jefferson on, 107
    Tuiliers Palace attack (1792) and, 113–14
Louis XVIII (dauphin of France; king of France), 112, 141–42, 211
Luzacs, Jean, 27

Maclay, William, 74
Madison, Dolley, 188–89
Madison, James
    Albermarle County settlement of, 26, 202

French Revolution and, 202–3
Jefferson and, 12–13, 54–55, 61, 78–79, 80–81, 90, 103–4, 105, 113, 188–89, 193, 208
Morris and, 99–100
as president, 194–95
as secretary of state, 188–89, 191, 193
Short and, 37, 202–4
Virginia state politics and, 42
War of 1812 and, 202–3
Malone, Dumas, 106
Marie Antoinette (queen of France), 127–28
marriage. *See also* infidelity
American, 45–46, 56–57, 58–59, 60, 67, 69–71, 133–34
companionate marriage's increasing prevalence in post-revolutionary Atlantic World and, 69–70, 133–34
French, 28, 45–46, 54–56, 58, 62, 69–70, 133–34, 138
republicanism and, 56–57, 58, 70–71, 133–34
Short on the virtues of, 67–68
Maury, Walker, 52
Mayo, John, 64–65, 67–68
Mazzei, Philip, 31, 34–35, 47, 61–62, 141, 158–59
McKean, Thomas, 4–5
Mercier, Louis-Sèbastian, 54–56
Merry, Anthony, 188–89
Merry, Elizabeth, 188–89
metayer (sharecropping system of land tenure), 42, 143–44, 166–67, 179
Missouri Crisis of 1819, 12–13, 199–200, 210–11
Monroe, James
    Albermarle County settlement of, 12, 26, 169, 202
    Congress's relations with US delegation in Paris and, 31
    Giles Resolutions (1793) and, 96

Jefferson and, 96, 169
as minister to France, 99–100, 146–47
Morris and, 90
as president, 202–3
Rosalie and, 131, 146–47
Short and, 90, 146–47, 202–3
Monticello
fire damage (1819) at, 200–1
French books and wines at, 208–9
Jefferson as patriarch at, 1, 11, 26, 58, 139–40, 195
Lafayette's visit (1825) to, 204–5
La Rochefoucauld-Liancourt's visit to, 149, 172–73
naillery at, 16–17, 160, 174–76, 177
Short's comparison of Limagne to, 151
Short's discussion of settling near, 164
Short's visits to, 3–4, 184–85, 203–5
slaves at, 172–75, 177
Montmorin, Amarnd Marc de, 37, 83–84, 101, 117, 119, 159
Monville, François de, 46–47
Morris, Gouverneur
abolitionist views of, 88
Flahaut as mistress of, 88–89, 133
French culture as experienced by, 54, 64–65
French Revolution and, 88–89, 91, 94–95, 96–97, 101–2, 104–5, 107–8, 113–15, 116–17, 119, 122–23
Hamilton and, 89, 94–95, 96–97
Jefferson and, 89–90, 93–95, 113–14, 117, 121–23
La Rochefoucauld (Louis-Alexandre de) and, 48–49
Madison and, 99–100
as minister to France (1792-94), 89–93, 96–97, 121–23
Monroe and, 90
as presidential emissary to Great Britain, 88–89
Rosalie and, 141

salon of Louise, Countess of Albany in Paris and, 64, 133
September massacres (1792) and, 117, 119
Short and, 75–76, 87–90, 91–95, 96–97, 123–24, 133, 141, 142
Madame de Tessé and, 49–50
US debt to France and, 82–84, 93–94
Washington and, 89, 90, 96–97, 121–22
Morris, Robert, 4–5, 82–83, 88
Morven. *See* Indian Camp estate
Moustier, Count de, 73–74

Napoleon Bonaparte, 152–56, 191–92, 211
National Assembly (France), 82, 87–88, 109, 111–12, 114–15, 127–28
Necker, Jacques, 81, 82, 107
Nelson, William, 53, 62, 64–65, 67–69, 146–47
Noailles, Marie-Adrienne de, 55
Notes on the State of Virginia (Jefferson)
on cultivation of land, 180
Jefferson's views on race in, 33–34, 171–72, 174
on master-slave relationship, 5–6
Short's involvement in the publication of, 34–35

Orange, Princess of, 106–7
Orléans, Duchess d', 69

Paine, Thomas
French Revolution and, 75, 112–13
Jefferson and, 102–3, 105, 112–13, 187–88
Morris's appointment as minister to France and, 92
native country of England renounced by, 46
return to United States (1802) by, 187–88
Short and, 75, 112–13

Paradise, John and Lucy, 65–66

Parker, Daniel, 82–84

patriarchy
Atlantic World revolutions and
diminishing of, 133–34
Byrd on, 1
Jefferson's advice to his daughters
and, 58, 59
Jefferson-Short relationship and, 5,
6–8, 10, 12, 14–15, 23, 37–38, 42–43,
45–46, 96–97, 133, 217
Jefferson's vision for Albermarle
County and, 12, 56–57, 163–
64, 180–81
Monticello and, 1, 11, 26, 58, 139–
40, 195
republican notions of the household
and, 11
slaves' role in the household and, 11

Patsy (Martha Jefferson, daughter of
Thomas Jefferson)
abolitionist views of, 7
Botidoux's correspondence
with, 39–40
French language abilities of, 25
French Revolution and, 117–18
Jefferson's correspondence with Short
regarding, 38–39, 40–41
Jefferson's patriarchal advice to, 58, 59
marriage to Thomas Mann Randolph
of, 41, 77
Panthémont Convent School and, 38–
39, 40–41, 51–52
return to Virginia from France (1789)
of, 39–40, 41
Sally Hemings's social interactions
with, 9–10
Short's interactions with and advances
toward, 9–10, 29–30, 39–41, 42–43,
61–62, 133, 137
Simiâne affair in Paris (1787) and, 40

Peale, Rembrandt, 151–52, 153*f*

Peters, Richard, 4–5

Peterson, Merrill, 118

Pétion, Jerôme, 114–15

Petit, Adrien, 30, 38

Petit, Emanuel, 24

Pichon, Louis, 188–89

Pinckney, Thomas, 90, 98–100, 162

Plunkett Chastellux, Marie Brigitte de,
69–70, 114–15, 124

Polly (Mary Jefferson, daughter of
Thomas Jefferson), 1–2, 22–23, 29–
30, 37–39, 40–41, 117–18

Portugal, 74

Potomac Canal, 163–64

Price, Jacob, 179–80

Price, Joseph, 177–79

Prosser's Uprising (1800), 181–82

Prussia, 26–28, 115, 116, 118, 167

Psyché (ballet performance of 1791), 137

Puisieux, Madame de, 49–50

Pyvart de Chastellué, Adélaïde, 152

Quasi-War with France (1798-1800), 128

Randolph, Davies, 172

Randolph, Edmund, 98–99

Randolph, Ellen Wayles, 201–2, 215–16

Randolph, Peyton, 11

Randolph, Thomas Jefferson, 11, 205

Randolph, Thomas Mann, 6, 41, 77,
158, 164–65

Raynal, Abbé, 34–35

Remsen, Henry, 125

Researches on the United States
(Mazzei), 34–35

Revolutionary War. *See* American
Revolution

The Rights of Man (Paine), 75, 112

Riqueti, Honoré Gabriel (Count
Mirabeau), 32–33

Rivanna River, 163–64

Robert, Hubert, 46–47

Robespierre, Maximilien, 113–14, 125–
    26, 211
Robinson, Merit Moore, 67–68, 70
Rochefoucauld-Liancourt, Alexandre
    François, 116, 142, 152
Rohan-Chabot, Adélaïde Louise de,
    144–45, 153–54
Rohan-Chabot, Alexandrine-Charlotte-
    Sophie de (Duchess de La
    Rochefoucauld d'Enville). *See*
    Rosalie
Rohan-Chabot, Armand-Charles
    de ("Charles"), 111–12, 114, 115,
    116, 141–42
Rohan-Chabot, Louis-Antoine-Auguste,
    Duke de (Prince de Léon), 55–56
Romanzoff, Count, 193, 194–95
Rosalie (Rohan-Chabot, Alexandrine-
    Charlotte-Sophie de)
  Condorcet and, 49–50, 69–70
  correspondence with Short after
    second marriage in 1810 and, 154–55
  education received by, 49
  English language abilities of, 131–
    32, 139–40
  French Revolution and, 16–17, 115–17,
    124, 128–29, 134, 141–42
  imprisonment (1793-94) of, 115–16,
    128–29, 130–31, 133–34, 141–
    42, 146–47
  Jefferson and, 10, 49–50, 110, 124,
    145, 146–47
  "little society" envisioned by, 140,
    142–45, 154
  loan to Short by, 142–43, 145–46, 213
  marriage to Boniface Castellane
    of, 154–56
  marriage to Louis-Alexandre La
    Rochefoucauld of, 49, 55–56, 131–
    32, 138, 146
  Monroe and, 131, 146–47
  painting of, 130, 132*f*

Rousseau and, 49, 137
royalist sentiments of, 49–50
September massacres (1792) and mob
    killing of husband of, 115–16, 117,
    124, 128–29, 134, 141–42
Short's affair (1790-1802) with, 16–17,
    130–34, 136–49, 150–51, 153–55, 157,
    169–70, 177, 215–16
Short's friendship (1780s) with, 10,
    16–17, 41, 49–50, 56, 88–89, 114,
    116, 117, 124, 128–29
Rousseau, Jean-Jacques, 50, 63–64,
    137, 139–40
Royer, Alexandre-Marie, 29
Royer, Anne-Hipolyte-Louise ("Lilite").
    See Lilite
Royer, Henri-Raphael, 29
Royer family, Short's relationship with,
    28–29, 62, 107–8, 133, 136, 144–45,
    215, 218
Rush, Benjamin, 209–10
Russia, 192–94
Rutledge, Jr., John
  French Revolution and, 116
  Jefferson's correspondence with, 54–55
  marriage of, 66–67, 68
  sexually transmitted disease experienced
    during European travels by, 66–67
  Short and, 65–67, 116, 134–35,
    141, 146–47
  on women's roles in French culture, 60
Rutledge Sr., John, 51, 106–7

San Lorenzo Treaty (1795), 99
Savary de Valcoulon, Jean, 23–24
Schuylkill River, 163–64
Schweitzer, Jeanneret & Co., 83–84
Sénac de Meilhan, Gabriel, 35
*A Sentimental Journey Through France
    and Italy* (Sterne), 18–19, 65–66
September massacres (1792), 115–17, 119,
    124, 134, 141–42

Shadwell estate, 177–78

Shays Rebellion, 103–4, 105–6

Shippen, Thomas Lee, 65–66

Short, John Cleves, 216–17

Short, Peyton, 20, 53, 140–41, 160–61, 176–77, 216–17

Short, William. *See also* Jefferson-Short correspondence

  Adams (Abigail) and, 24–28, 30

  Adams (John) and, 26–27, 30

  on American culture's virtues, 45, 53

  American Philosophical Society membership of, 202

  American Revolution commemorative medals project and, 31–32

  anti-slavery views of, 5–6, 21–22, 33–34, 160–61, 165–66, 167, 168, 170–71, 176–77, 181–83

  as bachelor, 12, 43, 57, 60, 67–70, 133–34, 201–2, 207, 215–16, 217–18

  Bank of the United States investment by, 159–60, 162–63

  Brown's financial dealings with, 159–63

  canal company investments of, 163–64, 169, 176, 190–91, 198

  as *chargé des affaires* in Paris (1789-92) and, 8–9, 42, 75, 76–77, 82, 87–88

  Chastellux and, 33, 69

  College of William and Mary education of, 3

  Condorcet and, 34, 35, 69–70, 75, 202

  Continental Congress and, 19–20

  Cosway (Maria) and, 9–10, 36–37, 43

  death of parents of, 4, 21

  diplomatic meeting in Holland (1785) with Prussia and, 26–28

  Enville and, 37–38, 46, 110, 112–13, 117, 124, 131, 133, 135–36, 138, 144–45

  family members' correspondence with, 140–41, 216–17

  financial challenges faced by, 123–24, 128–29

  French culture as experienced by, 44–46, 50, 53, 60, 63–64, 70–71, 78, 100

  French language abilities of, 23–25, 30, 72–73, 131–32

  French Revolution and, 5–6, 16, 87–89, 91, 92–93, 94–95, 96–97, 101–2, 107–9, 111–14, 116–24, 126–29, 141–42, 189, 202, 203–4, 213

  Giles Resolutions (1793) and, 95–96, 194–95

  Hamilton and, 75–76, 82, 83–84, 85–88, 91, 92, 94–97, 113–14, 126–27, 189, 203–4, 217–18

  Humphreys and, 91

  Indian Camp estate and, 16–17, 131, 143–44, 157, 160, 169–70, 177–79

  Jacobins and, 111–12, 118, 123–24, 189

  Jefferson's financial dealings with, 3–4, 5, 10, 16–17, 23–24, 157–60, 162–65, 169–70, 173–77, 181, 183, 184–86, 190–91, 195–97, 205

  as Jefferson's private secretary in Paris, 4–5, 7–8, 15–16, 23–24, 27–28, 31–32, 35, 37, 160–61, 187

  Lafayette and, 37, 89, 108–9, 128–29

  La Rochefoucauld (Louis-Alexandre) and, 46, 108–9, 112–13

  La Rochefoucauld family and, 47, 74, 78, 100, 101–2, 110–12, 117–18, 134–36, 140, 141–42, 144–45, 146–47, 155–56, 218 (*See also specific family members*)

  Lilite Royer's unconsummated affair with, 10, 23–24, 28–29, 36–37, 41, 62–64, 133, 136

  loan from Rosalie to, 142–43, 145–46, 213

  London travels (1785) of, 26–27

  Louise, Countess of Albany and, 64, 133

  Madison and, 37, 202–4

  on marriage's virtues, 67–68

  Monroe and, 90, 146–47, 202–3

Monticello visits by, 3–4, 184–85, 203–5

Morris and, 75–76, 87–90, 91–95, 96–97, 123–24, 133, 141, 142

Mush Island estate sale by, 160–61, 176–77

Napoleonic Wars and, 155–56

Ohio and New York land holdings of, 180

Paine and, 75, 112–13

patriarchal nature of Jefferson's relationship with, 5, 6–8, 10, 12, 14–15, 23, 37–38, 42–43, 45–46, 96–97, 133, 217

Patsy's interactions with, 9–10, 29–30, 39–41, 42–43, 61–62, 133, 137

Peale's portrait of, 151–52, 153*f*

Philadelphia as home after 1802 of, 12, 202, 213, 215–16, 218

Polly's travel to London (1786) and, 29–30

popular democracy opposed by, 17, 197–98, 202, 207, 213–15

portrait of, 214*f*

preparations for departure to Paris (1784) by, 20–23

proposal to convert slavery into serfdom offered by, 17, 143–44, 165–66, 167, 168, 170–71, 182–83

proposal to write authorized biography of Jefferson by, 207, 216

race and miscegenation views of, 171–72, 173–74, 187

as resident minister to Holland (1792-93), 16, 75, 85, 90–94, 136, 139–40

resignation from foreign service (1795) by, 99

return to France (1795) by, 144

return to France (1808) by, 154

return to United States (1802) by, 142–43, 151–52, 175, 184, 186

return to United States discussed by, 42, 43, 140–41, 150–51, 165–66, 170, 172, 181–82

Rosalie's affair (1790-1802) with, 16–17, 130–34, 136–49, 150–51, 153–55, 157, 169–70, 177, 215–16

Rosalie's friendship (1780s) with, 10, 16–17, 41, 49–50, 56, 88–89, 114, 116, 117, 124, 128–29

Royer family's relationship with, 28–29, 62, 107–8, 133, 136, 144–45, 215, 218

Russia diplomatic mission proposal (1808) and, 192–95

Rutledge Jr. and, 65–67, 116, 134–35, 141, 146–47

Sally Hemings's interactions with, 9–10, 30, 43

September massacres (1792) and, 116, 117–18, 124, 128–29, 141–42

sexually transmitted disease experienced during European travels by, 66–67, 146

Smith (William Stephens) and, 53, 97, 141, 189

Société des Amis des Noirs and, 33–34, 88, 167

as special envoy and resident minister to Spain (1793-95), 75, 90–91, 92–93, 96–98, 117, 122–24, 130–31, 133–34, 144

St. Germain as French residence of, 23–24, 25–26, 27–28, 31, 35, 62

Madame de Tessé's friendship with, 9–10, 35, 37–38, 70, 133, 135–36

travels in France during revolution (1792) of, 117

travels in southern Europe (1788) of, 40–41, 42, 64, 65–66, 68, 133

travels to United States (1798) of, 147–49

US debt to France and, 78–87, 93–94, 100, 123

Virginia Executive Council seat of, 22, 26

Washington and, 75, 88–89, 98, 121–22

Short Wilkins, Jane, 151–52
Sierra Leone, 170–71
Simiâne affair (Paris, 1787), 40
Skipwith, Fulwar, 30
Skipwith, Henry, 162–63
slavery
    hereditary forms of, 168, 173
    international slave trade and, 182
    Jefferson's financial dealings with
        Short and, 173–75, 176–77, 181–82
    Jefferson's ownership of slaves and,
        1, 11, 20, 21–22, 166–67, 168, 172–
        75, 177
    Jefferson's views regarding, 166–67,
        168, 182, 218
    at Monticello, 172–75, 177
    patriarchal conceptions of the
        household and, 11
    sex between masters and slaves
        in, 173–74
    Short and Jefferson's proposals of
        serfdom as alternative to, 17, 143–
        44, 165–68, 170–71, 182–83
    Short's views regarding, 5–6, 21–22,
        33–34, 160–61, 165–66, 167, 168,
        170–71, 176–77, 181–83
    uprisings against, 181–82
Small, William, 11
Smith, Abigail, 189
Smith, Samuel H., 197
Smith, Thomas Rhett, 60
Smith, William Stephens
    French Revolution and, 122–23, 189
    Hamilton and, 189
    Jefferson and, 56–57, 90, 91, 103–4
    marriage to Nabby Adams of, 56–57, 90
    potential nomination as minister to
        Great Britain of, 90, 91
    on Royer family's relationship with
        Short, 28–29
    Short and, 53, 97, 141, 189

on Spain's royal court, 97
Société de Quatre Vingt Neuf, 108–9, 111
Société des Amis des Noirs, 33–34, 48–
    49, 167
Society of Friends to America, 82–83
Spain
    Congress's funding of US diplomatic
        presence in, 74
    French Revolution and, 97–98, 123
    Great Britain and, 97–98
    Pinckney as presidential envoy
        to, 98–100
    San Lorenzo Treaty (1795) and, 99
    Short as special envoy and resident
        minister to, 75, 90–91, 92–93, 96–
        98, 117, 122–24, 130–31, 133–34, 144
    US border and Mississippi River trade
        negotiations with, 90, 98, 191
    US efforts to establish an alliance with, 98
Staël, Madame de, 57–58, 87–88, 202
Stanhope, Philip, 63
St. Domingue, 33–34, 93–94,
    142, 157–58
Sterne, Laurence, 18–19, 64–66
Sterrett, Edward, 60
Stiles, Ezra, 209
Stockdale, John, 34–35
Stolberg-Gedern, Princess Louise
    (Countess of Albany), 64, 133
Strickland, William, 165
Stuart, Charles Edward, 64
Sutherland, Lady, 87–88
Swan, James, 82–84

Taggart, Samuel, 193, 206
Talleyrand-Périgord, Charles-Maurice
    de , 88–89
Taylor, John, 165
Temple Franklin, William, 72
The Terror (French Revolution, 1793-94),
    16–17, 50, 101–3, 122, 125–26

Madame de Tessé
  abolition of aristocratic titles endorsed
    by, 49–50
  on American marriage, 70
  French Revolution and exile
    of, 128–29
  Jefferson and, 9–10, 28, 37–38, 49–
    50, 57–58
  Morris and, 49–50
  Short and, 9–10, 35, 37–38, 70,
    133, 135–36
Thulemeier, Baron de, 26–28
Ticknor, George, 208–9
Tott, Madame de, 64, 70
Travels in America (Chastellux), 33
Trudaine de La Sabliere, Charles-
    Michel, 115
Trudaine de Montigny, Charles-
    Louis, 115
Trumbull, John, 7–8, 9–10, 31, 36–37, 42,
    45, 189
Tucker, Frances Bland Randolph, 171–72
Tufton, Caroline, 39
Tufton, Elizabeth, 39
Tuileries Palace attack (1792), 49–50, 113–15

University of Virginia, 12, 199, 212
US debt to France
  annual interest payments on, 78–79,
    81, 84–85
  Assemblée des Notables debates
    regarding, 78–79
  Confederation Congress's neglect
    (1786-90) of, 78–79
  Congress of the United States and, 81,
    82, 84–85, 93–94
  Dutch banks' loans to the United
    States and, 16, 78–79, 80–83, 84–
    87, 93–95, 126–27
  France's financial crisis (1780s) and,
    78–79, 81, 83–84, 85–87

  French Revolution and, 94–95,
    123, 162–63
  Hamilton and, 82–87, 94, 95
  Jefferson and, 32, 78–87, 93–95, 100
  Morris and, 82–84, 93–94
  Parker and, 82–84
  pension obligations to French
    soldiers from Revolutionary War
    and, 78–79
  Short and, 78–87, 93–94, 100, 123
  Society of Friends to America
    and, 82–83
  US Constitution's full faith and credit
    provision and, 82–83
  US government credit jeopardized by,
    79–80, 81
  Washington and, 84–85, 86, 162–63

Valmy, battle (1792) of, 120–21
van Hogendorp, Gisbjert, 27
Van Staphorst banking house, 78–79,
    81–82, 84–87, 94, 142
Versailles, march (1789) on, 102–3
Volney, Count de, 173, 180–81
Voyage dan les États-Unis d'Amerique
    (La Rochefoucauld-Liancourt),
    149, 172–73

Wadstrom, Carl Bernhard, 170–71
Walsh, Robert, 13–14
War of 1812, 196–97, 202–3
Washington, George
  diplomatic appointments by, 72, 78,
    89–90, 91, 96–97, 98–99
  French Revolution and, 121–
    23, 126
  Humphreys and, 19, 91, 99–100
  Jefferson and, 74, 76, 108, 165, 168
  lack of male heir of, 1–2
  Morris and, 89, 90, 96–97, 121–22
  Short and, 75, 88–89, 98, 121–22

Washington, George (*cont.*)
    US debt to France and, 84–85,
        86, 162–63
Wayles, John, 157–58
Webster, Daniel, 202
West Florida, 191
Whitcomb, Samuel, 208–9

Williamos, Charles, 24
Wood, Gordon, 213–15
Wythe, George, 3, 11

XYZ affair, 128, 147–48

Young, Arthur, 46–47, 48–49, 165